The author at age four

STICKS, STONES
&
Songs

The Corey Story

A MEMOIR

Eleanor Corey

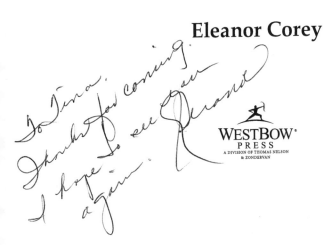

WESTBOW®
PRESS
A DIVISION OF THOMAS NELSON
& ZONDERVAN

WestBow Press books may be ordered through booksellers or by contacting:

WestBow Press
A Division of Thomas Nelson & Zondervan
1663 Liberty Drive
Bloomington, IN 47403
www.westbowpress.com
1 (866) 928-1240

ISBN: 978-1-4908-5976-7 (sc)
ISBN: 978-1-4908-5977-4 (hc)
ISBN: 978-1-4908-5975-0 (e)

Library of Congress Control Number: 2014920429

Printed in the United States of America.

WestBow Press rev. date: 1/20/2015

Family, History, Hardship, Children, Rural America, Olympic Peninsula

Sticks, Stones & Songs is written in honor of my parents,
Arthur and Margaret Corey.
It is dedicated to my grandchildren,
Zaid, Zia, Zac, Zella, Neveah, Nolan, and Niko.
Because of you, I am able to see the world
once again through the eyes of a child.

CONTENTS

PHOTOS

ACKNOWLEDGEMENTS

I express my gratitude to those who opened for me a treasure trunk of documents, maps and old stories—Susan Koehler and Kathy Monds at the Clallam County Genealogy Society as well as Mary Pfaff-Pierce and Margaret Owens, of the Joyce Depot Museum; to starting-point mentors of the Whidbey Writers' Lockdown Retreat—Margaret Bendet, Priscilla Long, and Andrea Hurst; to editor David Jacobsen who helped me see what was important and what was not; to literary agent Heidi Mitchell, who believed in the story; to Elizabeth Dolhanyk who assisted with graphics; to Margaret Phillips and my family members who gave attention to details; and to Shelby D. Zacharias, who dredged out many bloopers of style, grammar, and punctuation.

I am indebted to my mother for her diary that began in 1954, and my five sisters who helped me wade through its pages; my second cousin Charles Phenicie for genealogies he compiled; Naoma Spottswood, who hoarded Mother's letters to her; Aunt Eleanor who took pictures every time we saw her; my father who recorded portions of his early ministry; my nine siblings and their spouses who answered hours' worth of questions and were quick to straighten me out if I didn't get their stories straight; and especially my sister, Marilyn, who transcribed her faded pencil diaries for each day of fifteen years and then trusted me with the text. In the same breath, I also include a disclaimer for any errors in the timeline and stories included, fully aware that every memory has its circle of limitations, and every event has its leeway for interpretation. Some names and details have been changed for concerns of privacy, but the events included are as close to the facts as the information gleaned has allowed.

I am thankful to my husband, Ron, who understood the importance of this project and didn't take it personally when he got the same leftover soup three nights in a row. And, finally, I am grateful for the patience of all who waited while I finished one last sentence.

"I don't like to talk about those times," my brother said.

He meant those times in the thirties, the forties, the fifties, times of hunger and cold and of angst and fear. Yet talk we did—all ten of us siblings—of the resourcefulness on the other side of hardship, of rivalry transforming into camaraderie, and of chores lightened with songs. For two years we talked by phone, by email, and over potluck parties. We remembered. We cried. We roared with laughter. And we heard my brother admit—at the end of it all—, "Now that was good."

_____*Eleanor Corey Guderian, 2014*

PROLOGUE

In the living room, nine-year-old Zaid catches my attention. Rubbing his hands over gold-etched words, my grandson asks, "What's a White Rotary, Abuela?"

"It's a sewing machine. This is the one I learned to use as a kid, when I was even younger than you."

"Will you show me how it works?"

I pull a frayed leather belt from the side drawer and hold it up. "I would, but the belt is broken."

"You should get a new one."

"You're right—I should."

While tucking the belt around the upper wheel, I explain, "See, here's where the belt should fit on the top. Then it goes down and around that wheel on the bottom."

I kneel down and move the treadle with my hand. "When you want to sew, you push your feet back and forth on the treadle plate. That makes the belt turn both sets of wheels so the needle will go up and down to make stitches in the cloth. This machine needs no electricity."

"Well, you should buy a new belt and make it work," he answers, still staring at the machine with its intricate design. "It's cool."

A few days later, Zaid's six-year-old sister Zia stands in the bathroom, opening and closing the tiny doors of a model outhouse. She looks up at me and asks, "What's this thing?"

"It's a pretend bathroom, kind of like a Porta Potty at the fair."

"You mean where we go pee after the rides?"

I move my hand to touch the roof of the toy I have displayed and dusted for twelve years—ever since my brother-in-law had fashioned it for me in minute detail out of a cedar shingle from the farm, and my sister had planted a cedar sapling in an earthen pot behind it.

"It's the kind of bathroom we had when I was a little girl like you," I tell Zia. "We called it 'The Outhouse' because you had to go outside to use it. We didn't have a warm bathroom and a toilet with water you could flush."

She reaches inside and picks up a tiny rectangle of paper labeled, SEARS, and looks at me. I see in her eyes a question to be answered. "And we used the pages from a catalog to wipe. We didn't even have enough money to buy toilet paper."

"Oh."

She shrugs and follows me to the music room for her piano lesson. The ebony upright also has a history, so—since we're on the topic—I ask her, "Did you know my mother—your great-grandmother—learned to play on this piano over a hundred years ago when she was your age? Your great-grandmother even taught me music, same as I teach you."

Zia looks at me with a blank face. She can't imagine her mother as a child, much less me—so how would she ever comprehend a child called Great Grandmother? I'm reminded how different her childhood is from any of the mothers before her. And yet she represents the continuity of our family, the strength of our lineage, and the permanence of our songs. As I open the music book on the piano in front of her, a bell rings in my brain. *That's it—I'll write for my grandchildren! The Book will be a gift for them.*

The seed of inspiration to write had actually been planted the previous year, when my five sisters and I spent a week together poring through our mother's diary. The kernel had grown as I studied letters Mother had written during the 1930s and 40s to her cousin, and it came into full bloom as I researched genealogies, questioned friends and family, and studied photo albums. Then, when I talked with Zaid and Zia about the emblems of my early life—the treadle machine, the miniature outhouse, and the antique piano—the book's purpose and plan unfolded.

I would write the tale in three chronicles: Chronicle One would include the years 1937 to 1946, my family's history as I learned it from those who preceded me; Chronicle Two would begin in 1946 with my first memory, and end in 1958, with the completion of a milestone of our lives; Chronicle Three would bring all of the players and their offspring together many years later for the first family reunion.

What follows is for my descendants[1] and my siblings' descendants, just as it is for everyone else who wants a glimpse into the middle years of the 1900s, and into a family of twelve whose fortitude and ingenuity took them through the harshest of times, and whose songs of fun and faith spilled out from never-ending duties.

CHRONICLE ONE
1937-1946

CHAPTER ONE
The Auction
(Fall 1937)

"**W**hat should I bid?" My father, Arthur Corey, turned to ask the man standing next to him.

"The amount of the overdue taxes."

Arthur's hand went up. "I bid twenty-eight."

"I hear twenty-eight. Who'll bid fifty? Forty? Anyone? Any amount? I have a bid of twenty-eight."

"Going. Going. Gone. Sold to Mr. Arthur W. Corey."

It was 1937, near the end of the Great Depression, when twenty-eight was even less than the thirty-five dollars college-bound Arthur had paid for an overcoat in 1924.[2] But at the Clallam County court house, a few blocks up from the waterfront in Port Angeles, Washington, Arthur was bidding on something far more significant: an abandoned, defunct grange hall, and the quarter acre out in the country where it stood.

Arthur paid the auctioneer, buttoned his threadbare tweed overcoat, pinched the front creases of his brown fedora, and settled it on his head. He bounded down the courthouse steps and scurried up the sidewalk, document in hand. At the cottage on East Second Street, three girls met him at the door, calling back to their mother, "He's here! Daddy's home."

Their mother Margaret—black-haired, slim, and nearly as tall as her husband—held chubby, six-month-old David. Daddy took off his hat, brushed the other hand through his receding sandy brown hair, and told his wife about the auction.

She looked through her glasses, straight into his eyes, and nodded silently. She had seen the grubby yard and tumble-down shack on their trips out in the country. Her bright-eyed daughters didn't notice the hesitation. They only saw the sparkle in Daddy's eyes and heard the lilt in his voice. Marilyn, the five-year-old, jabbered to her sisters, "We'll be living in the country! It'll be an *adventure* and I can't *wait* 'til we move!"

She put her hand over her mouth, fearful she had spoken too loudly and Daddy would be cross. Virginia, two years older and that much wiser, cautioned under her breath, "The place is a mess. Mother said so, and I'll have to go to a new school."

Elizabeth, at three, said nothing. She blinked back and forth at the others, nervous about the change and scared the nights would be dark.

1

But it was a done deal. With the cash in his pocket Daddy had purchased a building that would become the family residence. On a parallel scale of significance, it would also become the place for him to answer God's call—the commissioning that had burned deep in his spirit for nearly two years.

The Call had come in late winter 1935. Daddy was feeding chickens at the Wilcox Farms near Hart's Lake, Washington. The job was a dull one compared to the position as store manager he had held prior to the depression, or his role as truck driver that he had lost because he wouldn't join a newly formed union. Yet the chicken job was a way to pay the bills, and for that he was grateful. One morning, as he measured out the grain to the chicks, he heard a voice say, "Do you love me more than these?"

He looked up, and the voice continued. "Feed my sheep."

The words were as clear as if his brother had spoken. Yet no other person was there, only the sense the Lord stood nearby. He went back to feeding the chickens, aware that he wasn't being called to a sheep ranch, but that God was echoing the message given to Peter, one of Jesus' disciples.

The next day, in nearly the same setting, Daddy heard the voice again. This time, the message was "Feed my lambs."

My father spoke out loud, even as he considered that God already knew his answer. "I am doing that already, Lord. I preach in the little church and speak at the jail. I witness to everyone you bring our way. We're all involved. My wife helps with the music, serves food to the poor, and our children sing at the rescue mission. What more are you asking?"

The third day, when he again heard "Feed my sheep," Daddy knew God was calling him to become a full-time minister and that he, God, would furnish what the family needed to live.

Daddy anticipated how Mother would respond. This decision would not only involve his faith, but hers as well. His wife was strong and resourceful, yet times were tough and work was scarce. In fact, before applying at the chicken farm he had been without employment for nearly a year. He remembered how hard it had been for his wife to see him come home day after day without landing a job, and how painful it was for her to sell several of their wedding gifts to make ends meet. He remembered how appreciative they had both been for this pauper's occupation, even though it paid next to nothing and kept him away from home six days and nights each week.

Daddy's heart burned within him as he repeated verbatim to Mother his chicken-yard conversations. Mother looked at him—rather seemed to look through him—before she spoke. "But how can you give up the little bit you earn to have no regular income? Think about your three children and the fourth that's coming. How will we live?"

Daddy didn't argue. Instead, he waited on God, waited on Mother, and continued feeding the chickens. It wasn't long before Mother looked up at him from prayer. She shook her head as peace began to fill her heart; shook her head at the unrealistic decision. But she told my father, "I believe that *you* believe. Your faith will be enough for both of us."

That day, a check for ten dollars came in the mail from a young lady my parents had not seen in several years. She wrote, "Margaret, are you in trouble? Do you have need?"[3]

Mother held the check in hand and said to Daddy, "This is enough confirmation for me. I will serve with you."

My father quit the chicken business. He did not reconsider when the owners offered to increase his salary and give him more time off for ministry. He did not blink when most of his friends and nearly every relative on both sides of the family said he'd lost his mind, and he'd become irresponsible as a father and a husband. Instead, he sold the home he'd built for Mother in Tacoma and gave away many of the furnishings. He took her and the three girls to live in a dank, dinky rental in the small town of Roy, not far from the Wilcox chicken farms. Within a few months, he moved them into the vacated McKenna Charleston Inn where they slept in the hospitality rooms, cooked in the tavern kitchen, and turned the dance hall with its green bar stools into a church sanctuary.

People came from all directions to hear "the new preacher" tell how God had called him to this town, to this tavern that had been a hall of sin and degradation until the day Daddy implored God to close its doors. The congregation outgrew that center and services were moved to another location. Soon after the move, a young couple from Canada visited and asked if they could assist in the services. "No," my father said, "I don't believe God has brought you here to assist. He has brought you here to lead. It is time for us to move on."

Daddy concurred with Mother that they wouldn't move on until after the baby came. David Arthur was born in Tacoma on March 24, 1937. Then move on they did, to Port Angeles, a busy mill town on Washington's Olympic Peninsula. The family settled into a cottage, a pillbox parsonage, on Second Street. Daddy would assist at the Independent Bible Church during the sabbatical of Pastor Hutchinson, hold services at the Clallam County jail, and begin an outreach to folks in the country.

Within a few weeks the outreach was established. Each Sunday morning, Daddy, Mother, and their four young ones left town to lead Sunday school they had started in a rural one-room school house. The trip took them seven miles west and up Dan Kelly Road. They entered Eden Valley, a rolling plateau of verdant fields divided by hand-hewn fences and speckled with grazing herds of cattle, woolly flocks of sheep, and cocky roosters with their harems of hens.

Daddy stopped to pick up kids along the way. Gladys Bolling was one of them. She and three of her siblings—Hazel, Harvey, and Audrey[4]—would be waiting by the road, after having crossed the creek, climbed the hill, and crawled through the barb-wire fence. Before they could see Mr. Corey's car, they could hear the sputtering motor. When the vehicle stopped for them, it was already filled with at least six people, a box of songbooks, and an accordion. But Mr. Corey could always make room for one more . . . or four.

At the meeting place, the Bollings emptied the nickels and pennies from their pockets into the offering basket while a few other locals stoked the fire in the wood stove and swept the floor. Everyone made a joyful noise of singing the hymns Mrs. Corey played on the accordion, and paid quiet attention to Mr. Corey's Bible messages.

One Sunday Daddy asked if anyone wanted to accept Jesus, and Gladys ran to the front. Afterwards, she skipped all the way home, not even stopping to notice the weather. She knew on no-rain days Mr. Corey would ask her and her siblings to walk all the way home so he could coast down the mountain by the other Eden Valley road and save on gas.

But, she thought later, *I was so happy that day I didn't even notice if it rained or not.* [5]

One night a week, my parents held meetings in homes farther west on Highway 9A, toward the community of Joyce. The McNally place at the top of Dempsey Road was a favorite. For at that home, Beverly and Joan McNally would be watching at the window for Virginia, their newest best friend, and waiting for Mother to sit down at their piano and play.

It was on the trips to the McNally home that the Coreys passed the decrepit grange hall that was up for sale. "If we live here," Daddy had reasoned to Mother, "we'll be close to Joyce. And Joyce is where we need to be."

Joyce. A pretty name to match its magnificence. Rugged white-capped Olympic Mountains to the south; sleepy sand-framed Crescent Beach to the north; and everywhere, sky-high evergreens, perfume-laden flowers, trout-filled streams, and forests full of animals in their natural habitat.

Joyce. Named for a settler who had helped establish a community of hardy pioneers, old country immigrants, tough loggers, and subsistence farmers. Joyce was exactly right for the Coreys, not because my father was looking for a place of pristine beauty, nor because he was of the same fiber as these residents; rather, because these people and their children were—he believed—the sheep and lambs God had called him to feed.

His belief was affirmed by a local who said, "We have never had a resident pastor here, just a visiting minister from time to time, and our families have been here now since our grandparents first laid claim on the land."[6]

So Daddy had gone to the courthouse and placed his bid for twenty-eight dollars. When he skipped down the steps, he carried a paper that declared the quarter acre and the building in Ramapo, three miles east of Joyce, belonged to him. It would be home, church, and the place to reach out to neighbors, friends, and passers-by. If Daddy heard Mother's silence about the purchase, he never let on.

Within days, Daddy surveyed the derelict, dilapidated dump. Piles of non-descript junk languished in the corners and layers of filth lined the floors. Grime covered the windows and weeds camouflaged the steps. A maze of spider webs crisscrossed the inside of the outdoor toilet, and signs of earlier usage encrusted its floor, walls, and seat bench.

Even Daddy, with his endless enthusiasm, was overwhelmed. So he called on a friend in Tacoma, Mr. Art Berg. "I've purchased a place to fix up. Can you come and help?"

The two shoveled garbage, scraped rubbish, and scrubbed excrement. They repaired floors, re-nailed walls, and rebuilt stairs. They washed windows, chafed the chimney, and dumped the ashes. For weeks, through the dead of winter, they worked as many hours as daylight permitted. The pair of Arthurs reveled in Christian camaraderie in the midst of chaos. Their fellowship would turn out to be spiritual preparation for an encounter of quite another sort.

Soon after Art left to return to his home, Daddy was putting away his tools when he turned to see his new next-door neighbor advancing down the rutty driveway—the driveway that cut through the front yard of the former grange. Peter Johnson stiff-walked in the manner of a uniformed soldier—his bearing like that of a warrior on assignment.

Earlier, while Daddy and Art were working, Johnson had driven by nearly every day, to and from his turn-of-the-century farmhouse. At first he had saluted with his hand or stopped by to talk. Then he quit giving any form of greeting and faced the other way.

That day, as my father walked to meet the neighbor, he ignored the man's scowl and the vintage musket-loading rifle anchored on his immense shoulder. Daddy held out his hand and smiled. Johnson ignored the gesture, pointed toward the structure, and growled. "Preacher Corey, that piece of your building juts out onto my property."

He turned to face Daddy and added. "What are *you* goin' to do about it?"

My father studied the room in question. He didn't know when nor by whom the eight-by-eight foot addition had been built, but he assumed Mr. Johnson had known. Daddy spoke with calm, measured words.

"Mr. Johnson, I'm sorry the room of our home has encroached upon your land."

He paused, and spoke again, "I would gladly cut off any part that is causing offense, but my saw is not big enough. If you will bring yours, together we can remove whatever lumber crosses the line."

Johnson turned around. Within the hour he was back, leading a team of horses attached to a wagon. He hoisted the crosscut saw onto the shoulder that had earlier carried the gun. Without words, the two men lined up the walls with the boundary and marked the overhang. They went to work on opposite ends of the saw, *scrunch-scratch, scrunch-scratch, scrunch-scratch.* The slight-framed minister on the inside was no match in size or strength to the farmer outside, but he kept his end of the saw moving until the walls and roof were separated. Johnson dropped the saw on the wagon, hooked a chain to the disconnected piece, and led the horses out into the field. The wall of the side room toppled over and tumbled along behind the wagon. Daddy looked at the gaping hole in his building and walked toward the neighbor.

When Johnson took note of the troubled look on my father's face, he mumbled his rationale for hauling away the demolished wall. "The lumber on *my* side of the property line also belongs to me."

Daddy waited a moment for his own initial reaction of anger to subside, waited for the right answer from God. "Sir, I am unable to purchase lumber to cover this open space, and the end of our home is now in your yard. I know you are a respected man in this community. What will your neighbors and friends think if you leave my family of four small children without protection against the elements?"

Johnson, without lifting his eyes, answered, "All right, Corey, you may have the lumber."

He turned, unhitched the wall from his chain, heaved his bulk onto the wagon, and snapped the reins of the horses.

Daddy took the fallen section apart, straightened the nails, sorted the boards, and reconstructed an outer wall on the narrow strip that was left of the room. He stacked the extra bits of splintered boards and the scraps of broken shingles onto the porch for firewood.

As Daddy told Mother of the encounter, he added, "In early conversations I introduced myself as a preacher of the Gospel and invited Johnson and his family to come to our meetings. He just told me he wasn't a religious man and that this place wasn't built to be a church or a house. I'm not sure what caused his outburst."

Mother nodded. She wondered if Daddy had preached to the neighbor with a mite more intensity than was wise. She'd at times heard the passion of conviction in her husband's voice and had watched offense cloud a listener's eyes. Yet on the subject of this possibility she remained silent. Instead, Mother suggested that perhaps Johnson's demeanor had to do with the history that connected him to the building. She knew the land had once been his and he had helped establish the Ramapo Grange, which for a time had also been used as a schoolhouse. She also knew that in recent years, rats and bats had taken residence and no one had paid the taxes. She finished her musings with a reminder to Daddy, "We'll just trust God to change his spirit."

Within days of the confrontation, Daddy moved the family from the cozy parsonage into the grange building. Peter Johnson was nowhere to be seen that day. Yet his unnerving attitude and action served, perhaps, as a foreshadowing of what lay ahead for the Corey family in their new habitation—their Grange House.

Ramapo Grange used as secondary school 1921[7]

CHAPTER TWO
The Grange House
(Spring 1938)

The storm spit at the family of six as they rushed from the car to their new home. March winds howled down from the mountains and across the neighbors' fields, whining under the eaves and wheezing through the gaps around the windows and doors. Rain pelted the single panes of glass and hammered on the roof. Waterfalls poured off the eaves into streams that chiseled trenches around the sides of the building and spilled into overflowing puddles.

Daddy led the way and Mother carried one-year-old David. Three girls followed close behind, stopping on the small porch outside the back door of the kitchen to shake off the rain. Inside the kitchen, they walked past a chipped, brown-stained porcelain sink with a drain hole and no faucets. Next to it, pale light leaked through an east-facing window onto a scabby counter. Across the room stood an institutional-size iron cook stove with an upper warming tray. To the left of the stove, an empty cupboard with shelves awaited staples and dishes; to the right, a bin held firewood and kindling. Behind the stove a steep, narrow stairway led to the attic. The girls had to hold on to the wall or to the unstable open-side railing to climb the stairs. The floor of the attic was laid out in two decks, one a couple of feet higher than the other. The ceiling was peaked enough for Mother to stand in the center, but the eaves on the edges connected with the floor. The upper room, which had been used for storage, became the Bedroom.

Next to the kitchen, a second room had just enough space for a few chairs and Mother's wedding table with the pullout ends. Little more than a passage, this area had served as a meal hall for the grange and a lunchroom for the school. The family called it the Dining Room, though most of the year it was too chilly for sitting down to eat.

An opening from the Dining Room led to a large hall with a lofty ceiling. This had once been the community center—the place where farmers met and where young people went to school or danced. A black pot-bellied stove with corroded silver handles was stationed near the inside wall, its flue connected to the same chimney as the kitchen range. The opposite wall with its two north-facing windows became the designated location for Mother's prized piano and a davenport sofa. The girls named the spacious hall the Big Room.

Daddy crumpled pages from a catalog into the kitchen stove, topping them with shingle bits and bark scraps. Fingers of smoke reached upward, and he added wood that crackled into flame. In the Big Room, he lit the potbelly stove to take off the chill, but said it would take too much wood to keep that room warm unless there were guests.

A frightful distance from the house was the Toilet, sometimes called the Backhouse. It had been sanitized, which meant there were no spiders or cobwebs to assault the face and no garbage on the floor. The girls tested the facility right away. It was the same type of smelly shed as they had used in Roy before moving to Port Angeles, with the same type of frigid hole that froze their backsides. The shiny pages of a Montgomery Ward catalog were stacked near the seat. Many of the softer pages—the black and white newsprint type that would have been a bit more absorbent for wiping—had been removed for starting fires. Elizabeth, at barely four years, was so tiny she had to hang on to the front edge to keep from falling through. Virginia, going on eight, held her sister by the shoulders as guarantee of safety. Marilyn, nearing her sixth birthday, crossed her legs and danced around. "Hurry, hurry," she urged. "I can't wait."

In the backyard, a rusty pipe and pump marked the location of a well. Daddy braced his legs and battled with the screeching handle until he had drawn enough water for Mother to fill the kettle on the stove, cook soup, and wash the first round of dishes. He placed buckets under the eaves to harvest rain.

There was no electricity, which meant there were no lights to turn on. After dark, a kerosene lamp on the kitchen table threw shaking light under the stairs and onto the kitchen stove. It cast creeping, slithering shadows into the far corners of the kitchen and dining room—shadows that seemed, to the girls, like jungle animals or even snakes.

At bedtime, Mother lit a second lamp and followed the girls up the stairs. At the top, they passed the section set aside for their parents' bed and the baby's crib, and crossed the cavernous space to a mattress on the floor. The mat was covered with blankets wide enough to envelope all three if they stayed close together. Mother placed the chamber pot nearby, but not so close a sleepy child would knock it over. Marilyn, who had to "go to the toilet" at least once during the night, could crawl toward it from her side of the bed, and Mother could reach it for her own needs without disturbing the sleepers.

Elizabeth, tucked between her two sisters, prayed, "Dear Father, thank you for the new house. Help me not be afraid in the dark. Jesus-name-amen."

Marilyn dragged out her prayer—and her time with Mother's lamp—by listing all the immediate and extended family members she could remember, finally finishing with, "Thank you we don't have to go outside to the toilet in the night. In Jesus' name, Amen."

Virginia said she was thankful to live close enough to the McNallys to walk.

Darkness hung heavy as tar in the attic after Mother carried the lamp downstairs. Just a sliver of light crept through the stairwell behind her. The trio of girls snuggled tight and buried their faces, becoming a single mound beneath the heavy blankets.

When they opened their eyes it was already light. The sun was shining through spaces under the eaves, accompanied by the whirring of a frosty breeze. They jumped out of bed, tucked the covers around the mattress, and scampered down the stairs to the kitchen. David, delighted to see them, toddled after them as quickly as his short legs allowed. Next to the kitchen range, his sisters dressed in their play clothes—their oldest dresses covering loose knit leggings.

Mother put David into the highchair and Virginia set bowls of steaming oatmeal on the kitchen table. The kids were starving, but first things first. Daddy pulled a small card from the scripture box. He read it, and led out in a chorus of thanksgiving to God for his love and provision. He prayed, and gave assignments. "We've a lot of work to do. Virginia, Marilyn, you are responsible to pick up wood around the place to keep the kitchen fire burning." He saw Elizabeth's consternation at being left out, and added, "You can help too."

After the kitchen was cleaned up, the youngsters grabbed their coats and pulled over their shoes some rubber galoshes—what Daddy called low-slung boots. Mother bundled up the baby in his red wool Santa suit and Daddy went to pump water from the well.

The girls skipped down the driveway—the opposite direction from Pete Johnson's house—with Mother and David close behind. "It will be a treasure hunt," shouted Marilyn.

They crossed Highway 9A[8], listed on maps as Piedmont Road or the Olympic Highway, and headed for the clearing beyond. A wide swath of land with railroad tracks slicing it lengthwise was the place to find wood. The search party got busy, with Marilyn and Virginia placing the largest pieces in the crooks of their arms and giving the small sticks to Elizabeth.

They heard a rumble in the distance. The sound got closer and louder until they could distinguish a *clackety-clackety-clackety*. A deafening two-blast whistle shrilled in their ears. Around the corner roared a black engine, clouds billowing from its smoke stack, and sparks arcing from its wheels. Behind the engine, a snake of flatbed cars squealed and twisted, each piled high with fresh-cut logs. The girls counted until a battered red and yellow caboose signaled the end of the noisy parade. A brakeman engineer in the caboose saw the troupe and saluted with his hat out the opening in the back door. They waved back until the train was past the bend. They could still hear the clatter of the wheels passing over the spaces between the ends of rails and a fading echo after the train thundered across the tall trestle to the east. Then it was silent.

David clapped his hands and pumped his feet. His sisters chattered. Mother lifted her face and took a deep breath. "Can you smell it?" she asked, and then she answered her own question. "That's the smell of tar and creosote that preserves the wooden railroad ties underneath the rails. It smells strong right now because of the heat of the train."

Beaming faces met Daddy back at the house. David hugged his piece of bark and the others dropped theirs on the porch. Marilyn pointed to the pile, "Look Daddy, we found gold on our treasure hunt."

Elizabeth squeaked, "The man in the *caboosh* waved at us."

Marilyn corrected her sister, "You mean caboose."

Virginia emphasized her new word. "We could smell the *creosote* on the railroad ties."

Within a short time, the children knew which day and what time to expect the train. At the first rumble in the distance they ran to their staked-out spot on the corner. The train was their friend. It talked to them and they answered back. It whistled its greeting and tossed gifts of firewood and bark. For many years the logging train clattered past the Corey kids. First there were four, then five, then eight—and most often a small child held up by a bigger one. The driver smiled as he blew the whistle for the cheering crowd, and the brakeman in the caboose chuckled as he waved his cap. The interaction must have afforded the engineers a brief intermission in the isolated trip from the logging camps to the mills in Port Angeles, and their greetings provided entertainment—as well as kindling—for the youthful audience on the hillside.

Each day that the train passed by, the sisters filled gunny sacks with the bark. They tried to balance on the track without falling off and tried to remember the words to a song they'd once heard about whistling while you work. When the words didn't come, they attempted to whistle, but that also met with little success. Nonetheless, adding music to the chore took the hardship out of it, at least for a few weeks.

The girls travelled farther and farther along the tracks to the west, past the Nordstrom Road and up the hill towards Joyce. To the east, they stopped at the Salt Creek trestle—an extensive stretch from one side to the other, and so high you could barely see the water below. It was a fearsome place—fearsome enough to nag Marilyn to show her grit. But not yet, because Elizabeth was a fraidy-cat and Virginia had to go to school.

Within a few days of the move into the Grange House, Virginia caught the bus for the three-mile commute west to Crescent Consolidated Schools at Joyce. Two months remained of second grade. Still only seven years old, she was facing the fourth new school, the fourth new teacher, and the fourth new batch of strangers. But this was her first school bus—a long yellow bus filled with all types, from runny-nose six-year-olds up to smart-aleck teenagers. Mother and the younger kids walked to the highway with Virginia, and waved as she climbed the steps.

The first day, Mrs. Hall discovered that Virginia didn't read as well as the others in her class. She stumbled over her words and could not sound them out. Mrs. Hall presumed the child had been subjected to the progressive no-phonics philosophy of reading promoted in city schools. She sent a note home telling Mother she would tutor Virginia during recess until she caught up with the rest of the class.

Virginia brought home her reading lessons and her phonics flash cards. She caught on quickly, studying with Mrs. Hall and practicing with Mother. The younger girls said it wasn't fair that they couldn't ride the bus to school and have their own reading books. So they fixed a classroom upstairs near a window, and occupied themselves for hours with scraps of paper, a few crayons, and pencils. Sometimes Virginia gave them lessons from her schoolwork and read her primer books out loud. But more often she went to her own corner on the opposite side of the upper room, or headed outside to hide near her favorite stump. If they followed, she would say, "Leave me alone—I have to study."

That's what she said one morning when Elizabeth begged her to read. Elizabeth, looking towards her sister with scolding, disappointed eyes, backed toward the stairs. In an instant, her foot caught and she tumbled down, catapulting out under the railing, through the air, finally landing face-first on the kitchen floor. She sat up and howled. Blood covered her eye, her cheek, and her chin. Mother picked her up and carried her to the sink. Marilyn flew down the stairs and brought a ragged roll of adhesive tape. Virginia stayed out of sight until Mother had anchored the gash, covered it with a patch of torn threadbare sheets, and stationed Elizabeth flat on the davenport. Virginia, out of guilt, promised to read her a book, but Marilyn served as nursemaid for the next few days. Hour after hour she hovered, fixing the blankets, tipping the spout of a teapot with water into her little sister's mouth, and offering to help change the dressings. Stitches would have helped the healing and lessened the scarring, but the car had a flat tire, and a trip to the doctor was never discussed.

By the time Elizabeth recovered, Marilyn and Virginia had braved the first part of the trestle. They encouraged the youngest to try.

"Please don't go," Elizabeth whined, "there's no bark on the trestle."

But Marilyn kept going. She called back, "I dare you, double dare you."

Virginia, feeling her own fear, prompted. "Don't be afraid. Y-you can do it. I'm right with you."

Close together on their hands and knees, the two eased out onto the trestle. Elizabeth was sure she would be sucked through the gaps between the sticky black ties. She bit her lip to keep from crying. Marilyn saw them coming and crab-legged back to secure the vulnerable side. "See, we've got you in the middle of a sandwich where you're safe. It's not so bad. You're very brave."

On each subsequent trip to the trestle they counted off a few more ties over the chasm. They discussed a strategy for safety in case the train came before they had time to return to the west end. The plan was to climb onto a small shelf jutting out at the middle of the trestle. It held a big water tank they could hang onto while the train passed by. It was a formidable thought, even for Marilyn.

The day came when they had crawled far enough to be just above the creek, right next to the water tank. Marilyn whooped, "Lookeeee, we're past the middle! It's closer to the other side—come on!"

They hobbled on their hands and feet over the gully until they could almost touch the ground below. Then they stood, grabbed hands, and ran the last few yards. Elizabeth, her legs jiggling like jelly, pointed at the railroad bed and at an open space where a passenger depot had once stood. The area was strewn with bark and splinters of timber from the logging loads. The girls stuffed the gunnysacks and headed to the highway just a few steps from the depot clearing. Virginia and Marilyn would have preferred traveling on the railroad where they wouldn't have been seen by passersby, but no way could the two older sisters convince Elizabeth to return via the trestle. Instead she skipped ahead and they dragged the loot a quarter mile home on the road. Elizabeth had mastered one measure of fear. It was enough for that day.

Daddy, meanwhile, was upgrading the well to give it a multipurpose use. Not unlike the earliest settlers, he was turning it into a cold storage vault—into Mother's new Frigidaire. He constructed a platform exactly the size of the well, cut a hole in the middle for the water pipe, and secured the framework about six feet into the hole. He fixed a hook to a rope that lowered or raised the food-filled containers and tins of milk. The children weren't allowed to play in the cold room, but they were primed to climb down the ladder and rescue the rope if it fell, or to clean up food if it spilled.[9]

That is, if there *was* enough food on hand to store or spill—supply of which, it seemed, there was less and less.

The kids, within a few weeks of the move, had learned not to ask "what's for dinner?" Better to be busy about other things, like exploring the countryside, like getting to know the neighbors, and like being resourceful in finding food to eat.

Virginia Marilyn David Elizabeth 1937

CHAPTER THREE
The Neighbors
(Spring 1938)

They got a chance to be busy with all three—explore, visit, and eat—one Sunday morning when the car wouldn't start. Daddy still led Sunday school at Eden Valley, but seven miles was too far for all of them to hike. So Daddy said he'd go alone, and Mother told the rest, "We'll take our *own* hike through the woods."

Hiking. It had been the pastime of Daddy and Mother before they were married; and of Mother's parents, aunts, and uncles the generation earlier. In fact there is a memorial near Mount Rainier in honor of this clan of avid explorers. The site is a rippling waterfall—Edith Falls—off the trail at Mount Rainier named after Mother's mother.[10]

So Daddy picked up his Bible and walked to the highway, while Mother and the children donned jackets and headed up a rutty logging road and across the fill over a small brook. The youngsters played follow the leader, dodging or jumping over the puddles that filled the chuckholes. When Mother shushed the children, frogs began to resonate in the spring ponds, first a solo, then a second, and a third, until the sound of the ensemble became a choir. The music echoed through the air—air laden with the aroma of recent rain, fresh growth of evergreens, and salmonberry blossoms.

The trail ended at the Smith[11] farm that had been deserted decades earlier when a fire destroyed the cabin. Weeds and branches covered a tumbledown shed and pieces of broken machinery, but nearby stood a hay barn still intact. Inside the barn, the girls discovered a wagon—the kind with large wooden-spoke wheels that an owner would have hitched behind a horse to ride to the store or to the neighbors. Marilyn begged to climb on the wagon, but Virginia had something else in mind. "I think we're really close to McNallys. Can't we go see them?"

Mother negated both options. "It's getting late, and if Daddy got a ride, he'll be back by now. I never left anything ready for his lunch."

Mother then hurried the group towards home on a shortcut, cross-country through the woods and pasture. The path took them close to Pete Johnson's home, and Mother stopped. "I'd like to meet Mrs. Johnson," she said.

The girls held back—they'd heard Daddy's stories about Peter Johnson—but Mother stepped onto the porch and knocked. The door was opened by a round, grandmotherly lady clothed in old country style, a scarf around her head and a worn apron nearly covering her ankle-length flowery housedress. Mother put out her hand. "I'm Margaret Corey and these are my children," she said. "We want to apologize for trespassing on your property. I—I didn't realize we'd come out of the woods so close to your home."

Mrs. Johnson answered with a heavy Scandinavian accent, her singsong voice almost like music, "Goot day! I'm Mrs. Yonson. You must come in vit your lovely children."

Mother knew politeness required her to receive the hospitality—not only the black-as-tar coffee long brewed in the pot on the cast iron range, but also the cardamom-scented feast of baked goods that Mrs. Johnson put before them. Not that Mother was averse to eating treats and drinking coffee—it had been awhile since she'd had any grounds at home to brew. "Eat goot now." Mrs. Johnson encouraged.

The girls inhaled. Breads, pastries, cheese, and a full glass of creamy milk for each child. They were so busy trying to eat like young ladies and not gobble the food that they only caught snippets of Mother's questions and Mrs. Johnson's lilting answers. But, as she drank the last of her milk, Marilyn heard Mrs. Johnson say in her sing-song, "After ve bought da land from da homesteaders, it vas such a mess of logs und stumps."

Mrs. Johnson shook her head. "So hard da life, back den."

Marilyn muttered to herself, "Still is hard. I wish *we* had some mess of logs to cut up for firewood."

On the way out, the children tripped over themselves to shake the woman's farm-calloused hand. "Thank you, thank you, thank you."

"I hope you vill come again, und you are velcome any time."

Mother smiled back, scooped up David, and led the troupe home. By the time they arrived, Daddy had already fixed a sandwich for himself. Mother put David, who had fallen asleep on her shoulder, into the crib. "I'm sorry we're so late," she said. "But I was glad to finally meet Mrs. Johnson. She seems quite different from her husband, so open to talk, and so kind. I wonder if our accidental visit was God's plan for us to become friends."[12]

Marilyn said, "I wanted to see Walter, but he wasn't there."

Everyone liked Walter, Pete Johnson's grown son. He wore a friendly smile, talked to the girls, and patted David on the head.

As dinnertime arrived a few hours later, the girls could think of nothing apart from Mrs. Johnson's food. They couldn't remember the last time they had eaten so well. Sometimes visitors dropped off a meaty soup bone or an armload of vegetables. But offerings of money were small and irregular, so staples were usually in short supply. Mother didn't complain about the challenge of getting meals on the table. She even made jokes about it, at least these first months. "You wondered how we were eating and if the children are getting enough milk," she wrote in a letter to her cousin Naoma. "We are getting a gallon of good milk a day from a local dairy. It is only 30¢ which is certainly reasonable. And we haven't missed a meal yet."[13]

When she told the girls what she'd written, Marilyn said, "Oh, yes, lots of times I don't get enough to fill up."

Virginia frowned, "Well, I didn't get enough to eat when you sent me upstairs for being naughty."

In spite of Mother's early optimism and humor, her unease about the shortage of money to buy milk and eggs was simmering. Soon, thirty cents was more than she could afford for milk and she told the dairyman not to stop by any more.

The day came when even the flour was gone and Mother could not make bread. She'd fixed oatmeal for three days straight—oatmeal three times a day for three days! Virginia said, "I will throw up if we have to eat oatmeal again for dinner."

That evening Daddy called all of them into the kitchen and Mother pulled open the empty flour bin. They sang the doxology.

> Praise God for whom all blessings flow.
> Praise him all creatures here below.
> Praise him above you heavenly hosts.
> Praise Father, Son, and Holy Ghost. Amen.[14]

Like Daddy, everyone in that circle believed—or at least hoped—God would replenish the bin. Virginia managed to eat her oatmeal again without vomiting, and a gift of food arrived at their door the next day.

Sometimes God did flat-out miracles, producing bags and boxes of food on the porch unannounced. But Mother had ideas too, and conceivably her ideas were part of the miracles. She took her brood with her to visit local farmers, including the Nyholms and Nordstroms, where she would offer the coins in her hand to pay for any milk they might spare. Each of the neighbors welcomed Mrs. Corey and her well-behaved children, and offered them a snack. The kindly host would motion with her hand, "Sit down here so I can serve you coffee and."

Coffee and was the old country way to say, "Coffee is ready and I will find something to go with it."

The ladies charged Mother little or nothing for the milk—especially if they had already separated out the cream for delivery to the Port Angeles Creamery. On occasion the quest for milk brought a bonus. Such occurred when Mother sent Virginia, Marilyn, and Elizabeth to the Nordstroms to pick up skim milk. In the separator room where the milk was stored, they saw a large box of potatoes. Virginia couldn't stifle her outburst. "Oh Mrs. Nordstrom, I don't know when I've seen such wonderful potatoes. Did you grow them?"

"Yes, we grew them. Would you like to take some home with you?"

"Thank you so much. Are you sure? Mother would be *so* happy to have them."

The trio was tempted to skip down the hill, across the bridge, along the highway, and all the way home, but the milk was too precious to spill, and the sack of potatoes too heavy. They belted out a blessing instead—one that Aunt Hazel had taught them.

> We thank thee for our daily food
> God is love, God is love
> But most of all for Jesus' blood
> God is lo-o-ove, God is love.[15]

Three out-of-breath girls burst through the door and plopped the potatoes on the floor of the kitchen in front of Mother. "Can we cook some right now, Mother? Please?

"Please, Mother?" echoed Elizabeth.

David picked one up and hugged it to his shirt. "Peas, Mudder?"

Summer came, and Daddy and Mother discussed the problems of the water system. The well was running dry and the pump barely holding together. The handle squeaked on the upstroke and whined on the downstroke. *Eek-waa, eek-waa, eek-waa.* It dropped red and brown rust into the water bucket. Daddy planned to dig the well deeper and repair the pump. But while he did it, the girls would have to carry water from the creek—the creek that was across the highway, on the far side of the railroad tracks, through a barbed wire fence, and down a steep bank.

Every day of the summer, the girls took two trips to the creek with their tin buckets. The spring-fed stream danced and rippled across the rocky bed, its sparkling surface reflecting the sunrays that filtered through the alder trees. The trio filled their pails in a clear pool, trying to nab the slippery minnows that zipped to and fro. With buckets full, they competed to climb out of the gully, up the slippery bank, and through the fence without spilling their slopping cargo. They got better with practice.

On some days—after the household water had been carried—they returned to the creek with dirty diapers. Twenty feet below the pool where they collected the drinking water, Mother had pointed out smooth rocks on which to kneel. Hands in the icy water, the girls dunked, shook, scrubbed, squeezed and scoured, all the time singing at the top of their lungs. Their favorite song, or at least Marilyn's, was a rhyme in the round to the tune of *Twinkle, Twinkle Little Star.*

> Rub-a-doo-doo, rub-a doo,
> Wash the smelly Number 2.
> See it float, or see it sink.
> Never worry, just don't drink.
> Rub-a-doo-doo, rub-a doo . . .

"Shhh, Marilyn, not so loud." Virginia cautioned one day. She could see Daddy coming down the path. If he heard the silly words and the shrill voice of Marilyn, Virginia knew her sister would *get it.*

No matter how far away the girls were, Daddy would hear his middle daughter's voice above all other sounds. Her voice had been a malediction for her since the time she was two, and likely before that. But Marilyn still couldn't curb her gusto, no matter that she knew her noise could bring a reckoning. She'd come to expect that her father would quote the scripture, "Foolishness is bound in the heart of a child, but the rod of correction will drive it far from him"—after which he would apply that correction to her.

So the girls switched to a hymn that was supposed to be loud.

Onward Christian Soldiers, marching as to war
With the cross of Jesus going on before
Christ, the royal master, leads against the foe
Forward into battle, See his banners go . . . [16]

This was Daddy's first trip to the Laundromat. In his arms he carried a hand wringer. The girls watched, speechless, as he nailed the portable device to a log near the washing pool. The rubber-roller invention was almost as clever as the modern electric wringer washing machine Mother had left with her friend in Port Angeles, because there was no electricity at the Grange House.

Daddy stood by as the girls took turns feeding the dripping diapers through the two rollers and twisting the handle. It was less effort to extract water, less wet-diaper weight to carry, and infinitely more fun. Daddy helped them tote their payload back to Mother, who had staged the next step.

On the porch, Mother had filled the round, galvanized washtub with hot water from the stove-top tin boiler; then had added soap she'd brewed from beef tallow and lye. The girls plopped in the pre-scrubbed diapers. Up and down, up and down, counting all the way to a hundred, as they took turns pumping the plunger. David practiced counting with them, so he would be able to pump when he grew tall enough.

The soapy diapers were squeezed and returned to the tin pails—not the same ones used for drinking water, of course—and carried back to the creek for a final rinse before delivery to Mother at the clothesline.

Mother was particular to the point of persnickety when it came to laundry on the line. She had the spiffy diapers flapping on the outside for all to see, with the unmentionables hidden behind. One day, for no apparent reason, a car braked to a stop in the driveway. A tall woman in a gray and purple striped dress got out, walked up to Mother and declared, "I've never seen such white diapers. How *ever* do you get them so clean?"

Mother didn't explain the process. She just thanked the lady and turned to the girls, "You can see how your effort has been rewarded."

With bucket delivery of drinking water established and diaper service fully functional, Daddy pulled the pump out of the well, gathered the pick and shovel, and hacked away at the hardpan and rocks. Marilyn, recently turned six, was his right-hand "man." She shoveled the mud he threw over the edge. And, if Daddy didn't put too much slurry in the pail, she could haul it up and dump it for him. Marilyn pumped up her muscles. "Ha," she bragged to her sisters, "I'm stronger than you."

"And I don't care a whit." Virginia retorted. "I'm going in to help Mother."

Mother was seated at the kitchen table, a blank paper in front of her. She looked up as her eight-year-old asked, "Will we be able to visit Grandma Phenicie this summer? Do you think?"

"I don't know," Mother said. "There's so much to do before winter. Besides getting the well working, we need to fill the cracks around the windows and put paper under the floors to keep out some of the cold. And Daddy says he doesn't think the car would even make it that far."

She turned back to her blank letter, but as Virginia walked away, she heard a catch in Mother's whisper, "But I need to see my mother, I really do."

Mother had been anxious about her mother, Grandma Phenicie, for nearly a year, almost since the move from Roy to Port Angeles. In the fall of '37, Grandpa Phenicie had been diagnosed with lung cancer. He'd undergone surgery, but his suffering only worsened until he died on Feb. 25, 1938.[17] Mother had been unable to leave the children during those months and could only offer comfort and consolation to Grandma in the letters she wrote.

Then in the summer of 1938, when Daddy was working on the well, Mother also needed care. She found herself, more and more often, flopped in the rocking chair or going to bed early. She sighed at the prospect of another day full of cleaning house and canning vegetables the neighbors had thinned from their gardens. She was grateful for the children who worked hard to fit baby carrots into jars, snap the ends off green beans, haul wood for the range, and shoo David away from the hissing pressure cooker—but she was still the one in charge of all of it, and it never seemed to end.

Mother leaned over the table, finding it hard to explain how she felt, even to her cousin, the one person with whom she could be completely honest. "Arthur says he guesses I shouldn't be on my feet canning and I don't know but what he's right," she managed to write that day. "Our living room, though it is July, is very cool – even this morning a fire would be comfortable. We've so much work to do before winter hits us again, so it doesn't seem possible that we will get to Tacoma to see you or my mother."[18]

Margaret and her mother
Edith Phenicie ca 1912

The weary one held her head in her hands, yearning not only to comfort her mother, but also to rest and recuperate from an ailment to which she alluded, but gave no name.[19] And deep in her heart, she felt an ache of homesickness.

CHAPTER FOUR
The Relatives
(Summer 1938)

Near the end of July, Mother and the children were able to make the trip to Tacoma. Daddy took them to Grandma's place[20] at 115 East 34th, and left on a traveling mission with another preacher.

The girls tiptoed into Grandma's home, a stately structure that was as silent as a cat-guarded mouse hole. It seemed so different than when they had last been there, nearly a year earlier. Grandpa was now gone and the walls did not echo with his mirth. He was not there to make their visit like a carnival as he once would have. Back then, it didn't matter that Grandpa had labored twelve hours moving baggage at the train station; he would recover his energy in the leather and oak recliner as his granddaughters teased, giggled, and climbed all over him. Now the recliner was empty.

The girls were quiet, but 16-month-old David—Mother's "he-man"—paid no attention to the dreary mood. He ran, laughing, from one room to another on his stubby legs while Aunt Eleanor, Mother's younger sister, chased after him. David was Grandma's first grandson and Aunt Eleanor's first nephew. His free spirit was what they needed.

After that, the girls' reserve wore off and they explored every nook and cranny of Grandma's dignified three-story house—including the dark basement that held truckloads of sawdust for the furnace. They climbed the wide, oak staircase with the leaded glass window that glittered as a rainbow in the sunshine. They entered the bathroom with the claw foot tub and used the toilet with the wooden box on the ceiling that held the water until one of them yanked the handle. The girls weren't supposed to, but they even snuck from the second floor up the narrow staircase into the attic that had been Uncle Herbert's room until he got married the year before. Now, the attic was all theirs to explore—the trunk with mothballed coats and the clock that didn't tick. They studied the boat-making plans Uncle Herbert had drawn before constructing a 30-foot yacht, and the photo of a crane dropping the unwieldy watercraft into Puget Sound.

Best of all, at least for Marilyn, in the attic they discovered Mother's childhood tea set. Marilyn caressed the cups and saucers, holding her pinky out just so, while touching the fragile edge to her lips and pretending to sip. "Someday I'll have white china, someday I will." She whispered.

After dark, the girls gazed out the narrow windows of the dining room at the bay that glimmered with reflections from a pulsating lighthouse and passing ships. They watched the flamingo hue of sunset clouds and the fickle shape of smoke from the pulp mills below. The vista at night almost made up for dingy daytime skies and the infamous rotten fumes of the mills sometimes referred to as the "aroma of Tacoma."

The threesome slept in Aunt Eleanor's oversized room—in the iron bed that had once been their mother's. In the morning they pretended to be asleep in order to spy on beautiful Aunt Eleanor who prepped by the mirror for her job at the dental office. They were awed by the bright red lipstick that glistened as their aunt rubbed her lips together and blotted them on a cloth. Mother didn't wear lipstick and the girls knew that Daddy didn't approve but, oh my, it surely enhanced Aunt Eleanor's glamour.

Now with Grandpa gone and Uncle Herbert married, Aunt Eleanor came home from work to shovel mountains of sawdust into the furnace or shove the stiff push mower up the steep hill in the backyard. The three girls didn't think it right that such a gorgeous lady didn't just marry one of the handsome men who came to see her and let *him* take care of such matters.

At breakfast in the kitchen, arthritic, bow-legged Grandma put brown sugar on the oatmeal. *Brown sugar on the oatmeal!* Elizabeth couldn't squelch her songs. She twittered non-stop in a voice that was high-pitched and clear as a bird whistle. Grandma said it wasn't proper to sing at the table and Elizabeth quit for a while—until the spontaneous song bubbled out of her again. And Grandma let it go.

One day, Grandma met the iceman on the front porch. Four stair-step observers stood guard as he hooked sharp talons onto a block of ice, hefted it from his truck, lugged it through the house, and dropped it in the metal-lined wooden container on the back porch. The icebox would hold milk, butter, and meat until the next delivery or until all the melted ice dripped out below. Grandma's cold chest was much more convenient than the cooler room down inside the well back home.

Grandma had a phone on the wall beside the door to the living room. When you pulled the crank, an operator answered, and you could call, for instance, Cousin Naoma to see if she would like you to visit. She always did if she was home from the Pacific First Federal Savings and Loan office. She lived just around the block at 115 East 35th in a cramped bungalow with an ebonized piano and a muddle of paraphernalia. Naoma saved everything—every paper, every letter, every magazine, every memento. In her place, you could hardly get around. But Naoma was as warm and cuddly as any relative could be. The girls understood how Mother loved her so much, as if she were a favorite older sister. They had seen the picture of Naoma as the flower girl in Grandma's and Grandpa's wedding. They knew she had taught Mother to play the piano and been her confidante while growing up. And they loved her too.

Through all the early years, Naoma was the recipient of Mother's longest, most detailed letters—letters that generally included counsel to the older cousin in regard to a couple of long-term suitors whom Naoma held at bay. In her return letters, Naoma refrained from criticizing Arthur, even though she was concerned for the children's welfare. "After all," she said to herself, "Art is dear Margaret's husband."

The girls didn't visit Great Uncles Charlie and Joe and their wives who lived on either side of Grandma. Mother said not to bother them. What she didn't say was that she lacked the fortitude to face her relatives' raised eyebrows—eyebrows lifted at her husband who had quit his job and gone off the "deep end of religion." Mother needed more time, more strength to rebuild those relationships, but she knew she could, and one day would.

Mother filled the week, sitting with her mother, drinking coffee and recuperating. Then she got busy. Daddy's sister Hazel Bruck, who supported Daddy's call to ministry, took her and the children to the Brucks' country cabin to pick beans. The next day they canned 48 quarts and nearly as many pints. That seemed like too much canning for one day, but Aunt Hazel had the right equipment. Her husband Emil, a machinist, had built from heavy steel an industrial size custom canner that would hold 24 quarts on the bottom with a layer of pints on top. He had manufactured wing-nut bolts to hold down the solid lid. Even empty, the pot was almost too heavy for the ladies to lift—and Aunt Hazel forbade Mother to even try.

Energetic, jovial Aunt Hazel had Mother joking in ways she hadn't for months. Mother hummed in the car on the way home and didn't hush the gigglers. It seemed the visit with Grandma and the amity of Aunt Hazel had put to rest the unnamed infirmity and the grief of Grandpa's death.

Back at the Grange House, Mother and the girls put the quarts of Aunt Hazel's green beans in the cupboard, lowered the bushels of fresh produce into the well cooler, and unpacked a box of pre-worn shoes, coats, and dresses Naoma had sent along.

"Did you ever hear of a missionary barrel? That's what this gift is like," Mother wrote to Naoma. She said how pleased she was with the fit of the red dress and the black one, "considering the body they are going on."[21] And how the shoes would save her the need to buy new winter ones for herself—not mentioning the lack of money for such extravagance.

Naoma and Aunt Eleanor sent packages every few months. Mother took the dresses and coats apart, redefined the shapes, and sewed the new pieces together. Her feet flew back and forth on the treadle of the sewing machine, her agile hands gliding to-and-fro with the fabric until an outfit was finished.

Mother sent Marilyn off to first grade in a hand-me-down from Virginia, and Virginia to third grade in a re-constructed dress from the missionary barrel. By October, she added newly altered coats: a brown one for Marilyn—it matched her eyes—and a red plaid for Virginia. No one would have guessed they had once been worn by Naoma, an elderly lady of 43 years.

With her alteration expertise, Mother never let her offspring appear as poor as those whose mothers weren't so clever. She said, "Lots of people are poor but we'll not look or act as if *we* are."

Sometimes the missionary barrel gifts opened the door for jesting. Once Naoma sent a bag of thick rayon stockings full of runs with instructions for Mother to fix what she could. Teasing, Mother wrote back she might be able to repair some with a latching gadget and return them so Naoma could wear them longer. If not, she would keep them herself. She added these words, "I wonder how big the runs can get before you have to throw the stockings away."[22]

The fall of '38 turned bitterly cold. Daddy thought to winterize the Grange House by stuffing the walls—a task that turned out to be impossible. Even if he had raided the Port Angeles pulp mills he wouldn't have found enough paper to keep the wind from whistling through the walls, the drafts from creeping through the floor, or the heat of the stoves from filtering up-and-away through the roof. The whole place, except a few inches from the stove, felt like a cold cellar. Virginia told Mother the only place she could take off her coat was at school.

Daddy never quite figured out how to make the place comfy for living, but he did have creative ideas to give the place a more up-to-date design. While winter still wailed outside, he began his first major remodel. It involved rotating the entire home by 90 degrees. The sawed-off addition would face north—the coldest side—while most of the windows of the upstairs and downstairs would face the direction of the winter sun, letting in more warmth and light. Daddy borrowed a heavy-duty crowbar, immense jacks, huge blocks of wood, and enormous planks. He set up a scaffold to hold the weight of half of the structure while he cranked up the jacks on the other side. Back and forth he went, moving the jacks, moving the blocks, moving the scaffold, and ultimately rotating the creaking construction inch by diminutive inch. Back and forth he went, taking care that the joints didn't break and the corners didn't sag. Back and forth he went, and Marilyn, his assistant, went with him. She wasn't much help, but she told Mother, "I just keep guard and pray the whole thing doesn't come falling over on him."

Once the house was situated in its new position, the shortened closet-size room—the one that Mr. Johnson and Preacher Corey had reshaped—was loose, leaving large fissures where it had been attached to the Big Room wall. Daddy spent hours building supports and sealing the worst cracks but frigid air still flowed through, almost unabated. His frustration with the task grew, as did the tension in the room. Mother could see Daddy's tight lip and picked up David. Virginia followed them to the kitchen with her books. But Elizabeth didn't read her father's mood. She had been playing with Marilyn and turned to engage with him. Back and forth she ran chanting, "Silly Daddy, silly Daddy."

At first, Daddy didn't look up, so she repeated. "Silly Daddy, silly Daddy."

Her father stopped what he was doing and called out, "Marilyn, get me the pepper shaker."

Marilyn knew Daddy had reached the end of his temper fuse, and knew Elizabeth would be punished. But pepper? That was cruel. Marilyn didn't know if Daddy had told Elizabeth more than once to stop, and she didn't know if he'd quoted the scripture about foolishness or the one about honoring your parents. All Marilyn knew was that if she didn't obey she would get a whaling too. She shuffled toward the kitchen, hoping her father would get over his anger before she got back. But no. He held fragile, barely-five-year-old Elizabeth by the shoulder and told her to open her mouth. He shook the pepper onto her tongue. Elizabeth cried for hours. Marilyn suffered with her, and Mother's eyes were wet.

For a long season, the littlest girl kept a safe distance from her father, and swallowed her thoughts instead of speaking them. She was afraid of Daddy.

After the house was turned, the ground looked as if a plow had been hitched to the back end of a wayward mule. The scraped-off sod left patches of bare mud and foot-deep ruts. The timing was perfect. Mother declared, "We'll plant a garden."

Elizabeth lit up. She didn't know how to read Heidi books like Virginia, she wasn't strong enough to help Daddy move the house like Marilyn, and she got into trouble when she ventured close to his jobs. But she could plant radishes. Elizabeth never left Mother's side as they smoothed the soil, raked the rows, and tucked in the seeds. Every day when her sisters left for school, Elizabeth hurried out the back door to check the soil for signs of green. Then, almost overnight, starts shot through the ground and Elizabeth was beside herself. "Can we plant more seeds?" she begged.

So, in the little space left, Elizabeth planted carrots, parsnips, and squash. She didn't need to go to school. She could watch, weed, and water her garden.

Mother and Elizabeth tidied up the north side of the house with ferns they dug from the creek banks, and decorated the scruffy west corner with transplanted Douglas fir and hemlock seedlings. Mother said a woodsy area would wrap up the edge of the property and—after a few years—provide a piece of privacy.

Daddy constructed a second-story cubbyhole above the narrow closet that had tested his temper twice—first when he held his anger while sawing off the end with Peter Johnson, and later when he lost it with Elizabeth. Virginia got the new upstairs nook. She crawled through an opening from the bedroom, pulled a curtain and disappeared with her books. She was the only child with a *piece of privacy* to call her own. "It's not fair," Marilyn protested to Elizabeth, "we'll just leave her out of our fun, okay?"

Elizabeth shrugged. Her garden was all that mattered.

Daddy's next project was to build a woodshed for chopping and storing firewood. David, at two years, ran for his hammer and begged to pound nails too. Daddy started a nail for him and went to work on the other side. The carpenters were only half done with the building when the first of the animals—Bantam the hen—moved in. Near the chopping block, the little mother made her nest and began to lay her eggs. David toddled after Mother to check on the nest and helped her stack chunks of wood to protect the brooder. When it appeared that Bantam was not perturbed by the chopping of wood and nailing of shingles, Mother tucked in several full-size fertilized eggs from a neighbor's coop and wrote to Grandma, "Am thinking these probably won't hatch tho, because the eggs have been jarred so much, so if anything comes out of this brood they ought to be tough chickens."[23]

Tough chickens? Of course they would be tough. Everything on the Corey property was tough, by necessity—even David. Whatever others did, he'd say, "I do it too." He washed dishes and mixed bread with Mother. He stacked wood and pounded nails with Daddy.

A crash, bang, and boom one night that spring wasn't one of Daddy's new projects or David's hammering. It sounded as if the train had roared through the bedroom. The girls jumped up. Mother was holding David in front of the window. Outside the sky pulsed with light. Streaks of lightening zigzagged to the south and zipped down behind the towering black mountains. Thunder clapped at the fireworks and kept up its applause. Then, with a flash as bright as a sunny day and a blast as loud as ten shotguns, an enormous snag exploded. Flames soared above it.

David cried, "WaWa house, WaWa house. Fiya, fiya, WaWa house!"

The children had never seen such a display. The fiery torch seemed close enough to feel. They worried out loud, "What if it burns our house?"

"Where'll we live?"

"I'm scared."

The fire was out by morning, just a wispy reminder in upward swirling smoke where the snag had stood. The Johnson's home had not even received a singe to the shingles, but broad, brawny, strapping, twenty-five-year-old Walter had been given a new name. "WaWa."

A few days after the storm, Mother and Daddy caught a ride to town with neighbors, leaving Joy Belle Wetherald to watch the children. Joy was the daughter of my parents' friends, Mr. and Mrs. Wetherald, who had been some of the earliest neighbors to welcome the Coreys into the community. The teenager often stayed at the Grange House to help Mother. On this day, Marilyn and Elizabeth had their fingers in flour-water paste, and Virginia was cutting red paper with a pair of scissors, when David crawled onto the dining table and announced. "I do it too."

"Oh, no you don't," reacted Marilyn, reaching out to smack the tot's bottom. At the same moment Virginia threw out her hand to protect him. Stuck to her fingers was the open pair of scissors that stabbed deep into the palm of Marilyn's hand.

Blood spurted everywhere. Joy came running. She rushed the child to the sink, but could not stop the gouts of blood. She grabbed a cup of flour from the bin and stuffed the cut palm as full of flour as she could. Joy held Marilyn tight with her hand propped above her head. What to do? There was no phone, no vehicle, and no way to get help.

Virginia couldn't stomach the sight of blood and disappeared with David. Elizabeth wiped up the splatters on the table and the floor with a tattered towel. She ran back and forth to the window until, at last, she saw a neighbor's car stop in the driveway. Mother and Daddy emerged from the back seat, and she shrieked, "Here they come! Mother and Daddy are home!"

Mother took charge, tearing strips from the bandage sheet and wrapping Marilyn's hand. Daddy prayed, fully believing God would heal the wound. That night Mother found the child in a pool of blood, her sheet soaked red. They moved her to the living room, and for the next several nights, one parent sat next to Marilyn, keeping the hand wrapped tightly and the arm in a sling they fastened to the back of the sofa.

As Mother changed the bandage one day, she saw that Marilyn's fingers had begun to curl up. Daddy cut a piece of wood and placed the splint inside her hand and eased open the fingers. The packing and the splint held and they left it untouched for several days. Marilyn agonized that her hand was not healing, and she fretted about school—especially when Virginia said, "You'll probably flunk if you can't finish the first semester."

Mother's friends were disturbed too—not about school, but that the little girl was getting worse. They whispered that she should go to the doctor. Mother told her friends Mr. Corey had not wavered in his belief that God would heal Marilyn. "Yet," she said, "I would feel much better if the injury were checked."

One day, as Mother sat next to Marilyn and mopped her burning face with a cool wet cloth, Marilyn blinked her eyes and mouthed, "Mother, I can barely see you. Your head is so small."

Mother looked at Daddy. Without a word, he picked up his brown felt hat and gray tweed overcoat and left the room. In half an hour Daddy tucked Marilyn into the back seat of a big car. It was Peter Johnson's automobile, with the owner in the driver's seat. Daddy had gone to ask the formidable neighbor for help, and Mr. Johnson had kindly obliged.

In an examining room at the hospital, the doctor removed the splint and the discolored packing that was stuck in the middle of the stiff, swollen hand. A purple and amber colored pocket, the size of a flattened tangerine, began to ooze putrid goo. The doctor caught the pus in a pan, and the artery began to spurt blood once again. Marilyn passed out.

She came to in a white room engulfed with blinding light, where nurses in their starchy stiff hats and scary masks looked down at her. Her arms were tied and she couldn't move. Mother and Daddy were not there. She squirmed and tried to call out, but one of the nurses put a mask over her nose and mouth, and said, "Breathe now."

After the surgery Marilyn was placed in a ward where nurses checked the stitches, changed the bandages, and brought her food. She described the menu for her sisters later. "It was delicious; the best food I ever tasted. And I could have as much Jell-O and juice as I wanted. But I really wanted an ice cream cone like that girl in the next bed. Her parents brought her an *ice cream cone*! I wanted one so bad, but I knew I shouldn't ask for it."

A few days after returning home, Marilyn had to go back for a dressing change. Daddy didn't look to Pete Johnson for a ride. Instead he and Marilyn started walking the fifteen miles to the clinic. People picked up walkers and hitchhikers in those days, and the two did not wait long for a lift. The doctor said the fever was gone and the hand would be fine.

Daddy thanked the Lord for saving Marilyn's life and her hand. It was the same prayer of thanksgiving he had prayed after the accident. That's how Daddy's faith worked. He had believed for a miracle of divine healing, but he also read Mother's eyes and heard God's voice that told him to ask Pete Johnson for a ride to the hospital.

By Christmas, Marilyn was almost back to normal. The family celebrated the occasion all week. Friends in the community sent two turkeys, one all dressed in tissue paper and ribbons. There was enough to eat for several days, along with more to can. Everyone sang Christmas carols over and over since Virginia had learned a few on the piano. Joy Wetherald was there too—for Mother to teach her a piano lesson, but mostly to check up on the child whose hemorrhage of blood she had stopped with a handful of flour.

• • •

CHAPTER FIVE
The Whippet
(1940)

At some point, the family's first car—the boxy dark-colored one that had carried them up the Eden Valley Road and had transported them from Port Angeles to the Grange House—had broken down one time too many. When Marilyn had needed medical care, this rattletrap had been dead for quite some time. A friend, after seeing the difficulty the Coreys faced in that emergency, donated to Daddy an oddly-shaped 1920s-something called a Whippet.

Unfortunately, the Whippet had already been through its prime of life and beyond. For a few months, Daddy kept it running with prayer, willpower and jerry-rigged solutions, until there was no money for parts. That's when Daddy polished a manner of travel that allowed someone *else* to purchase fuel and manage repairs. He began to ride in dairy trucks and bread trucks, timing his trips to coincide with their exact schedules. The drivers would stop if he waved at them, and two or three even slowed down and looked toward the house to see if he was coming. He became first-name friendly with the drivers, several of whom considered him to be their personal itinerate pastor who counseled them and prayed on-the-go. The system gave him a captive audience and cost him nothing—factors which suited the traveling minister just fine.

But not his wife, at least not when she needed to be somewhere. Mother was expecting a baby in July, and she told her husband that babies couldn't be counted on to coordinate *their* delivery schedule with the bread or milk trucks. Conceding to her wisdom in that matter, Daddy set out to make the Whippet road-ready. He tested it by taking the three girls to Tacoma to stay with Grandma and Aunt Eleanor until after the baby came. They were ecstatic, Mother was relieved, and the car met the challenge.

The Coreys' fifth child was born in Port Angeles on July 25, Virginia's 10th birthday. Daddy, pleased to be presented with another boy, announced, "His name is John."

Daddy's declaration sounded as if had come from the Biblical story of Zacharias, and thus appeared to have the weight of scripture behind it. Mother was quick with a counter.

"Well then, his middle name is Wayne."

Daddy had selected a hero from the Bible; she had chosen a hero from the western movies she'd seen years earlier on the reel-to-reels at the theater. And so John Wayne Corey entered the family, a younger brother to challenge the attention given to three-year-old David and a baby for the big sisters to babysit, at least until it was time for all three to go to school.

Or so they thought. Daddy had almost decided to keep the children home, since there had been disturbing reports of inappropriate behavior on the buses and at the school. However, just before classes started, a few changes had occurred. There was a different bus driver, who was the parent of a student, and two new teachers.[24] The girls never knew their attendance at school had been in question. Elizabeth had waited *forever* to get on the bus with her sisters and to have her own books. As nervous as she was—with extra trips out to the toilet—she was ready long before bus time, long before breakfast, and long before her oldest sister was even dressed.

In November 1940, Grandma and Grandpa Corey celebrated their 50th Wedding Anniversary. Daddy's siblings planned a shindig at his parents' home in Tacoma, and everyone was invited. The party was a significant event—the first opportunity in several years for Daddy to reconnect with his brothers and sisters, most of whom had disparaged him for his decision to leave a job and go traipsing off to the wild country to follow—as he titled it—"The Call."

At the festivities, Virginia babysat John upstairs. While he slept, she listened to the goings-on through the heat grate and snooped through the nice clothes and personal things in the suitcases of her older cousins. The rest of the cherubs stuck close to Mother. She looked quite elegant, wearing her best silky dress and a fur-collared coat Naoma had given her. She had spent extra minutes in front of her mother-in-law's mirror, combing her bobbed hair and noticing more silver streaks than she'd seen before. Mother wondered for a moment if she should have put on her diamond engagement ring so she fit in better with the society ladies. She had set aside the jewelry years before, back when she felt it to be too showy for a preacher's wife. She had even considered selling it, but when there was no market, she tried to give it to her cousin Naoma. Naoma didn't want it either, since a boyfriend had already given her a diamond. So Mother had left it in the drawer at home, thinking to herself, *What's the point of trying to appear as someone I'm not?*

Mother fixed the children's plates with treats and found them places to sit. She greeted the relatives with her usual warmth and watched to see how they would receive her family. Several of Daddy's siblings stood aside with their cigarettes and drinks, but Grandma Corey was as warm as if there had been no breach of relationship. She reached out and pulled the little ones into her ample arms and bosom. Even Grandpa grinned around the edges of his colossal cigar at Marilyn sitting next to him. The child was embarrassed by this display of affection. She'd heard Daddy tell how the call to ministry had been impossible for his family to understand, how the uncles had called him fanatical and negligent, and how Grandpa had all-but disowned him. She wondered, *How can they put on a phony happy face after they have been mean to my parents?*

Grandma asked the three girls to sing, but Marilyn shook her head, and Mother didn't insist. Soon after, Daddy said it was time to go home, and Marilyn was first out the door.

The youngsters fell asleep in the car, but Daddy and Mother talked a long time.

"I'm glad we went," Mother said. "I could tell it meant so much to your mother that we were there."

Daddy said, "There were things I started to say to my older brothers, but God checked my spirit, and I kept still."

Mother agreed, "It seems right for us to live a godly life that they can see. Perhaps that is the message that will reach their hearts."

Daddy was quiet for a time. "Yes," he said, "We'll be faithful, and God will do the rest."

Back home, it was the season to get ready for Christmas. The Coreys had been invited to perform as part of the Christmas program at Joyce School. It was almost a tradition that had begun before the move to the Grange House. Daddy would go to the school and ask if they would like to include in their agenda a brief reading of the Christmas story and a carol sing. Some years the school administrators agreed, and some years they didn't—it all depended on who was in charge.

Mother wrote to Naoma of the preparation for the school presentation, and included in her letter the Christmas wish list that her cousin had asked for. With five children plus Joy Belle Wetherald, who lived with them most of the time, Mother was hesitant to write each child's specific need. But Naoma insisted on shopping, and Mother wanted to be sure the gifts were practical. So, on the top of two pages of instructions listing the appropriate items and sizes, she wrote, "If I give a few things under the name of each child you won't think I mean (for you to buy) the whole bunch, will you? No. It's just to give you something to pick from. And nothing, please, for anyone but the children. Thank you."[25]

Mother asked for a Bible for Joy and piano music for Virginia, pajamas for the younger girls and play clothes for the boys. She gave secondary options, just in case the first suggestions didn't pan out. Then, no doubt embarrassed by the lengthy inventory, she added a postscript. "It's certainly getting pretty awful isn't it—when my family increases in size so fast. Maybe John is the end!!! Or caboose as one teacher said David ought to be!!"[26]

The requests certainly didn't overwhelm Naoma. She itemized a list and headed off to the store. By the time she returned home, having spent the sum total of $12.65, she was ready to send a clothing item and a toy for each child, the Bible for Joy, and a dollar for Margaret and Arthur. She tucked her record of that shopping spree inside the envelope with Mother's Christmas list and filed it in her keep-forever box of "Letters from Margaret."[27]

Naoma didn't spend much, but there were Christmas gifts for the Coreys and Joy Belle to open. Mother dressed John in his new rompers, David found a board and nails to pound with his new hammer, and the girls passed around their treasures before tucking them into their own spaces.

Mother was glad for the Christmas celebration with her children. It took her mind off the growing burden she felt—a burden for the country and the safety of all of them. Rumors were spreading. She heard them from neighbors and from the school children and from shopkeepers. The mood in the community had become dark, and people said it was only a matter of time before the United States would be at war.

· · ·

CHAPTER SIX
The War
(1941)

For several years, conflict had raged in Asia and Europe. Canada had gone to aid Britain in 1939, but the United States declared neutrality. As German invasions and government takeovers continued throughout European countries, and Britain was under siege, the tension was building on all fronts. Even if the U.S. military could keep from crossing the ocean, there was concern that the Olympic Peninsula, surrounded on three sides by interconnected waterways—the Pacific Ocean, the Straits of Juan de Fuca, and Puget Sound—was vulnerable to attack. Defenses were being designed and installed.

The army began construction of Camp Hayden, a 518-acre military base at Crescent Bay, less than three miles from the Grange House. Crescent Bay, with its silver beach, was the locals' playground—a place to fish or jump the waves, to comb the beach for shells and driftwood, to watch the seagulls, and to smell the surf. A half century earlier, Crescent Bay had been the port of entry for the first explorers and settlers, and the site of a short-lived, but booming logging town.[28]

Out of security concerns, Camp Hayden was closed to all civilians, but everyone understood that the camp's mission was to protect the entrance to Puget Sound, as well as strategic sites on the Canadian side. Of course, all the activity was top secret.[29]

The Camp Hayden Road, leading from Highway 9A to the installation, was less than half a mile from the Grange House. When the children hiked the railroad tracks for wood, they watched the long lines of trucks carrying supplies and troops to and from the camp.

And they fretted. What would they do if war came to Joyce when they were at school or riding on the bus? Or—heaven forbid—if the roads were wrecked and they couldn't go to school? But most distressing of all, what if the army told Daddy he had to become a soldier and go away to war? "Dear Father," the girls added to their prayers, "please don't let Daddy have to fight."

Daddy kept right on with his travels and projects. He removed the steep stairway from behind the stove and built a wider, safer flight of steps on the east end of the room. This opened the space beside the range for a set of new cupboards—well-conditioned by its former owner, but complete with tin drawers, enameled bread-kneading shelf, upper dish cupboards, and flour and sugar bins. It was a Kitchen Queen set, made popular in the 1930s by housewives who had come to believe that kitchens should not only be convenient but also pretty enough for a queen.

During the kitchen improvements, David, at four, was his father's shadow in construction with his own apple-box lumber, a saw, a chisel, and his Christmas hammer. David was Mother's shadow too. He carried the empty half-gallon aluminum milk can while she pushed the baby in the buggy to the neighbor's. "Busy, busy boy," Mother labeled him.

When John got big enough to sit up, Mother said, "A wagon would be useful. I don't anticipate that we will need the carriage again."

So Daddy put two wheels of the baby buggy on the bottom of an orange crate and hitched it to the back of David's toddler-size tricycle that had no pedals. Mother tied John into the wagon and David wheeled the babysitting box outside on dry days and inside when it rained. Mother watched them and chuckled, "The carriage was turned into a caboose to carry the caboose of the Corey train. I'd say five is certainly enough children for this family."

Summer came, school let out, and the Grange House was awhirl. The family was going on a vacation—the Coreys' first vacation ever—to Daddy's summer cabin at Hart's Lake.

The girls knew of Hart's Lake. It was near the Wilcox farm where, back in 1935, Daddy had fed the Wilcox chickens. Hart's Lake was also near Roy and McKenna, where Daddy had turned the Charleston Inn Dance Hall into a church. And it was near the Brucks' summer cabin.

The girls didn't know about the land and the cabin their father owned; nor that Uncle Emil Bruck had bought the land for Daddy from the Pattons with the agreement that he and his brother-in-law Arthur Corey would build cabins; nor that during Daddy's trips, the two had completed the construction.[30] So many surprises.

For the trip, family friends—most likely Joy Wetherald's parents—loaned a big truck.[31] It was large enough to take the whole tribe and all the basics to live for two months. Pot and pans, dishes and cups, spoons and forks, boxes of clothes—not to mention the accordion—and everything topped with bedding and mattresses. Mother tucked the boys in the cab. The girls crawled up the summit of possessions in the back with just breathing room under the coarse, musty, canvas tarp. There they rocked and rolled into each other on every bump and curve, while the wind flipped and flapped the fabric above their faces. For the entire six-hour journey, fumes stung their noses and made them cough. But so what? They were going on *vacation*.

Daddy stopped the truck at regular intervals for toilet breaks, a picnic lunch on Hood Canal, and even a few minutes to get the wiggles out at the Tacoma Power and Light Hydroelectric plant at the south end of the canal. Then at last—*bounce, bump, bang*—the truck shuddered to a halt. The girls piled out of the back, anxious for fresh air and open skies, only to have the dust of the gravel road whirl around their skirts and into their eyes.

The cabin was a miniature summer castle. It boasted covered porches on two sides, a kitchen sink, a hand-pump to a well, a small wood-burning stove, a home-made table and chairs, and a narrow stairway up to the second floor. The villa overlooked the Pattons' fields of rustling grass and lowing cows— multi-colored cows, contented cows, a whole colony of cows!

As soon as the outside toilet was tested, the floors swept, the boxes placed, and the mattresses laid—a few in the upper room, others on the porch—Marilyn and Elizabeth ran to the Patton's pasture. The two followed the herd, patting heads and scratching flanks as the bovine bunch mowed the grass. Every morning the girls searched for the cows, but some days they were too far away to reach during play time. So Marilyn planned a strategy with Elizabeth and presented it to Daddy and Mother. "Wouldn't it be a good idea if we had the cows come into our yard to cut the grass for us?"

In the discussion that followed, the two cowgirls-in-training agreed to clean up every pile the cows dumped in the yard. Virginia said, "That's a really dumb idea. I don't want to clean up cow pies."

Marilyn retorted, "Well, you don't have to. You can go read your books!"

The next time the cows were nearby with their heads stretching for the tall grass under the barbwire fence, Marilyn pushed open the gate. The herd accepted the invitation and the girls had the cows nearby. No need to chase the livestock half a mile through the fields and yodel blue grass songs in their ears. In addition to those advantages, the grass got mowed.

The next morning, Marilyn and her accomplice surveyed the scene. There must have been a thousand piles and runny smears from the overfed cud-chewers. Mother said the two girls' part of the bargain had to be done before any *little shavers* could play in the yard. So they shooed out the herd and picked up the shovels. Singing and crowing, they threw the messes over the fence. No big deal. They were used to making games of hard jobs.

However, not everyone thought this was a suitable activity for a Sunday morning. Driving up the dirt road on the way to Sunday school in their 1927 pall-bearer-size Packard, Uncle Emil and Aunt Hazel observed the cleanup operation. When their aunt saw the girls in mucked-up dresses and bare feet shoveling cow pies, she had a full-blown *hissy* fit. "Look at you. Why are you in this mess at church time on Sunday? Where is your father? Why, I have a mind to . . . "

Elizabeth stood stock still, and Marilyn bit her tongue so as not to be disrespectful. Then, once the black limo was out of sight, they resumed shoveling with slightly less merriment. This was the first time they had heard Aunt Hazel speak out with words and tone as strong as her brother—their daddy—used.

Dear Aunt Hazel! Despite her strong opinions, she was happy-humored *most* of the time, and generous *all* of the time. That summer the girls joined her in the market-style garden. Aunt Hazel would spend hours under the shade of her hat, kneeling along the sandy, blistering rows—weeding, watering, picking, and weeding again. Marilyn said you could die out there with the sweat running into your eyes, but Aunt Hazel explained that the heat was worse for her because she couldn't sweat. "Well," Marilyn muttered, "If Aunt Hazel can do it with no sweat running, anyone can."

Furthermore, helping in the garden meant there would be vegetables and fruit for everyone. Peas to shell, carrots to scrape, beans to can, corn to husk, radishes, lettuce, cabbage, strawberries, raspberries, blackberries, blue berries, and best of all, apples for pie. From Aunt Hazel's flower patch you could pick dahlias, daisies, and delphiniums for the table. Living in Hart's Lake, next to Aunt Hazel's garden, felt to the girls like living as royalty.

The surrounding property presented a plethora of places to play. The earlier lumbermen had removed all the virgin timber—mostly huge firs and cedars—and had dropped and left to rot the trees up to two feet thick. So the children could run for miles on the stumps and logs that lay scattered through the region, without ever touching the ground. Cousin Don Bruck, three years older than Virginia and twice as big, taught the kids how to play wood tag. The rule was, if you fell off a log, you were "It" and would have to tag someone else on the logs. You could never catch long-legged Don, who kept just ahead by intention, so you wouldn't give up and quit.

But fun could turn to folly in an instant, as it did one morning when Elizabeth was running as fast as she could with Marilyn at her heels. Mother was in the yard chopping wood, and Elizabeth darted headlong for her skirt. She reached out just as the axe came down on a block with the child's finger on top of it. Blood gushed and the tip of the finger dangled, attached only by a small piece of skin.

Marilyn was sickened, not only by the sight of the severed finger, but also by her anticipation of the walloping she was sure to get. Her worst spanking ever had come not long before when she was carrying a bag of jars and accidently dropped them. Daddy's provocation hadn't been the broken jars as much as the loudness of his daughter's laughter before the accident. In Daddy's mind, it was her noise that equated to foolishness. If she had been serious, there would have been no boisterous behavior, no foolishness, and no broken jars. In his book, there was only one way to deal with foolishness—the rod of correction. At the sight of Elizabeth's injury, Marilyn knew it was coming, and she expected it would result in welts and bruises to her behind.

But Mother didn't say Marilyn was to blame for Elizabeth's accident, and no retribution followed. Instead, Elizabeth got all the attention. Daddy prayed and didn't delay, saying to Mother they would get this cared for by the skilled hands of a surgeon. So he and Mother took her to a doctor in Tacoma to sew back on the finger; then left the patient at Grandma's to recuperate.

Virginia also had a near disaster that summer. It happened at the Nisqually River, just a trek through the woods from the cabin. Although the river was full of strong and twisting currents, a swimming hole had formed inside a big sandy spit. Cousin Dorothy offered to give Virginia swimming lessons, so the girls headed to the river.

Cousin Don had planned to go fishing in Hart's Lake that day with a pastor and his sons, but his plan fell apart when they forgot their can of worms. So the fishermen jumped into their swimsuits, pulled on their jeans, and headed to the swimming hole. While still walking through the woods, Don felt an urgency to run ahead with his friend. The instant Don and Jim broke out of the brush they saw Dorothy and Virginia struggling in the water.

Virginia was in a state of panic, grabbing Dorothy around the neck and trying to climb on her back. Both were going under. Don dropped his jeans and rushed into the water. Reaching the struggling girls, he grabbed Virginia, allowing Dorothy to go free. Don tried to pull Virginia's head above the water, only to have her put a chokehold on him, like she had his sister. He kept shouting, "Don't do that. Let go! I'll pull you in!"

Don was forced to push Virginia loose so he could gain a few breaths of air, but she kept clawing at him until he too was on the verge of drowning. Just then, he found his toes could touch the bottom, and he was able to tug Virginia to shore.

In the meantime, Jim took off after Dorothy, who was drifting out into the current. When the pastor came out of the woods onto the dune, he saw the struggle and ran into the water, hurling his fishing pole toward the lifesavers in a useless gesture, only to see it sink beneath the waves.[32]

The boys were exhausted when they got Virginia and Dorothy onto the sand. But the girls looked gray and nearly lifeless, so Don and Jim leaned over them and began artificial respiration. The girls improved quickly and sat up. Don told them, "It is a miracle that you girls didn't drown."

"It is true. God did miracles," Virginia said to Mother later. "I was praying my heart out when my feet didn't touch the bottom. God made Don forget the worms so he didn't go fishing; God told Don to get to the river as fast as he could; and God made Don and his friend Jim tall enough, strong enough, and smart enough to keep us from drowning."

Far too soon, the family's sojourn at the cabin came to an end, and they packed up to return to the Grange House—to the cold rooms, the never-ending search for wood, and the water buckets and laundry detail at the creek. On the way back, Marilyn moaned, "I sure wish we could live at Hart's Lake forever."

Virginia corrected her, "The house is too small and our friends would miss us."

Elizabeth piped in, "We have to go to school."

If the child had known what was ahead, she might have preferred to avoid school that year at Joyce. A few days after classes began, Elizabeth came home sick. She had stayed in the nurse's resting room most of the afternoon and told Mother after school that her head ached and her stomach hurt. By evening she seemed better, but in the morning she said, "I'm not feeling good. I'd better stay home."

Minutes after the bus picked up the other children, Elizabeth told Mother she thought she could eat something, that her stomach was better.

In third grade at age seven, Elizabeth was the youngest and by far the smallest child in the class. Marilyn had tutored her so well in the attic that the teacher had skipped her past second grade. Elizabeth fretted about making mistakes in her papers and having to recite in front of the classmates. She recoiled from the older boys who bullied her. Anxiety and fear wreaked havoc with her digestion. Mother declared that the waif was too thin, and began giving her cod liver oil and tablets of brewer's yeast fortified with iron. Elizabeth hid in the corner or cowered behind the stove. Those horse-size pills were impossible to swallow, but she didn't want to miss the bus, just like she didn't want to get behind in school. So she choked down the pills and felt sick all over again—about going on the bus, about getting bullied, about her schoolwork, and about having to do it all again the next day.

This was the same year Elizabeth got lice at school. Daddy shaved her head in the yard, after which Mother covered her bald scalp with a stocking cap. The hat emphasized her pinched cheeks and accented her other chronic condition of red and crusty eyelids. With a nervous tic, she picked at the scabs, making them look even worse. The boys, especially those who were in sixth grade with Virginia, harassed her even more.

It was a hard year for Marilyn too, on account of her little sister. The third and fourth grades were in the same room, so Elizabeth sat just a few feet away. Marilyn regretted that she had taught Elizabeth everything she, herself, knew. Now her smidgen of a sister could do everything in third grade that Marilyn did in fourth—and the imp was two years younger and half her size. "Besides", Marilyn stewed under her breath, "the reason Mother gives my sister the pills is because she is a picky eater and doesn't like very many of the foods that we have. She only likes pickles—dill or bread and butter, maybe even beet pickles. I hate beets. Ever since canned beets were the only thing we had in the house to eat, the thought of them makes me gag."

Yet Marilyn suffered with her sister too. When Elizabeth got lice and Daddy used his cure of the razor blade and kerosene, Marilyn agonized. She hated the bullies who taunted her sister at school and said it wasn't fair that no one else got shaved for lice, not even the girl who brought it to school. *Why is there no justice, no justice at all,* she wondered. Marilyn puzzled over her paradox. She wanted to hide from her little sister, but wanted to help her too, and didn't know how.

Marilyn, by nature, looked out for underdogs. One day, the poorest girl with no other friends brought Marilyn a piece of birthday cake. The rotten smell of the pastry was overpowering. Marilyn took a nibble—it was all she could stomach. An idea popped into her head, and she said to the girl, "It's so delicious I would like to take it home to my mother."

She told Mother that canned beets were easier to eat than the birthday cake. Mother replied, "The smell is rancid butter, so you can dump it in the toilet."

That took care of the matter, with no offense to the less-fortunate child. So these two sisters had their ailments, anxieties and embarrassments in third and fourth grades. Virginia was in her own world of sixth grade and books. David followed Daddy around like a puppy and Mother kept close tabs on John who, at 17 months, could run to the highway almost faster than she could—especially now that she was pregnant again. It was all to be expected.

What wasn't expected was the visitor who knocked at the door on Sunday evening, December 7, 1941. Daddy had heard the vehicle in the drive and opened the door immediately to a uniformed officer from the Clallam County Sheriff's department. Mother came from the kitchen and the children followed her. The officer was a tall man with serious eyes who touched his hat toward Mother and shook Daddy's outstretched hand.

He said, "I've come to tell you that the Japanese have bombed Pearl Harbor. Many of our military have been killed and the United States is now at war."

Mother lifted her hand to her mouth as the speaker continued. "All homes and businesses on the West Coast are under immediate blackout order. After dark, all windows are to be completely hidden so no light escapes. All cars driven at night are to have their lights covered."

He finished with, "There will be neighborhood watch groups to ensure compliance."

Daddy said, "Thank you for telling us."

Mother added, "Lord have mercy!"

The visitor dipped his head as if in agreement, and turned to go.

A shock of silence lasted but seconds. Marilyn asked, "How'll we cover the windows? All the blankets are on the beds."

Mother said, "Oh Jesus, comfort the families of those whose loved ones have been killed or injured. Bring a quick ending to this war, for your glory."

Daddy added, "'Thou shalt not be afraid for the terror by night; nor for the arrow that flieth by day; nor for the pestilence that walketh in darkness; nor for the destruction that wasteth at noonday.'"

Mother turned to comply with blackout orders. Although her quilts were already occupied, Mother cut a large, scratchy wool blanket to hide the glass in the living areas. Within the hour, she had located sufficient materials for Daddy to nail on all windowed walls. Then Daddy, followed by a handful of kids, checked the windows from outside. He pointed out moth holes or gaps to Mother who, on the inside, was ready with a needle and thread.

The news that day changed everything on the peninsula. At school the students were told what to do in case of an attack. They practiced the air raid drills, dropping under their desks at the sound of the alarm. At all homes, parents discussed where to go, and how to get there, if evacuation orders came.

Daddy and Mother talked about going to Hart's Lake. Daddy said, "I'm not sure the location—so close to Puget Sound and Fort Lewis—would even be acceptable."

Mother agreed and added, "I'd surely feel better if we could keep the car in running order, just in case.

Daddy promised to fix the Whippet, but reminded her, "God will provide a way. 'He is our refuge and our fortress; our God; in Him will we trust.'"

Every prayer at the Grange House included a remembrance of families who had lost loved ones, a request for safety of relatives who were serving in the military, and a plea for God to bring peace to the world. And many people in the community, who were not used to praying, began to talk to God too.

A few days later, the family called on God urgently—yet it was no longer as much for the war as it was for baby John. At just a year and a half, he was desperately sick with whooping cough and pneumonia. He burned with fever. His chest wheezed. He choked. He hacked night and day. Mother sat with him hour after hour, trying to coax a little water through his lips, only to see him gasp and go into fits of coughing all over again. Elizabeth tried to keep David occupied and away from the baby, while Marilyn exchanged hot cloths for cool ones. She hovered over the crib and ran errands for Mother.

Mother whispered to Daddy, "He is very sick. Without medicine or a miracle, I'm not sure he will make it."

Daddy looked at her for a moment and moved toward the crib. He laid his hands on John and exclaimed, as if he already knew God's answer, "Lord, thou hast promised to hear when we pray in faith. Thou hast said, 'By thy stripes we are healed.' We bring John to thee for that healing."

He stood silent; then raised his eyes to Mother. "God has heard. But he has also made it clear to me that you must release him to his heavenly father."

He didn't wait for her response, adding, "I want you to leave John with the girls and we will drive to the lake. God has promised to heal, and you need to come away with me for a while."

Mother looked back at John. She stood still, a handkerchief at her face. Daddy waited, believing that God was confirming the message to his wife. Then Mother bent down, tucked the blanket around the child, and lifted him in her arms. With tears in her eyes, but resolve in her step, she turned and handed the baby to Marilyn. Her nine-year-old would know how to care for John.

Marilyn heard the rattle-trap sputter to a start and clatter down the driveway. She held baby John gently—oh so gently. It would take Daddy and Mother two hours to drive to Lake Crescent and back, *if* the car kept running. Marilyn would be the best nursemaid John could possibly have. She crooned to him, cried over him, and begged God to make him better.

He opened his eyes, ever so slightly, and his sister dripped water between his lips. He didn't cough. She dripped a little more and waited. He stirred but didn't choke. Elizabeth brought a fresh cloth for his forehead. Marilyn whispered, "Look, his eyes are open. He didn't cough when I gave him water. Bring me a little orange juice, but add some warm water first."

Marilyn just knew he was better. He didn't seem as hot. He took several drippings of juice. He smiled. He wet his diaper. The nurse was beside herself with excitement for Mother to get home. Virginia fixed food, but Marilyn couldn't eat for the bursting bubble in her stomach. Elizabeth and David ran back and forth to the window, watching for the folks' return. It was getting dark when the car stopped. Elizabeth flew outside. "He's better, he's taking juice, and Marilyn says his fever's less!"

Marilyn handed John to Mother. Mother smiled for the first time in weeks. "Thank you, Jesus," she whispered.

It was close to the New Year before Mother wrote to Naoma, "Am very thankful John is better. David has whooping cough too, but doesn't feel bad. Takes it as a joke when he goes outside to cough and loses a meal." She continued the letter with her thanks for the Christmas gifts her cousin had sent. "Joy likes her apron. Elizabeth's cap and mittens are just right. John has his sweater on—it fits and looks fine. And did I tell you how much I was pleased with the can of cookies. They are delicious with their sweet centers."[33]

John was getting well. Mother, David, and the girls partied with Naoma's cookies—*store-boughten* cookies, complete with creamy frosted filling. Nineteen forty-one had been a hard year—a year with valleys of deep darkness—but the light of a new year was dawning.

Margaret David John Arthur

David pulls John in the orange crate caboose 1941

CHAPTER SEVEN
The Guests
(1942)

In January, Daddy left on a lengthy trip. Mother was grateful he had stayed close by while John was sick, but now she sent him off without an objection. He would see his parents and her mother, all three who—by this time—had worked through their disapproval of his choices and had come to welcome his visits. He would see other people to whom God would lead him, and God would lead these people to give offerings to meet the needs of her family. That was the promise she had received when she had told Daddy she would serve with him, even if her faith hadn't been as strong as his.

When Daddy was home, he no longer went to Eden Valley for services. Instead, he led Sunday service at the Grange House. The meeting always served as church for the Coreys, while attendance by others was sporadic. Sometimes there were strangers Daddy occasioned to meet along the roads, or friends like Virginia Norman who walked all the way from the Lyre River. About once a month the Samuelsons or Mrs. Branson drove out from Port Angeles; and sometimes the Wetheralds came, or Doreen Taylor and Joan and Bev McNally. It didn't matter who or how many showed up. What mattered was that the doors were open to all who came, and all were being taught the Word of God.

When Daddy was gone, Mother usually led the meeting. She played the piano for singing and asked for testimonies but gave no sermon, saying she wasn't a preacher. However, in the wake of John's illness and in the weariness of a pregnancy, she said, "I'd prefer to cancel the service entirely. I'm not even up to leading the singing right now."

So on his way out, Daddy promised to stop in Port Angeles and announce the change to Hester Branson—the only one likely to come the distance.

But Mrs. Branson came anyway. The girls saw the lady—weird Hester Branson—climb out of her car, wearing a dress in a color none of them knew how to describe. Was it brown, or gray, or dusty rose? "Just call it out-of-style and homely," Marilyn said.

"Mother," she called, "It's Mrs. Branson. We're going upstairs."

Mother met the lady at the door. "Didn't Arthur tell you there would be no service?"

"Yes, but I thought you might need some company, being alone and all."

Mother grinned. She was never alone, not for a minute at the Grange House. But she ushered Hester in.

The girls stayed out of sight. They hadn't forgotten the actions of this strange lady a few weeks earlier. After everyone else had gone home from the Grange House meeting, she had remained. Marilyn had stood in the doorway, transfixed by Hester's behavior. Her netting-brimmed hat bobbed up and down; her hands went this way and that; her body swayed to and fro; her voice uttered gibberish; and her lips parted and closed, popping and slurping in air like a fish out of water. Marilyn had whispered to Elizabeth, "She's gone off her rocker."

Elizabeth had just shuddered and gone to find Mother.

On this visit, a few minutes after the girls had disappeared, Mother called them to come down. She said that Mrs. Branson had offered to take her to the store, and that they were to watch the little ones.

Mrs. Branson bought Mother a bag of groceries and the children a carton of ice cream, both contributions inspiring a chorus of thanks from the children. As she headed out the door for home, Hester invited the girls to help her make cookies in a few days. True to her promise, she drove out to pick up Virginia and Marilyn—Elizabeth didn't want to go—and brought them home later with a bag of cookies. The two fidgeted around the house, acting polite and waiting for Hester to leave so they could tell Mother the *real* story of how the day had gone.

The moment Mrs. Branson's car door slammed, Marilyn piped, "She put all the stuff into the bowl and mixed it with her hands, dirty fingernails and all. Worse yet, she licked off her fingers and stuck them back in the dough. If I did that, kneading bread, you'd swat my hands."

Virginia added, "It was disgusting. I don't want to eat any of these cookies."

Mother ended the sniveling. "They are cooked, so we can eat them. Just be grateful."

Mother was grateful, not so much for the cookies, but for the generosity of Mrs. Branson, who brought gifts and helped with the expenses nearly every month. While the lady sometimes behaved in strange ways, Mother knew she was one of God's needy sheep. Mother wrote to Naoma that the lady's visit this time had been a "blessing without histrionics."[34]

After Daddy returned, Seth Davis came to visit. The fusty, feisty fellow lived up Grauel Road[35], south of the trestle where the girls had picked up their biggest loads of bark. They had seen him before, but never close up—never observed his long, matted beard discolored by food, chewing tobacco, and other unknown droppings. He walked up the driveway with a cane, pausing to pinch one side of his nose and blow out the other; then wipe his finger down the side of his coveralls. Daddy invited him in and talked about the Lord. Seth was okay with that, especially since Mother set another place at the table. Mother could always make room for guests, no matter whom, and no matter what there was to serve.

Watching the character eat, now that was a jaw-dropping experience for the children. The young spectators' eyes followed each movement of Seth's hands as he pushed the food around, even the tiny canned peas, until he had a portion balanced on his knife. Back and forth he aimed the knife, from plate to mouth, except when he took it on a detour for a slab of butter to spread on his bread. If the kids hadn't been so stupefied at the sight of that grimy hand bringing the germy knife to their butter plate, they might have allowed themselves to snicker. Instead they peeked at Mother, anxious to see how she would react. She never let on.

A few days later, Mother took the children to call on Seth Davis. People in the neighborhood didn't have phones in those days, so calling around without previous announcement was considered friendly. Seth lived in what had once been a two-room schoolhouse. He lived alone—unless you counted his bees and his goats. And the goats were as comfortable inside the house as out! The children had to be careful where they sat, and even where they walked—and not just because of the bees and goats. Mr. Davis smoked, chewed, and spat, layering piles of ash and pools of tobacco spittle in a slithery mound at the front of the potbelly stove. He rocked back and forth in a creaky chair, his mouth oozing on the sides, and his scabby hand scratching the neck of his polka-dotted dog.

The old man, like all hospitable neighbors, offered a snack to the visitors. His menu options were simple. Among all the critters and mounds of garbage stood two five-gallon buckets, one filled with honey and one filled with peanut butter. From the cluttered table he lifted a loaf of dry bread, a section of honeycomb, and a pail of goat's milk.

He reached out to Elizabeth—such a petite thing she was—to share a chunk of honeycomb. She backed off from the flies buzzing the piece and the stains on his hands. She squeaked, "No, thank you," and hid behind Mother.

Marilyn didn't want to offend. She just squeezed her eyes shut at the sight of the crusty overgrown fingernails and opened her mouth. Elizabeth told Marilyn as they left the place, "I'd rather starve to death than eat that stuff or drink goat's milk with hair floating in it."

Marilyn hadn't liked it a bit either, but snorted at her sister. "Oh piffle. You're just a baby."

In Seth's yard, David stopped to scrutinize an amazing machine—a giant grinding stone that stood at his eye level above a chain that was attached to bicycle pedals. When Daddy took his axe to be sharpened, David went along to watch Seth pump the pedals and send sparks flying in every direction like a spitting firecracker. David wished his father had a pedal-run grinding apparatus at home.

The family never saw Seth Davis clean or shaven, but it was rumored that at least once a year he went to town for a shave, a haircut, and a new set of long johns and coveralls. After that he was good until the next time.

On March 19, just a few days before David's fifth birthday, Phillip Raymond was born. Cousin Dorothy Bruck came to stay while Mother was in the hospital. In those days, a new mother would rest for a week or ten days while the nurses helped care for the baby. Mother needed the pampering this time. At home she would be facing some wearisome months with Phillip, who was colicky from day one, and 20-month-old John, already in the terrible-twos and engaged in Olympic-style competition for her attention.

Mother's hair was turning gray and she began to roll it around a tied and twisted cloth. Gone was the dark bob that she had worn as a smart-looking professional, and as a young wife and mother. This donut-shaped roll, popular ten years earlier, required no cuts and kept the stray hairs out of her eyes.

When Daddy took Dorothy home to Tacoma, he took John and David to stay a few days with Aunt Hazel. Mother had said, "It'll be easier to manage a fussy baby with the other boys gone."

A fussy baby, but he was a cute one—a replica of his father. Fine features, coal-black hair and a smile—when he was happy—that drew a line from one ear to the other.

Beverly and Joan McNally came to help with the cooking and cleaning. Joan was ecstatic at the invitation. It hadn't been all that long since her mother had left her to stay overnight at the Coreys. Joan would never forget that experience—an incident that bonded her forever to Mrs. Corey. It happened when she, Marilyn, and Elizabeth had started to read together in the upstairs bedroom. Suddenly, a surge of homesickness hit like a flood, and Joan couldn't even open her mouth. Marilyn had run downstairs to Mother, "Joan can't read out loud, something's wrong."

Mother had gone up, sat down, and put her arm around the dumbstruck girl. She said to her daughters, "Joan has a little lump in her throat and can't read right now. You girls can read to her."[36]

Joan's older sister Beverly also had experienced the compassion of Mother. The child had been running down the driveway toward the highway when her feet slid out from under her. She'd skidded, and skinned up the whole side of her leg. Mother had comforted her, cleaned up the wound, and wrapped it with a piece of sheet. As Bev felt the gentle hands, she looked up at Mrs. Corey and thought, *she is just an angel in a pretty dress and pretty shoes.*[37]

So Joan and Bev beamed with pride that they were *needed* at the Coreys.

With five efficient cooks and babysitters in the house, Mother felt the urge to re-start her Wednesday afternoon Women's Christian Fellowship that had not met for at least a month. She sent the girls to invite the neighbors, half hoping that most would not show. But they came and she sensed God giving her the words to speak. Afterwards she wrote to Naoma that it had been a blessing in more ways than one. "I made coffee for the ladies and we ate bread but had no cake as there was sugar rationing. My own fault for failing to put it on the grocery list the last time Art went to town. Well, several neighbors insisted that I send the children over to get some sugar."[38]

Rationing had become a way of life. Mother didn't fret about it since she didn't even have enough currency to buy the rations anyway. Instead, in a barter and trade, she exchanged her coupons for the neighbors' surplus. They gave her farm milk and even cans of *government-recommended* Spam. Mother sliced and fried the canned meat in the iron skillet until it sizzled and gave off an aroma that filled the house. Her plate-holding onlookers said Spam was the best sweet-salty meat ever invented, perfect with pancakes or ground up with potatoes to make hash.

Mother's neighborhood friends talked about the citified Victory Gardens—a remarkable new wartime concept of growing your own food—that caused much amusement in the rural households. These old-time farmers had been growing their own food, canning it, and sharing it since they were big enough to help their own mothers. Most of them also scoffed at the idea of spending a few pennies to try the latest fad—Kraft Dinners, the macaroni and cheese-in-a-box—that the papers touted as a nutritious alternative for meat and dairy.

Neighbors talked about other implications of the war, especially unusual occurrences in their neighborhood. Highway 9A was the coastal route to far northwest points of Washington. One day, hundreds of troops with loaded donkeys marched in rhythm, *clip-clop, clip-clop, clip-clop*, past the Grange House, past the neighbors, past the school. Beverly McNally was waiting for the bus when they marched by in military dress and formation. "What cute boys they were," she said, "It was fun to make eyes at them and watch them wink back."

Mother wrote Naoma about that military parade and the rumors that surrounded it. "In the past week there have been hundreds of mules and soldiers go past our place—where? I don't know. Some think to the hills where cars or trucks can't go. Others surmise they are sent across the water. Many think we will be evacuated this summer—if not because of enemy landing here—but because they anticipate that 5th columnists will be starting forest fires to scare people, cripple the logging industry, etc. So all we can do is live one day at a time and trust the Lord to keep and direct us."[39]

Daddy brought David and John home from Tacoma in the Whippet car, which was once again in need of repairs. David had become his father's right hand in those repairs, his reliable "gofer" whenever Daddy needed a wrench or a screwdriver. Yet Daddy was becoming increasingly agitated with the Whippet. He was not a patient man when things, machines, and people did not do what they were supposed to. David stood by as his father got in the car and drove out of sight. He'd wanted to go too, but didn't ask. When Daddy returned on foot hours later, David ran down the driveway to meet him. He frowned, "Where's the car?"

"I sold it to a man in Sequim."

"How much money did he pay you?"

"$50.00"

David gasped. *Wow—Daddy must be rich!*

Then the little guy mumbled to himself. "I wish I knew better how to help Daddy fix the car so he didn't have to sell it."

So the Coreys were carless, and once again depended on friends, delivery drivers, or strangers on the highway. Daddy traveled easily with that kind of arrangement. He didn't have to wait in line with coupons for gas he couldn't afford, and he no longer felt beholden to the independent-minded Whippet. Instead, even though he never raised his thumb as a hitchhiker, he expected the right person to pull over and offer a lift. Daddy never walked the highway very long before he would get his "divine appointment."

A long, dreary winter slouched into a gloomy will-this-rain-ever-quit spring. Neighbors were enlisting or being drafted into military service at an increasing rate. Even young women took wartime jobs at Puget Sound businesses such as Boeing. There was honor in becoming part of the Rosie-the-Riveter force. The children worried again that Daddy might have to go to war and prayed about it. They worried about having food to eat and prayed about that too.

And God answered their requests—at least about the food, and at least on this occasion. The family had been on a diet of Aunt Hazel's canned green beans for three days when, at dinner, Daddy asked Mother to give thanks. She paused a moment, then implored, "Dear Lord, will you give us our daily bread?"

That night, when everyone had gone to bed, Daddy heard a door close. He went down the stairs to discover on the table three loaves of bread. The next day a car drove up and Daddy met a daughter-in-law of the Wetheralds at the door. She said, "Mr. Corey, would you come to the car to carry in a sack of flour? It is too heavy for me."

After the flour and other staples where laid on the table, he asked the young woman, "Did you bring bread last night?"

She looked surprised. "Let me tell you what happened. In the night when I was sound asleep, I heard a voice drilling in my head, 'Coreys need bread, Coreys need bread.' I turned over several times, but the voice didn't quit. 'Coreys need bread, Coreys need bread, Coreys need bread.' I woke up my husband; we dressed and left in the car. When we got back to bed, my mind kept working, *If the Coreys need bread, three loaves will barely last them a day. I knew I had to do more.*"[40]

The parents of this young woman's husband had been friends and partners in ministry with Daddy ever since the beginning. They had arrived from the Midwest in 1935, driving a canvas-covered truck—arguably the one Daddy borrowed for the Hart's Lake trip. The Wetheralds brought with them a batch of grownups, several of them married; teenagers that included Joy Belle and Onolee; and a handful of younger boys. In those days, the Wetheralds had more offspring than Arthur and Margaret Corey.

After their daughter-in-law's charitable act, Mr. and Mrs. Wetherald invited all of the Coreys to dinner. The house was overflowing and the noise was deafening. Daddy turned the conversation into a sermon and the prattle subsided. He said, "I was not surprised that God awakened the young lady from her sleep. That is what faith is all about. When you pray, you know God hears and you expect results. But, I have to admit, her second trip with more groceries did surprise me. God answered with even more results than my faith imagined."

Meanwhile, the youngest boys, two rabble-rousers, waited for Marilyn and Elizabeth to go out to play. They snuck up from behind and pursued the girls on a full-out race. That startled the rafter of gobble-squawking turkeys, and they, too, joined in the chase. Elizabeth was bawling by the time she and Marilyn got in the door to safety.

Mabel Wetherald, married to Bill Jr., gave rapt attention to Mr. Corey's messages. She wanted to have the kind of faith he talked about and wanted to know more—she always wanted to know more. It was said of her, "Mabel took such pains."

Mabel was a singer, and you could hear her solo voice above everyone else. Hers was the only voice you heard when there were just a few people in the meetings. Mother accompanied Mabel on the piano or accordion as the soloist sang from the depths of her being, often dabbing a handkerchief behind her glasses.

Mabel joined Mother as she prayed and wept for the people who were suffering in Europe—the starving babies, the persecuted families, the displaced millions. They prayed and wept for their country that people would turn to God. They prayed and wept for neighbors and their wayward youth. Mother counted Mabel as her soul-mate sister.

Thus it was that the friends and relatives and guests came and went, along with the seasons, bringing with them a cartload of changes that were quite unexpected.

• • •

CHAPTER EIGHT
The Downs-and-Ups
(Summer 1942)

In July, the family returned to Hart's Lake. This time the borrowed car wasn't as roomy as the borrowed truck of the previous year. Daddy and Mother tied boxes and sleeping mats on top; then crammed the inside to the ceiling with more stuff and kids. Daddy turned the crank; then turned it again and again. Not a sputter from the engine. Without a word, three barefoot girls piled out to push the car down the hill and onto the road so Daddy could start it while rolling. In the searing July heat, tar squished between their toes and burned their skin. By the time the engine coughed enough to get chugging, three pairs of feet were covered with gunk. Then it was back into the house for a lamp fuel scrub, the vapors of which stuck with them the entire six-hour trip, through even the picnic lunch and the toilet stops. But cleaning fumes didn't do anything to diminish the anticipation of summer at the Hart's Lake cabin.

The children unfolded themselves from the car. Something was different. From the cabin they could hear sounds that had not been there the year before. Trucks rumbled non-stop, sending up clouds of dust higher than the treetops and leaving a pall over the region. Guns popped in the distance. At night, lights searched all directions in the sky. The country was at war; young men were preparing to fight; and the family was not far from the scene of intense military training at Fort Lewis Army Base. It was all very nerve-wracking.

Perhaps Mother's nerves were on edge, or perhaps it was Daddy's that got the best of him. One afternoon, the two of them were in the yard—alone they thought. But Marilyn had gone out the back door. She stayed out of sight, startled by the sound of a heated discussion. She couldn't make out Mother's words but was disturbed in hearing the argument—Mother never argued with Daddy. Then she saw Mother reach up and whop Daddy on the forehead. For a split second Marilyn thought he would smack her back, but he didn't move. Mother blurted, "There was a mosquito."

Marilyn crept back inside so no one would know she had eavesdropped. For a long time afterwards she could still hear the sound smacking in her ears of Mother slapping Daddy and see the fire in his eyes that made her expect him to return the whop. She didn't know what she would have done if Daddy had hit her mother.

Yes, it was all nerve-wracking. Soldiers—just young boys—learning to fight, and Mother and Daddy arguing. But what could Marilyn do about all that? Life just had to go on when the chickens chattered and the cows called.

This time Mother said the Pattons' animals were not permitted inside the yard, but she let the girls go find them. Each day they watched as Mr. Patton rode his horse to corral them into the pasture. Virginia said she wanted to ride the horse, so he helped her climb on. Before she was even seated, the horse took off at full run to the barn, leaping over logs, dodging around stumps, and racing through the weeds. Virginia didn't even have her hands on the reins. She clung to the horn of the saddle, her legs whipping up and down with each gallop. If it hadn't been so scary, it would have been hilarious. Virginia had barely recovered from horseback riding when she caught her leg on a barbwire fence and tore a five-inch gash. Hart's Lake vacationing was taking a serious toll on that twelve-year old.

The end of August came. It was time to go home, out of the dust and mosquitoes, and away from the noise of Fort Lewis. David and Elizabeth ran to check the rows they had planted in the spring. Not a "Victory Garden" any more. The enormous radishes were bitter and woody as logs, the ground was parched, and the well was dry. The summer had been as arid on the peninsula as at Hart's Lake.

There might have been many things to complain about, but Virginia and Marilyn weren't grumbling. They had been waiting to get back for one long-anticipated event: They were going to be baptized.

Virginia knew the time was right. Two summers earlier, she had gone to Sammamish Bible Camp on scholarship. Her counselor wanted to be sure that her charges knew they were ready for heaven, and asked Virginia if she was. Virginia answered, "Yes, I'm a Christian."

"When did you accept the Lord as your Savior?"

"I can't remember exactly. I just know I did."

Later on she remembered when it had happened. That's because one day Daddy discovered a note in Virginia's handwriting. He brought it to her and she read it. *"I see the light."*

Ah, she thought, *that's what I should have told the counselor about.* The "light" had come to her like a bolt from the sky—the realization that she had to make her own decision to follow the Lord. She could not ride on the coattails of her father and mother. Their faith did not cover her, and she had to believe for herself. So she did.

The need had been building in Marilyn's mind too. For as long as she could remember, she had struggled to behave the way she thought she was supposed to. She'd heard Daddy connect his punishments to her will to do wrong, to her inability to act like a Christian. She'd thought, *If I can't act right, how do I know if I really am a believer?* In a state of anguish one night, she'd called Mother up to the bedroom. "Mother, I need to know for sure I'm a Christian. Will you help me?"

After the two had prayed, Mother encouraged her, "Salvation is a gift from God. It does not depend on how good you are, but on Jesus' death for your sins."

So Marilyn knew, no matter what, she was going to heaven, and she would be baptized as soon she could.

About the same time, some of the Wetherald teenagers asked if Daddy would baptize them. So the plan had been set for August, after the family's return from Hart's Lake.

Finally, the day came, and everyone met at the Elwha River. The Wetheralds had selected a quiet pool of milky aquamarine water that also served—on other days—as a Laundromat for travelers or local construction crews. After a hymn led by Mabel's inimitable voice that echoed up and down the gorge, Daddy confirmed the faith of each young person. Thigh deep in the water he tipped the candidate under the water, and declared, "I baptize you in the name of the Father, the Son, and the Holy Spirit."

Virginia felt the shock of cold as the water rushing from the Olympic glaciers covered her face. But she came up smiling. She had waited a long time to be obedient to God's Word. Marilyn also felt the chill, but her heart was warm. She had confirmed in her spirit and before her family and her friends: *I will never doubt again that I am a Christian.*

Fall ushered in another round of guests, the most significant being Mr. and Mrs. Samuelson. Vern Samuelson owned the Port Angeles Ford dealership. He was a conscientious man—a handsome and dashing professional—who drove slowly into the dusty yard in his spiffy new car with velvety seats. "He probably gets a new car every year and we don't even have an old one," Marilyn whispered. Mother ignored the remark, knowing that without the friendship of the Samuelsons, her family would be in far worse straits.

Vern and his wife Rene depended on Daddy for spiritual counsel in decisions. In turn, they often paid for groceries, Daddy's travel expenses, and the car repairs—when there was a car to repair.

In December 1942, Mrs. Samuelson invited all of the Coreys for dinner. The children scrubbed themselves, even though it wasn't Saturday. Virginia and Marilyn unwound their perennial pigtails and left their hair down in braid-designed waves. They wore their best clothes that Marilyn had touched up with the stove-heated "sad irons."[41] Marilyn loved to use those hot, heavy clunkers, and she was careful not to touch them to anything but the clothes. She'd never forget the time she tested the heat of her play iron on Elizabeth's leg, back when she was five—what did she know?—and her sister was three. That test had left behind an iron-shaped tattoo on the younger child's leg, leading Marilyn to think about the sadness that could accompany any iron. *You can burn your fingers, burn your clothes, or even your little sister, and any one of those burns will make you painfully sad.*

Mr. Samuelson drove out to pick up the family since the Coreys had no car. What a sight to see when Mr. Samuelson opened the door. The dining table was covered with a white long tablecloth and decorated with red poinsettia flowers and lit candles—even though the Samuelsons, with their electric lights, didn't need candles. Glossy red rings to match the flowers held rolled-up white cloth napkins. Mrs. Samuelson showed each child where to sit . . . except the baby of course. Daddy blessed the food and each member of the Samuelson family.

Mrs. Samuelson and her two teenage daughters brought out small plates, each with a leaf of crispy green lettuce topped with a red Jell-O square full of tiny fruit pieces—the kind you could buy in a can. They set the salad on the big matching, shiny-gold-rimmed, plate in front of each person. It looked like dessert was being served first. The girls watched to see how Mrs. Samuelson ate, and copied her every move, just as Mother had taught them. The genteel lady ate most of her red Jell-O but, to the astonishment of her imitators, stood to clear the plate with the lettuce leaf still on it. The girls had been savoring the thought of the crisp greens—the kind they hadn't tasted since Aunt Hazel's garden at Hart's Lake—but they were forced to watch in anguish as Mrs. Samuelson threw the lettuce away.

She then brought out a banquet of turkey, mashed potatoes, gravy, sweet potatoes, green beans with bacon, and soft white buns with butter. She poured red juice in the dainty crystal glasses. When her daughters collected the plates, the guests were stuffed—they had eaten two helpings. Yet still there was more: pumpkin pie and snowman-shaped globs of whipped cream. The kids made room in their stomachs, and not a morsel was wasted—except for their pieces of lettuce!

The Samuelson's bathroom was a dream world, much prettier than Grandma's functional "Water Closet." Before the evening was through, the girls *had to go* at least twice each, and they *had to go* together. Real toilet paper hung beside the gleaming white basin. The flush made a splendid swooshing sound and washed everything out of sight. Next to the sink in a heart-shaped dish, a bar of soap radiated the fragrance of wild rose bushes in the summer woods. Fluffy towels, as soft as baby robin feathers, hung on the silver bar, just waiting for the girls' soaped, rinsed, and wild-rose-perfumed hands. The young ladies preened in front of a glistening mirror lit by an electric overhead light. They weren't the same girls who appeared in the scratched mirror back home beside a flickering kerosene lamp. Virginia admired the new glasses perched on her nose. She had needed glasses for several years—the school nurse had sent home a note after each eye test. This year, when public assistance was made available, Daddy agreed to get them. In this exquisite boudoir-like bath, with her new spectacles, Virginia could see her face and hair from at least three feet away. She fussed with the big white bow that held back her long waves. Elizabeth pulled at her bobbed locks that had grown at least six inches since all her hair was shaved off. She announced, "I want to grow my hair long too."

Marilyn tucked a stray strand behind her ear and said, "Maybe someday we'll have a flushing toilet. Maybe someday we will."

After dinner, Sammy, the youngest Samuelson daughter, invited the girls into her bedroom. They saw stacks of shimmery Christmas paper and rolls of red, green, and white ribbon on the ruffled bed. Sammy placed a lady's miniature jewel in a stamp-size box, wrapped it in paper, and tied it with a bow. She put that present into a larger box and covered it with new paper and ribbon, repeating the process again and again. Sammy giggled with anticipation of her mother opening many boxes before finding the gift in the bittiest box. The Corey girls' consternation grew with each layer. So much new wrapping paper cut and wasted. At home you always wrapped gifts in paper that had been used other Christmases. You always meticulously removed, folded, and boxed each piece. You could make it last for several years.

The girls returned to the living room. The Samuelsons' conversation with Mother and Daddy stopped mid-sentence. Phillip, with his face-crinkling smile and unruly coal-dark hair, wiggled on Mother's knee. John and David looked up from the floor where they played with a stack of picture books and bag full of wooden blocks. Mother suddenly declared it was late, and bundled up the children. Mrs. Samuelson sent home gifts for each to put under the Christmas tree. The kids whispered in the car about the food, the wrapping paper and—most of all—the bathroom, but Mother was silent.

She didn't tell the girls until later how the Samuelsons had ended the evening. When she finally did, she repeated for them Vern's exact words: "Rene and I know how hard it is for you to meet all of the needs of your family. If you are in agreement, we would like to adopt Phillip."

Grief was a heavy weight in Mother's heart and mind. *The Samuelsons must think my husband is not providing for the family! Was this whole ostentatious dinner display somehow designed to heap coals of inadequacy on our heads? How could the Samuelsons presume we might want to give up our baby for adoption!*

To add to her incredulity, as well as to her melancholy, Mother had just begun to feel within her body that she was once again pregnant—pregnant with the seventh child. *What would the Samuelsons think about that, and what about other friends who gave donations? What would the neighbors say, and the teachers at school? How would her mother, her sister, and her cousin respond?*

But equally distressing—*how would she and her family cope with the additional demands of another baby? Another baby, and so soon!*

David Margaret John Phillip 1942

CHAPTER NINE
The Toilet
(1943)

The girls, 9, 11, and 13, could hardly bear to go to the outside toilet after visiting the Samuelsons and experiencing the pleasantries of their cozy, perfumed bathroom. The smelly shed seemed worse than ever, even though Mr. Samuelson had supplied newspapers that were better for wiping than catalog pages. The problem with newspapers was that they left ink smudges on hands, as well as other body parts.

Each time the chamber pot had to be emptied—that was now the older girls' task—the caldron below bubbled and sloshed and splattered up the sides. Mother, who rarely spoke up on these matters, told Daddy it was unsanitary for the girls to sit out there, and that she felt like vomiting whenever she had to go. "This condition makes you feel sick, and that place makes it worse," she said.

Daddy did a survey and dug test spots. He had already moved the outhouse at least once, and he looked hard to find a space to dig another hole that would allow the contamination to seep away from the house and not pollute the well. He promised to dig when the weather improved.

Meantime, the children used the woods on Pete Johnson's property whenever they could. Even if the fresh air froze their bottoms, they preferred to *go* behind a tree. They took turns with at least one sibling stationed as a lookout for Mr. Johnson or his son WaWa.

They also used the woods for play. On Saturday, after the chores were done, and Sunday, after service, Mother was glad to send the whole caboodle out of the house. The girls tucked the boys into the wagon—a substantial homemade structure Daddy had recently assembled on top of spoke wheels—and ventured out. The girls, sometimes two at a time, gripped the bent pipe handle and pulled the wagon up the neighbors' driveway, through the fields, and into the woods. If Pete or Walter Johnson drove past the little caravan, everyone waved and smiled. Long gone were the confrontations of an earlier season.

The first place to investigate in the dead of winter was a shallow, frozen pond where David was the ice tester. He never minded falling through and getting his feet cold and wet. Mostly, they all played hide and seek, follow the leader, and a game they invented: "Hunters and Bears." Through the woods they, the Hunters, would sneak. One of them would spy an imaginary creature behind a stump, under a bush, or around a log, and then yell, "Bear, there's a bear!"

Up the nearest trees they would scuttle to get out of reach of the wild animal. Marilyn thought it was the most fun to holler "Bear!" when Elizabeth was hidden behind a bush with her pants down. Frantic to get put back together and up into a tree, she was in a perpetual state of wide-eyed alarm, much to the amusement of her bigger sister.

One afternoon, the youngsters returned late from an outing in the woods just as their father came up the driveway. He was carrying a box that held a new light for the Grange House—a Coleman lantern. The whole family circled the table to watch, as if they were a parliament of round-eyed owls. First Daddy took off the glass chimney and set it on the table. He attached a new mantle—a small circular bag of silken mesh—to the inner ceiling of the lantern. He cinched up the string with his fingertips, tied a square knot, and cut off the ends. He took a match and set the mantle on fire. It flared up, the flame as colorful as one on a shiny-colored catalog page. Then it fizzled out, leaving the fabric shrunken to a gray fiber ash. "Shhh," he said.

It was Daddy's way of warning, "Don't move, don't talk, and don't wiggle the table."

He lifted the glass, eased it down over the mantle, and tightened the screws on the vented roof. He pulled the stopper from the spout on the side and poured in the pure white gas. "You have to use the right kind of gas, not the kind used in cars," he explained.

Daddy set the valve and pumped the knob up and down until he was satisfied the pressure was just right. Then he opened the valve and everyone could hear the hissing of gas as it filled the chamber. He lit a match and held it to a small opening under the glass. *Whoosh*—the chamber lit up and flame flew out of the vents on top. Daddy tweaked the valve back and forth until the flame was gone and the mantle shimmered white—a white that was so dazzling the children had to look away.

The lamp illuminated the room like a streak of lightning that did not fade. It brightened up everything: the stove, the table, the sink, the cupboards, the stairway, and even the cobweb hanging in the corner. Marilyn scurried to the spot and swiped the swinging web with the towel. She scowled. "I just cleaned yesterday. I can't believe I missed it."

Those on duty washed the dishes and cleaned up the kitchen in a flash. Elizabeth brought her school tablet, Marilyn gathered her quilt pieces, Virginia grabbed a book, David picked up his tool kit, and Mother sat two little boys—albeit briefly—on her round expectant lap. The kitchen table, with its spectacular centerpiece, became the place to study, play, read, and talk every day after the sun went down.

The light had another illuminating feature. For Marilyn, it showed the shabbiness of the house and furniture, and the dreariness of her clothes. No matter how zealously she washed and ironed and changed them around, they were still just tacky missionary barrel clothes that had been altered to fit or belted in to disguise their shape. How she longed for the outfits other parents bought for their daughters—dresses with tall shoulders, black boleros, and cinch belts.

Her shoes were scuffed and smashed down. She thought if she could somehow rub a hole in the bottom, Mother would have to use a ration coupon to buy her a new pair. So each time she was alone in the restroom at school she stood over the heat register, swiveling her shoe back and forth over a jutting metal knob. Her action only made her shoes look shoddier.

Virginia, on the other hand, didn't think as much about how she looked, and Elizabeth could change out her clothes every day of the week since she inherited what her *two* sisters had outgrown. She was just thankful her hair had grown back and she didn't have to take horse pills and cod liver oil.

But, if Elizabeth's clothes didn't embarrass her at school, her lunches did. Other kids had soft Velveeta cheese and bologna in white store-bought bread, so Elizabeth and her sisters tried to conceal their sandwiches made of a thin layer of butter or jam or peanut butter spread between slabs of dry homemade bread. On occasion they were surprised to find in their sandwiches ground-up raisins mixed with Kraft Miracle Whip. It was a sweet-tart treat that they might have shared with their friends, if only it had been spread between slices of snowdrift Wonder Bread.

At least their grades were top-notch. All three worked hard to show that—while they didn't have new clothes or fancy food like others—they had brains that were better. On top of that, Grandpa Corey always gave them a dollar if they got all A's and B's. This term Virginia got a C in Arithmetic and had to write him a letter.

> Dear Grandpa Corey,
> I am writing to tell you that I got a C in one of my classes because I didn't work as hard as I should. I promise to work very hard and bring up the grade for next semester. I really need the dollar so I hope you will forgive me.
> Love from your granddaughter, Virginia Corey[42]

The letter paid off. She got her dollar and she didn't slough off any more in her assignments. However, about this same time, Virginia did have a run-in with her father that cost her more than money.

One morning at breakfast, Daddy confronted her for wearing lipstick. Virginia said, "No, I'm not, Daddy. I don't have any lipstick."

"You are lying. You *have* painted your lips. I won't have a daughter of mine going to school looking like a Jezebel."

Then Virginia remembered. The night before she had opened her watercolors and brushed on bright red paint. She had wiped it off, but the stain remained. She put her hand to her mouth, but said nothing.

"You will stay home from school today—not so much for the lipstick, but for the lie."

Tears welled up. She wanted to argue that she needed to be at school to keep up her grades as she had promised Grandpa Corey. She even thought a spanking would be better than the penalty Daddy imposed. At least a licking would not have lasted so long.

All day at home Virginia kept to herself, finding excuses to hide away with her books and saying she didn't feel well. By evening, her father told her she was developing a sullen spirit and that he might need to give her a spanking to deal with the attitude. Marilyn was stunned to hear him say that to Virginia—*Virginia*, the obedient, compliant, respectful young lady who was already getting *that time of the month.* "Daddy," Marilyn scolded, "You can't spank Virginia. She's grown up now!"

And Daddy didn't lay a hand to his teenage daughter.

Spring passed into summer. Mother was miserable with pregnancy and worn possum-weary by three little boys: David, a fireball of endless energy; John, a hot-tempered time-bomb; and Phillip, speedy as a road runner while still wearing diapers. She said she couldn't plant a garden. She couldn't do anything extra until the baby came.

The girls told Daddy they didn't need anyone to look after them when Mother went to the hospital. They were big enough to take care of the boys, cook the meals, pick up wood, and wash the clothes. It wouldn't be too hard since there was still spring water in the well. Marilyn said, "I will assign David to help with the chores and to keep Phillip off the highway."

The new father came home from the hospital and announced that Mother had a baby girl she named Eleanor Joy. The news of a seventh kid, even though she was named after Aunt Eleanor and Joy Wetherald, excited precisely no one. However, the girls were excited to brag to Daddy about all that they had done while he was away. Virginia boasted she had baked bread, "My first time ever all by myself."

Marilyn showed him the pile of wood she and David had collected, and Elizabeth pointed out the mountain of clothes she had scrubbed by hand in the washtub, hung on the line, and folded.

That first night, dinner was a bit discombobulated, considering how busy the cooks had been listing their accomplishments. When the family finally sat down, John bobbed his head, blinked his eyes, and pronounced, "Amen, let's eat."

The McNally girls, who had come to help, thought *Amen, let's eat,* the funniest thing they had ever heard from a child. They tried it out at home, and their parents chuckled too, so "Amen, let's eat," became a password to merriment at their meals.[43]

After a week, friends brought Mother home with baby Eleanor Joy. The girls told Mother they were worn out from chasing their brothers and managing the housework, but Daddy countered that they had been so efficient and so proud of themselves that they were to continue as if Mother were still away. So it was that I—Number Seven—came into the family.

Three weeks later, Daddy and Mother packed up a loaner car for Hart's Lake. It was to be a short stay, just enough time to introduce the baby to Aunt Eleanor and Grandma in Tacoma and to stock up from Aunt Hazel's abundance. Everyone picked and canned produce, and watered and weeded the patch—all except for Elizabeth. She stayed at the cabin to look after the month-old baby. "Don't worry, Mother," she said, "I can do it while you pick berries."

It was easy to babysit during naptime, but not so easy to change a messy diaper—especially when the contents of the diaper escaped their confines. At nine years, it was Elizabeth's first time to do that kind of clean up all by herself on an infant so squirmy and so mucked up, all the while swatting at a blur of buzzing flies attracted by the odor.

The family returned to the Grange House in time for school. David was starting first grade. He dragged his feet to the end of the road and told Mother, "I just want to stay home and help Daddy. He needs me."

Mother coaxed him with the promise that Virginia would sit with him on the bus, take him to his class, and meet him at the end of the day.

Meanwhile, Daddy couldn't put off the toilet pit any longer. He took the pick and shovel to a new hole near the intersection of two well-travelled roads. Everyone driving by on the highway and everyone going in and out of Pete Johnson's drive could see Daddy at the dig, but no one knew his plan. Until, that is, he pulled the toilet shed off the used hole and stationed it on top of the new. Then everyone did.

Pete Johnson charged down the road to tell Preacher Corey what he thought about the stench-emitting putrefaction so close to his drive and within full view of the highway. Daddy listened and apologized. "But," he countered, "This is really the only place to dig since the ground everywhere else is so hard."

The neighbor stewed and steamed and spouted every time he drove by. And who could blame him? Over the years he had gotten used to Mr. Corey's unorthodox ways and he'd become friendly with the youngsters. But this outhouse setting was beyond the sphere of common sense. What if he drove by when the door happened to open? And what would it be like when the full heat of summer hit? To avoid the outhouse, Mr. Johnson cut a new driveway straight to the highway, right through the middle of his hayfield. And not one of the Coreys squawked about that.

When the kids got home from school, Daddy gave them the task of covering the old hole with dirt from the new. That meant hauling it on the wagon or pulling it on a piece of cardboard up the hill, across the front yard to the opposite side of the house. They asked Mother for clothespins to pinch their nostrils shut, all the while yodeling hymns in the twang of the hillbilly singers they had once heard on Grandma's radio. It was kind of fun until Marilyn ribbed her little sister. "Ha ha, Tin Lizzie—I'll push you in the pit!"

Marilyn sniggered at her own wisecrack. She only called her sister "Tin Lizzie" to really, really tease. Then guilt set it. *I didn't really plan on being mean, the words just popped out of my mouth. I don't know why I forget to think before I say stuff.* She started to say sorry, but by then Elizabeth had run whining to Mother, "Marilyn said she would make me fall in the toilet hole. I don't want to help her anymore."

Daddy overheard, sent the boys off, and told Marilyn she would do the rest of the shoveling by herself. As the girl hurled the dirt and sputtered under her breath, repentance gave way to resentment. She forgot about apologizing and began to plan how she would get even. Then she recalled a joke Virginia had pulled on her. Maybe she would copycat that act with her tattle-tale sister.

Marilyn would never forget Virginia's trick as if it had been yesterday. One night she had run out the back door and into the toilet to do her business as fast as possible. Finished, she had slung the door open, only to have a body leap out of the shadow, and shout, "Boo!" right in her face.

Marilyn had nearly had a heart attack, while Virginia whooped and howled. "Gotcha, Mare." She had finally bested her sister, the one who fought with Elizabeth and bossed her little brothers. And she had called her the most-hated nickname in the process—Mare, as in "The Old Gray Mare."

As Marilyn pelted dirt down into the hole, she felt the terror and fury all over again. Yep, that's what she would do to Elizabeth. She could scarcely wait for the right time to pull it off.

The girls didn't like the location of the new Backhouse—now a Fronthouse in the front yard—any more than Pete Johnson did. But at least he'd provided a slight pay-off by moving his road. They fussed that friends would have to use that shed, fumed that it would be sickening for the people driving by with their car windows open, and fretted that everyone in the whole wide world would see them going in or out.

Since it wasn't going to up-and-move, however, they devised a procedure for keeping their toilet trips unnoticed. At the door of the house, they'd check for cars both directions on the highway. Once it was *all clear*, they'd run as fast as their legs could carry them to the shed, and leap inside. And once they were finished, they'd make sure to peek both ways out the toilet door. All clear again? They'd fly back to the house.

Halloween came. The toilet shed was opportunely perched for the prowling boys from Joyce School to perform a trick—without waiting for the option of treats to be offered. The previous year they had turned over the toilet and it had not even been close to the road. This time Daddy was ready. He didn't have a gun, but he did have his Bible. In the dark of night, when the hoodlums came sneaking up the drive, Preacher Corey met them head on. His impromptu sermon of sin and damnation was heard by those boys, as well as all the Johnsons, the Baars, the Nordstroms, and even the McNallys clear at the top of the mountain. Word got around that messing with Mr. Corey's toilets just wasn't worth the price.

As Christmas approached, Marilyn was trying to be good. She hadn't even scared the wits out of Elizabeth at the toilet, even though she planned to do so several times. Perhaps her good behavior influenced Daddy to let her spend the night with her friend, Doreen Taylor, or maybe it was because Doreen and her mother came to Sunday school. Marilyn didn't know the reason her father said yes, but she was euphoric. It was an exquisite sleepover. She got to eat as much dinner and chocolate cake as she wanted. And before the girls went to bed, Mrs. Taylor rolled Marilyn's long hair up on rags. The next morning, cascading waves bounced on her shoulders. She felt beautiful.

Marilyn's good behavior didn't last for long however. Daddy left on a long trip. There wasn't enough food, the weather was nasty, the boys were testy, and Mother was weary. Marilyn and Elizabeth were caught in a cyclone of teasing and tattling. Mother noted Marilyn's infractions on the calendar behind the kitchen stove every day. "Your father will deal with you when he gets home," She said.

It used to be that Marilyn could clown around, invent some cockeyed tale until Mother would get to laughing. Then she wouldn't mark the calendar. But, this December of 1943, the tomfoolery didn't change Mother's mind. Her patience had petered out, the marks were adding up, and Daddy would soon be home. Marilyn shuddered with thoughts about the "day of reckoning" that would come when Mother showed him the calendar. Then a letter came from Daddy with cash to buy groceries. In the same delivery arrived a new calendar. Marilyn looked at all the gloriously clean pages—a wild hope growing in her heart. She pulled herself together, played with the boys, helped Elizabeth without pestering her, ran errands for Mother, and rocked the baby. She cooked lunch, swept the floor, heated the sad irons on the kitchen stove, and pressed the pillowcases—along with Mother's aprons and her sisters' dresses.

Then, at a quiet moment when Mother was feeding the baby, Marilyn sat down in front of her with the new calendar in hand. She held it up. "Look," she said. "This calendar starts with December and will be good for all of next year. Can I, can I hang it up already?"

Mother peered over her glasses at her second daughter. "Yes, you may," she said.

Marilyn held her breath and eased toward the opposite wall. She removed the red-smeared calendar and replaced it with a snowy white December scene. She opened the kitchen stove, stuffed 1943 with all its symbols of bad behavior into the flames, and anchored the cast iron lid. Through the crack in the cover she watched the fire blaze until only amber and ruby coals remained.

She eased out her breath. The icon of this difficult year with its sting, stress, and struggle had been burned to ashes. For Marilyn—and perhaps for Mother as well.

Eleanor Ruth Phenicie and Eleanor Joy 1943

CHAPTER TEN
The Songs
(1944)

Mother's music echoed within the walls of the Grange House once again. The children heard it and their friends heard it. "Amazing Grace, how sweet the sound, that saved a wretch like me,"[44] she sang. When she forgot the words or when her thoughts wandered, she hummed. Her voice moved from one hymn to another all day and into the night, often ending with her favorite: "When by his grace I shall look on his face; that will be glory, be glory for me."[45]

Mother seemed to have a newfound tranquility. In three years, she'd added two more cabooses to the end of her train, two more gifts from God to bring the total to seven. She would not stew. She would sing.

At the same time, she knew her seven gifts were sprouting like seedlings—the older girls already at adolescence, and the boys not far behind. "Arthur," she asked, "What will we do about the need for privacy? The hanging sheets really aren't adequate anymore."

The Grange House, with its dormitory attic, was becoming less and less suitable for sleeping the entire family. The only child to have a guaranteed personal mattress was the baby who slept in a crib next to Mother, and that security was short-lived. John had been less than two years when newborn Phillip bumped him out. Each night after John threw his tantrum, Elizabeth, only eight, but gifted with a prodigious maternal aptitude, comforted him until he slept. When I was born in 1943, Phillip was barely more than a year old, and he was heart-broken to be shuffled away from Mother. He cried nonstop and stuffed both thumbs into his mouth, until Marilyn tucked him into her bed. As the toddlers grew, they formed daytime alliances with older siblings to determine who would sleep with whom. If there was an argument, Mother dictated where the younger child would bunk. Sleeping arrangements created more tension than rest.

Even the older girls moved around. One day, Marilyn talked Elizabeth into moving into her space—she was forever pushing her next sister into some change or some crazy new idea. She said they could make a darling room by putting their mattresses together and arranging the orange crate dressing table kitty-corner. But alas, the next day Elizabeth whined at her even though, as Marilyn told her diary, "I caught myself twice and stopped before I said something mean."

Marilyn talked every day to her diary now that she had received one after Christmas and was turning twelve. She wrote that while Elizabeth was sleeping next to her, she got sick in the night and threw up all over the floor. And that she didn't want to miss school, and begged Mother to let her go. And Mother asked, "Do you feel well enough to clean up the mess?"

The vomit and the drama were too much for Elizabeth, and she moved her bed away from her sister. Marilyn tried to make amends, and even suggested that they start a Nature Club so they could search for new specimens in the woods. But Elizabeth was fed up, and they were back to squabbling over everything, even the few curlers someone had put in a package. Mother said, "I'll take those curlers."

Marilyn wrangled the next day with Virginia, over the set of jacks the girls were supposed to share. Mother took the jacks too and said to Daddy, "I'm exhausted from the bickering. It would surely help to have more rooms where these girls could get away from each other."

Daddy went to check out a place with several bedrooms. He returned late that night and told Mother. "It cost too much. But I'm thinking that we can increase the sleeping space upstairs and give privacy by adding dormers."

He explained to the girls that the dormers—a raised roof extension with two windows—would give Elizabeth and Marilyn each her own partitioned bedroom. He listed the lumber, shingles, nails and windows required, and the cost—if purchased new. The supply of money or, more likely, the provision of used materials, became the ticket item for prayer. And these were prayers offered by those who knew that a God, who could awaken people to deliver bread, could easily provide dormers.

While waiting on God for the materials, Daddy started on another idea. He would move the Grange House off the back of the property—where it butted up against Pete Johnson's fence—to the flat gravelly ground to the north. A generation earlier, the flat had been used by the Grange for parking horses, wagons, and cars, and by the school for a playground. For the Coreys, however, the flat parking lot was useless for a garden and too hard to dig for a toilet.

"With some poles as skids," figured Daddy to his audience, "we can shimmy the house into a far better location."

Marilyn stifled her comments about what she thought was a preposterous proposition, and Mother sighed. But Daddy went right ahead and recruited a shovel squad. They dug all the sod in front and along the sides of the Grange House; then excavated soil from the hill and under the building, dumping it on the north side and widening the flat surface.

This project was put on hold when someone delivered a washing machine—a gas-powered wringer-topped Maytag. Daddy spent hours getting it to run the first time. It spewed dusty gray smoke and jangle-jerked like the Whippet, but eventually it worked.

It only took half a day, rather than the normal two-days-straight, for Marilyn and Elizabeth to do up the bin full of dirty clothes. After that, the back-and-forth swishing of the agitator replaced all the hand-plunging and scrub-board scrubbing. So efficient! The same soapy stove-warmed water washed multiple loads—the white clothes first, followed by the coloreds, ending with dark, muddy work clothes. The powered rubber-roller wringer squeezed the washed items as one of the wash maids fed it shirt after shirt, sheet after sheet, while the other stacked piles of the lathered clothes. They drained out the murky water, filled the washer or a rinse tub with buckets of cold, clear water from the well, and followed the same order for rinsing— whites to coloreds to darks. Then they hung everything on the clotheslines outside or behind the kitchen stove.

In sync with the modernized laundry machine, an iron that burned kerosene came to the house. Turquoise colored—slightly deeper than a robin egg—it had a wood handle and a round bulb that held the fuel. When you lit the wick inside the iron, you could adjust the flame to burn as hot or as cool as needed. If you had a kerosene supply you could iron all day without ever having to switch out a cold sad iron for a hot sad iron from the stove. Mother cheerfully turned over Daddy's white starched shirts to Marilyn's nimble fingers, and the 12-year-old saw to it that the ironing never piled up.

The new laundry scheme was in full swing when someone brought by a truckload of used bricks that Daddy mortared around the chimney. He'd barely finished that job when the Nyholms donated a set of cupboard doors, which took him another week to alter and install. Then he left on a trip.

When he returned, Marilyn met him at the door. Out of breath with excitement, she said, "Daddy, we saw fish in the creek that are big enough to eat. Can we go fishing? We asked Mrs. Nordstrom and she said it's okay with her."

David came running up. "Can we Daddy?"

Daddy said he had never seen anything large enough to fry, but agreed to help them get tackle fixed for fishing. He hiked with them along the stream and showed them how to pick an iron bush stick with the exact amount of flex. He helped them bend straight pins from Mother's sewing drawer and tie them with string to the poles. Lo and behold, when they hung the wiggly worms in the water, fish did come out of their hiding places—and some stayed to nibble. David watched Marilyn jerk her pole from the water and pointed, "Look—you got two at the same time!"

One trout still thrashed on the hook, while the other flopped on the bank. No one could figure out how one worm on a flimsy sewing pin had nabbed two trout. But alas, for all the fish Marilyn and David caught, not a single trout was the required six inches in length. Nordstrom Creek was not going to provide fish as a dietary supplement, at least not for a long time.

When the fishing didn't pan out so well, Marilyn began to talk about getting a cow. Mother was in favor. To have fresh cow's milk every day for the little ones without having to ask neighbors—that would be a mercy. Marilyn promised Daddy she would keep up with her jobs, do the milking and care for the cow. She would even ask the neighbors for their leftover hay.

"But first," she said, "I have to learn how to milk."

Mother let her ride the school bus to the Wetheralds so she could practice on their cows, help with the farming, and assist Mabel with her new baby, William Ralph.

If someone offered a ride, others of the family went to the Wetheralds, sometimes to help with the farming tasks and sometimes for a meeting. On one of these trips, David sat counting—counting up to 9 on one hand, and up to 34 on the other. He stewed, "I don't know why I have so many warts. They hurt when I do the work; they hurt when I play baseball. They are miserable and embarrassing. I wish I could cut them off." He went on and on, complaining and whining and counting a second time to be sure his numbers were accurate. Being accurate was fundamental.

Daddy didn't even look at him. "David, your problem is that you have a bad case of the gremlins. When you get rid of your gremlins—Grumpy, Grouchy, Gripey, Grumbly—your warts will disappear."

His father's prescription made no sense but David knew better than to disagree. He mused, *Maybe I should quit some of my bellyaching.*

Late spring, the Wetheralds auctioned a few cattle, but Daddy didn't have the cash to bid. Marilyn kept rehearsing her skill anyhow, knowing God would supply the money someday, somehow, for her to have a cow. Then summer came, and Mother commented it was providential that we didn't yet have a cow. For, with an animal to care for, the annual excursion to Hart's Lake would have been in jeopardy. Someone at the last minute had donated to Daddy a new car . . . well not at all new . . . but it was a car—a dull green coupe with a rumble seat that popped up out of the trunk. It needed immediate repairs and everyone offered to help fix it up. So Daddy had Marilyn hold onto some gizmo inside the car while he worked under the hood until the engine sputtered to life.

Then, Mother and Daddy crammed the rumble seat with supplies and scrunched part of the family into the coupe. The three remaining—Virginia, Marilyn, and David—were left behind to fend for themselves until Daddy could drop off the first set of passengers. The threesome, alone in the cavernous Grange House, listened to the creaking of the floor and walls, to the sound of the neighbor's barking dog, and to the crowing of off-schedule roosters that announced midnight instead of morning light. The worriers watched at the window, walked along the tracks, climbed the hill and counted the hours. David stewed, "What if they had an accident and nobody knows we're here by ourselves."

Marilyn contemplated the same, but said, "Daddy'll be back soon and we have good neighbors."

The feeling of abandonment lasted three wasted days and three creepy nights. Finally, Daddy arrived. Marilyn, who figured she'd earned a dispensation by helping in repairs, begged to ride in the rumble seat. "I love to sit in the wind, and besides, that way the car won't be so crowded."

"No," Daddy said.

But the rest of the jam-packed summer at Hart's Lake made up for it. The vacationers were so busy they scarcely noticed the dust, lights, and target practicing from Fort Lewis. Instead of chasing on logs and playing with cows, they cleared parts of the field between their cabin and the Brucks. Mother got a fire permit for a week, and they lit so many old-growth stumps at a time that smoke filled the valley as if a forest fire raged. The young loggers left the bonfires to cool down and helped Aunt Hazel plant tomatoes, spinach, corn and flowers. They took their pails to pick berries. They helped Mother and Aunt Hazel can cherries, plums, and green beans until wee hours of the morning. They hauled snags and logs of cedar and helped Daddy and his friend, Bert Prestwood, split the cedar into shingles—shingles designated for the yet-to-be-provided dormers back home.

On Sunday, everyone went to church in Roy, the first church Daddy had started. The trio of girls, now 10, 12, and 14 sang all five verses of, "There's not a Friend like the Lowly Jesus, No not One."[46] It was the song they had memorized seven years earlier so Mother would let them sing at the Tacoma rescue mission and the Tacoma jail. In memory of those places, Daddy took them once again to sing at the mission and the jail. Singing for the down-and-outers in Tacoma as they had way-back-when was like coming home from a far-away land. "But you can never really go back, can you?" Virginia asked Mother. "Everything changes, doesn't it?"

All summer long, Daddy came and went from the cabin. He brought back friends, along with wieners to roast on the stump fires. He took Mother and me, now a year-old toddler, to visit the relatives. He hauled home loads of shingles piled to the roof of the car and tied on top of the rumble seat.

As July ended, he took all of us home except Virginia and Marilyn. The two girls were lined up to help Aunt Hazel lead Vacation Bible School in Tacoma. Hazel was a professional VBS facilitator and knew how to train volunteers and how to make the classes, the lessons, the crafts, and the games a delight for everyone. Most importantly, she knew how to draw children to faith in Jesus.

Daddy had said helping his sister would be hands-on missionary training, and he promised to help Mother with her handful at home. After the second week, Daddy came to pick up Virginia and Marilyn, not realizing they still had a week to go. He told Aunt Hazel he needed his helper Marilyn for the outdoors and Virginia to lighten his childcare load, but Aunt Hazel told him she would not be able to find replacements for them. He started to quibble, but quit mid-sentence. He knew his older sister to be as tenacious as he. So he drove home to face Mother, who had tried to tell him she knew the girls were expected to stay for three weeks. But Mother was not one to say "I told you so," and welcomed him with a smile and a kiss.

The following week, Daddy returned to Tacoma as the final VBS presentation ended. He loaded the car with boxes of fruit, and the girls packed up their things. The weighted-down rumble-seat car left in the wee hours, arriving at the Grange House: in time for breakfast; in time to pick a bumper crop of pears and plums at the neighbor's orchard; in time to can Aunt Hazel's tomatoes before they rotted; and in time for school to start.

David sat on the school bus, studying his hands. He couldn't believe how smooth they were. Oh, there were calluses, but all of his warts—all 43 of them—were gone. The summer had been so full of activity, he'd forgotten about those sore lumps that had caused him pain and embarrassment. *Could it be*, he thought, *I've rid myself of those gremlins of complaining. Did my father's remedy really work?*

David was still thinking about these things when he got off the bus. As he walked up the drive, he saw that Daddy was digging under the Grange House. He knew his father had given up the idea of moving the structure, but had talked of turning the partial gap on the north side into a cellar for storing the produce and canned goods. David poked his head under the foundation. He gasped at the cave-like hole, "Daddy, won't the whole house fall down if we take out too much dirt?"

Marilyn grabbed a shovel and began to smooth the wall where shelves would go, and that activity gave David more anxious thoughts. *What if she is under there and it crashes on top of her.*

Then Mother came around the corner with concern on her face and a letter in hand. It was addressed to Arthur Wheelock Corey. It said he was to report to the Selective Service Office within a certain number days.

Daddy had been concerned about that possibility since the beginning of the war. He had said he could not fight, could not kill another person, and he had prayed that it would not be necessary for him to file as a "Conscientious Objector." Shovel in hand, he was once again facing that dilemma. He put the tool in its place and went off to pray. All of the family prayed and worried. *What would we do if Daddy went to war?*

God answered. The next day word came that there had been a mistake. Daddy would not have to enlist. He was too old and had too many children.

"Too old and too many children!" Mother praised the Lord and laughed at the same time. "I never thought that being too old and having too many children could be such a blessing."

Another blessing came in the mail about the same time. It was an announcement that electric lines were being installed westward along Highway 9A toward Joyce. It had been ten years since President Franklin Delano Roosevelt had established by executive order the Rural Electrification Administration (REA) as one of his New Deal initiatives. We would be a beneficiary of that act if the Grange House was wired when the hook-up trucks trundled past our driveway. Daddy promised Mother we would be ready.

Amidst the excitement, we were prepping for another transition. Virginia was going away . . . maybe. The maybe was because Daddy was still waiting on the Lord for assurance. Virginia would see him, sitting for hours with his Bible on his lap—reading and studying and praying and waiting. It was his pattern—reading, studying, praying, waiting—and not only when there was a decision to make, but also every day in between.

While she awaited his answer, Virginia had been accepted at Prairie High School, a Christian boarding institution in Three Hills, Alberta, Canada, where Cousin Donald Bruck was starting his senior year. A long-time friend of the family promised to pay Virginia's room and board and the Wetheralds took her to town to buy store-bought clothes—a jumper and two blouses. Virginia packed her trunk. But Daddy still wasn't sure he wanted his daughter at just fourteen to go so far, even though he valued the idea of her being under the influence of godly teachers. He said to her, "If I wake up at 4:30 and have a message from God, you can go."

At precisely 4:30, Daddy sat up in bed. He opened the Bible and a verse from Micah jumped out at him. "Arise and depart."

Everyone was up to wave Virginia off as she and Daddy caught their ride to the ferry in Port Angeles—the ferry that would take them to Victoria on Vancouver Island, where they would catch a five-hour ferry for Vancouver, BC.[47]

It would be a daunting journey—all day of travel on the water, after which Daddy would see his daughter off on the Canadian Pacific Railway for Alberta.

Mother and the kids turned back to get on with the day. It was a droopy, dumpy, gloomy day—in the kitchen, on the bus, and even at school. The first of the Coreys had left home.

It was mid-October. Daylight was decreasing and weather was chilling. Not much time to build the dormers before it would be too late. While Daddy was still seeing off Virginia, Mabel's husband Bill delivered windows and nail-studded lumber from a demolished building. After school until dark, David and Marilyn yanked out nails and pounded them flat. David said, "We should teach Bill Wetherald how to straighten bent nails. When he pounded his brand new nails and they bent, he just threw them away."

"Well, why didn't you grab them? They'd be a lot better than these rusty ones."

"I didn't have the nerve."

When Daddy returned from Vancouver, he found the recycled windows, boards, and nails waiting, alongside the shingles from Hart's Lake, each for its own new role in the dormers.

The next day the beds were rearranged on the far side of the upstairs bedroom, away from the dormer wall on the east. Daddy took his handsaw to the roof and sliced two parallel lines from the eve to the peak. The next day, with Mother's help, he raised the disconnected section of the roof as high as the two-by-fours would allow and anchored the new structure with the largest of the straightened nails. Everyone helped after school and, within a week, outside walls were built, windows installed, shingles attached, partitions put up, and whimsical curtains—altered from missionary barrel drapes—hung in place.

At last, Elizabeth and Marilyn each had her own private room with a window. Each could decorate her own space as she wished, and each could ignore the other if she wanted to. Both of them wrote long letters to Virginia, explaining how they had fixed up the rooms and telling her what she was missing.

When a return letter came, Marilyn read it at least five times. She missed her sister more than she ever thought she would. Everyone missed Virginia; everyone wanted to hear how she was doing.

Elizabeth was in sixth grade with the strict Mrs. Wilder, while Marilyn was in seventh grade next door. Marilyn eyed her former teacher, heard her stalwart steps, and scuttled the other way. She felt as if the steely gray eyes of the woman pierced her inner soul. For Marilyn was weighed down with the guilt of a lie she had told Mrs. Wilder two years earlier in fifth grade.

The burden of guilt grew to an intolerable level when, one Sunday, Marilyn heard an evangelist preach of the hellfire and brimstone that awaited liars. She knew she wasn't going to hell, but she also knew she needed to get this sin straightened out. So, the next morning, she told Mother and Daddy about the lie and asked them to pray that she would go tell Mrs. Wilder and ask her forgiveness. All morning in Mr. Green's class, the twelve-year-old twisted in her seat and twiddled with her hair. She couldn't concentrate on studies for the war going on inside. She delayed the inevitable all morning long, but she knew she had to confess because her parents would ask. Finally, she raised her hand to be excused. No problem with Mr. Green. He liked the girls, and they could do anything.

Marilyn stopped at Mrs. Wilder's room, paralyzed. Then sick. She ran for the washroom and cleaned up her face. She crept back to the dreaded door and tapped four brave taps, heart hammering and knees knocking. A student opened the door and said Mrs. Wilder was teaching arithmetic.

"But I n-need t-to t-talk to her now."

Mrs. Wilder came out. She frowned. "What do you want?"

Marilyn swallowed. "Mrs. Wilder, I have to confess that I told you a lie in fifth grade and I want you to forgive me."

The teacher started to interrupt, but there was no stopping now. "Remember when you were talking about Santa Claus being a dear old man who might bring us wonderful gifts? Well, I said under my breath, 'You are crazy' and I didn't mean anyone to hear me, but Marlene told on me and you called me in after class and asked me if I had said that, and I swore I only said 'it's crazy.' But that was a lie. I really did say 'You are crazy' and I am sorry—will you forgive me?"

Mrs. Wilder put her hand on Marilyn's shoulder. "It's nothing. Don't worry anymore."

"Th-thank you," Marilyn stammered; then ran again for the washroom, her eyes and nose dumping a deluge down her face. She decided then and there she would never tell another lie. Confession was the worst punishment in the whole dim-witted world.

Santa Claus was no longer a problem between Marilyn and Mrs. Wilder. But he was a problem between Mr. Corey and the school. If the Christmas programs focused on Santa and the reindeer, not on the true meaning, Daddy said that his children could not participate. His notes put pressure on the teachers because his daughters had the truest and brightest and strongest voices. They could read notes, sing in harmony, drown out the tone deaf, and play the piano or accordion. The staff knew that without Marilyn and Elizabeth, the music portion of the Christmas entertainment was destined to mediocrity. In 1944, Mr. Corey's input prevailed. The committee selected to honor the birth of Jesus.

Mother was glad when the controversy at school was settled, for she had another issue drawing her attention—an issue she had not shared with a single soul, save perhaps her husband. In the kitchen, over tea with her friend Virginia Pennoyer, Mother whispered her secret. "You understand . . . I get pregnant so easily. All Arthur has to do is look at me."

The joke amused both of the women, and Mother allowed the mirth of the moment to mitigate the reality of her pregnancy with child Number Eight.

Outside the walls of the Grange House, the war was taking its toll on the neighborhood and the country. There was increased rationing of food. Commodities such as rubber, sugar, and shoes were scarce. Butter in the stores had gone up from 4 points to 24, making it out-of-sight expensive. Skirt hems had gone up too, but that had the benefit of longer-lasting outfits, since the girls didn't outgrow their clothes so quickly. And there was omnipresent reconnaissance of the military. Soldiers, stationed in strategic locations, monitored the waterways, skies, and roads. They guarded the bridges and checked loads carried in the back of trucks.

We learned of such goings-on from the Singhose family. Mrs. Singhose and her two daughters, Leola and Hannah, liked to come to our home for fellowship, and Hannah was a favored babysitter to little John. The girls rode the bus to school and Mrs. Singhose was the school cook. The Corey children would see her in the kitchen, and wish they had money to buy the hot tasty dishes she prepared for the school lunches.

Usually two soldiers were stationed at the Singhose house, located at the bottom of Eden Valley Road. One of the soldiers slept in the kitchen each night. His commission was to listen for the telephone—one of a handful of phones in the entire area. Mr. and Mrs. Singhose welcomed the service men and treated the young soldiers as if they belonged in the family. These kitchen guests were temporary surrogates for their son, Charlie, who had joined the US Coast Guard in 1941. Young Hannah and her sister Leola watched the uniformed boys from a distance. Each night, the girls laid out their shoes beside the bed in case evacuation orders came. Hannah even anticipated which shoe she would put on first if the call came.[48]

In the same kitchen as the wired link to the world, Hannah, Leola and their mother prepared for Christmas. They baked flat molasses cookies and constructed the walls of a gingerbread house. They shingled and shuttered the spicy cabin with frosting and added a kaleidoscope of colored candies fit for a fairy tale. They packed up the masterpiece and carefully delivered it to the Coreys for Christmas.

Mother accepted the gift with a smile for Hannah and Leola. "This will be a very special treat for the children," she said. "We'll make it last for several days."

Mr. Singhose placed on the porch a sack of potatoes harvested from his patch. Mother held out her hand. "I don't know how to express our thanks for your generosity. God bless you."

Other Christmas gifts arrived, including a check from Naoma designated for the purchase of presents. Naoma had long given up the shopping trips of earlier years. Receiving money instead of gifts was easier for Mother. She could find the best deals and then make her decisions about what to buy. This year she was pleased with her purchases and how much she had saved.

She was also pleased that the children woke up on Christmas morning to find it snowing. It seemed God had smiled down and sent a Christmas day with snow! After breakfast, after the Christmas story, and after the gifts, all went out to make snowmen. That evening four-year-old John prayed God would keep Virginia and Grandma and the snowmen. Mother asked what he meant about keeping the snowmen, and he said, "I don't want them to die. Want them to be there in the morning."

Mother wrote to Naoma to thank her for the gifts that she and Daddy had purchased with the money. "Eleanor Joy is enjoying (and so am I) an unbreakable dish with 3 partitions and a broom to do her own sweeping. The dish was rather expensive ($1.25) but when I figure up what she has broken of our dishes it isn't so much. We used your gift to buy electric fixtures for Marilyn's, Elizabeth's and David's bedrooms. The children couldn't have received a more appropriate gift."[49]

And she wrote of her anticipation of what the New Year was about to bring. "If the car will start (and the poor thing is in such a worn out condition it should be run into a wrecking place) Arthur is going to town to notify the electric company that we are ready to be hooked up. Hadn't minded so much the kerosene lights until now when we have visions of something better."[50]

So Christmas 1944, everyone upwards of four years had visions of something better dancing in their heads, something far better than kerosene lamps that smelled, a Coleman lantern that cost too much to use all the time, and candles that burned out in an hour or two and left behind a drippy mess of wax.

What would it be like to live with electricity? The oldest could remember the lit-up parsonage in Port Angeles and some of the youngsters pictured the Samuelson's. But imagining lights at the Grange House, and lights at their neighbors? That was puzzlement beyond the power of their speculation.

• • •

CHAPTER ELEVEN
The Electricity
(1945)

By the first days of January 1945, the children made excuses to run down the highway or the railroad tracks to see where the utility trucks were parked. The day came when the men lifted the wire near the corner of the Camp Hayden Road.

"I think they'll be here tomorrow!" shouted Marilyn as she ran through the door.

David wanted to agree, but that seemed too good to even hope for. "I don't know," he hedged—all the while thinking, *when you are anxious, these things take forever.*

The day finally came. When the school kids climbed off the bus, John came whizzing down the driveway. "The lights are on! We have 'lectricity!"

Phillip wasn't far behind, his legs pumping and his arms waving, "lecticity, 'lecticity, 'lecticity!"

The little boys turned and rushed to point out where the electrification squad had hooked up power to the circuit box on the outside wall.

John wanted to show them how the disc turned in the glass meter box, but they couldn't wait. Mother met them at the door and everyone followed her through the kitchen where the hanging bulb glowed. They couldn't stop there, and sprinted up the stairs. They went from Mother's bedside, to David's, and to the dormer bedrooms, pulling the chains on the Christmas-present light fixtures. Sure enough, they sparkled even as the Sears Roebuck label guaranteed.

"I'll be able to do my homework upstairs now."

"Me too."

They headed down the stairs and Marilyn said. "I'll put away the lamps."

David went straight to Daddy and asked, "Can I turn on the radio?"

He'd been thinking about the radio with its faded blue and gray woven face and brown wooden knobs ever since the first promise of power. He'd even known where it would be plugged in.

With a radio, we finally had a direct source for happenings outside the community. For seven years, since the move from Port Angeles, information had come in flyers from school, reports by friends, and hearsay of neighbors. Now, with a light bulb shining overhead, everyone huddled around the little box to listen to news broadcasts.

Even so, radio listening was regulated. Daddy said most broadcasts were not edifying. Mother said the news was worrisome and we shouldn't waste electricity. But she said we could listen to music of The Haven of Rest Quartet and sermons by First Mate Bob of the Good Ship Grace, or Charles Fuller of The Revival Hour. When Daddy was elsewhere, those radio preachers became our in-house Sunday school teachers.

When the Samuelsons heard we had electricity, they brought moving pictures to show on their reel-to-reel machine. Where else might they find willing watchers that would sit without fidgeting through hours of their travel adventures to places Corey kids could not even imagine?

Mr. Samuelson suggested that Arthur—he only called him Arthur—tune in to KONP, the radio station in Port Angeles that had just begun broadcasting. From 6:15-6:30 PM, Samuelson Motor Company sponsored the series about world peace entitled, "What are We Fighting for?" The program promoted the Moral Rearmament philosophy that contended the world would be better and peace could be attained if those in power would practice high morality in their public and private lives. Vern's perspective on morality as a solution to world problems, though diverse from our father's message of repentance, allowed for many hours of deferential discussion.

The Samuelsons had never again mentioned adoption, and Mother carried on as if the proffer had never been presented. If the girls looked askance at the Samuelsons, Mother reminded them, "Rene and Vern just didn't understand how much we love Phillip."

Electricity provided new options for housework. Daddy pushed aside the gasoline washer that spewed exhaust fumes or didn't start at all. He plugged in an electric wringer machine—the one Mother had loaned to friends in Port Angeles because the Grange House had no power back then.

This machine had three plunging arms, each attached to a brass rod that connected to a shaft in the center of the washing tub. The shaft went down through the tub where it attached to the transmission. The three plungers worked in rhythm, like drumsticks with no hands, and beat the clothes with a vengeance. That first day, the girls washed eighteen loads. David was hypnotized by the mechanical action. When the girls were at school, he begged, "Mother, please can I do the washing?"

He didn't care about getting the clothes clean—he just wanted to watch the gears turn underneath and the plungers go up and down. "You can help me or the girls if you like," she answered, "but not by yourself. The wringer doesn't know the difference between a body part and a pair of pants."

Electric lights also showed the distress of the plank floors, and Daddy brought home gallons of varnish. Everyone pitched in to move the entire kitchen and dining room—except the stove and built in cabinets—into the Big Room. Marilyn and Elizabeth scrubbed the floors twice with brushes and cleanser. For a week the whole tribe camped next door to the fresh, tangy, nose-biting fragrance of varnish, all the while anticipating floors as smooth as glass and shiny as satin.

Marilyn was hoping all her hard exertion with the floors, the laundry, and the woodpiles would earn her the right to go to the school roller skating party. But Daddy said no. She snuck off to her room and sulked in silence. Next day she said to her friends that it simply wasn't fair, especially since only two other students weren't going and they weren't the popular kids. Since Marilyn couldn't go, her friend Donna sidled up to her and asked. "Can I borrow your white circle skirt with the strawberries for the party?"

Marilyn would have worn that cute skirt, a prized Christmas gift from Naoma, if she could have gone. Instead she loaned it to her fancier friend, who wasn't so much her friend—just one of the girls who had lots of pretty clothes. All evening, she pictured Donna spinning round and round on roller skates with the strawberries swirling high around her legs like red on white streamers, and she imagined the dancer was herself. When she couldn't bear it any longer, she stood in her little dormer room with her eyes closed, swirling in circles and humming the only happy tune she could remember. She only managed a few notes of "Tea for Two,"[51] then flopped on her bed, pounded her pillow, and sobbed.

In March, Mother talked about the arrival of the baby and told Daddy this one might even come early. "I'd surely feel better with plans in place—someone lined up to stay with the children and a car ready to go."

Daddy had an idea that would take care of both exigencies at once. "Maybe this baby can be born at home."

Daddy might have been half joking, but Marilyn believed he meant what he said. She knew in her heart he would be no help to Mother at all—none at all—why he couldn't even butcher a chicken. She turned with fire in her eyes and declared, "You can't do that to her, Daddy. You must take her to the hospital where she'll be cared for. *I'll* look after the children!"

"Then you will need to stay home from school in case Mother has to go quickly."

The other obstacle was the dead car. Mother wasn't kidding when she had written to Naoma that the current car—the green rumble seat job that the owner had junked to the Coreys before the last vacation to Hart's Lake—was a useless piece of rubbish that ought to be driven into the junkyard. From the start, Daddy had fussed with it many times, resurrecting it in the driveway or along the highway. Marilyn had even offered to hold the thingamajig inside the car, so he could work under the hood, but now it had a different problem.

Daddy knew when Mother said she was ready to go, there would be no time for pushing, towing, or repairing the car, and no way to delay the event. Mabel and Bill Wetherald solved the transportation dilemma when they brought over their car, and Bill said to keep it "until Mrs. Corey is safely situated in the hospital."

On April 5, Merton Henry, named for Grandpa Corey, was born. Grandpa was also the father of eight, and Daddy was pleased to have as many. "It is scriptural to have a full house, a full quiver," he liked to say. He backed his doctrine with the Psalm: "As arrows are in the hand of a mighty man; so are children of one's youth. Happy is the man that has his quiver full of them."

While Mother was in the hospital, Marilyn and Elizabeth both stayed home from school to do the laundry, cook the meals, bathe the youngest, and manage bedtimes. But John, at five, disobeyed his sisters and acted out a tantrum at the slightest provocation or for no reason at all. The two toddlers, Phillip and I, whined non-stop for Mother. The babysitters were exhausted after the first day. Aunt Hazel had written to say she would keep John for a bit, so Daddy took her up on the offer. He delivered John to Tacoma and returned the Wetheralds' car to its owners. After that, he sometimes caught a ride on the highway to visit Mother, while other days he counted on her friends to check in on her and the baby.

While racket reigned at home, Mother had a restful week at the hospital—except for April 12, the day that President Roosevelt died. The hospital was abuzz with whispers of the staff who, along with the country, mourned his passing. Nurses reminisced—as did the newspapers and the town folk—about the President's visit to Port Angeles in 1937.[52]

The next day, friends brought Mother and Merton home. The household settled into somewhat of a routine with Elizabeth or Marilyn staying home to help with the baby, and sometimes even David skipping school to entertain Phillip and me. It was at least two weeks before Mother asked Daddy to borrow a car and retrieve John Wayne, who no doubt had reveled in the personal attention of his Aunt Hazel.

On May 8, less than a month later, Victory in Europe (V.E.) was declared. On the radio we heard President Truman announce that all V.E. Day celebrations would honor the former president. "Who," he said, "should have lived to see this day." Over and over, that phrase was repeated on the newscasts and around the community.

For the celebration at Joyce School, the teachers called an assembly and showed a black and white—but gruesome—war movie in which the "Japs" were the bad guys. "At least we couldn't see any red blood," Marilyn told Mother.

But the mood of celebrations at school and around the region was muffled. On the west coast, Japan still loomed as the enemy. Japanese submarines prowled the entrance to the Straits of Juan de Fuca, and Japan had been launching balloon bombs for more than a year with the intent to start forest fires in the Northwest. Reports were circulated that a few small fires had been started but quickly extinguished. However, in Oregon this same month, May 1945, an explosion of one of these incendiary devices claimed the lives of a mother and her five children.[53] According to some reports, the woman was related to one of our local families.

At the same time, Japanese-Americans were returning to the west coast from the internment camps where they had been locked away after Pearl Harbor. The paper reported that groups of people didn't want them to come back and treated them hatefully, while others argued for their rights.

What we knew for sure was that instead of military presence and activity slowing down, it was ramping up. Blackout rules heightened and surveillance along the coast increased. There was still plenty of wartime stress to go around.

Even at home, all was not well. Mother's trip to collect the mail brought the doctor's bill for services at Merton's birth. It was $65.00—yet what a relief when she read in the fine print that it could be paid over time without interest.

The relief was short lived and inconsequential, however, when she reentered the Big Room. There was Daddy, lying still on the sofa, his face void of color. She dropped to her knees, held his hands, and pleaded with God for his life.

An hour or so later, Mother, with the baby in her arms, spoke to the panel of six other children around the table—Marilyn, 13; Elizabeth, 11; David, 8; John, 5; Phillip, 3; and me, almost 2. "Daddy is having some trouble with his heart. We need to be quiet and pray for God to heal him."

Daddy was only 40, and Mother still 39. "What if Daddy died?" "How will we live?" "Who will care for us?" Marilyn and Elizabeth whispered those thoughts until Marilyn said, "We have to have faith that it's God's will to heal Daddy."

We children worried, whispered, and prayed—when we went to bed, when we got up, when we ate, when we washed dishes, when we set the table, and when we gathered bark, sawed wood, cleaned house, and watched babies.

Daddy got up after three days and we knew: It had been God's will to heal him, and Daddy wasn't the only one who could pray for healing and have God answer—God had answered our earnest prayers too.

My father was back to normal, ruminating on yet another plan for the Grange House. He would have it licensed as a chapel. We didn't understand all of the reasons, just knew that there was no *real* church in the community and, if our Grange House was a church, there would be a church and more people would attend and it would be their church.

Daddy rode the bus to offices in Port Angeles and gathered the required paperwork. He visited Mr. Wetherald, Mr. Hall, and Mr. Norman—the men whom he had selected to sign as trustees. He assured Mother if the application went through, he would be home on weekends—at least most of the time—to lead the services.

He scheduled the official inauguration and began cleaning the yard. He and his helpers dug a new toilet hole on the west side of the house, as far as possible from the conspicuous corner where it had revived the ire of Pete Johnson. He tore down the clothesline by the front door, moved it to the back, and fixed the fence where the Johnson's broken down gate had floundered. Phillip wanted to help with the fix-up, so he took a hammer and pounded nails into the window sill. Mother said it was a miracle that he didn't pound right through the glass. Nonetheless, the front door was ready and welcoming, and the distraction of clutter in the yard was gone.

Just in time for the distraction of church dissention to descend. Only days before the scheduled opening ceremonies, one of the trustee couples and Daddy had a vociferous disagreement with gestures to match. This wasn't the first time Mother had seen and heard Daddy get into doctrinal disputes. When her husband knew he was right and quoted scripture to prove it, he would turn up the volume and the fervor of his conviction until there was no retreat. Mother never told the children what this upset was all about, but she sighed and murmured, "I don't think some of our friends will be coming anymore."

And that was the beginning and the middle and the end of the plan to turn the Grange House into a chapel. Except a few benefits remained—the yard was tidied up, the toilet was in a discreet location, and the window sill was decorated with three-year-old Phillip's nail art.

The derailed pastor didn't stew—at least not more than a few hours—over the dispute. He said, "Praise the Lord"—just like he did when he dropped a brick on his toe—and got ready for another trip. Ten years before, God had called Daddy to feed sheep, and that call had not changed. He would continue to serve God's flock wherever the Good Shepherd sent him.

Daddy headed out by foot with plans to meet Virginia who was finishing grade nine at Prairie High School in Alberta. He'd already left when Mother got a letter from Virginia telling that she had a ride to Tacoma and what day she would arrive there. Mother had no way to contact Daddy to tell him not to go all the way to Alberta. So, when he got there, he had to turn around and catch rides the entire 750 miles back to find her in Tacoma.

At home, no one could even guess when they would arrive. For two long days, we kids raced from window to window, watching the road like hawks, all the while reminding ourselves that our sister would arrive when it was God's will. Finally, the bus stopped at the driveway. With a cacophony of calls and squeals, all of us whooshed out the door and down the driveway. There she was, in her summery dress, carrying two bags on her arms. She'd grown up, not quite a lady, but no longer a girl. We didn't know what to do so we all talked at once. Tried to tell her about the 'lectrity, about the chapel that didn't pan out, and about the new baby who was taking a nap. Marilyn got in close and said, "I fixed up my room real nice. Do you want to sleep there with me?"

Later, when it was time to go to bed, Virginia decided to bunk with one of the other kids, and Marilyn grumped to her diary, "I shouldn't have taken all those pains to make my room nice for her."

Of course, Mother, as much as anyone, was glad to have her eldest home. At the same time, she was more than ready for a reprieve from the uproar. So Daddy agreed to occupy the biggest kids for a day. Together they hiked for miles down the railroad track and gathered bark on the long-cut home. They climbed to a logged out area at the top of a hill above the old Smith place from where they could see Victoria across the straits, nestled beneath Vancouver Island's snowy mountains. To the west, they pointed to the rust-colored bricks of Joyce School, and to the east they could imagine the gorge of the Elwha River. Behind them, a cool breeze floated down from the rugged peaks of the Olympics and across the underbrush. In a few months' time, the mesa with its stumps, logs, and highland flowers would be laden with blackberries, waiting to overflow Crisco-can buckets.

The hikers returned home in time for Mother's meeting with the ladies who were arriving from the neighborhood to coo over Merton. They seemed to agree that he had features of Marilyn and John, but his curly hair was fair-colored, like mine. Daddy and the girls put on a concert for the visitors. They belted out hand-clapping and toe-tapping southern gospel quartets from the hymnal they called the "Arkansas Book." The guests—most of them attired in flowery old-country dresses—nodded their scarf-bound heads to the syncopated rhythms. Such a celebration! Everyone loved the baby, Virginia had come home . . . and The Tandem bike had arrived from Tacoma by Auto Freight.

The girls had watched day after day for the bike's arrival, ever since Aunt Eleanor wrote that it was on the way. Months earlier, Grandma Phenicie had written that she planned to sell it for scrap to the junk man, prompting an urgent letter from the girls, begging her to send it since so they could easily run errands to the store for Mother.

Finally, word had come that the bicycle crate was sitting at the freight office in Port Angeles. Daddy and Mother went to town with a neighbor and brought it home. A whole bevy of heads poked in close as Daddy took the crate apart. There it was—the two-person bicycle that Grandma had nearly junked. The girls couldn't imagine that dreadful possibility. They knew all about its history—how Grandpa had purchased it about the time he married Grandma and the two had ridden it everywhere, including dozens of trips throughout Mount Rainier Park where all the relatives socialized; and how Mother and her sister and brother had grown up riding all over Tacoma and in the Point Defiance Park. There it was, disassembled for travel and looking every bit like a parts factory. The tandem had been idle for decades. Daddy said it needed new tires, new chains, and a set of brakes. He didn't know when he could get the parts and do the repairs. And, on top of that, he was leaving the next day for a trip.

The Tandem—that's what the girls called it because they could never agree on a proper name—sat in pieces for the rest of the summer. All that anticipation of going to the store, visiting their friends, and just going, going, going, wherever and whenever—all that excitement in vain. What a letdown!

In time, Daddy got The Tandem running. But it was complicated. Both sets of pedals were connected by chain to a direct-drive hub—no freewheel on that bike—so there was no way for the riders to let their feet rest and the bike coast without the pedals continuing to turn. It had no real brakes, so if you were going fast and lost your footing, the only option was to aim for an upward hill. No sooner had Marilyn and Elizabeth returned from one of their first trips to Joyce Store than speed got the best of them, and they ended up in the roadside ditch. They pulled themselves out of the grass to discover on the highway a scramble of the dozen eggs they'd purchased. The eggs were a total loss—a loss more painful than the scratches on their legs and the ding to the bike.

But the girls, and later the boys, put mile after mile on The Tandem. For wheels to ride, it was more consistent than a car and less costly to run. And it represented a first-ever measure of freedom and independence for the Corey kids.

On July 2, Mother turned forty. Daddy agreed with the girls that everyone should pitch in and give her the day off. Mother smiled and sat down. With eight children—and four of them under the age of five—the well-intentioned gift lasted less than ten minutes.

That summer there was no family trip to Hart's Lake. We had no car, and none of our friends had a vehicle to loan that was big enough for the army of us. Instead of vacationing, we sang while Virginia played her repertoire of hymns, picked wild blackberries and gardened for Mother, hauled buckets of water for Mrs. Nordstrom who was sick, chopped wood for Mrs. Taylor, cheered up other neighbors, and did our best to make games of it all.

Daddy went by himself to Hart's Lake. He needed time alone, time to fast and to seek God's guidance about an extensive tour of ministry. This would not be the usual trip that took him to Tacoma, Seattle, or Ellensburg. Ahead of those, Daddy would get a call in the night from the Lord, or he would receive a clear picture of someone in need and a sense that God had given him the vision. He would be gone a day or two and back home for the Sunday meeting, reporting that the divine appointment had been just as he had seen it. So this trip was unusual for at least two reasons. He would be leaving his family for weeks, and it was his friend, Hillary Marx—not God—who had initiated the call.

My father had known Mr. and Mrs. Marx since his early days of ministry. In fact, Mrs. Marx was the first sick person—sick with cancer for which the doctors had no further treatment—who was healed when Daddy prayed. The telling of that miracle is for another time—except to indicate that since Mrs. Marx had been restored to health, Hillary Marx had wanted to be mentored in the type of itinerate ministry for which Daddy was gifted. This summer, he told Daddy he wanted to go across the country following his mentor's lead. Each would carry only a handbag—a grip, Daddy called it—and a Bible. They would take no car and carry no cash. God would lead them to souls who needed their prayers and counsel, and to people who would offer transportation, food, and lodging.

Daddy returned from Hart's Lake and told Mother that God had confirmed the call. He continued to pray for guidance, sometimes hiking the road to be free of the ruckus. One day—just a few hundred yards from the Grange House—he heard a voice say, "Turn in here."

He stopped in his tracks and looked to his right. The voice continued. "I am going to give you this land."

Daddy nodded his head and walked into the woods. He knew there was no house on the land, but knew, as clearly as God had spoken to him, that one day there would be a large, sun-filled home for his wife, and bedrooms for his children.

The next day, he looked up the woman who held the title. He told her that he was interested in purchasing the land and wondered how much she would charge for it. Instead of answering his question, she anchored her hands on her hips, glared at him, and pronounced, "When the weather turns cold each year I bring my cattle down the mountain to winter in the fields. Moreover, I plan to build my own home on the property. There is no way you are going to get this land . . . except over my dead body."

Daddy was surprised by her answer—he'd been so sure of God's voice. But he was respectful. "Thank you for your time. God bless you."

A few days later, Daddy handed Mother a bit of left-over grocery money from his pocket, picked up the gripsack that held his Bible and two changes of clothes, and headed out on foot to catch a ride, planning to meet up with Hillary Marx.

We didn't hear from Daddy for at least two weeks. Then a letter Daddy had sent from Dodge City, Kansas, arrived with several dollar bills enclosed. He explained that a man who had been blessed in one of the meetings had donated the money for whatever needs he had. "Of course," he wrote, "I am concerned for the needs at home."

Mother held the bills in her hand and thanked the Lord. Although friends like the Wetheralds and Mrs. Branson had brought us produce and staples, she was running short. This donation meant she would not have to face the humiliating task of asking for help.

Other than concern for Daddy's safety and return, or what's for dinner, life at home was pretty much the same while he was away on short trips or long. However, during this absence, two monumental events transpired. The first might not seem earth shaking to most people, but to the Coreys on Highway 9A, it brought heart-racing excitement. On August 6, Jimmy Norman, his sister Lucile, and her husband brought us a puppy. The plump Spaniel mix had baby-soft obsidian-black hair, and his ears flopped on the ground when he bounced up and down. The bigger kids tried out lots of names. None of them sounded right to enough members of the panel, until Marilyn burst out with, "He's just a Skeezix!"[54] After that, the vote was unanimous, and a new ditty to the tune of "Bingo" was sung to christen the puppy.

> There was a family had a dog,
> and Skeezix was his name-o,
> S-K-E-Z-X, S-K-E-Z-X, S-K-E-Z-X,
> And Skeezix was his name-o.[55]

Skeezix was pure entertainment. Even Mother grinned at his antics and lined up all eight of us, along with Skeezix, for a rare family photo, shot with her Brownie camera. "Someday," she promised, "I will get the film developed."[56]

The second astounding event happened just days later. The news blared and the papers headlined:

THE US DROPS ATOMIC BOMBS ON JAPAN. JAPAN WILL SURRENDER.

President Truman declared August 15 and 16 as holidays and announced that the 19th would be a day of prayer. Mother didn't wait for the 19th. She immediately got down on her knees for the families who had lost loved ones and for those who were injured. She mourned the death of innocent children from the bombings and said out loud, "I am so sorry bombs had to be dropped on those cities, but so thankful for peace in our country."

"Does that mean no more air raid drills at school?" Elizabeth asked.

"Sure," answered Marilyn, "and it means we can take the blankets off the windows!"

Mother fixed a victory dinner with blackberry pie, and Marilyn dressed in her best clothes even though it wasn't Sunday or a school day. For the younger set, the best part was seeing the smile on Mother's face. Virginia said, "It's too bad Daddy isn't here to help us celebrate."

We all agreed, and Mother said. "I think we'll hear from him this week."

Two days later Daddy's letter arrived from Springfield, Missouri, with another donation, and we celebrated again.

We weren't the only ones in a good mood. People throughout the entire region were jubilant. The fear of Japanese invasion in the Straits of Juan de Fuca and in Puget Sound had dissolved. The military had begun to clean up and de-militarize the Camp Hayden Army Base. Guards had walked away from roadside and bridge checkpoints. Everywhere, the cloud of apprehension had lifted and the blaze of celebration had exploded.

School started on September 4. Elizabeth was right: there would be no more air raid drills—no more startling alarms to scare her out of her wits. Then the school declared September 6 a holiday of memorial.

We declared it a holiday for another reason. That evening most of us were already tucked into bed when Marilyn said, "I heard a car." She flew down the stairs just as Mother opened the door to Daddy and Mr. Marx. The rest of us . . . except the baby of course . . . scurried down to get in on the excitement. Daddy was finally home! All too soon, Mother sent us to bed, saying, "Daddy needs to rest. He'll still be here in the morning."

That night, we could still hear their voices as we drifted off. It was a comforting sound.

The next morning, Daddy overflowed with the reports of meeting former friends and of connecting with strangers on the highways and byways. He talked in rabbit trails, with one story leading into another, leading into another, and another, until he would get back to where he started. Mr. Marx was there at breakfast to help him keep on track. They shared stories of meeting up with people who had been praying for someone to teach them, of catching rides in the oddest places, and of going to cities they'd never heard of before. They talked about going hungry all day, about sleeping under the stars accompanied by mosquitoes, and about walking miles and miles in the hot sun.

Mr. Marx jumped in with his take on the adventures, "Remember that blistering day when I took you to task about the heat? I said, 'I thought God gave you a verse about the sun.'"

My father grinned, "You did catch me off guard—but not for more than a split second. I told you, 'That's right. God did give me the promise that the sun shall not smite you by day!'"

Daddy turned to face his family, and continued the story. "So I lifted my hands and looked to the sky. I said, 'Now, Lord, thank you for your promise that the sun will not smite us.'"

Mr. Marx nodded, "I could scarcely believe my eyes when I saw a cloud come up from the horizon and cover the sun."

Daddy finished the recounting. "And on the rest of the trip, Mr. Marx and I were never again oppressed by its heat."[57]

We'd sat at the table a long time—it was Saturday—and then Mr. Marx said he needed to get home, that he'd hardly seen his wife when he picked up the car to drive Daddy back. Mother said, "Thank you so much for bringing Arthur home."

Mr. Marx replied, "God blessed many people, most of all me. Thank you too."

The jobs couldn't be put off any longer and the big kids went to work. Everyone was glad to have Daddy home and to hear his stories, though no one was surprised at the miracles. We were used to those.

It was time for Virginia to go back to Prairie High School in Alberta for grade ten. We'd gotten accustomed to having her around, to hearing her play hymns on the piano and sing with the big sisters. But she was so sure that God wanted her to go back that no one could argue. Except Marilyn, who teased, "I just think you have a boyfriend up there."

This year Virginia had a ride lined up with Uncle Emil and Aunt Hazel, our Hart's Lake companions, who were going to volunteer at Prairie Bible Institute, the Bible and missionary training center located near the Prairie High School. So when the Brucks with their son Don came by for Virginia, it seemed as if everyone was moving away, and everyone was sad, and everyone had to sing, "God be with you 'til we meet again." And at home everyone older than six had to go to school and leave us little kids all alone with Mother. And, for a while, we just didn't know what to do with all the emptiness of that quiet.

Marilyn and Elizabeth were in Mr. Green's seventh and eighth grade room together. By this fall, they had figured out how to get along, how to do things together without all the teasing and tattling. That was a relief to Mother and to the two girls themselves. In the classroom Elizabeth was as shy as ever, but Marilyn was the teacher's pet. Mr. Green asked Marilyn to stay after school to help him with secretary tasks. And, at noon, he excused her early from class to wash dishes in the lunchroom and assist Mrs. Singhose, the cook.

Marilyn loved kitchen duty. It was not only a way to skip class, but it was also a profitable job with benefits. They paid her six dollars a month and let her have a hot serving of food, plus the leftovers for free. She relished the crusty pan scrapings of macaroni and cheese or scalloped potatoes—all eaten with no competition from her brothers. Every day she filled her stomach and equally began to fill out her frame.

In October, practices for the school Christmas program began. The girls brought home the theme and music for Daddy's review. By this time, a ritual of negotiations had been established that would determine whether or not the children could participate. Except that the negotiations didn't allow for much leeway from the Corey side. There would be no further discussion if the primary focus of the program was a secular version of the season. This year, after looking at the script and songs, Daddy sent back a note with Marilyn saying his children would not be involved. The teachers were skeptical that anyone would deny children the privilege of performing, and sent him another note, requesting that he reconsider. To the chagrin of his daughters, he returned a lucid explanation for his decision which—he assured them—was final. "It is not Santa who sees you when you're sleeping, nor is it Santa who sees when you're awake. Santa does not know when you've been good or bad. These are lies and we will not have our children perpetuating them."[58]

Marilyn dropped the note in the school office and ran out the door, her face crimson with disgrace. She could just imagine the look on the teacher's face when she read the words. At the end of the day, the teacher told her how sorry the school was that Mr. Corey would *not* let his family be part of this important traditional school and community event. She said, "Tell your father the decision has been made, and the theme has been chosen!"

Marilyn told Elizabeth and the two of them commiserated in misery. During practice times after that, the girls were sent to help out with younger classes, which included looking after their brother who, likewise, would not be performing. And thus the matter was settled for the season.

About the same time, Daddy told the girls to look after the youngsters while he took Mother on a walk. It was almost dark when they strolled up the drive. We younger ones danced at the door, and everyone asked questions about the unusual event. Daddy waited for quiet. "It will cost $1,000."

The children bounced up and down. "What? *What!?* What will cost a thousand dollars?"

"Mother and I walked through a piece of property that God has told us will be ours. Three months ago, before my trip with Mr. Marx, I first heard that message. But Mrs. Grauel, the owner, said it wasn't for sale and that we would only get the property over her dead body. Now Mrs. Grauel is gone.[59] In truth, her death has come as a complete surprise."

He went on, "I have spoken with her son and daughter, and they are ready to sell us the piece of land—the whole twenty-one and a half acres—for $1,000. Mother and I believe God will supply every cent in the time we are permitted. We have two months to pay the first four hundred."

Mother said nothing. The teenagers were silent too. They knew Daddy had lots of faith, but they wondered if his faith was as big as $1,000, which was almost as big as the cost of a brand new car. We little ones didn't understand what it was all about, or how much money that really was. All we knew was that miracles of dollars were to be expected.

One week later, a gift of $200 arrived in the mail. Three days after that, $100 arrived. We were only short by $100. But the hundred dollars didn't come. Every day we prayed, and every day we watched for the mail lady at the highway. Time was running out for the down payment to be delivered.

Thanksgiving arrived, but still no checks for which to give thanks. So, Daddy, Mother, and the older kids switched the traditional feast for a fast. Marilyn wrote in her diary that at least while working in the kitchen at school she had eaten Thanksgiving, "a feast of potatoes, gravy, cranberries, baked ham, beans, and cake."

After the urgent praying and fasting, everyone was certain the required amount would come immediately. It didn't. What came was a wild windstorm that lifted shingles off the roof, broke pots, and blew over the toilet. It knocked out the transformer and returned the Grange House to the dark rooms and kerosene lamps of its former years. It rained sideways and then the rain turned into a blizzard of snow. But still the well was dry and the kids had to haul water and rinse the clothes in the creek. It was time for the school Christmas play, but no one was permitted to go. Mother wondered out loud, "What do you think God is saying to us?"

Then, in the calm after the cleanup of the storm, God provided the final $100. Daddy answered Mother's earlier question. "Just remember Elijah. God sent the wind, the earthquake, and the fire. But he did not speak to Elijah in the wind, or the earthquake, or the fire. It was after the display—after God got Elijah's attention—that he spoke in a still, small voice."

Daddy and Mother took the down payment to town. The kids went searching for a Christmas tree along the railroad track. The girls made hundreds of red and white bows and tied them to the tree as it stood, confident and regal, in the Big Room. They draped cedar boughs in windows that were no longer blackened for war. The Christmastime house, with its heady evergreen perfume, welcomed our parents upon their return from the courthouse, a receipt in hand. Daddy read the document out loud.

> Contract between Anna Kreaman and Herman Grauel, the heirs at law of Elsie Grauel, and A.W. Corey and Margaret L. Corey. Volume 177 Page 300. 20th day of December, 1945. The purchase price is $1000 of which $400 has been paid. The following terms and conditions: $50 on or before the 20th of June, 1946 and every 6 months thereafter with interest to date of payment until the full purchase price both principal and interest has been paid in full.[60]

We celebrated Thanksgiving and Christmas that day. The down payment on a property, big enough to be a farm, had been made. Mother didn't say the thoughts that were in her head. *Where will the rest of the payments come from? And how will we ever have the wherewithal to build a home?*

She knew God was able and that Daddy believed. It would be enough for her.

Eight kids and Skeezix

CHAPTER TWELVE
The Promised Land
(1946)

On January 11, 1946, official papers of ownership were signed, notarized, and certified. Daddy confirmed with the Lord. "Does this mean we are free to use the land?" To his mind came words from Deuteronomy. "Behold, I have taught you statutes and judgments . . . that ye should do in the land whither ye go to possess it."

Possess the land. Yes, indeed. On Saturday, January 12, an assembly of Corey investigators—not unlike the Israelite spies of Bible times—scouted out our Promised Land. I was included in this party, since at two and a half years, I was grown up enough to appreciate the excitement and decidedly big enough to walk on my own two feet.

The property was located about the length of two city blocks east on Highway 9A, bordering on the Phillips Road that we had hiked many times. On this expedition, we veered off the road through a rusted barbwire fence and followed a path into the woods. Once a logging rail grade, the neglected path led through trees of all sorts: Shady firs armed with winter brown cones; droopy cedars designed with overlaid branches; wide-armed maples attired in elegant moss; and lacy hemlocks dripping with remnants of rain. The path opened to a clearing through which a seasonal stream slithered. Water soaked the feet of a stand of naked alders streaked with black pearl paint. Weathered, fire-blackened old growth stumps stuck out like volcanic eruptions on a green incline. On top of the grassy hill, a peek hole through towering Douglas firs revealed the sun-touched splendor of the Olympics. We stopped to gaze.

We followed the stream as it snuck through a gorge. Overhead, youthful cedar trees stood guard above a bed of soft needles they had been depositing since their first generation parents were removed. The canopy of cedars ended at the top of a ridge from which the stream tumbled and bounced on its way towards a rushing, splashing fork of Salt Creek. The smaller clear-water stream was sucked up by the murky winter run-off of the larger creek. Then both were swallowed by two culverts—one of corroded steel, the other of concrete.

This section of Salt Creek would be Corey Creek—our own place to draw water, to swim, and to catch fish. Phillip said, "I wanna go fishing now."

Daddy said, "Next summer, Lord willing."

Mother nodded her approval. Eye-level with the highway, we could see beyond to the railroad trestle. The trains didn't go by as often anymore. They were gradually being replaced by colossal logging trucks that barreled down the highway and blasted their air horns to let everyone know they had the right-of-way. A partially rotted cedar stump on this ridge near the culverts would be our new lookout for trains. We would be able to watch them rumble across the trestle and shoot sparks from their wheels. We would be able to signal our greeting to the engineers and hear them blow the whistle and wave their hats.

Below the look-out stump, in the "V" created by the two creeks, a blackened cedar snag with super-size knot holes where birds could nest stood straight and proud and tall—taller even than the highway. David studied it for a few moments, thinking about all the snags he'd seen on other properties. *This is a neat snag. I'm glad we have one of our own.*

That winter there was no way to cross the big creek that surged through the valley, except by a single slippery log that lay across the span. So we crawled through the fence, walked east on the highway over the culverts, past the corner where a snow-collapsed chicken house lay in ruins, and turned right on Grauel Road. We could see up the road to where Seth Davis lived, and beyond to the mountains. We'd skirted this section many times—when we'd visited Seth and the John Johnsons, and when we'd hiked even farther up the steepest hills to pick blackberries. We never imagined that one day this Promised Land would belong to us.

Daddy pointed to the left, "This field is also ours."

The grassy pasture, shaped as a triangle, was separated by Grauel Road from the 20-acre piece. At the far corner of the acre-and-a-half there were a few charred stumps and a handful of young trees, while in the middle stood a ramshackle shed. Otherwise the field was bare.

Marilyn said, "I remember seeing a bunch of cows last winter."

Daddy explained, "Those would have been Mrs. Grauel's. She wintered her cattle here because of the snow at their farm's elevation. In fact, she bought this property for that precise purpose. From what I've learned, her husband returned to Germany, leaving her and two young children to farm alone on the mountain."[61]

He continued. "I wish there had been opportunity to reach out to her . . . reach out to give her a hand."

The property surveyed, we spies returned home by the highway, overwhelmed with the thrill of discovery and full of wonder at God's blessings. Yet, not even remotely aware of what toil lay ahead or of what labor would be required to inhabit our Promised Land.[62]

In the following days, weeks, and months, we approached the property step by step, rather like proving up a claim. The girls had learned the definition of "proving up" in history class and had heard the neighbors tell how their ancestors had gained title to most of the land in the Ramapo region. They learned that the earliest pioneers first filed their homestead request and paid a few dollars of fees. Then they had to clear sufficient land for agriculture, build a domicile of acceptable proportions, and live at least five years on the property, before they could gain title to the land.

Our first proving-up step would be to build a domicile—a living place, not for the Coreys, but for the cow. Marilyn, who had practiced milking for two years at the Wetheralds, had been promised a cow within a month. The heifer would be nearly ready to deliver a calf and afterward would dispense milk for the children. *That* mother and her child had to have a domicile of acceptable proportions.

Mother wrote to Aunt Eleanor of plans to cut poles and build a small barn, and of thoughts to clear land for a garden. She spoke of her gratitude for the never-ending supply of firewood the children were bringing from the new property, and of her relief that it would no longer be necessary for them to gather bark and wood on the railroad.

In response, our aunt immediately sent a parcel. The package contained several pairs of ladies' trousers—1930s-style baggy pants our aunt used to shovel sawdust and to ride horses with her "Galloping Gerties Club." Included was a note directed to our father whom she had heard quote a scripture about women not dressing in men's clothing. Aunt Eleanor's message clearly pointed out that the kind of heavy farm work the girls were doing "cannot be done in dresses. It's not appropriate."

The words must have made sense to Daddy, because after that, the girls wore pants for their scut work, for logging, for construction, and—hurray!—even when they rode The Tandem.

The pressure was on to be ready for the cow. For two weeks, everyone big enough stayed home from school to build the barn. They cut down young trees, skinned the poles, and dragged them by hand to the flat part of a railroad spur[63] in the corner near the Phillips Road. For additional materials, they pulled parts off of three former structures that were available at no cost. The first was a burned out cabin in which a man named Mike Laszlo[64] had died in a fire. The ruins were hidden on the mountain beyond the end of Grauel Road on property that was part of the original Grauel holdings. The descendants of Mrs. Grauel had told Daddy he could take whatever was salvageable, which turned out to be next to nothing. The second was the caved-in chicken coop on the corner next to the big maples, and the third was Mrs. Grauel's broken-down cow stall in the triangle field.

It was during the disassembly of the cow stall that Marilyn called out, "Look what I found!" She cradled a hand-painted pitcher in her dirty fingers. "I'll be back in a sec."

Within minutes, she had returned from the creek with washed-clean hands and a gunk-free goblet. That night, she displayed the collectible on top of the starched and pressed cloth covering her orange crate dressing table. She cleared the space of all her other trinkets, for those had no value whatsoever. This pitcher, on the other hand, was a precious antique. Alas, within days, a younger sibling dropped the treasure and it smashed to smithereens. She held the pieces in her hands, her face distraught with grief. "Why can't they stay outa my stuff!"

Seth Davis saw the demolition team at the cow shed and came down the road to supervise. He followed us home at mealtime and back out to the job, telling us that his house—the former schoolhouse—had been sold and that new owners would be moving in. Within days Seth, the wizened old geezer, gentle goat herder, and kindly neighbor, moved out. We would miss the character that he had been in our neighborhood—the character whose history in the region was longer than ours by at least fifty years.[65]

The heifer arrived the first week of February. Marilyn blabbered nonstop about *her* Betsy. Every morning, long before the rest were up, she and Skeezix went to find *her* Betsy. In spite of the frequent effort put into fence repairs, *her* Betsy could find the weak spots and truck as much as a half a mile up or down 9A.

One day, as Marilyn was heading out to feed Betsy, that highway took its toll on Skeezix. Marilyn picked him up, enfolded him in her arms, and carried him back to the Grange House. Tears flooded her face and she could barely talk. "Skeezix was running along with me as I-I-I went to take some grain to Be-Be-Betsy. He ran up Pete's road and before I could stop him he zipped back out onto the highway and straight into the path of a car. H-h-he didn't have a chance and I-I-I couldn't save him."

Elizabeth cried too, and boys ran to see what all the bawling was about. They dug a grave between the highway and the railroad tracks and laid Skeezix to rest. They held a memorial and talked about how tenderhearted and gentle he was. How his tail made his whole body wag. They thanked God for the few months they were allowed to have Skeezix as a pet.

Phillip was sad too, but he stood back. He didn't enter into the burial proceedings. The dog that had been so much fun was now dead and stuck in the ground. *This is a scary place,* he thought to himself, *I'll not go anywhere near that black stump—not ever again.*

Marilyn, however, mourned every day when she went to the woods for Betsy. Her hard-working companion was gone, gone for all eternity. For comfort she reminded herself by writing in her diary that "God knew best and Skeezix didn't suffer."

Soon after Skeezix died, a beautiful cat came calling at the Grange House. Perhaps she knew that this family needed some cheering up. "Please can we keep her?" Marilyn begged. "We'll soon have our own milk."

Just in case that wasn't enough rationale, David added. "I saw a mouse yesterday."

Mother had always said there were enough mouths to feed and she couldn't be buying milk for cats, but she had to admit circumstances were changing. Besides, Mother had been saddened along with the rest of the family at the loss of Skeezix. "All right, you may keep her. But she may have a family to go home to, so don't get your hopes up too high."

The cat never left. Within a few days she had become an honored member of the family with a name to match her glamorous fur coat—Calico. Soon after, Calico honored us by presenting her family of five kittens, allowing each of us older than Merton and younger than Marilyn to adopt one.

Early spring is the time for the agricultural part of proving up. Under Daddy's tutelage, Marilyn, Elizabeth, and David became horticulturists, of a sort.

Daddy taught them how to lay out the orchard fences so they were parallel, and helped them mark spots for trees that were already on order from the Co-op. "The most important thing is organization," he said. "You must line up the trees in rows and set them equal distance apart."

So the young people fenced in the selected section after cutting another round of trees and skinning the poles. They lit a bonfire that Phillip and John maintained with the branches. They dug holes that were ready for Daddy's inspection and for the saplings—Yellow Transparent apples, Italian plums, and Centennial cherries. To dedicate the new orchard, Mother brought us younger ones for a picnic at the bonfire and the whole family relished raisin pie for dessert.

Sadly for all of us, most of the trees died within a few months. They had been set in exact symmetry, but in a clay-bottomed swamp—the kind that should have been left to nature's sun-colored skunk cabbage. And if the muck didn't get the trees, mountain beavers did. Those ebullient, overgrown rodents discovered that the freshly-turned soil facilitated underground travel, not to mention that the young roots and stalks of the orchard trees furnished effort-free meals. Marilyn and David borrowed heavy-duty traps from Walter Johnson, and Daddy helped set them in the runs. Shouts of triumph burst forth when the trappers found a deceased fat-from-overeating critter awaiting them the next day.

It was not such fun, however, when the trap caught a creature by the foot or leg, and left it thrashing. On those occasions, Daddy steered clear and David deferred to his intrepid sister. Marilyn, all bravado—or at least pretending—raised her sledgehammer. "I can butcher chickens," she growled, "so I can dispatch these beasts."

Eventually David also took his hand to the hammer, though he made sure to tell Daddy, "A gun would be easier."

After school and on the weekends, all who were big enough to work traipsed back and forth to the new property to clear land, battle critters, and plant produce. At school, however, David was developing another skill—one that required fine-tuned dexterity. He became the star marble competitor in third grade. Because the classmates played for keeps, David's bag of marbles grew every time he took out his shooter. It was almost a source of pride, except he'd heard Daddy warn that "pride could come before a fall." So he kept a low performance profile at home, with no bragging at all. John, however, was jealous of the stash. One day the younger brother initiated a melee of marbles. He—being five and not so wise!—grabbed and ran, yelling at David, and throwing the treasures. Daddy, catching wind of what was happening, stopped them. "Give me those—all of them. This collection has become an idol and has to go."

David started to say that his daddy was the one who had taught him the winning technique, but he knew better than to argue. Daddy took the entire collection of steelies and shooters, single-colored glass, multi-striped, and cat's eye marbles, and dumped them down the hole of the toilet. David didn't witness the action, but he spotted the pock holes left in the pit as evidence. Fortunately, Daddy didn't forbid the boys from future play, so the next day David borrowed a shooter and began to restock his inventory.

Daddy was alarmed by what he considered to be idols in the lives of his offspring, whatever form they took. "Thou shalt have no other gods before me," he would quote when some object got too much attention or became the center of a fracas. One year it was dolls, while another year it was the Christmas tree. Daddy did change his mind about dolls after a respected relative told Daddy that dolls helped little girls become good mothers. And, anyway, the girls rarely played with dolls, given all the real babies around to dress and care for. But the loss of the Christmas tree was punishment beyond comprehension. Mother intervened in that instance, telling Daddy, "The children don't worship the tree. They just want to bring inside the smell of the forest, and to decorate the evergreen with their crafts."

Mother's cautious pep talk prevailed, and Christmas trees were never outlawed again.

By early April, Marilyn primed everyone for the birth of Betsy's calf. Each evening she invited different siblings or even her friend Doreen to sleep in Betsy's new shed, just in case Betsy might go into labor and need assistance. Each morning before school Marilyn looked Betsy in the eyes and scratched her forehead and ears. "Now you stay close by, don't go gallivantin' around. You need to have this baby where it'll be safe."

Her birth coaching prevailed, and Daisy June was born next to the shed on April 25, just one week after Marilyn's own 14th birthday, prompting Marilyn to record her as "a slightly-delayed gift, dark brown or black with white coloring."

Everyone looked after Daisy June. Once she was weaned to a bucket, we brought her close to the house and gave her all the mothering she could possibly need.

Daddy did the first milkings, while Marilyn held Betsy's head to calm her. Then Marilyn took over the milking, with help from Elizabeth. But this was Betsy's first experience with someone pulling and twisting on her teats, and she did not like it one iota. She marched back and forth, swatted her tail, lifted her foot, and kicked at the milk pail. Daddy built a stanchion, but even that didn't stop Betsy's meandering.

One day Mrs. John Johnson[66] stopped by. She had become Mother's friend early on, and had occasionally walked the distance to attend the women's meetings Mother led. She followed a pathway to the Grange House that cut across the fields, down the Phillips Road, and through the bottom corner of Pete Johnson's place. On this trip to visit Mother, Mrs. Johnson saw Marilyn struggling to catch the milk in a pail, as Betsy rotated her rear end. The lady walked up, gave the cow a pat and took Marilyn's head in her hands. "Here's how da Yonsons do it," she said, moving Marilyn's head into the curve of

Betsy's flank. "Hold your head firmly in place, vit your forearm pressed against her 'tigh. Ven she tries to kick, you can move da bucket out of da vay."

Such a simple procedure, yet such a profound improvement. Once Marilyn had the technique down pat, she became the sole caregiver: Find the cow, feed the cow, and milk the cow. It was her primary commitment. Besides, it got her out of washing the dinner dishes.

Betsy didn't get Marilyn out of the gardening, however. Every Saturday and every weekday after school, we all cleared land, tilled soil, and put in raspberries, lettuce, cabbage, carrots, beets, and potatoes. When the weather warmed, we added peas, corn, squash, and cucumbers. I use the pronoun "we" in its generic meaning. I was still less than three years old and would have been more bother than benefit. But it was all hands to the hoe, all the time, as we worked to ready our Promised Land.

Spring waned, the garden was growing, the cow was producing, the calf was fattening, and our parents were deep in discussion. Long into the night, for several nights in a row, they talked. Apparently, Mother was not completely in favor of the proposal, and thus the drawn-out debate before Daddy eventually declared, "We are going to build a place to live on the new land. It will be a temporary cabin that will serve us until God grants the wherewithal to build a real home."

Two milkmaids and Betsy in the field

He explained that we would begin to disassemble the Grange House while we still lived in it, removing just the parts we could do without. What we took off, we would carry to our new land to construct our dwelling. And we would do so that very summer, before the rains came and the cold set in.

While Daddy announced the plan to us, Mother remained silent.

Ramapo Map 1946

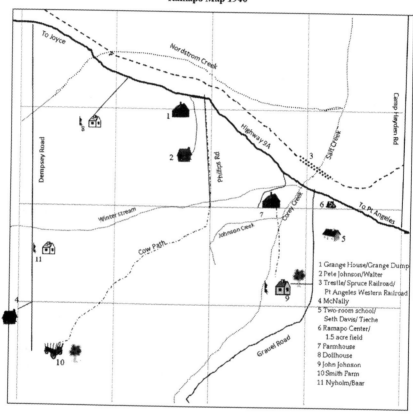

1 Grange House/Grange Dump
2 Pete Johnson/Walter
3 Trestle/ Spruce Railroad/
  Pt Angeles Western Railroad
4 McNally
5 Two-room school/
  Seth Davis/ Tieche
6 Ramapo Center/
  1.5 acre field
7 Farmhouse
8 Dollhouse
9 John Johnson
10 Smith Farm
11 Nyholm/Baar

Not to Scale

CHRONICLE TWO
1946-1958

CHAPTER THIRTEEN
The Move
(Summer 1946)

"**Q**uick! Down in the ditch!"

I did as I was told—dropped the shingle I was toting, slid down the bank, curled up, and buried my head deep in the grass as fast as I could. I was three years old, so hiding was easy for me. Not so easy for nine-year-old David, who, in addition to covering himself, had to disguise the heavy plank he was carrying. I peeked. A car was coming around the corner on Highway 9A. It was the color of overripe raspberries—the kind you don't see until you step on them.

This is my first memory—an eye-scorching memory buried deep in the tunnels of my brain—a memory that, for the rest of my childhood, surfaced with a spasm of fear at the sight of any dark-reddish car, like the one that had sent us into the ditch.

At the time, I thought David was terrified like me. But David was not afraid. I learned later he was embarrassed to be seen by anyone—stranger or friend. Seen—moving our house, battered board by battered board, smashed-straight nail by smashed-straight nail, down the highway and around the corner.

One month earlier, before my memory kicked in, Daddy had decided that we would move our house to the farm, and we would have to do it without a vehicle, without a mule, and without new materials. Our father knew exactly where it would fit on the land, and how the boards and shingles we took from the Grange House could be put to optimum use in a structure that could—one day—be turned into a barn. The drawings were in his head, as clear as an architect's blueprint. Who could argue?

He had given further rationale, "When the move is complete, we will live close to our garden, our orchard, and our cow; and we will have our own creek full of running water."

Mother had agreed—albeit with concessions. She needed to be certain that this would be a temporary dwelling, not a permanent home. Daddy gave his assurance. Then he took his first step in the house-moving transition. He cleared out a place in the cellar under the Grange House and moved in a bed for himself. He led us children to believe his motivation was the hot weather, but in all likelihood it was one of his concessions to Mother—that she would not be having a baby as per her most recent schedule of deliveries.

At the selected building site, Daddy laid out the footprint and gave construction lessons to David, Elizabeth, and Marilyn. He said they could get started while he went to meet Virginia on her way home from boarding school. Fortunately, Joyce School was already out for the summer so the youngsters could work all day, every day, except Sunday. But we'll get to the Sunday part later.

The day after Daddy left, David was the first logger out the door in his work clothes, a hatchet and rolled up measuring tape in hand. "I'll measure the trees," He called back to his sisters who carried the crosscut saw and axe.

Daddy had told them that the trees—preferably cedar—needed to be solid, straight, and eight-to-ten inches thick. He had pointed out some examples on the new property not too far from the construction site, so the kids knew where to begin. They dropped a few, lobbed off the branches, and cut the 22-foot lengths. They rolled, shimmied, and shoved the poles off the hillside to the flat. Then David remembered. "We have to skin the trees too. Come to think about it, they'll be easier to move without the bark."

After that, they took to the logging site a drawknife to remove the bark. David liked that task. He could straddle the log pulling the drawknife blade by its two handles as he backed up to the end. "Look," he hollered at the girls, "I stripped the whole side of this pole in one swipe."

Marilyn looked back at him from her project and nodded. She had tied one end of a rope to a prepped log and the other end around her middle. She chugged and tugged, her forehead beading with sweat. Suddenly the pole took off by itself. Elizabeth yelled, "Look out," and Marilyn jumped out of the way just as the log rolled past. It pulled her the rest of the way down the hill. Most logs didn't give the kind of assistance that required a "watch out." Instead, they resisted, rebelled, and held their ground as long as they could.

For breaks in the logging, the workers pulled the little kids' wagon all the way from the Grange House down to the new creek—not for the fun of it, but to collect cornerstones for the foundation. Loaded with rocks, some of which required two sets of hands to lift, Marilyn pulled the loaded wagon up the steep incline with Elizabeth and David pushing from behind. It took all the energy they could muster.

The rock pile wasn't the end of the preparation Daddy had called for. There were chicken coop planks to carry from the far side of the creek and up the face of the steep hill. There were foundation stones to lay out, poles to notch, fit, and level; and then to notch some more, fit, and level again. For the youngsters, ages 9, 12, and 14, the multi-faceted job of getting the site ready to build was an awesome assignment. Daddy and Virginia arrived home in time to attach the joists, complete the foundation, and lay a subfloor of weathered chicken coop lumber.

It was time for the contractor and his staff to begin paring apart the Grange House. They started with the dormer bedroom partitions—which had only been in place for eight months. After that, they pulled off other least-needed parts: the front porch and the roof over the Big Room. Mother kept an eye out that Daddy didn't tear down too much structure at one time. She reminded Phillip to stay out of the way and to watch out for Merton who'd just learned to run—without ever bothering to take normal walking steps first.

Back and forth down the highway bit by bit, item by item, everyone big enough to carry got in on that—Marilyn, Elizabeth, David, and even John. All except for Virginia, who pulled and straightened nails since she had injured her foot and couldn't walk.

It was in the middle of these goings-on that I picked up three shingles to match my three years, and asked, "Mother, can I carry too? Please? I'm big."

"No, it's too dangerous."

"But the rains will come and wet my bed. Please let me. Please?" I begged.

Mother relented, but took away two shingles, saying, "One is enough to start with."

So I stood, shingle in hand, peering up at the open sky through the gaping roof, and waiting for David to quit dawdling. I wanted to go as badly as he didn't. I wanted to help move our house too.

Within a few trips, the ditch-diving by David and us younger ones had flattened the tall grass along the road, so hiding places became harder to come by. Our sisters, however, were too big to hide, and just had to ignore the indignity of the job that had to be done. Their plight was noticed by neighbors and friends, whose offers of assistance trickled in. Harold Baar and Mr. Taylor came by with their vehicles to carry a load or two. The Nordstroms loaned their truck for a few hours now and again, and Mr. Samuelson offered his station wagon when he came to visit. Mr. Tudor, once even brought his ancient truck with big wheels made of solid rubber. David had to stop what he was doing to rub his hands on those remarkable tires.

There was no direct route to our construction site, so each ad hoc delivery vehicle entered the twenty acres from Grauel Road. They backed down a flattened path that had once been used by Mrs. Grauel's cows, and then dropped the loads on the opposite side of the creek. Everything transported on wheels then had to be muscled across the water and up the steep hill, the same route as the lumber from the chicken coop and the foundation rocks from the creek. But that was child's play compared to hoofing it a quarter mile down the highway as well—and it saved David and his older sisters, at least part of the time, from the flushed faces of public exposure.

The vehicle-assistance program was sporadic, and the carrying still had to continue every day, from first morning rays until we tripped over our feet in the dark. Bundles of shingles on The Tandem bike, chimney bricks on the wagon, and boards on each back.

While we concentrated on the move, taxes in the amount of $4.96 became delinquent. Daddy didn't know about that part, but he hadn't forgotten it was time to pay the first installment on the mortgage, a bi-annual amount of $50 plus $18 interest. Daddy paid the bills, but remarked that he was puzzled God had not supplied the amount he needed to pay off the loan entirely.

The burden of debt was lifted in July when Uncle Emil and Aunt Hazel came. As our uncle helped Daddy put two-by-fours into place, he asked, "Art, how much is still owing on the property?"

Daddy answered. "I just made the first payment plus taxes, but we still owe nearly $600. I know to some people six hundred might seem like an unattainable amount, but I also know that 'with God all things are possible.'"

Uncle Emil reached in his pocket and removed a large round roll of greenbacks. David, the money watcher, stood stock still. His eyes bugged as his uncle counted out six $100 bills and handed them to Daddy. "I've just sold my home in Tacoma," Emil said. "This is the tithe, and God has told me it's for you."

The light of relief lit up Daddy's face as he spoke. "I've been asking God for the whole amount. No question he led us to buy, but somehow I couldn't reconcile this payment system of mortgage and interest with the command, 'Owe no man anything.'"

His brother-in-law grinned. "Well, I likely had this money before your first payment was due, just no way to get it to you."

The two discussed the scripture in question, Emil suggesting that there was more to the verse than could be tucked into one phrase and that perhaps further study of the context would clarify Art's concern.

When the Brucks left, they took John with them. Of all Mother's eight, he was the one most volatile, the one most prone to disobedience and temper, the one most wearisome. Aunt Hazel would give him some of the personal attention that was lacking at our zoo of activity.

We began to dig a new driveway from the highway to open a direct access that would eliminate the long roundabout through the creek and up the steep bank. We excavated by shovel for a couple of weeks, after which Mr. Samuelson loaned us his tractor and scraper. The process was better than shovels and picks, but the implements were far from efficient. Every time Daddy drove over a bump or turned a corner the gadget holding the scraper in place flipped loose. So while Daddy drove, Marilyn or David took turns walking behind with a crowbar to fix the scraper when it went *bockety*. They'd been at this for days and the path was barely smooth when unexpected, unplanned-for rains came. The new road turned into a slippery skating rink with a river flowing where the culverts were to be placed.

We'd left the de-construction at the Grange House longer than anticipated, longer than weather wise. The mid-summer torrent that messed up the road came after the roof was in halves—half still attached to the Grange House where we lived, and half in pieces at the new property. We were camping with puddles all around us, not only puddles, but also sheets of rain that the wind blew through the vast openings onto everything—the clothes, the quilts, the cupboards, the curtains, and, worst of all, Mother's piano. Over it, she draped dark green army blankets. They were the best water repellants available, though hardly adequate. We jammed beds, dressers, and clothes under the remaining partial roof in the attic and prayed the rain would stop.

While we huddled out of the weather, we called and called for Calico and all her tribe, both adolescents and babies. It turned dark and they still didn't come. We worried that they were without coverage in this soggy mess of weather and wondered if the confusion of the torn-apart house made them feel unwelcome. What a relief when Calico brought home her trail of rain-soaked, rat-smooth cats. We moved over to give the traveling family a dry corner.

Calico and her kittens—she had more kittens than there were foster homes in the neighborhood. In fact, before her last batch, Daddy had said we couldn't keep so many cats. So he had given Calico away. She had found her way back home and Mother said, "She is a pretty smart cat. We'll let her be for a while."

So Calico, unaware of Daddy's earlier ordinance, had her next batch where she knew there were still lots of kittysitters. We had been careful not to fight over the babies and draw Daddy's attention to them. Thus, during those first weeks of roof ripping, nail pulling, and board hauling, she had been raising the latest litter without much ado.

The cattle, on the other hand, were the source of the regular grind, rain or shine. Daisy June had to be corralled and returned to the property every few days after she broke through the fence, and Betsy had to be called to her stanchion and milked twice a day. Then, one morning, Betsy added much more challenge to Marilyn's milking task. Betsy was in heat, and what a tizzy that put her into. Her eyes darted in circles and she shook her head. She stomped and paced and bellowed. Daisy June didn't know what it was all about and kicked up her heels too. Betsy, in heat, provided an education for anyone big enough to grasp the significance of her behavior. Marilyn gathered a couple of assistants and took Betsy to *visit* the Nyholms' bull. After the *visit* Betsy was calm once again. She flopped down to the ground and munched her cud while toddler Merton climbed up one side and slid off the other.

It was time to get back to the main task, but first we welcomed the arrival of a new puppy from Harold Baar. After great deliberation, we christened him Tig—for Tiglathpileser, the Bible king that Virginia had studied in her grade ten ancient history class at Prairie.

We'd just given Tig his formal initiation into the family, when Aunt Eleanor showed up on the bus—Aunt Eleanor, the beautiful lady with the bright red lipstick who wore white uniforms and a stiff hat in the Clorox-clean dentist's office. But at our place, Aunt Eleanor changed out of her dress slacks with the straight creases to become one of us. She trekked back and forth from the Grange House that was half way in shambles to the new construction that was held together by what the Grange House had lost. She hauled two-by-fours and armloads of shingles. Or she carried a window. That's because Marilyn said if Aunt Eleanor carried a window and it broke, no one would get in trouble.

It didn't bother Aunt Eleanor to use the woods for a bathroom or the creek to wash her face. She just invented jokes that made us think our life wasn't so bad after all. Then, while she was available to supervise, Mother let the older kids carry mattresses down the road and set up a dormitory on the new floor. I begged to go sleep next to my aunt, since I had the same name, but Mother said no.

As much fun as Aunt Eleanor brought, her greatest contribution the summer of 1946 was the roll of photos she filled. She shot pictures of the Grange House while it served as our dwelling place—even though it was only half a dwelling. She took pictures of the new place before there was a roof and second floor walls. She lined us up for pictures with the cow, the calf, the kittens, and The Tandem. Her photos guaranteed that many details of our move, and of our family during that season, would never be lost.

After Aunt Eleanor left, it rained rivers again. This time there was more coverage at the assembly site than at the Grange House so Mother moved everyone down the road to sleep. Slop everywhere and drip, drip, drip all night long, except where we slept in the first-floor dormitory that Aunt Eleanor had helped set up. After that, we never went back to sleep in the Grange House. It was a disaster zone of soggy stuff and scraps everywhere, leading to its new name—the Dump. A garbage pit it was, yet, each morning Mother herded us back up the highway to what was left of the kitchen. There she would cook our meals and wash our clothes under a small portion of attic floor that remained. Mother said, "We really can't live much longer in this condition. But we can't complete the move until there is a toilet down there."

She said it again, "We have to have a toilet, Arthur."

So the outhouse couldn't be put off any longer. Marilyn wrote her description of that. "Started the Backhouse and got the dung hole about 3 inches above Virginia's head."

Daddy said the toilet would need another foot of depth, but then he was distracted by the state highway men who came to put in the culvert. Once that was in place Daddy smoothed the new driveway, opening up a much closer cargo route to what was left at the Dump. While he was completing the road, his mind was gearing up on another plan. "We are nearly finished with the basics," he told Mother. "I believe we should set up the new place for a Vacation Bible School (VBS)."

Nearly finished? Mother would have laughed had he not been so serious. There were no bedrooms, no stairs to the second floor, not even a kitchen for making bread. There was no wiring for electricity and no way to get it hooked up even if the wires had been in place. But she also knew there was no point in offering a second opinion. Daddy promised her, "The toilet will be ready, and the stairs installed. We will move the stove so everything is convenient for you."

For the two weeks of VBS, Daddy used a borrowed bus to pick up dozens of kids, from four years like Phillip, to fourteen like Marilyn. There were Wasankaris from the east, Normans from the west, Cedars from the south, and Rosie Tieche from across the road. There were classes at tables by the creek for the teenagers and classes on the grass for the little people. I loved to listen to Aunt Hazel teach Bible stories while she moved figures around on the flannel graph board. My favorite was the adventure of Jonah in the belly of a big fish, and I wondered if he was slimy like vomit when the whale puked him onto the land. There were pictures to color and crafts to glue. So much fun.

In the morning recess, a few of the kids took off their shoes and played in the creek, and some of them ran races. Then everyone got back into order for singing. On one of the last days, John asked Daddy if he could sing his favorite song. The six-year-old stood straight and strong on the trunk of the maple that hung out over the field and sang of the Savior who had knocked on his heart to let him know to open up.

John wanted to sing that song because of the knock he'd heard a few days earlier at Aunt Hazel's. Well, not really a knock, but a voice, he explained. At the time, he had been out playing in the yard and heard someone speak. He couldn't see anyone, so went into the house. He asked Aunt Hazel, "What do you want?"

She said, "I didn't call you."

John was puzzled. Uncle Emil wasn't there either, so he kept talking to Aunt Hazel.

"But I heard a voice call, 'John.'"

When she shook her head, John told Aunt Hazel he knew the story of Samuel's call, and wondered if it was like that story. She said she didn't think it was God's voice he'd heard. Yet, somehow he felt it was—but he knew better than to argue with Daddy's sister, Aunt Hazel. So, instead of disputing her word, he decided he would show her his new heart by being "quick to obey."

Yes, John knew God had spoken to him, and he was changed. So that day at VBS, John wanted the rest of the children to know that they, too, should listen for God to knock on the doors of their hearts.

The last day of VBS, as we prepared for the final picnic, the sky opened up and poured out its contents. Parents, teachers, and kids crowded the roughed-in house for a lunch that parents provided. The party was topped off with apples from the neighbors, popcorn supplied by Mr. Samuelson, and fudge made by Mr. Corey. Daddy's chocolate treat was unforgettable, melt-in-your-mouth fudge that he cooked to perfection with sugar, cocoa, milk, butter, and a dribble of vanilla. Add to that popcorn and apples, it was a celebration. And VBS at our new place—at our Farmhouse—was worthy of celebrating.

The thrill of a new address, the activity of Vacation Bible School, and the taste of fudge came to an abrupt ending with the beginning of school. Especially for John, who entered first grade. Compared to his mountain heights of the summer, school was a dung pit full of rats. Within a few days, a band of sixth graders selected him to be their target. They'd hide near the playground, waiting for the little kid to come out. John cowered and tried to stay out of sight, all the while knowing they would find him, call him "Rabbit Teeth" and chase him crying back to the room. No one helped him, no one seemed to care. He wanted to go back to Aunt Hazel's and hear God's voice again. Or maybe he could go with Virginia to Prairie. Virginia always had time for him, didn't pick on him, and didn't make him lose his temper. But then she went away without him. He was all alone.

The sun of summer and picnics by the creek had ended for the rest of the family too. The weather turned frigid and the walls of the house lacked even a layer of tar paper to cover the cracks between the bare boards. The floors were one layer, just the subfloor with spaces as big as those in the walls. There were no partitions on the second floor, so privacy was no better than the original dormitory of the Grange House. Daddy wrote to get his helpers, Marilyn, Elizabeth, and David, excused from school for a week. John welcomed the work and the cold that kept his siblings home from school, because Mother let him stay home too, and he was safe from that gang of eleven-year-olds.

Even with everyone working all day, every day, the Farmhouse was nowhere near ready when a blizzard in November sent snow through the fissures like powdered sugar sifted onto a torte. The cold stayed a long time, but lumber still had to be torn off the Dump and carted down the road to cover floors, make partitions, and build stairs to the attic. During VBS Daddy had used the Brucks' car or the borrowed bus for hauling, but those vehicles were gone. Fortunately for the cargo kids, Daddy seemed to have gotten over his reticence to ask for help. When he had a pile ready to be moved, he would summon a friend or neighbor to haul a load or two.

For the cows, the summer party of sweet grass was also over. Not only was Betsy short of food, but in the middle of the snow storm, she came down with an ailment. She was sick, swollen and suffering. Then overnight she was better, and we knew God had answered our prayers. But Marilyn fretted for her cows—fretted out loud that Betsy would get sick again. "Please Daddy. The cows need a better barn, one close by where they have protection from the cold, and where Betsy can be milked. Their shed's too far away."

Mother agreed. So, even though we hadn't finished the shingling and could still see light of day under the eaves and around the windows, the cow and the calf got Marilyn's wish. We laid a log foundation and patched together scraps from the usual sources to build a barn with two stanchions. So the twice-a-day milking task was at least closer by and Betsy had a roof over her head.

The travail of the farm didn't let up, except for Sundays—when it always did.

Sunday mornings at the Farmhouse we had our service. Daddy had moved the Sunday meeting from the Grange House as soon as the living room of the new place had walls and a subfloor, even before we'd moved the beds and the stove. The new living room was much smaller than the Big Room had been, so it filled up each meeting time with neighbors and friends, including the Taylors, the Nyholms, the Wetheralds, the Possingers, and the Myers. Most of the kids who came along sat with us Corey kids on the stairs, facing the side of the living room where Mother played the piano and Daddy preached.

There was a growing sense of camaraderie in the congregation, a sense that God was blessing this new home and place of meeting. Then, on the first Sunday of December, a near disaster occurred that could have ended it all. That day the song service was well underway when someone hollered out, "I smell smoke!"

Marilyn pulled open the door at the top of the stairs and a cloud of acrid gray-black smoke billowed out. Immediately, the congregants scattered. Ladies pulled the youngest of us far from the house. Daddy and Mother ran up the stairs with drinking water from the kitchen, while the rest of the men and teenagers grabbed buckets and raced to the creek. Flames licked up the inside of the framing and across the unfinished underside of the shake roof. Marilyn and Elizabeth whipped blankets off the nearest bed, and engaged in all-out combat against the crackling fire. Within minutes, buckets were being passed up the hill along a fast-moving line. Mother opened the window, and the girls tossed smoldering coats and dresses to the ground; then hoisted the containers of water back through the same window.

When the fire was out and the guests had left, we surveyed the scene. The backdrop on the second floor had been permanently altered. The two-by-fours holding up the roof were scarred with splits of shiny black charcoal, and the shingles were etched to match. The area Mother had set up as a closet for her coats and dresses and for our best clothes was bare, save for puddles of water and the pungent odor of burnt wool.

How did it happen? How did the fire start? I watched from nearby as Marilyn collared Phillip. I could see that she thought he was guilty. They came down the stairs together and she cornered him between the bottom step and the front door. "What did you do, Phillip?"

He looked at the floor. "Nothin'."

"You know what happens to people who tell lies. Liars go to the lake of fire and burn forever."

I imagined that my brother would not tell the truth and he would go to hell. But Marilyn was almost as perspicacious as her father, and even more persuasive. "You can tell me. I won't report to Daddy and Mother. It will be our secret."

Soon enough his eyes watered up. "I was just trying to find my s-s-sailor suit to wear for Sunday school and I-I-I couldn't see and I lit a match an-an-and I thought I wiped out the spark on Mother's dress and the fire's out now."

Then he smiled up at her. "And I'm wearing the sailor suit and it didn't burn up!"

The truth was told. What would Marilyn do with it? I stayed out of the way as she stomped straight to Daddy and told him Phillip had confessed. Perhaps she thought her deception had not been a real lie—just the means to a holy end. Her brother would not be eternally judged. He would get his punishment now, rather than forever.

And punishment now he certainly got. Daddy pulled him into the living room with one hand. In the other was the switch he'd retrieved from behind the kitchen stove. Phillip was sure the spanking was more for the lie than for using a match after Mother said not to. He was sure of two more things. That his sister told a lie as big as his and that he would never confess to *her* again.

Marilyn was torn between the hurt she'd caused her brother and the need for him to confess the truth. Now she needed to find a way to mend his damaged feelings towards her. She grabbed the first opportunity. John and Phillip were skinning poles in the yard when they got in a squabble over the hatchet. Phillip ran hollering toward the house, a gash in his ankle. Mother held him, while Marilyn got in the bandaging part, insisting that was her role. "Oh, Philtoose." She was the only one who called him that. "I will go find the piece of meat you cut off and we can fry it for dinner."

Phillip laughed so hard about cooking his ankle meat he forgot to be bitter.

As a result of the fire, Mother's clothes, along with the kids' Sunday best, were ruined. That loss was felt more than the singed rafters. However, it wasn't long before Genevieve Possinger, along with some other friends who had been at the fire, brought clothes by. Our relatives—once they heard—sent boxes of clothing too and, in next to no time, we were all dressed up again in fine missionary-barrel style.

Dressed up and ready for the Joyce School Christmas program. Daddy had approved the content and all eligible Coreys would be allowed to participate. What a relief for Marilyn to tell the teachers she could sing in the sextet, the glee club, and the chorus; and that Elizabeth and the grade-schoolers could do their parts. The night of the performance, all ten of us Coreys, including Daddy, Mother, and three preschoolers—Phillip, Merton, and me—rode the school bus to Joyce. After the program ended, three students dressed as Santa Clauses ho-ho-ho'ed onto the gym floor. There they handed out to each child a bag of goodies. I looked at Daddy, afraid that he would make us get on the bus before we got our treats. But, no, he waved us forward. "Merry Christmas," the Santa girl said as she handed me an orange, a candy cane, and a bag of peanuts.

"Merry Christmas," I replied. "Thank you."

I peeled the orange as soon as we got home and ate it section by section. I would have left half for the next day, but I didn't want to chance that Merton would steal it. I hid the candy cane under my pillow, and ate it the next day because I couldn't wait for Christmas. But I allowed myself to nibble on the peanuts—just one at a time—so they would last.

It was a happy Christmas, except we were sorry Virginia couldn't come home. We sent her a gift with a handkerchief and "toilet water" cologne. "Toilet Water? Toilet Water!" Phillip couldn't quit saying, "Toilet Water."

Somehow those two words, "toilet" and "water," didn't match up to the whiff of perfume Marilyn had allowed us before packaging it up for Daddy to put in the mail.

During vacation we found a thick fir tree in the woods and trimmed it with our homemade ornaments. Elizabeth and Marilyn hung the strands of silver foil—they had to be just right. Then on Christmas Eve, those two girls went caroling with the Possingers, the Wasankaris, and Mabel Wetherald—the one who made sure the carols could be heard. On Christmas morning there was a stack of gifts piled under the tree—more than the older kids could remember from the Grange House Christmases. And Mother cooked three chickens for dinner to have enough to feed us and the Possingers, who came to spend the afternoon.

By the end of 1946, we'd nearly finished with clean-up at the Grange House Dump. We lived on our own farm, ate produce from our own garden, drank milk from our own cow, watched our own calf grow, and gathered eggs from the nests of our own chickens. We had no baby sister or brother born that year, and we didn't lose everything in the fire.

Yes, Merry Christmas and Happy New Year to us.

Dismantle Grange House

Reassemble as Farmhouse

CHAPTER FOURTEEN
The Chapel
(1947)

The New Year came and the growing group of Sunday morning faithful—now up to 20 adults and 15 children, including us—decided it was time to move the service out of the Coreys' front room. It was time to build a real chapel that would offer a larger space for meeting and better access to the community. Daddy offered to turn over the one-and-a-half acre field for that purpose. It made sense, since the field was right on the highway; it had plenty of parking space; and had its own registration that could be transferred. To follow up the discussion, Daddy took a contingent on tour of the location. We kids tagged along—down the hill, across the creek, up the bank, over Graul Road, and into the field. Daddy pointed out the building site, a place hardened with gravel and punctuated with bits of fire-forged glass.

"Do you know the history of this piece?" one of the long-timers asked. "This was once much more than a cow pasture."

Everyone turned to listen, and she continued. "It was the center of Ramapo."

She paused and pointed north, "There used to be a train depot where my relatives and their friends would catch rides to and from Port Angeles."

We knew about the depot near the end of the trestle, but got in closer to hear the rest of the story. "So many people walked by here to the depot that someone decided to build a post office, store, and social hall. They gave the place its name, Ramapo. They even built their kids' school up there."

She turned again, pointing south to the two-room where Seth Davis had lived. "This was quite a booming center, they say, especially during the first war. Then the war ended, and everything closed but the school. I think this rocky spot must have been where the store and post office burned to the ground."[67]

Before the visit was over, plans for a chapel were confirmed by the Possingers, the Myers, the Wetheralds, the Duncans, the Baar girls, the Taylors, the Pennoyers, and likely others whose names have been forgotten. They agreed to start construction that week, visualizing that the Ramapo Center would once again be the hub of activity—not for dances and parties, but for worship and prayer. It would be the sanctuary to fulfill the need in the Joyce community for a church of its own.

Mother said nothing during the meeting or the tour, but later commented to no one in particular, "I suppose this means parts on our house will be open to the elements for the rest of the winter."

In the weeks that followed, members of the planning group brought planks, four-by-fours, and all manner of supplies for that chapel in the field. David,

John, and Phillip hauled sand and gravel from the creek bed to mix with mortar for cement blocks. The foundation began to take shape.

At the same time, the winter cold howled through the gaps in the Farmhouse walls, and darkness lasted hours longer than daylight. Snow came in a blizzard, switched to rain, and turned to ice. In those miserable conditions, the friends didn't come to construct the chapel, leading Mother to comment, "That's a blessing. Now, maybe, we can finish a little more of this house."

So despite the cold, we attached more tarpaper and shingles. Daddy installed a sink in the kitchen with pipes to a drainage ditch. We still had to lug the water from the creek, but washing dishes in the sink was not as sloppy as having dishpans on the counter. I begged to help with the dishes, so Mother tied a towel around my middle, and let me stand on a chair. "I'll wash every day," I told her.

Phillip smirked, "Ha ha! You'll soon get tired a' that!"

What did he know? He was only five, hardly more than a year older than I. Mother gave him a towel to dry the silverware. We bickered as usual; then sang about rowing our boat down the stream, while making a mess of the counter and the floor. Mother cleaned up after us, hung our towels next to the stove, and changed her meal-making apron for a clean one. Mother's aprons were the kind that had bias tape trim in coordinating colors and wide shoulder straps that crisscrossed in the back. Mother wore an apron all the time, except for attending church, going shopping, or visiting. And sometimes she even forgot to take it off for those events. Her aprons covered her front from the collar blade to the knees, disguising her torso all of the time. Not that I, still less than four, would have noticed a change in her shape. But somebody must have noticed, because the chapel ladies hosted a full-scale baby shower with party food and a new stock of muslin diapers. Mother told them the diapers would replace the ones she had scrubbed to shreds with eight babies and retired to dust rags after Merton was born. The party and the talk about diapers is how I learned that Mother had a baby growing in her tummy.

Nobody talked about the timing back then, but with a little calculation one could figure that Mother had become pregnant within a month of the move to the Farmhouse that put her husband back in the same bedroom. He must have done some *lookin'* at her, as Mother had told Mrs. Pennoyer.

The baby shower, the growing attendance, and the construction of a chapel—to all appearances, the locals and the Coreys were on the same track of service and ministry to each other, rather like a family of its own sort. Yet, like a family, this group had its disturbances, its difficulties, and its disagreements.

So it was, one Sunday morning in March that a furor broke loose. One of the women—the same old biddy who had picked a fight in the Grange House chapel—started making demands. "Several of us," she said, "have met together and we believe that the church should be run like the other churches we have come from. We should . . . " The lady began to list how the elders should function, how decisions should be made, and who should have the final authority.

Daddy listened for a moment. His face turned ashen, and then color began to rise from his neck. He interrupted the woman. "That is not how I read it in God's Word, not . . . "

No one recorded the rest of what was said. But some memories have never dissipated—that it was the lady who started it, that others nodded their heads in agreement, and that Daddy was livid. His eyes searched the walls, the way they always did when he spoke with intense certainty. Once Daddy got started, he could not back down. Once the lady got going, she could match his timber and out-shout his volume. The rest of the people picked up their Bibles and their coats. They, along with the loudmouth who let out one last invective, went out the door, leaving behind my father and his family in shock.

Daddy sat down and Mother went to the kitchen with Phillip and me. David and the older girls walked out the back door, not speaking the thoughts that thumped in their minds. *Why did Daddy have to get so mad? Why couldn't he listen to people, and talk in a soft voice if he didn't agree? Why does this have to happen, just when things are going well?*

Elizabeth stewed for days. *Our friends will never be our friends again.* Before this had happened, Elizabeth had been sneaking looks at one of the boys who had just started coming to our meetings. But after the fight, when she was on the school bus and in class, she couldn't bear to look in his direction. She knew her own face was flushed with disgrace at the woman's diatribe and Daddy's denunciation. And Marilyn, too, avoided her friends. She wrote to Virginia at Prairie High School, "You should be glad you weren't here that day."

A few days later, Mr. and Mrs. Myers came to see us. Wilson spoke to Daddy in a soft, kind voice. "Ruth and I are sorry that the issues of some people were brought up during the meeting. We have been so grateful for your teaching, and know that God gave you a message that has spoken to our hearts and helped us grow in our faith."

Daddy responded, but I didn't hear his words. I was too busy looking at Mrs. Myers. She was a sweet lady who nodded her head as her husband spoke to Daddy, though she didn't say anything. I noticed Mrs. Myers wore an apron over her dress, and wondered if she forgot to take it off the same as Mother sometimes did. Mrs. Myers rolled her long, shiny brown hair around a rag, also the same as Mother. At church services and out in public places, she usually hid her rolled-up hair under a white cloth with a knot in the front. Mother sometimes tied her hair that way too, only she usually wore a black cloth. I didn't know what the cloth meant, but I had seen other women wear them too. Perhaps these ladies didn't have proper hats to wear to church. Mrs. Myers reminded me of my mother, only she was years younger and didn't have gray hair. I was glad she and Mr. Myers had come to apologize to Daddy.

Those who had instigated the altercation did not return, and within a few weeks they started meeting in another home, inviting others to join them. Several who'd been at our place began attending churches in Port Angeles, and one couple quit going to church altogether.

Mother and Daddy didn't talk about the argument and its fall-out in front of the children, and the youth did not talk about the heavy weight of school gossip they felt. Mother didn't speak of the pinch of having lost the offerings that had given us a nice Christmas, helped to pay farm bills, and buy food. So all of us quietly mourned the loss of a dream for a chapel in our field where our friends, neighbors, and even strangers, could come together.

It wasn't until the hurt lessened that Mother reminded us of something we already knew, "Your father just doesn't realize how strongly he speaks when he is convinced of something."

And it wasn't until the shock wore off that Daddy said, "It took me a long time to get over the sting of what happened that day. Those who came with an agenda to present had not brought any of it to my attention ahead of time. In front of everyone they made demands that contradicted what I believed God had in mind for this church and for my role in it."

In the season that followed the break-up, we returned to a quiet Sunday school with just the family and one or two neighbors. With Mabel gone, the music didn't reverberate, though the rest of us sang louder to drown out our sadness and to cover the hole left by all our friends who had left.

Daddy increased his traveling circuit to be on the road several days a week, usually starting out by foot and ending up with God's appointed rides. Even as the chapel plans ended, God seemed to be reminding him that the sheep on the highways and byways were his first calling. Not a neighborhood church—at least not at this time, and not in this place.[68]

We also returned to our labors—once again focused on the Farmhouse and the cleanup at the Dump. Spring vacation filled up quickly with jobs, of which there were so many that Marilyn bemoaned to her diary, "I don't like vacations all you do is work."

Up at the Grange Dump, we ceremoniously burned the last toilet—that three-times-moved outhouse shed still stationed over David's embedded marbles. At the creek we panned sand for the Farmhouse chimney instead of the church foundation, and built a picnic stove from the rocks. We dammed up the creek for a laundry hole so it would be easier to scrub the clothes on our rippled-glass scrub board. And we dug more garden space and started the spring planting.

Mother, however, didn't engage in the outside toil or the creek laundry, and she could barely keep up with the cooking. Her legs and her back ached with the pregnancy. Friends, including Mrs. Pennoyer, Mrs. John Johnson and Mrs. Myers came by to check on Mother, and see if she needed anything. On one of Ruth Myers' visits she found Mother sitting near the creek where Elizabeth and I were scrubbing and plunging our clothes. Mrs. Myers said, "I don't know why I didn't think of this before. How about loading up my car and we'll do laundry at my house?"

So Elizabeth and I did just that. We hopped in the car, along with our baskets of dirties, to go to the Myers' place. Mrs. Myers' electric wringer machine was right in the middle of the kitchen, hooked up to her sink. But the quick motion of the machine wasn't the only treat that day. Mrs. Myers served us sweet rolls with cinnamon and raisins buried inside and brown sugar caramel oozing all over the bottom. I must have licked my fingers fifty times.

Later I went outside to play on the swings with Alice and Carol Myers, who were about my age. Then when baby Linda woke up from her nap, Mrs. Myers let me hold her on my lap. After that, I couldn't help but think, *I have my own friends, have eaten gooey cinnamon rolls, and cuddled Mrs. Myers' baby. What more do I need? Certainly not people who yelled at my daddy and made him lose his temper.*

In May, nearly a year after we had moved into the Farmhouse, electricity arrived. Finally! We'd had electricity at the Grange House just long enough to get used to it, long enough to realize we'd never want to live without it again. Then with the move, we'd been back in the dark ages all through another long, dismal winter. So that day in May, when the PUD workers arrived, Phillip was thrilled out of his mind. David and John were in school, so there was no competition for the role of supervisor. Phillip stood guard as the men stepped up the poles with their spiked boots, and hooked the wires to the green glass insulators. He was on duty, as close as Daddy would allow, when they hooked the connection to the fuse box in the kitchen. His eyes turned to the light nearby—the one and only bulb in the Farmhouse—until it lit up. Then Phillip studied the slow-ticking wind-up clock, counting down until he could race to the bus stop and shout to his siblings, "We got the 'lectricity in!"

John—who remembered he'd been on hand for the Grange House hook-up—ran back with Phillip. David acted a little cool about the whole thing—so as not to behave like the little boys—but was quick to suggest to Daddy that he'd go get the radio from the Nordstroms who'd been storing it since the move.

Marilyn and Elizabeth helped Mother clean up and stash away the kerosene lamps and Coleman lantern that came out of storage after the move. Mother had already brought out the toaster and electric iron, but the girls thought they should test them too. They hooked up the washer and hauled water to do up the stack of laundry. They couldn't wait to tell Mrs. Myers that we wouldn't need to wash at her place anymore.

Daddy said it wouldn't be long before he would get more wire to install for lights in all the rooms and more outlets for the kitchen and living room. He added, "Lord willing," as he usually did, when money was required.

In the doldrums after the excitement of electricity, Phillip had a falling out with Mother. "I'm so mad," he stomped, "that I'm just going to cut down this *whole* house!"

Mother walked to the tool shed and returned with a dull, rusty carpenter saw. "You will need this," she said. "Where do you want to start?"

Phillip trudged out the back door to the piano nook that stuck out from the side of the living room. He started sawing until a solitary cedar shingle was notched. Mother paid no attention. So the sawing progressed, and the notch got bigger. Still nobody seemed to care what he was doing to the house, so Phillip shrugged his shoulders and put the saw away. For years after—as he got taller and taller—he would lean down to rub his finger over the totem-type carving that marked the second row of shingles, and remember his act of defiance soon after he had turned six and the 'lectricity came.

Meanwhile, at Joyce School, Marilyn and Elizabeth were practicing music for the Mothers' Day Tea—a long-standing tradition within the community. Marilyn loved singing with her sister and the other girls, but hated the rehearsal of modeling for the style show. Being looked at—ogled, as she called it—made her feel conspicuous. "All that parading with fussy hats and prancing in homemade party gowns in front of the ladies is dumb," she muttered.

Mrs. Blore, the teacher in charge, took her muttering seriously. "Okay, then, you can be stage manager instead of model. You will set up the platform, pull curtains, and prompt." Mrs. Blore meant it as a punishment for complaining, but Marilyn took it as an opportunity to organize everyone. She fretted all week over the details and whether or not the girls would do their parts correctly. But when the day came, *her* Mothers' Day Tea went off without a hitch.

Late spring also meant that preparations were underway for Elizabeth's graduation from eighth grade. Virginia Pennoyer drove to our house in her nearly-new station wagon and took the young lady and Mother to town. When they returned home, Elizabeth carried her first-ever brand-new outfit, a blue taffeta dress with an overskirt of fluffy, swirly chiffon. She couldn't wait to show Marilyn. The older sister would never have chosen blue for herself, but had the grace to show interest. "This dress is perfect for you. It highlights your blue eyes so they look just like the summer sky."

She talked that way, even though Elizabeth's gown was a reminder to Marilyn that she, herself, had never been given a new store-bought dress. A reminder that she was born different—with olive skin and black eyes—between two blue-eyed sisters with creamy skin who didn't get nearly so many spankings. *I just know*, she'd once thought, *I was adopted.*

By the time Elizabeth showed up with the new dress, Marilyn had long before given up her birth misgivings. She'd seen the infant David come home with a shock of black hair and dark eyes like hers. Then John came along and began claiming just as many lickings as she received. Nonetheless, she still felt as if she were the black sheep that didn't quite belong in the flock of white.

A few days after graduation, word came that Virginia Pennoyer's father, Mr. Norman, had been killed in a logging accident. His was the first death close-to-home, and we all felt terrible. The Normans had been kind when others were critical; had shared produce from their farm, and game from their hunting trips. Sometimes they had invited us to have picnics or services on their secluded, driftwood-covered beach. It was near that beach, in a pool of the Lyre River, that Elizabeth was baptized.

Jimmy Norman, the son who had given us Skeezix—our first dog—asked Daddy to help plan the service and to sing Mr. Norman's favorite hymn as a solo. Mother attended the funeral. She reported to us afterward, "Mrs. Norman looked bad."

Mother leaned against the counter, her body weighed down with nine months of Number Nine. "I look bad too, and wouldn't have gone if they weren't such close friends."

A few days after the funeral, Daddy borrowed the Pennoyer's station wagon to take Mother to Grandma's house in Tacoma to wait for the baby. Mother had informed him that she wanted to be under the care of the physician who had delivered her first four babies, not the doctor in Port Angeles who delivered the last four. "He charged too much," she said, "and looked at me like, *Oh it's you again, Mrs. Corey.*"

Marian Ruth was born on June 15, 1947. Daddy had left Phillip and me with Virginia and Fred Pennoyer, whose children were close in ages to the two of us. He traveled twice back and forth from Tacoma during Mother's stay, once because she insisted he stop in Port Angeles on the 18th to wish me a happy fourth birthday. Daddy told me that Mother's gift was a baby sister. *Nice,* I thought. *After those four brothers, a baby girl like Linda Myers is a good idea.*

On the 20th, Daddy brought everyone home, including our oldest sister, who was returning from boarding school. The neighbors came to bring gifts, and to meet this black-haired rosy baby, who appeared to be the living image of her mother's baby picture.

Mrs. Tieche was one of the first to arrive, bearing for Marian a frilly pink layette. Mr. and Mrs. Tieche and their daughter Rose had moved into the Ramapo two-room school across Grauel Road after Seth Davis vacated it. We had gotten to know Rosie right away when she attended the first VBS in our pasture by the creek. She was a year ahead of David in school and caught the bus at the bottom of Grauel Road one stop before ours. On occasion, she would bring us cookies or cake her mother had made and would stick around awhile. She said she liked to get in on the excitement of our big, noisy, happy family and to hear our music.

It had taken awhile to make friends with Rose's parents. The first time Daddy and Mr. Myers called on the Tieches to invite them to our home services these neighbors said they were not interested in religion. But we knew they needed it, for we could hear Mrs. Tieche's voice all the way across the valley giving her husband the "what for."

Daddy and Wils Myers returned on a regular schedule to visit those neighbors. They would take sweet rolls from Mrs. Myers or a jar of jam from Mother, and would visit for a brief time. Daddy had a gentle way of talking with people who needed the Lord; seemed to find them better listeners than the church people who already had their religious minds made up. So, as days went by, friendship with the Tieches flourished. Mr. Tieche would offer our parents rides to town and would escort Mother, along with Mrs. Tieche, to the

Mother's Day Tea. Later, when the Tieches got a telephone, they said we could use it whenever we needed to.

The Tieches had partitioned one room into their living quarters with bedrooms for themselves and for their daughter.[69] Mr. Tieche had turned the other room into a machine shop with an impressive set-up. He had a gasoline engine with gears to control the speed of his various tools. Shafts, lathes, and pulleys protruded from the engine in all directions. Daddy and David would go over there to visit, and Mr. Tieche would use his machine to make or fix parts that we needed at our place. David was intrigued when he heard Mr. Tieche tell about the barge full of machinery he had once owned. "What's here is all I had left after the Coast Guard sank the barge during the war."

David's eyes lit up as Mr. Tieche added an afterthought. "I suppose they thought it was enemy equipment and ammunition."

The lad couldn't imagine what the rest of the machines might have included—and he wished he was brave enough to ask.

To celebrate Marian, Mrs. John Johnson greeted Mother with a milk bucket brimming full of ruby-colored strawberries. Although the Johnson property also bordered Grauel Road, she came by short cut: A path through her field, past her barn, into the woods, down the steep bank, and across their section of Salt Creek on a chiseled-flat single log bridge with a skinned alder pole handrail. She trudged up the bank on our side and plodded along an early logging grade, coming out of the woods not far from our toilet and kitchen door.

Since we moved to the Farmhouse, Mrs. Johnson had become a regular visitor. Sometimes she came so often that Mother would frown and fuss under her breath, "I don't have time to sit and talk." Then she would smile and invite the neighbor in to have coffee. John heard Mother grumble and saw how she switched from a frown to a smile, after which she would usher Mrs. Johnson through the door. At first, it seemed to John that Mother wasn't being honest. However, he came to realize that by the time our neighbor reached the house, Mother had overcome the inconvenience and could show that she really did care for the elderly lady. John was watching one day when Mrs. Johnson picked up the jam jar, stuck a spoon into it, and put the whole spoonful on just one bite of bread. She repeated this delicious process until the slice of bread was gone and the jam depleted. He looked at Mother, who seemed to be unaware. John thought to himself, *That's not fair. We only get a smidgen of jam scraped across our bread, and sometimes we don't even get any.*

But, if Mother was generous with the jam, Mrs. Johnson was munificent with much more. Peas, new potatoes, cardamom breads and treats from her pantry—and, oh, the apples from her orchard! She grew trees with transparent apples that were ready in August for pies, and sweet apples in the fall for eating. On one of her trees she had a gigantic grafted branch of Red Delicious, a kind I'd never tasted before. If we planned our hikes up Grauel Road at the right time, we might see her in the orchard and pay a visit. Then she would share from the wealth of her orchard, including the juicy Red Delicious.

On one visit to our place, Mrs. Johnson asked about the animals. Mother told her there was no hay in the shed to feed Betsy, Daisy June, and the new calf. "Ah," the neighbor said, "Den you must come und get as much as you need. Ve have plenty in da barn."

Elizabeth stayed with Marian, Merton, and me so that Mother, Marilyn, and the boys could go for the hay. At the Johnsons, the boys stuffed gunnysacks, and Mother filled two open tarps of sewn-together burlap. She wrapped them around the hay and tied the ends. She put one on Marilyn's back and hoisted the other onto her own. They headed homeward, chattering about nothing in particular. Just before the bridge, Mother stepped to the side of the trail and into a yellow jacket nest. A swarm of bees shot out from beneath her feet, surrounding her in a furious cloud. Mother dropped her load and yelled, "Run, run, get out of here. Go home!"

The others turned and gaped at the sight of Mother scuttling down the bank, pulling off her clothes as she ran, then leaping into the creek, and sliding under the water.

At the house, Mother counted more than 200 stings to her head, arms, legs and mid-section. Marilyn hurried to mix a paste of baking soda and water to plaster on the swollen, ruddy-purple welts, and hovered until Mother shooed her away. "I'll be fine."

Marilyn wasn't sure and twisted her hands. Still wanting to help, she offered, "David and I can go for the hay you dropped."

"Not now," Mother said. "Wait until dusk when the bees are asleep. Go on now and let me be. Go! Go make cookies!"

It was also in the summer of 1947 that Willard Skaugseth and his 14-year-old son, carrot-topped David, arrived. They had biked all the way from Tacoma. Mr. Skaugseth, a long-time friend to Daddy, worked in the Ruston Smelter. Our David had gone there once. He said you could see the smoke stack of the smelter from Grandma Phenicie's house. In fact, you could see it from nearly anywhere in Tacoma. The plant was filled with machines and everything was gray, except the shimmering molten metal that poured from the furnaces. Not every furnace was hot the day David visited, but Mr. Skaugseth told him that during the war years the smelter would run at full tilt because of the need for copper bullets.

When the cycling pair arrived at our place, Mr. Skaugseth explained that he had wanted to do this trip as a way to know his son David better. It turned out that this trip was a way for all of us to know David better. Getting to know him meant getting to know those bikes. We went everywhere on them that summer: To the store, to the beach, to the neighbors. Merton and I rode in the baskets, while our older siblings and David Skaugseth doubled up on the seats and luggage racks behind. No one questioned whether it was safe for three or four on a single bike to ride down the busy country highway.

David Skaugseth tolerated the rest of us, but he had his eye on Marilyn. She wrote in her diary every day about his attention—noting on the last day that she and David S. had gone to the creek alone, where he gave her a picture of himself, took pictures of her, and promised he would write. At the creek side, in the moment, Marilyn said she too would write. Then David disappeared down the highway on his bicycle. Marilyn turned back, tucked away the photo, and watched the arrival of dark swirling clouds. Marilyn knew that flaming-haired David Skaugseth wished for the friendship to blossom, but for her, the wild thunder and lightning storm provided the final exclamation point of that idea.

This same tempest also marked the beginning of a new commitment in our household. At dinner, Mother said, "By the Lord's help we are going to support a leper child."

The declaration that we would finance care for a leper in China had come from Mother's burden for the poverty stricken, the sick, and the orphans. When missionaries talked about the needs, she would say, "Oh Jesus, what can we do?" She lit up this time when the answer came to her heart. She would put a jar on the shelf and we would trust God to supply enough for us to give a ten-dollar donation each month.

It wasn't long before another call came for help in Africa, and Mother listened to that one as well. After that, there were two Mason jars side-by-side on the shelf next to the sink, where all of us could see and be reminded.

Mother's vision inspired Marilyn, who first said she felt called to be a nurse and to go to China to help lepers. Then she agonized over orphans in Africa. Back and forth she went between the lepers and having an orphanage. Even as she went back and forth about which plan was God's will, the fifteen-year-old had been holding onto a nickel she'd been given, knowing she should put it in a jar, but wanting to buy an ice cream cone. The jar for the orphans won out.

Soon after, Grandma Phenicie came with Uncle Herbert Phenicie, Aunt Edith, and their nine-year-old twins Richard and Roger. We gave extra attention to cleaning because this was the first time Grandma had come. She'd not come to see where we lived in the entire nine years since the family had moved from Tacoma. Mother fixed Grandma a place in the living room to sleep because she couldn't climb the stairs, and asked if she wanted to have her own chamber pot nearby. "No," Grandma said. "But you can give me your arm to get to the water closet."

Phillip and I thought *water closet* was a funny name for the toilet that wasn't a closet and didn't have water. We tried out the name a few times, and Mother reminded us that we weren't to be foolish about these things. At our house, it wasn't *wise* to be *foolish*.

Two days with Grandma and our other relatives were packed. They took pictures and we had marshmallow roasts and picnics by the creek. David took Richard and Roger, who were almost his age, on long hikes, and they helped him pile wood. Virginia, Marilyn and Elizabeth went with Daddy and Uncle Herbert to the county jail for a service. Daddy still went to the jail when he was out and about, or when we had guests who could take him. However, since the move from Port Angeles, Mother had not gone much of the time. On this occasion she was glad to send the girls to sing, because there were protective escorts and the assurance of a ride back home.

The next day, when Grandma and the other Phenicies prepared to leave for Tacoma, they and our parents dragged out the inevitable all morning. They ate a long breakfast that grew into a Bible study and prayer time. They lined up everyone for a photo shoot; then talked some more—mostly about Uncle Herbert and his family going as missionaries to Cuba. It got so close to lunchtime, Mother fixed a substantial snack to hold them over.

Uncle Herbert loaded up the car and everyone stood in the yard to talk again. At last, Daddy led the singing of "God be with you 'til we meet again." I looked at all the tears running down the grown-ups' faces, and even my sisters' faces, and thought, *Why are they so sad? Nobody's died and gone to heaven for all eternity like Mr. Norman. Uncle Herbert and his family are only going to Cuba, but they aren't even going yet.*

David wasn't sad, however. He was waiting for the farewells to finish so he could get on with things—things like going for a long ride on one of the skinny-wheeled bikes that Richard and Roger left for us because Uncle Herbert said they couldn't ship bikes to Cuba.

Then the Phenicies drove out. David walked away, pushing one of the bikes, and Mother pulled her handkerchief from the pocket of her apron. Her mother had seemed frail and her only brother would be leaving for a foreign land in a few months. "God be with them and keep them safe—all of them," she whispered as she went inside and closed the door.

The details of life once again took our full attention. Mother talked with Daddy about making a back porch—a place for working crews to take off muddy shoes, a place to keep wood dry for the stoves. "We need to make it a big porch," she added. "Someday we will have running water and can leave our washer hooked up to it."

Daddy agreed, but said we'd have to remove the big stump first. Located close to the house, the blackened old-growth cedar was the size of a toilet shed with roots the shape of elephant feet. Every day we dug and chopped, but no piece would budge. Phillip said, "We could use dynamite."

Phillip had heard David telling how the John Johnsons blasted their stumps to clear a field, and the story had been replaying in his mind all afternoon. *The homesteaders would tuck bundles of dynamite into holes under the roots, and then make a big blast. Leftover roots they would winch out using a stump puller powered by a mule or horse. As the animal marched 'round and 'round the machine, the cable would coil up and pull out the pieces.*

Phillip could just imagine the explosion sending fire and rocks and roots into the sky. He added, "And we could set up a winch, and tromp like the mules."

David smirked like he did when one of us had a harebrained idea. He only said, "And blow up the whole house?"

Everyone who came by joined in the tug of war with the stump until, splinter by splinter, root by root, it came apart.

Meanwhile, Daddy was figuring what supplies would be needed for the porch. He told Mother that we would use the materials left in the field by chapel planners. He explained that after these four months, it was apparent none of them intended to retrieve their supplies. "So I feel at peace to make use of them," he said. "But before the porch, we'll build the bridge."

So we tugged and shoved and shimmed a Douglas fir log into place, parallel to the cedar that had fallen years earlier, and laid planks from the chapel to form a tractor-worthy bridge. We all agreed. *Someday we'll have a tractor, someday we will.*

Then we built the porch—the farm-size porch. We set up the wringer machine next to a wooden dirty clothes box so big I had to climb inside to reach the socks and nose rags on the bottom. Mother didn't use the washer very much though, since all of the water had to be hauled up the steep bank from the creek. But the machine was stationed in plain sight to remind Daddy that she was waiting for him to get the place plumbed.

In the middle of setting up the porch, without time for preparation, Daddy decided we would host another Vacation Bible School. He borrowed the bus and sent us around to tell the neighbor kids when to be ready. The whole event was fraught with malfunction. Several mornings the bus wouldn't start. Twice, Mr. Tieche got it going but then he ruined something on his tractor. Another day, the bus stalled on the highway and a logging truck towed it until the engine kicked in. Daddy was so late those days that most of the kids decided not to come. But I was glad for VBS. I remembered that John had sung his special song the year before so I asked, "Daddy, can I sing?"

He stood me on the table in my sunshine yellow dress and I led the motions with my feet and hands, while singing in my best voice:

> Jesus loves the little children,
> All the children of the world.
> Red and yellow, black and white.
> All are precious in his sight.
> Jesus loves the little children of the world.[70]

A lady told me what a strong voice I had for such a small person. I smoothed the front of my skirt, acting shy, but thinking that I must sound as good as my big sisters.

Phillip also had a memorable episode with the VBS of 1947. He loved riding on the bus to take the children home, and his favorite seat was in the back with the girls. On the last day, the five-year-old leaned over and gave one of the six-year-old girls a kiss on the cheek.

At home, John chanted, "Phillip kissed a gir-ril, Phillip kissed a gir-ril." I joined in, along with another sibling or two, and the chant echoed throughout the house, until Mother said, "That's enough."

And Phillip swore to himself he would never kiss a girl again.

In our field, no longer a chapel site, the hay was ready. After sharpening the scythe with a hand stone, Daddy wielded the blade back and forth, laying the crop in rows. When his arms gave out, David took a turn, then Marilyn. It took several days to cut and then pitchfork the hay into stacks, carefully overlaying the top in the form of a thatched roof—just in case it rained. When the shock was dry, they loaded the pieced-together burlap tarp, tied up the corners, and carried home the load on their backs—not unlike the harvest of sheaves in Bible times.

After our sheaves were in, the Kerrs, who lived some miles west of Joyce, offered us a field of their hay if we would do the harvesting. So we started the process all over again. Their fields were bigger than ours, but the Kerrs had a tractor for cutting the hay and a truck for hauling it to the barn. We simply had to rake, turn, shock, load, and unload. While the job wasn't so bad, the payback was. In exchange for the gasoline we'd used in their vehicles, Daddy gave the Kerrs our calf.

That calf had been born on April 18, Marilyn's birthday. She, while watching him getting used to his wobbly legs, had declared that he was her handsome guy and she'd name him Nebuchadnezzar, but would call him Neb for short.

Neb had been nearly as stubborn and headstrong as the Babylonian king for whom he was named, and every bit as independent as his mother had been when she first came. When he broke through the often-patched fence, we could hardly catch him. But he was as dearly loved and pampered as his mother had been, and his wayward ways were easily forgiven.

Marilyn wished there had been some other solution. "Neb's my birthday calf and they'll just butcher him for meat," she moaned.

At least the barn was full of hay for Betsy and Daisy June. We celebrated by sleeping on top of the sweet mounds that filled the loft almost to the roof. The next morning, as became a pattern throughout all hay seasons to come, David and Marilyn scratched, sneezed, snuffed, and snorted. It was bad enough working in the hayfields, but sleeping in it was a hundred-fold worse. The rest of us felt sorry about their hay fever, but what could you do? The haying was done, and sleeping in it was a reward to be reaped, allergies and all.

In September, the Brucks arrived and once again changed our lives. Uncle Emil and Aunt Hazel brought us a tractor. And it was a tractor unlike any other in the entire world. A few years earlier, Uncle Emil had taken his 1925 Packard car, cut off the top, and shortened the drive shaft. On the back axle, he put oversized Chevrolet truck wheels with chains. He added a second Packard transmission, increasing the number of gears to nine. Our cousin Don, who'd learned to drive that tractor when he was just a kid, said he geared it down so low he could actually get off while it moved. He would adjust the plow and then get back on again without ever stopping its forward progress.[71]

To get the tractor running once it was at our farm, Uncle Emil took Daddy and David to the wrecking yard in Port Angeles and found a ring and pinion gear set to rebuild the rear end. After that, Daddy drove the tractor to the store and filled the tank with gas. We had, for the first time, a machine to pull stumps, haul logs, transport haystacks, and plow fields—except no plow came with it. Uncle Emil and Aunt Hazel also left a whole trailer load of other stuff they had cleaned out of their homes. They were headed north on a permanent move to Three Hills, Alberta.

Virginia scarcely noticed the tractor and the cargo. Her full attention was on a young man named John McLennan who'd come along with the Brucks. She had met John at Prairie three years earlier when she was just fourteen. After that first encounter, she would sense him watching her until she looked back. At Prairie, boys and girls couldn't date, couldn't sit together, couldn't talk on the sidewalk or wink, but there was no rule about looking and smiling—though girls who smiled too much could expect a reprimand from Miss Dearing.

At the end of that year, John had figured out a way to connect with Virginia in Calgary before she boarded the train for home. Her memory of that event replayed like a broken record in her mind. She had walked with John through the city park where the song "Stormy Weather" flowed through the air. It was true romance and she wondered if she was sinning when she held his hand. Well, if that was sinning, she'd just have to ask the Lord for forgiveness.

After that encounter, Virginia arrived home for the summer, and the two high schoolers wrote letters. John would find Mother's note in the corner of Virginia's envelope, *Censored by Mrs. A. W. Corey.* During the following two school years at Prairie, Virginia had visited Aunt Hazel and Uncle Emil at their house every week or so, while John hung out with their son Don in the same rooms. Aunt Hazel had never caught on to the fired-up attraction.

She caught on in a hurry when John jumped out of their car at our place and ran towards Virginia. John with his "Sweetie" tried to take walks and find private places to talk, but Aunt Hazel kept her eagle eyes open, and a gaggle of us goofy Coreys traipsed along just a pesky distance behind. John played along with us, teasing and teasing. Marilyn thought John was so much fun she got over some of her reservation about attending Prairie. She started listening to Virginia's convincing arguments that this was the best place to get missionary training, and she began to think how going to boarding school with her sister would even get her out from under Daddy's tight thumb. Aunt Hazel said she was sure it was a good idea for Marilyn to go because Prairie was a school where young people got their preparation for ministry while being protected from some of the ways of the world. So when Marilyn sent in her application, Aunt Hazel gave her $50 for her train fare.

Aunt Hazel, Uncle Emil and John McLennan prepared to leave and we stood by the car to sing "God be with you 'til we meet again." I looked around for the crying people and there weren't any, except maybe Virginia. I wondered if the rest didn't cry because they were listening to John McLennan sing, like I was. His voice was baritone and loud, not like Daddy's voice, that was tenor and smooth, nor like my brothers' that were high-pitched like mine.

And then the Brucks and John McLennan were gone. It was hard to imagine that our uncle and aunt would never again live within driving distance. The older ones lamented that there would be no more vacations at Hart's Lake and we younger ones protested that we'd never get to experience that place. Virginia said that she'd be living near Aunt Hazel who would surely keep an eye on her if John was around. Nonetheless, at home we had a memento of their visit that Daddy assured us would serve for years to come—the two-transmission Packard tractor.

The Brucks had just left when Marilyn received notice from Prairie that she was accepted for grade ten. She packed her bags with clothes that were in compliance with Prairie requirements: Blouses and dresses with sleeves that covered the elbows; skirts no shorter than twelve inches from the floor; winter weight cotton stockings, and garters to hold them up.

She headed off with Virginia, Chuck Wetherald, his sister Onolee, and Don Hitchcock. On the ferry to Vancouver, they sang gospel songs and sermonized for the passengers who wanted to listen, as well as for those who didn't. The young people figured that since they were on their way to a school that trained missionaries, they might as well get a head start. In Vancouver, they caught the train that headed east to Alberta.

During the rest of 1947, Marilyn wrote regular letters home about living at boarding school. She liked to write about the fickle prairie weather. Expect to expect the unexpected, she would say—windy and hot one day, snowy and cold the next, followed by mud pies and dust storms. She wrote about girls who didn't like her—especially Virginia's friends—and boys who acted like they did; prayer meetings and testimonies that strengthened her resolve to be a missionary to the lepers or the orphans; ice skating for the first time; and visiting Aunt Hazel to cook treats for the dorm or send to us, which she did, just in time for Christmas.

At home, with Christmas coming, we missed our two sisters, but especially Marilyn who had been the main milkmaid and who added hoopla to everything we did. Mother didn't say much about the girls being away for Christmas—there was no manner or money for them to come home. But she tied up a Christmas package to send them. Someone had given her two dressy suits, a gray pinstripe she knew would be acceptable for Marilyn, and a blue linen that would fit Virginia. In her letters, sent separately, Mother let us add our notes telling our sisters that a package was on its way and that they were missing out on our Christmas plans this year.

In all honesty, however, they weren't missing much. Instead of going out to milk a cow in the frigid barn, they were sleeping in until they felt like getting up. Instead of shoveling manure, they were partying in the dorm halls with food parcels sent by their friends' parents. Instead of chopping and hauling wood, they were playing games in the dining room. And, instead of bucketing water to do the laundry on the back porch, they were washing, ironing, and folding their clothes in the steamy, soap-scented Laundromat at school. They lived in radiator-heated rooms and used indoor toilets. (The toilets were indoors, though they weren't quite up-to-flush type. They were chamber pots called "honey buckets" that sat under hinged wooden seats and had to be dumped every day.)

No, there was little comparison between our life and the comforts of the Prairie dorm, except for one thing: Everyone old enough to understand whispered about rumors that the United States might declare war on Russia. Even I could sense the cloud of doom in the radio voices and in my parents' prayers.

• • •

CHAPTER FIFTEEN
The Rumors
(1948)

Mother listened to the news reports from European countries occupied by Soviet troops. She talked about the people who were losing their farms, their businesses, and their freedom; and about the families that were shredded apart, the children who were orphaned, and villagers who were starving. She repeated to Daddy the declarations that western countries could no longer peacefully coexist with Russia. Then, she talked of how the Soviet communists had weaseled their way to take over the government of Czechoslovakia. "Such evil in the world makes me wonder that God doesn't just declare enough is enough."

Mother found it hard to pray as her concern grew. What if the United States declared war? What if bombs were dropped? What if her daughters could not get home? Yet, not wishing her apprehension to spill over, she penned her letters with restraint. To Marilyn, she echoed Merton's three-year-old voice. "Merton and I are anxious for you to come home. Christmas wasn't quite the same and the winter seems so long with you and Virginia far away. Besides, your little brother wants you to take him fishing."[72]

Mother didn't hear back for a longer spell than usual. If Daddy was home, he hurried out to the mailbox. "Any word from the girls?" she would ask.

If Daddy was not there, Mother let Philip and me stand at the top of the hill and watch for the mail carrier, so she would know when to check the box. She reminded us each time we couldn't cross the highway until we were six, and Phillip was still short of his sixth birthday.

Finally, three letters came from Marilyn on the same day that told us mail had not been going out from Prairie because of a snowstorm. Mother sighed with relief that communication had not been cut off for any sinister reason. Marilyn also wrote that Virginia had fallen on the ice and hurt her ankle. And she wrote that while Virginia was recuperating, she mended the girls' stockings—stockings they said were made of "French Lace." Marilyn joked about the name. "The stockings are made of cotton, in the color of dirty rags. But they get intricate patterns of runs and holes through which you can see the pretty skin of a girl's legs. Virginia takes her nifty hosiery hook in hand and the uglies are back to normal."[73] In the last of the three letters Marilyn wrote, "I heard a missionary speak and am more sure than ever that I am called to go to Africa. Please tell Merton I will take him fishing in the summer."

Mother began to write less often to the girls. It was hard to write without saying she was apprehensive, without saying she didn't want Marilyn to go overseas with so much unrest in the world, without saying she needed her daughters to come home . . . now. But talking about it with God smoothed down Mother's anxiety.

There came a time when she told the Lord she was willing to let Marilyn go wherever God called her, and that she would not push the girls to quit Prairie before the school year was out. However, she did ask Daddy to go see them at school, telling him she would feel so much better to have a first-hand report. She even conceded that she could wait a little longer for him to finish the pump hook-up to the creek, suggesting that David might be able to dig the water-line trench.

So Daddy caught a series of rides to Three Hills, Alberta. Virginia and Marilyn were in a meeting when they saw him come in on the opposite side of the tabernacle. They could scarcely wait to talk to him afterwards and ask about everything that was happening at home. When they caught up with him, they shook hands—in keeping with the standards of Prairie. He stayed four days at Aunt Hazel's and Uncle Emil's where they could visit. One day the two girls watched from a distance as John McLennan gave Daddy a tour of the Prairie facilities and took him to meet Mr. Maxwell, the principal of the school. Marilyn told Virginia, "Your John's just gathering Brownie Points, isn't he?"

Both girls wrote letters for Daddy to carry home to Mother and all of us. They wrote letters for him to mail to Naoma and Aunt Eleanor when he got back in the States. They were accustomed to writing to lots of people. All year, no matter what was going on, the girls wrote letters home and letters to other relatives. That way they would find a regular flow of letters in their mailbox, sometimes with stockings and sticks of gum from Aunt Eleanor, or five dollars from Grandma or Naoma to pay the bills, or a penny from Merton or me to bribe them to come home.

After Daddy returned home he finished connecting the pipes from an electric pump at the creek to a faucet hooked up by the sink. It was a pump that we had to prime, but once the flow started, the water just kept running. Now we had fresh water to the kitchen and a hose from the kitchen to the washing machine on the porch. Talk about handy. For most of eleven years we'd used a creek—first the Nordstrom Creek and then ours—for washing diapers and work clothes. For most of eleven years we'd hauled water by sloppy bucketful. Now we could bathe more often in the laundry tub in the kitchen—and not necessarily everyone on the same day of the week.

I was a big help with the laundry—that's what Mother said. I watched the stream from the hose splash into the washer tank and climbed on a chair to turn off the spigot when the water level was perfect. I helped sort the piles from the dirty clothes bin. I folded diapers for my little sister. I was as excited about the new water pump as Mother and Elizabeth. It was a new era, water at the touch of a hand, and I wanted to write about it to my sisters, even though I still didn't know how to spell. Elizabeth told me what letters to print on the bottom of her correspondence to Marilyn and Virginia. "WE HAVE WATER NOW COME HOME SOON. LOVE ELEANOR"[74]

With water to the porch, Daddy invented a refrigeration system so we wouldn't have to carry milk to the creek to keep it cool. He affixed a hose to a copper tub and attached a flush-toilet type float to keep the water level correct.

Phillip thought it quite ingenious and tested the mechanism from time to time by pushing down the float so the water would spurt in, then letting go so the float bulb would bounce back and the water turn off. Of course, he was reminded that this wasn't a toy and he shouldn't get dirt in the milk pails.

When Prairie school was out in June, my two oldest sisters caught a train back to Vancouver. Daddy's friend Vick Argenbright, who'd become a regular provider of transportation, took Daddy to meet them. Mother told us what time we might expect their arrival. When they didn't show as planned, we begged to stay up. But Mother sent us to bed, saying in a disappointed voice, "It is quite possible Daddy felt the need to call on someone."

But, no, when the scheduled train had docked in Vancouver, he and Vick learned from other Prairie students that the girls had missed a train connection. So Daddy and Vick waited for the next train, picked up the girls and drove all night to get home.

We kids didn't hear them come in, but in the morning, Phillip and I listened by the curtain for the first sounds from the bedroom. Then, when they opened their eyes, we were on top of them, welcoming, chattering about all the changes, and urging them to get dressed.

Marilyn was up and out the door to the barn, even before breakfast and even before unpacking and ironing. She'd not yet met the new calves—two of them, Betsy's third and Daisy June's first. And she needed to get her hands into the milking. Elizabeth gave up her stool next to Daisy June and stood by, pleased to have her bigger sister home and more than pleased to turn over the cow. David was milking Betsy, and John said, "I'm learning to milk too."

"Good for you," Marilyn said to John, who'd not yet turned eight.

Elizabeth commented, "Can you believe the gallons of milk we get now? I can remember when we had to beg milk from the neighbors. Now we have to throw it out."

That first day, we all celebrated the return of the girls. Others came too: Strange Hester Branson, the unhinged lady from Port Angeles who mixed cookie dough with her hands, Mrs. Taylor from up the road, and Mrs. Courtwright from Tacoma. Mrs. Courtwright was a little lady with curly white hair and a gentle face, who had known and respected my parents since the early days at the Presbyterian Church in Tacoma. Fact is, she was one of very few who understood—back then—that Daddy was trying to help the church people understand there was more to being a Christian than just Sunday morning virtuous faces and weekday good works. This time, when Mrs. Courtwright arrived on the bus, she carried her electric sewing machine, patterns in all sizes, cuts of brand new fabric, and spools of thread to whip up dresses for all of us girls and Mother. Were we ever glad to see her.

David welcomed home the girls by bringing out the Phenicie skinny-wheeled bikes that had by this time replaced The Tandem whose parts could no longer be repaired.

Of course, the farm duties were first on the schedule. There was wood hauling behind the tractor—Marilyn insisting she drive—and sawing, chopping, and stacking. There was twice-a-day milking, continual garden weeding and fertilizing—much fertilizing. With two milking cows in the two-stanchion barn, we had plenty of manure for the chard, corn, cabbage, carrots, beets, beans, and berries. We didn't fertilize the potato patch, however. That's because we'd set the potatoes in the location of the demolished chicken shed in the far corner, and one glance was enough to confirm that the plants were flourishing without cow manure. What a shock it was when it came time to dig, and we discovered that there were almost no spuds, just a few nubbins. It was one of those lessons we learned by experience: too much chicken poop feeds the plant, not the potato.

Unfortunately also flourishing were the daisies in the hayfield. We had learned by experience the previous year that the bitterness of the daisies flowed right through Betsy and wrecked the flavor of her milk. So this year Daddy said we would take care of those weeds before anyone took the scythe to the field. Mother joked, "I've seen daisies planted around homes. Can you imagine people in their right minds planting these weeds in their flower beds?"

For weeks we pulled daisies. We'd start at one corner and slog our way into the middle, doing our best to get the weed by the root. The sun was hot, the roots were stuck, and before we could even cover one acre, all the new ones were in bloom and we had to start over at the beginning. My way of helping, at the age of five, was to tell the boys when it was time to quit for lunch. I did that by hammering a piece of railroad rail suspended from a pole between two cedar trees near the back porch. That gong was so loud the ringing continued in my ears long after the vibrations of the railroad bar had stopped. Nonetheless, the clanging sound brought the boys home in a hurry no matter where they were occupied—but especially fast if they were doing daisies.

One morning, David checking up on daisy diggers John and Phillip, made some suggestion to help them improve their efficiency and walked away. He didn't pull a single weed. John grumbled to Phillip, "It's not fair that David can tell us what to do and how to do it, and then he goes off to tinker on the tractor. Dad lets him do what he wants and makes us do all the dumb, dirty jobs."

Daddy observed that David liked to be supervisor, and that the grown girls could manage the house. He reached a different conclusion than John. He said to Mother, "Let's go on vacation."

Mother agreed, on one condition. "We will need to take Marian with us."

They loaded up a borrowed car and left the same day that Daisy was itching to visit the Nyholms' bull. Or was she? When Daisy was in heat, she acted as if she couldn't make up her mind. She kicked, shook her head, and bawled. It took the three oldest considerable effort to encourage, entice, drag, and shove her up the Phillips Road, through the woods behind Pete Johnson's and into the Nyholms' pasture.

Getting her home a few hours later wasn't anywhere near as *easy*. They found Daisy in the middle of the pasture, close to her bull-friend. Marilyn hoped to attract Daisy and not the bull, so she whispered, "Daisy, come, Daisy."

Daisy looked up and tossed her head—as cows do when they are busy—and went on munching. The girls murmured her name again and again; they waited and waited. When she paid no heed, they crept silently into the field. Or almost silently, for they had not gone far when the bull lifted his head, looked their way, and charged. Three teenagers turned and ran. The fence was too far away and its barbs too sharp to climb through in a hurry. Virginia clambered up a cedar stump, while Marilyn and Elizabeth grabbed the lower branches of two alder trees and scrambled up, barely out of reach of the spear-like horns of the beast. Fire blazing in his eyes, steam seeming to snort from his nostrils, the bull pawed and stomped at the two in their scrawny, waving trees. He kicked the pail where it had fallen and scattered the remnant of grain. Then he headed to the stump where Virginia had begun to smack her legs and twist this way and that. Marilyn scowled at her sister, and scolded, "Don't move!"

"I have to. There are red ants everywhere. The stump is full of them."

The bull stormed back and forth for the next hour. Virginia tried to keep the ants out of her pants without knocking apart the fragile, rotted stump. The other two clung to the feeble branches, not even daring to scratch their itchy noses. They yelled, "Help! Help! Yoo-Hoo!" but that only made the bull stomp harder. "Dear Lord, don't let us be here all night," fretted Elizabeth, "and take care of David and the little kids all by themselves."

The prayer session ended when Mrs. Nyholm called the cows to the barn. The bull gave one last snort and turned to follow the herd. "Please," the girls whispered, "Please, Daisy, don't go with them. Come, Daisy."

This time Daisy listened, and the girls collared her for home, keeping the bucket far enough in front that she couldn't see it was empty.

A week later, Mother, Daddy, and Marian returned to discover Virginia had been offered a job at Clallam County Abstract in Port Angeles. She would be able to stay with friends in town or catch a ride home with neighbors or Virginia Pennoyer.

On one of Mrs. Pennoyer's trips to our house, she delivered a new chair and matching davenport. We had never owned new furniture, at least not in my years of recollection. The set was made of a mossy-green material called Naugahyde that had a feel of leather and was guaranteed to last. Both pieces had latches that held them upright. When the latches were opened, the furniture lay down flat, providing two new beds—one big enough for an adult, and the other sized for a child. Mother relegated the worn-to-the-springs couch to the back porch and kept it covered with a wool patchwork quilt she had pieced from coats, suits, and fatigue-green military blankets. The new furniture was so easy to clean that Mother said we didn't need a blanket to cover it. She simply told the boys to stay off it when they came in dirty—which was always.

In July, Daddy sharpened the scythe with the stone and we cut the field. The beauty of harvesting this year was pitching the hay onto a trailer and Marilyn pulling it down the highway behind the Packard tractor. No wrapping in the burlap, no hauling on the back, no stinging by the bees.

The hay was just in when Mrs. Courtwright, the lady who sewed new clothes for us, wrote that she wanted Marilyn and Elizabeth to look after her grandkids, Penny and Gary. The children's dad had moved out, and their mother worked long night shifts in a *drinking place.* Mrs. Courtwright wanted her grandkids to have our kind of Christian influence in their lives. So my sisters headed off to Tacoma, taking time first to visit lots of relatives—some of whom had once frowned at Daddy or told him off. Marilyn wrote they all now seemed happy to see the girls, and to load them up with gifts and clothes.

After that, the two teens and their five and six-year-old charges went to the cabin at Sunrise Beach, not far from Gig Harbor. They chopped wood, cooked, cleaned, and played on the beach. They sat in the canoe, but kept it tied to the shore because Aunt Eleanor had secured a promise that they would not move the boat from its mooring. She said, "If you let go, the tide might take you to China." And they believed her.

The cabin fridge was loaded with more food than the two girls had ever seen in one place. They cooked a whole chicken and then hoarded it until it rotted—such waste! They roasted as many hot dogs and marshmallows as they wanted, made fudge, and ate bowl after bowl of ice cream. When they returned to Grandma's house two weeks later, Marilyn had gained five pounds. When she told Grandma how upset she was at getting fat, Grandma gave her two new girdles.

The girls came home just in time for school to start. Liz—the preferred nickname Elizabeth had chosen for herself—took responsibility for Phillip, who was off to first grade. Virginia—who had become Gin over the summer—started classes at Simpson Bible Institute in Seattle. Mrs. Courtwright had helped pay her way, so she would be available to stay with Penny and Gary while their mother was at the bar.

Gin hadn't been at Simpson long when she wrote home with big news—she was engaged. It had happened one evening when John called her from Three Hills, using the pool hall phone—the only telephone in town. The background noise was so loud that Virginia couldn't hear him, forcing John to shout his question louder and louder. When at last she understood what he was asking, she shouted back, "Yes, *yes!*"

John's explosive proposal was overheard by the pool hall players as well, who broke into a chorus of guffaws that caused him to second-guess, *Did she say she would marry me or that she could hear me?*

John sent his savings for Virginia to buy an engagement watch—she had told him she needed a timepiece more than a ring. The watch's cheery face reminded her every time she looked at it that she was truly engaged to be married. The watch, however, didn't discourage the advances of another young man, a singer whom she accompanied at the piano. Gin had no clue how to hold the suitor at bay, so she asked Mother, "May I wear your engagement ring at school?"

Mother pulled her diamond out of the drawer. She hadn't worn the ring for years, nor had Naoma accepted it as a gift. It was just what Virginia needed.

Back at school, while sitting down at the piano, she floated her hand in front of the young man's gaze, and the message was communicated. She never had to say a word.

Meanwhile, Marilyn returned to Prairie High School to begin grade eleven. She'd barely completed the first week when she broke out with boils. The previous year she had developed a nasty one under her arm that chafed raw with every movement, but it had healed under Gin's medical intervention. This time the infection spread until her back looked like a battleground and burned like a branding iron. She wrote to Mother and Daddy to pray that she would be healed. Marilyn knew how God had healed her dad from the same affliction when he prayed. So, as she counted her feverish oozing sores, she thought about Daddy's testimony and listened to it replay in her mind. He'd been weak and sickly during all his growing up years—prone to break out with boils, styes and granulated eyelids. After he heard an evangelist say that God could heal, he went to the elders for prayer. They told him healing wasn't for today. But the boils and carbuncles became so bad he could hardly work. Daddy prayed and fasted four days with no food or water until he could hardly climb into the truck to fulfill his delivery. Late one night, in the darkness of the drive back from Olympia to Tacoma, he heard God say, "Turn in here. Go and eat." Daddy parked the truck in the lot of the Dutch Mill in Chehalis and ordered a full-course chicken dinner. Even though he'd not eaten for days, the meal didn't hurt him. When Mother checked his back that night, all the boils were gone and the skin was clear.

Marilyn didn't doubt Daddy's story or God's ability to heal. However, she did doubt her own faith and her discipline to go without food for days on end. So when the count of boils came to sixteen—one of which had grown into a carbuncle with multiple heads—she went to the Prairie Infirmary. She wrote to us all about it—how she had to take pills and get shots three times a day with a big one for the night and how she liked the stark and sterile infirmary with its beds laid out in a row, just the way she would keep her missionary leper clinic.

Marilyn's boils were starting to heal when Virginia in Seattle came down with a high fever and a tennis-ball-size boil under her arm. Rose Courtwright's doctor lanced it, squeezed out a cup of pus and blood, gave her shots, and sent her home. Both girls were healed of the boils and thanked the Lord for the medical miracle of penicillin. And we said amen.

About Thanksgiving time, Mr. John Johnson came to visit Daddy at the Farmhouse. Our neighbor was by then in his seventies, and his two daughters, Emily and Margaret, rarely came home anymore. Mr. Johnson got right to the point, "Mr. Corey, would you and David help me butcher the pigs?"

David was impressed that Mr. Johnson asked and that his father didn't refuse. Daddy hadn't taken care of the beavers when they were caught in the traps, he wouldn't chop the heads off chickens, and David had even heard him say more than once, "God called me to be a servant of healing, not an agent of death."

But a neighbor had asked for help, and Daddy answered the call. There were several pigs to be butchered. Mr. Johnson had a .22 single-shot rifle. He shot at one of the pigs and missed the tiny bullseye of the brain. With a sore head, the pig raced around the yard, squealing, while Mr. Johnson pumped bullets until it dropped. Then Mr. Johnson cut the throat and caught the blood in a pail. The scene about did Daddy in.

Mr. Johnson had prepared a 55-gallon drum of water that steamed over an outside fire pit. The butchers tied each pig on a pulley, hoisted it, and set it down into the water. After half a minute or so, they lifted it from the pot onto a wide board set on saw horse legs. Mr. Johnson handed out cup-shaped blades to scrape off the hair. When he cut up the animal, nothing was wasted. Mrs. Johnson saved the blood for sausage; kept the fat for lard, the kidneys for pie, the liver to go with onions, and various glands for who knows what. She took all the bits of head meat and brains and ground them up with spices. When the delicacy of headcheese was offered to us, Elizabeth turned up her nose and wouldn't even try it. David said to her, without realizing his own pun, "It tastes good—you're just a picky eater and it's all in your *head*!"

Headcheese was not a choice item for Mother, either, but when Mrs. Johnson handed her a smoked ham a few weeks later, she said, "I'll serve this for Christmas."

She told Daddy, "This makes all that work worth it. Don't you agree?"

Helping the Johnsons butcher ushered in a new era for the Coreys at RR1, Box 353[75], on Highway 9A—an era of more meat in our diet. Not that Daddy would soon want to repeat the experience at the Johnsons, but he had to admit their ham was the best he'd tasted.

Four brothers and Tig

CHAPTER SIXTEEN
The Twenty-Two
(1949)

Virginia Pennoyer heard about the pig slaughtering and said to our father, "I believe you should have a gun on your farm. As the boys get older they'll be able to hunt wildlife for meat, and when your animals are ready, the gun will help in butchering."

It took Daddy awhile to accept what she was offering and the rationale behind it. Eventually—with conditions of responsible behavior set for his eldest son—he answered, "Yes, you may give David a gun for his twelfth birthday."

Mrs. Pennoyer delivered a new J C Higgins single-shot, bolt-action .22 rifle, complete with a box of shells. She gave David a lesson in aiming, firing, and keeping safe. I stood by, watching wide-eyed, thinking of the day I could be trusted to aim at a target and pull the trigger. It would be up to my brother to decide when I'd earned the badge of responsibility. But I was still only five. It would be a long time.

That spring, Daddy sold Daisy June, who was already round with calf. He said the girls wouldn't have to deal with her in-heat tantrums, and the sale would outfit the Farmhouse and farmyard with a few conveniences. Out of the $174.00 payment we got an electric fence and charger to help keep track of Betsy and two yearlings. We circled a pipe through the firebox of the kitchen stove, connected it to a water tank behind, and ran a pipe to the kitchen. We added another faucet—a hot water faucet—at the kitchen sink. As long as wood was burning, we had hot water at the tap, enough for at least one service at a time: the dishes or the washing up or the white shirts in the laundry.

Daddy bought and installed a set of solid wood cabinets and cupboards with block knobs from Sears. I was ready to stack the dishes in their new home when Mother said we had to cover the shelves first. So she and I sorted through the stack of newspapers Mr. Samuelson had sent. We pulled out the tidiest pages—the ones with fine print and no pictures. We folded, trimmed, and laid them with all the text going one direction. The inside was as well-dressed as the varnished exterior. We set in the dishes, mostly enamel ware with dings, china plates with chips, and roughed up silver plate cutlery that had been kept so busy it never got a chance to tarnish before all the finish wore off.

To complete the renovation, Mother mopped the floors and I laid a layer of newspapers. We always put newspapers on the floor after a thorough mopping. As Mother said, "This floor never gets dry before somebody brings in filth from outside."

All of us missed Daisy June, yes, but all of us found the benefits made up for her loss.

That season the garden got a gift as well. Daddy's older brother, Jim, sent us his Gravelly Tractor. Uncle Jim had been one of the harshest critics when my father became a preacher. But this many years later, with what Daddy said was "a softened heart," Uncle Jim donated a farm implement he no longer needed. The Gravelly ran on the same type of tracks as a Caterpillar. Its traction and miniature size made it manageable in the woods, allowing us to create paths, pull logs, and clear brush. The Gravelly came with a one-furrow plow that was as primitive as those used behind the oxen in the days of the pioneers. The plow had a large wheel in front of the blade and a small one behind. A straight bar connected it to the Gravelly, meaning someone had to follow behind to lift the blade from the ground and turn it for a corner.

John McLennan, Virginia's beau, arrived at the opportune time to manage the Gravelly in the daisy field. After leaving Prairie, he had met up with Virginia at her job in Seattle. They went downtown to the Greyhound bus station and purchased their tickets for Port Angeles. While waiting to board, the earth began to move under them. Virginia grabbed John's arm and the two of them leaned against the wall. Everything was moving. The high-rises of Seattle waved back and forth, windows falling from the upper stories. Cars on the rolling streets swerved as if the drivers were drunk. Dust rose from the sidewalk where bricks crashed out of walls. Children cried and ladies shrieked. Then it ended. Faces near the two-some were white with shock, and theirs were too. An earthquake had struck. Later, they learned that Olympia was the epicenter of a 7.1 magnitude earthquake, and that even though Seattle was on the outskirts, it had received plenty of impact. After the dust settled and the driver got the go-ahead, the bus pulled out of the depot. All the way to Port Angeles, John held Virginia tight.

The lovebirds arrived at the Farmhouse and kept up their favorite pursuits: hugging and smooching. John's previous visit had been when he came surreptitiously with Uncle Emil and Aunt Hazel. This time he was engaged to my sister. Daddy, rather than telling the ardent suitor to slow down, suggested that John could help in the field. Gin could see the sweat pouring off John's face as he hoisted the plow off the ground and turned it so Daddy could keep going ahead with the machine. She was embarrassed that her father would subject *her* man to such a task, but she had little say in the matter, and John knew he needed to show himself worthy.

I was kind of glad when John McLennan got ready to leave. It was fine to have him help Daddy, and his teasing was fun, but to have him hanging around my sister with so many mushy-gushy goings-on nearly made me puke. When the time came for him to say his farewells, I plugged my ears and ran out the back. I didn't even wave goodbye. But neither of them noticed me. John was going back to Alberta and Virginia would not see him for a long time, so you can imagine what their goodbyes were like.

While all this was happening at home, Marilyn, at Prairie High School, was winding up for the end of her junior year of high school. She was in charge of the decoration committee for the Junior-Senior Banquet, and wrote in several letters about her litany of tasks: Calling the meetings, making the banners, reminding others to do their parts, scrubbing the wood floors, making dozens more banners, designing the place mats, constructing the corsages, meeting with the committee countless times, and speaking sternly to straighten out the goof-offs. On top of that, she scheduled her classes for the next year and took her tests in typing, composition, and Latin. She fretted in her letters about Elizabeth, who was going to parties, and about the tight pain in her own chest.

"It's no wonder," Mother commented to us, "that girl needs to slow down."

After the banquet was over—an astonishing success—Marilyn packed up for home. The twinge in her heart was gone. She waved good-bye to her friends, including Allen Thompson—her most recent eye-catcher—and boarded the bus.

As soon as she arrived at our place, Marilyn dropped her bags on the floor, found her patched farm pants, and joined us to clean out last-year's hay from the neighbor's barn. The labor was intense and physical—exactly what the brain-overloaded social planner needed.

The Johnsons had already used the top layers of the hay and needed space for the new crop. What was left was packed solid. But the Johnsons had a wavy-blade hay cutter that sliced straight down into the thick, heavy mounds. Once a section of the hay had been sliced, Marilyn and David—mostly— forked and rolled layers of the block, hauled it out of the barn, and pitched it onto the trailer behind the Packard tractor until it could hold no more. Daddy drove down the highway and those same two—mostly—pitched it into our barnacle-size barn. What a contrast of farming—the neighbors' and ours. We had a simple two-stanchion shed that held two or three animals and filled up with one trailer load, while the Johnsons had a gargantuan fifteen-stanchion shelter with mountains of hay to feed their herd.

Two weeks later in exchange for what the Johnsons had given, we helped rake their fields and load their trailer with new sweet hay. After they hauled it to their cleaned out barn, they speared the mound with their hayfork that hung from a pulley in the loft. When their tractor pulled the rope, a huge pile of hay lifted, slid through window and dropped. Our eyes filled with envy, almost covetousness, as their hayfork unloaded the trailer in minutes. "Someday we will have a hay fork." Marilyn said to David. "Someday we will!"

And David replied, "They cost too much."

In the course of haying with the Johnsons, Daddy casually asked Mr. Johnson what kinds of seeds he'd found were best to sow in his fields. Mr. Johnson said he usually planted three seeds together, so Daddy bought three types of seed for our field. Seed in hand, he scratched the balding part of his head, wondering how to plant all three varieties in an acre and a half, while simultaneously following the scripture that says: "Sow not your field with mingled seed."

After meditating on the matter, Daddy sowed the alfalfa, clover, and Timothy orchard grass separately in three sections. This was the only year my father planted in strips. Perhaps after that poorly produced crop, he had come to believe that the principle of the Bible was not quite that specific. What he—and we all—learned for certain: Alfalfa needs a longer, warmer summer than our field received. So, as our dad was gaining experience in farming, he sought the wise counsel of the neighbors. He listened, compared their expertise with what he knew from scripture, and made his decision. Thus, he explained from time to time, in any situation where there was more than one option, God's word had to be the ultimate authority.

That summer of 1949, Mrs. Courtwright asked if Penny could come to our place. Her brother Gary was going to stay with his father, and Virginia was moving home to look for a real job. I was ecstatic when Penny arrived. Her hair was the color of a brand-new one-cent piece, her face had more freckles than mine, and she was a head taller. Penny was seven and I had just turned six, but the differences didn't matter a bit. We were twins in dedication to our recreation, even as the older ones were to their labors. Mother felt sorry for Penny, who lived in a bad environment, which is probably why we got to play so much.

Penny and I washed and dried the dishes, then ran to pick strawberries, blackberries, raspberries, and boysenberries that Penny called "poison-berries." We ate so many poison-berries that the next day we had purple diarrhea, proving that the name she had invented was accurate.

The creek was our favorite place to play. There was clay along the side of the bank that we could form into sculptures of food, pots, or animals. We ran everywhere in our bare feet, not even noticing the stickers and rocks. We climbed trees and made sticky balls out of pitch, rolling them in dirt and plastering them like warts on smooth rocks or the sides of sheds. Once, when Penny fell into a nettle patch, I made a mud-pie poultice to rub all over her. It soothed the stings, but created a disturbance with Mother because I'd muddied the pump water in the process.

On hot days we went bathing in the swimming hole beneath the trestle. We crawled and crouched our way through the culverts—just like the boys did—watching for the seams and rusty bolts that would cut our feet or knees. Mother let us take a bar of Ivory so we could have our baths there. We dried off on the sunny bank, but by the time we made it back to the house we were grimy all over again.

Penny and I loved to play with a pet chick named Peep. Peep had been a clumsy runt when it hatched, and Mother didn't think it would live. But we held it and fed it tiny seeds and bits of bread until it grew strong enough to scratch for its own food. It was so tame that it followed us everywhere, squatting down next to our feet to be picked up.

Most of the chickens weren't lucky enough to be pets, and ended up as dinner instead. Phillip liked to put on a show for spectators, so he and John would pretend to hypnotize a chicken by moving the axe back and forth in front of its face. When they got tired of that game, down would swing the ax and off would come the head. If the boys held the headless chicken up by the legs, it would splash blood and flap its wings for a while, but if they dropped it on its feet it would run around blindly, demonstrating the truth of the cliché about a chicken with its head chopped off.

Sometimes Penny and I had to pick off the feathers, but we never had to clean out the innards. Marilyn said it was fun to put her hand inside the cavity and pull out the warm guts, but I told her she could save all that *fun* for herself.

The boys found their entertainment in pulling tricks. They talked us into lining up in a row. The biggest boy latched onto the electric fence and the smallest kid on the end jumped and squealed from the shock. Then we rolled on the grass and roared with laughter.

Penny liked having family devotions every morning before breakfast, but I was impatient to go play. She said, "My mother doesn't want to hear anything about the Bible, but my grandma loves the Lord."[76]

Before Penny went home, I *gave* her the itch—a recurring infection in the Corey household—that Marilyn slathered with her favorite remedy: kerosene. We two were still suffering from the cure when nine-year-old John came through the door, crying and holding his thumb. We watched as Marilyn turned the kitchen into an emergency room. She held the thumb together and washed the blood down the drain. Virginia and Elizabeth hovered near the sink, watching. John heard a noise and turned to see his oldest sister crash to the floor like a tree, her glasses flying across the room. Marilyn said, "Hold this tight," and left him at the sink so she and Elizabeth could revive Gin and get her to the couch.

In the excitement, John nearly forgot about his injured thumb. He couldn't wait to tell the folks when they returned. "You should have seen Virginia fall over as if she'd died—I had to hold my hand so Marilyn could take care of her first!"

At Mother's questioning, John explained that Merton and he were in the woodshed. They were arguing about which chopping block each would use to cut the firewood. Merton wouldn't quit yelling, so John ignored him and set his block for cutting. Merton lifted his hatchet and chopped down with all his force. John said, "When I pulled back my hand, there was my thumb just dangling loose by the piece of skin."

Mother was not surprised at the action of her youngest son. She'd come to realize that Merton could be every bit as obdurate as any of his older brothers. Even so, after the youngster saw John's severed finger and all the blood, the four-year-old didn't emerge from his hiding place for quite a few hours.

Marilyn emerged from the crisis as the one equipped to manage the medical emergencies—even two or three at a time, but she lamented to her diary and to the family that she was not one who could manage her diet. Ever since her junior high job with Mrs. Singhose in the lunchroom she had added pounds and dieted, never managing to subtract quite as many as she had added. So Daddy gave her a plan that he guaranteed. "Let's make a contract. You work seven hours a day in the woods, and you *will* get yourself into shape."

The farmer girl began to keep record of the hours she dedicated to physical labor. She took a hoe to the weeds in the garden and a shovel to dig a cave-like root cellar next to the woodpile. She felled trees and sawed them to specified lengths; she skinned the bark, cranked the Gravelly, and dragged poles to a pile. After that, she and David used the seven-foot crosscut to saw up two big logs, five feet and four feet in diameter, which had lain across the little creek since the homesteaders dropped them; and the two chopped enough firewood—18 cords to be exact—to last the entire winter. Marilyn's skin turned brown, her arms grew strong, and her fat turned to muscle. But the excess weight didn't shrink. Mother reminded her she couldn't eat more just because she was working hard, and suggested she not bake treats. Marilyn's resolve to avoid the kitchen lasted a week, until it was time to bake cakes for John's and Virginia's birthdays on July 25.

That same day, the 25th of July, 1949, the Johnsons came to help butcher our first yearling. As tough as she acted, Marilyn rebelled at the idea of butchering a calf born to Betsy or Daisy. So Marilyn took Merton, Penny, and me blackberry picking.

Daddy also steered clear of the killing. He returned to watch Mr. and Mrs. Johnson mentor the boys in the rest of the butchery—skinning the carcass, removing the guts, and preparing the quarters for the Port Angeles butcher man to put in the locker. The Johnsons took home all the delicacies that Mother refused to cook, which included the head and all the innards, except the tallow for making soap, and the liver. She only kept the latter part—*the liver*—because the boys liked it with onions and catsup, and it was a healthy way to fill them up. Just the thought of soaking and slicing and cooking the slippery organ reminded her of the waves of nausea she had felt during her pregnancies when Daddy would come home with liver for her to fix and eat so she would not be anemic. Well, after this butchering she wouldn't be forced to eat it for those reasons and she *could* serve it to her family.

Normally people would butcher in the fall when the weather turned cold. But we were short on food—not only for us but to feed a caravan of guests who would come that summer. The first guest, Hester Branson, came from Port Angeles—all of thirteen miles away—and stayed an eternity it seemed. Mrs. Branson was the religious lady who had shocked my oldest sisters with her histrionics of years earlier. She was also the kind lady who took two of these sisters home with her to bake cookies. And once she'd even taken them on the ferry to Victoria, along with her own daughter, where the girls had "crumpets-with-tea" for the first time. Yes, Mrs. Branson did nice things for us and helped with the finances, but she had emotional and mental disabilities. In Daddy's mind, many of these issues were also spiritual in nature. So when Mrs. Branson was in an *alarming* condition, Daddy would tell her to stay with us, where he and Mother could minister to her. If she got better quickly, she would go home in a few days. But this was a bad season for Mrs. Branson, and she stayed more than a month.

Mother curtained off the nook designed for a piano studio, and Mrs. Branson slept on the fold-open green davenport. I thought the woman hovered in every corner, just waiting to tell us what not to do. One time I bounded around the corner by the stairs and ran smack into her. I sucked in my breath and swirled to go the other way; then I realized she was just trying to take a fully-clothed sponge bath out of sight of the family. Poor lady! With no bathing place in the house but the sink or the round, galvanized wash tub in the kitchen, guests like Mrs. Branson just had to figure out how to get clean.

Sometimes Mother had a hard time with Hester Branson. More than once she remarked that Mrs. Branson was one of those women that gave Pentecostals a bad name—that she was big on religious experience and emotion, not wise in day-to-day living. Mother said, "If I can just learn to live in obedience to God's practical teaching—that kind of experience would be *wisdom* to me."

Next came the Art Bergs. Art was the man who helped Daddy clean the Grange way back in the beginning. He and his wife Ethel left their three girls with us for a week, and then Uncle Emil and Aunt Hazel came from Three Hills, Alberta. Those families were barely out of the house when Mother's brother, Uncle Herbert Phenicie, his wife, Aunt Edith, and the twins came. They'd spent more than a year in Cuba, and were preparing to return again, this time on permanent assignment.[77] David brought out the bikes Richard and Roger had left behind two years earlier. They'd had some use, but David made sure the tires had air so the cousins wouldn't think him irresponsible. After they'd ridden up and down Grauel Road a few times, the three boys built a dam in the creek. The rest of us hauled rocks, but only the big boys were allowed to do the construction. The water in the dam was deep, shady, and lined with stones. Penny and I didn't think it was as good as the pond beyond the culverts, where the sun was hot and the creek bottom was soft and squishy. Daddy appreciated the dammed-up pool, however, and decided an early-morning swim was just what he needed to start each day. None of the rest of us joined him, though we were impressed that he kept at it until winter rains knocked out part of the barrier.

We had another of those crying sessions when Uncle Herbert and his family left—you know, the kind that goes with the somber singing of "God be with you 'til we meet again." The tears must be contagious, because this year I even got wet eyes. I didn't notice if David was sad or not.

Probably not. For the Phenicies were barely out of sight when David invited Phillip to go on a biking and fishing adventure. Phillip, by then, spent as much time fishing in our creek as parents would permit. But to be taken downstream with his big brother? That was almost more than he could contain. Phillip climbed on the handlebars, and the two biked a quarter mile down the highway, a mile down to Camp Hayden, and headed west on a logging road to the Salt Creek Falls. The bike was going lickety-split down a steep hill when, next thing they knew, they were flying in all directions. Phillip's heel had caught in the front wheel, sending the bike and the boys somersaulting through the air. The two checked themselves for broken bones and walked the rest of the way to the fishing hole. It was a long trudge back home for the battered lads who had to carry both the catch of the day and the dinged-up bike.

After the summer guests had gone, our parents went on vacation to see relatives in Tacoma. This time they left two-year old Marian under the supervision of

Marilyn. Actually, they left all of us under her supervision. Our sister told us what we could do and what we couldn't—and sometimes changed her mind, like when we went with Mrs. Pennoyer to the Clallam County Fair and Marilyn told us afterwards she should have said no.

Marilyn turned us into scullery maids and cleaning slaves. We had to help her scour everywhere, wash windows, bake bread, get wood, make jam, can peas and chard, and cut up vegetables for a big pot of stew made from the scrappy meat and broth of the butchered animal. She did the ironing herself, claiming it was her therapy for the pandemonium—plenty of which she caused.

Marilyn wanted the garden to produce, so we watered and weeded. She didn't like squabbling so we tried not to squabble. All except for John, that is. His buttons were easily pushed, and Phillip knew how to push the wrong ones. John took off after the seven-year-old, down the hill to the creek and across the bridge. He yelled and threw rocks. Marilyn hollered at him to stop, then ran in pursuit. She tackled the out-of-control lad, holding him down until he quit struggling. "Please," John begged, "don't tell Daddy what I did."

She promised. But when the folks returned, she told Mother. Mother told Daddy, and so John found himself in the woodshed once again. After the punishment, John denounced Marilyn for tattling when she said she wouldn't. She laughed, "I only promised not to tell Daddy."

"You knew if you told Mother, it wouldn't be a secret from Dad." It was true. Mother may not have been as harsh, but she was nearly as strict, and there were few secrets between them when it came to our behavior.

John grouched that his sister, who had been so kind to fix his severed thumb, didn't care that Daddy would fix his backside. He thought, *if Marilyn is going to be a missionary to Africa like she keeps saying, she had better learn not to tell lies.*

Yes, Marilyn planned to be a missionary, and to be a missionary she knew she had to be obedient to the Bible and do the right things. It might be hard to imagine that she would want her younger brother, who was as feisty as she, to receive the severe punishments she had once felt. And, yet, she must have felt the right thing for him was to get his life straightened out and his temper under control. *Thus,* she rationalized, *my deception was not really a lie, just a way for righteousness to win out.*

Elizabeth wasn't as big and strong as Marilyn, but she too could get us younger ones in trouble. One day, when I was a little older than six, John and I were upstairs and he said to me. "Close your eyes and open your mouth."

"Oh no," I said, pointing to the half-full chamber pot, "You'll dump *that* in my mouth."

I hadn't even used a dirty word, but my sister was on the stairs and overheard. She headed straight to Mother and reported that I was being foolish about the Number One in the pot. Mother gathered the available kids in a circle for the lesson; then took the Ivory Soap and a washcloth to my mouth. I tasted Ivory the rest of the day and cried from humiliation. It's possible that

Mother chose this method of punishment because she didn't want to turn the foolish one over to my father and his rod of correction. Still, this chastisement stuck forever in the chambers of my memory, and not because of Mother. *Why didn't Liz mind her own business, and what right did she have to broadcast a foolishness citation against me?*

Washing the mouth was one of the punishments Mother could manage. So it was that nearly all of us—even David—at one time or another got a purification of the tongue with that "99.44 percent pure" soap known as Ivory. Mother's other favored behavior modification technique was not quite the organized production she provided at her mouth-washing events. When one of her sons was slow to obey or dallied when she'd given him a task, she would grasp an ear—or even two—between her fingers. If the kid resisted or tried to wriggle free, she pinched tighter and twisted the lobe or the cartilage until that errant offspring moved in the direction he was to go. It worked every time, without leaving a wake of tears or the shame of public disgrace.

When school began in the fall, I entered first grade. Mother pulled my hair into tight French braids and said I could wear the new dress she had sewn of white and gray stripes with red hearts and eyelet trim. Elizabeth ushered me onto the school bus and went with me to class. I didn't really need her, since I would be in the same room as Phillip, who was in second grade, but I was still glad for her company. I had been waiting . . . waiting . . . waiting for school to start, so when the day arrived I hugged my green lined tan-colored newsprint tablet and clutched the sharp-pointed new pencil Daddy had chiseled with his pen knife.

Elizabeth had already taught me to read and do arithmetic, so within a few weeks, Mrs. Tripp let me do the same studies as the second graders and told me to be quiet and read when I finished. Phillip griped to Mother, "Eleanor is a nuisance. I don't know why the teacher treats her like she's so smart."

Mother told him to do his assignments and pay no attention to me. However, she was much more sympathetic to his tears in the night for leg aches. "Growing pains," she called them, as she massaged his muscles. She explained, "I had them when I was your age. My mother told me it meant I would grow tall."

Phillip relaxed in the warmth and strength of Mother's hands. It was almost enough to make him forget his irritation that I'd caught up to his grade already.

I didn't have any homework, so I learned to sew. Aunt Eleanor had given me a little doll with a bright red circle dress, real human hair, and blue eyes that closed. I cut circles the same as the dress she came in, using scraps from Mother's sewing box. I cut a hole in the middle of the circle for her head, a slit down the back, and two slices for her arms. I learned to thread a needle and stitch a hem or add a bit of lace. I tied a ribbon around my doll's middle and carried her around to show her off in new outfits every day. I pointed out to Mother, "See, I've gotten good at sewing by hand. I think it's time to use the sewing machine."

Mother had told me she would teach me some day. So when I demonstrated my skill with scissors and a needle, she relented, even though she said, "I don't know if your feet will reach the treadle yet."

The White Rotary Treadle machine became my immediate friend, almost an extension of my hands and feet. Within weeks my black-haired beauty was the best dressed doll around, with lots of changes neatly laid out in her black leather squarish overnight case—a case decorated with flowery decals and labeled in silver with Aunt Eleanor's initials. After my doll's wardrobe was complete, I outfitted the naked baby doll that toddler Marian lugged around.

About the time school started that fall, Eddie Enser came to live with us. Virginia Pennoyer, who knew Eddie and his parents, had told Mother and Daddy that Eddie was having difficulties at home and troubles in school. "He needs to be with a good family," She said.

So Mrs. Pennoyer brought Eddie with his things. David moved over so there was room for an extra mattress in the attic. The next day, David introduced him to Joyce School and took him into the same classes. Eddie had barely settled in at home and school when David's brain popped a plan he turned into a convincing rationale. "Daddy," he asked, "Would it be alright if Eddie and I ride the bikes to school? I know we could get there as quickly as the bus and back home even faster."

For almost two years, David had been dying to show off his cousins' skinny wheel bikes at school, but Daddy had told him he needed to ride on the bus with his brothers. This time Daddy said yes to this request. David could hardly contain himself, but the twelve-year-old held his breath so as to downplay his enthusiasm, as was his nature. Eddie was not one to downplay his enthusiasm, not when it came to riding the bikes, and not when he bragged about his strength and his skills. He was taller than David, and his voice was lower, making him appear to have the upper hand in competition. "Alright," David said, "Let's see who's the toughest."

David pulled out a hardball. "You stand over there and I'll stand here. No mitts for catching, okay?"

So the two boys pitched the hard ball back and forth with as much force as they could muster, moving closer and closer with each throw. They were just fifteen feet apart when Eddie's face turned as red as his hands and David could tell he was dying to quit. So David let the kid off the hook. "That's enough for today," he said, glad to rub his own bruised hands together.

The challenge worked and Eddie calmed down. They did chores together and had cow pie fights. They even goofed around with nonsense talk until one day Daddy took a mop handle to their behinds to remind them that foolishness was a sign to the parent, and guardian, that action was required. David had not been one to get the number of spankings that some of us received—he wasn't wired with an impulsive trait—but this time he was joking along with his buddy and had not noticed his father listening in. Of course, after the punishment, David and Eddie got over their embarrassment by comparing the red welts on their backsides and legs.

The two rode the skinny-wheelers everywhere. They pedaled all the way to Port Angeles, discovering en route that those bikes could go up the Elwha River one lane road as fast as a logging truck. In Port Angeles they called on Mrs. Pennoyer, and spent the night at Eddie's home. It was at Eddie's house that David learned how to answer a telephone. His sister Virginia knew he would be there and phoned from her temporary lodging at Pennoyers to talk with him. When Eddie's mother handed him the phone, David did not know which part went to the mouth and which part to the ear. Eddie laughed, mumbling to himself, "How could that kid with all the smarts and muscle, not know which end of the phone is up?"

So once the competitions for bravery and brains were out of the way, and they'd shared a proper spanking, Eddie became almost like a twin brother to David as they adventured together on those twin bikes that David's twin cousins had given him.

That same fall, Virginia returned to Simpson Bible Institute in Seattle and John McLennan arrived to try out Seattle Pacific College. Marilyn left for Prairie to take her senior year of high school. So all the kids, except Merton and Marian, were back in the saddle of school.

Daddy, too, had climbed back in the saddle—the saddle of jailhouse services—going nearly every week with friends who would pick him up and bring him home. With rides available, it was easier for Mother to go with him, knowing she wouldn't have to wait by the roadside before or after the service. If she demurred, Daddy would tell Mother he could sense that God blessed in more profound ways when she was at his side, and others who were nearby tended to agree. Daddy had another reason for going to the jail every week. He had someone counting on him to be there—an inmate called "Slim." Slim would say to him every time, "See you next week, Mr. Corey." And Daddy would reply, "Lord willing, I will be here."

By the fall of 1949, Slim had been in jail for nearly a year. At first he had stayed out of sight when my parents were having services. Then he began to join in. Sometimes he would be ready with the Bible open to the passage Daddy planned to read even though he'd not been told ahead of time. Week by week, Slim began to tell Daddy of his own history—a history in which he had started out with Christian parents, but had chosen a trail of evil choices. Ultimately Slim had become a ringleader of the Port Angeles underworld, for which he had been thrown in jail. After God grabbed his attention, Slim began to talk about the Lord to other inmates and to help Daddy in the services.[78]

One day he told my father, "I am sick and will not live very long in this place. To date, they haven't charged me with any crime and I've never been brought to trial. Is there anything you can do to help?"

Daddy was pondering the request when he saw Judge Phillips on the street. He called out to him. Phillips turned and frowned. "Oh, it's you."

"Judge," my father said, "It seems like an odd thing to jurisprudence for a man to be in jail without charge or trial for sixteen months."

"Oh, you mean Slim. You have no idea what this man has done in our town for the past twenty years."

Daddy didn't tell the judge what he knew, but said, "Slim has changed his life. He has trusted in Christ and is not the man he used to be."

The judge said no more and turned away. However, the following week, Slim was paroled to the Port Angeles Rest Home. Soon the man influenced events in his new living quarters. When Daddy found him there, Slim said, "The people here need the message you brought to the jail. Can you come for services?"

Daddy sensed those words had come from God. So he asked the manager if he could hold a chapel. She replied, "These people are senile. You'd just be wasting your time."

"But," Daddy countered, "The Bible says we are to 'comfort the feeble-minded and help the weak.'"

My parents began services the next Sunday. When it was getting close to Christmas, Mother had me practice a song so I could sing at the Rest Home. The place smelled funny, sort of like the boys' mattresses at home that had been wet too many times. I had never seen so many old people, so many crippled in wheelchairs, or so many ladies in uniforms. The people who could get to the social room came, leaning on canes, walkers, or the arms of their nurses. Mother played carols on the grand piano and Daddy read the Christmas story. I sang all three verses of "Silent Night" with my hands folded in front of me, just like my big sisters. The people bobbed their heads, like elderly folks do, and hummed along. My heart was happy that I had helped them smile.

After the meeting, we went to visit people who had to stay in their beds. Mother held the hand of one lady with messy brown hair and spoke to her. The woman made groaning noises but could not talk. Mother told me later that the lady was only forty years old, but she was sick in a way that she could not move or speak. She had small children but could not care for them, and her husband couldn't care for her. I was sad for those little kids and I was sad for the sick lady.

Slim didn't live long after that, but Daddy and Mother went back to the Rest Home every possible Sunday *forever-and-ever-amen.*[79]

We had a full house for Christmas. The Bergs brought Marilyn from Prairie, and John McLennan came with Virginia. When our sisters arrived, Mother sent Eddie Enser home to spend Christmas with his parents, but said he could come back in January for school. We had a tree, gifts, food, and non-stop music. The piano was rocking all the time and the accordion went from one set of hands to another. John McLennan played his baritone horn and sang. All of us sang. We were one glorious family choir—greatly enhanced by the booming voice of John McLennan.

On December 27, Daddy turned 45. The guests made a big deal of the event. In the living room we set up the dining table with the pull-out ends and used our best tablecloth because Marilyn insisted. There were gifts for Daddy and a decorated cake. In earlier years, my father hadn't wanted us to celebrate his birthday. He would say, "We are supposed to 'honor God, not man.'"

But these guests wouldn't be put off, so Daddy joined in the festivities. He laughed at the bantering of Art Berg and John McLennan. We were dumfounded that Virginia's fiancé could get away with teasing Daddy, and even more shocked to see our father having fun with it. For us, teasing Daddy would have been disrespectful, but—as the party went on—we laughed respectfully at the jokes by others.

John and Virginia smooched even more than the last visit, and I overheard Mother agree that marriage was probably a good idea, considering all the kissing that was going on. John amened the comment and began calling her Mother Corey. The fact is: John had quit school to get a job with the plan for marriage in mind. He talked Virginia into doing the same, even though she was close to the end of the semester and would lose her credits. He explained, "Once we're married, you won't need to work, and your schooling will be a waste of time and money."

John headed back to Alberta where he could legally work, and Virginia got a job babysitting for the owners of Birney's Restaurant in Port Angeles. Once our sisters and all the other guests had left, Mother said to Daddy, "I suppose Virginia is too young to get married, but perhaps it is best. John is talented and committed to serving the Lord. I trust they will be happy, and that their marriage will weather the storms that are sure to come."

And Mother wasn't talking about the weather that would hit us a few days later.

The parents and nine offspring

CHAPTER SEVENTEEN
The Storm
(1950)

The decade began with a winter storm for the record books. It poured for days. Then, on January 12, the temperature dropped and snow began to fall. By the early hours of the next day, the storm had turned into a gale-whipped blizzard. Snow piled against the Farmhouse in drifts and swirled around the outbuildings. On the 14th, we ventured outside to play Fox and Geese and to bury ourselves in the banks. Daddy went with us bringing the dishpan for a sled. The steep snow-and-ice-packed hill made for a wild ride. If you caught it just so, you could fly clear across the bridge and into the field. If you didn't get it right, you could sail into a bank or roll head over heels most of the way to the bridge. We ruined Mother's dishpan, but it was worth it. Daddy said he would get her a new one and maybe next year we could get a toboggan.

But when the temperature kept dropping, Mother told us we had to stay in. We let in too much cold air when we opened the door, she said, and she couldn't keep the fires warm enough to dry our soggy mittens and coats.

School was closed for days. Mother found the chaos of cooped-up kids worse than the cold, so she sent us out and told us to stay. We tried to skate on the solid pond, taking turns with one pair of ice skates that we screwed onto our shoes. After the rest gave up and went to slide down the hill on a piece of cardboard, I kept at it. Halfway across the pond, my legs went one way and I went the other. When I came to, a knob stuck out on the back of my head and stars swirled across my vision. I lay there for at least ten minutes wondering if I should call for help, but I was used to looking after myself, so I went home. My head ached for two days.

A quick thaw followed by a rapid return to record sub-zero temperatures added to the dangers at home and throughout the region. Trees fell, pipes split, cars crashed, boats sunk, power lines snapped, and woodpiles disappeared. People died in accidents and animals died of exposure.

In February, the weather warmed up in a hurry—too much of a hurry. One morning we woke to find the pump not functioning and the creek dark gray. It swirled with logs, branches, and pieces of stumps. The debris was being sucked up tight against the culverts, and the muddy water began to back up. We watched as a lake grew, first filling the creek channel, then covering the flat area and lifting our bridge from its mooring. Water climbed the highway wall until it neared the blacktop. I said, "It reminds me of the Elwha dam, one side full of water and the other just a bare wall with bubbles at the bottom."

Phillip and I could see the water seeping out of beaver holes in the dirt and rock wall of the dam. David, John and Eddie came by to watch for a while.

They turned to go and David said, "You'd better not get too close, the whole thing could go."

We stuck close by, because that's what we were waiting for. Phillip said, "Just imagine all the water gushing through, knocking the trees out and flooding the Sands' property."

I said, "Just imagine what it would look like if a car was driving across when it went."

We even contemplated sitting in the middle of the trestle where the view would be panoramic, then double-vetoed that idea, commenting that the bursting dam might even knock out the entire rail system.

Before those apocalyptic events could transpire, the county road crew came with equipment. From their trucks, they sank cables connected to large pincher-type hooks. They tried to grab the intertwined stumps, branches, and alder trees, but had to give up. The next morning, the guys were back—just as we had to go to school. In the afternoon, we jumped off the bus and ran for the site, groaning to see culverts on both sides, and the creek flowing through at full speed. A log pile remained near the entrance of the culverts, the mouth of the corrugated pipe was twisted, and grungy gray muck covered the field—there would be no destructive deluge as we'd hoped to witness.

We learned that the engineers had brought in an explosives expert. From the lower end of the largest culvert, he had crept through the tunnel carrying an armload of dynamite. Phillip and I carped about him doing the job while we weren't there to watch. But Phillip and the older boys carped even more when the county workers came again and lowered the culverts, ruining the spawning ponds that the trout used.

The water pumps—ours and the Tieches'—had been destroyed. Mr. Tieche offered to help us replace our pump, and we offered to help him redo the pipes to his place. In his machine shop, he built our new pump entirely of solid brass and assured Daddy that no future flood would destroy his piece of handiwork.

In the Johnsons' gully above our land, the flood did even more damage. An avalanche of logs, stumps, and megatons of water roared down the upper creek valley, stripping trees off the banks and scraping a clean, deep swath through the ravine. The impact would have been worse on that land and ours if the largest logs had not tangled together into a crisscross logjam that slowed the surge. Still, the torrent that came past the pile knocked out their two crossings. The upper crossing—due west of their barn—had been constructed of old growth cedar logs laid in such a way that they formed an enormous natural culvert, big enough for the creek at its normal winter volume to flow unabated, and tall enough in the summer for adults to walk beneath. On top of this wood structure the Johnsons had built a dirt fill at least ten feet deep, across which they could drive their tractor. The flood completely destroyed this fill and tangled the cedar logs together with alder trees and stumps that had washed down through the gully.

The Johnson's other lost crossing was the footbridge to our side of the gully. We told the Johnsons we would rebuild that simple structure with a flat-top log and attached handrail. Their contributions in return came almost in the form of multiplication tables. They promised us the entire seven-acre field of hay located on the west side of the gulch where their fill had been destroyed. They gave us half a litter of recently weaned pigs to fatten with our oversupply of milk—since we had two fresh cows again. They also helped us get a contract with the Port Angeles Creamery to sell the cream. That led us to get a separator—a machine that by centrifugal force sent the cream out one spout and the skim milk out another. Daddy installed the galvanized contraption in the cold room off the kitchen, and we gave the space a new title: The Separator Room. The ones in the family with strong, steady arms were given the job of cranking the handle. We drank the skim milk and Daddy took the cream can to the highway for pick up. My job was to wash the milk and cream from a sink full of machine parts and little discs every time it was used. "If you don't wash off every speck," Mother warned, "The cream will sour, the creamery won't accept it, and we'll not get paid."

For many upcoming years, the few dollars we received each week helped Daddy buy grain for the cows and Mother buy groceries, which came to include white margarine—because we didn't make butter any more.

The Johnsons also helped us revolutionize our bread-making operations. They demonstrated their power-driven grinder that, with the flip of a switch, could crush wheat into flour in mere seconds. When Daddy checked on the cost of a grinder for us, he could only afford an $8.00 hand grinder from the catalog. We had to twist the red handle for hours to grind enough wheat for a batch of bread. Mother said, and even Daddy agreed, "This is too hard and takes too much time."

So Daddy took the motor and geared transmission from the three-plunger washing machine that had once fascinated David in the Grange House, and attached them to the hand grinder. He set it up in the Separator Room across from the cream machine. With the electric motor, our hand grinder became a whole new electrified wonder. Mother sifted out the coarse grain for the breakfast mush we ate daily. From the finer flour, she baked seven loaves of whole wheat bread at least twice a week, along with a batch of cinnamon rolls for the weekend. On baking day, the aroma reached us by the time we were halfway up the path from the school bus. We would rush into the house and argue over who would score the first hot crust sliced from the end of a loaf.

Meanwhile, anticipation of harvesting the Johnson hayfield was building. It would be a few months yet, but Daddy said, "We will have to build an addition to the barn."

Thirteen-year-old David disagreed. "But Dad, that would be terrible! We already have too many lean-tos and sheds that don't hold much. If we put on another storage space, there still won't be enough room for all that hay."

He paused and took a deep breath. "Why don't we construct a *real* barn?"

Daddy stopped in his tracks. "And how will we do that?"

"We can build a pole barn using skinned logs and cedar shakes."

Like father, like son. The plan was set. We would be able to start after school was out.

David was relieved that the job could hold off until summer vacation. He and Eddie were engaged in a rivalry quite different from the cow pie or hardball tosses. In this contest both of them were stars. The two were competing in marbles and helping each other improve. David hadn't played much since the infamous disposal of his set in the Grange House toilet, but Joyce was having a marble-playing tournament, and his passion for the sport was rekindled. The two boys practiced together and took their skills to the event. Eddie placed second and David got first place. Daddy then let them go to the regional championship, where Eddie placed third and David won second, earning himself a Radio Flyer Red Wagon. We all strutted proud as penguins, not only that our brother and Eddie were so talented, but that they were willing to teach us a couple of their best shots and share with us a few of their marble earnings—not to mention, that we younger kids fit in the wagon and David didn't.

Immediately after the marble victories, the school year ended and Eddie Enser went home. He had fit in well with the family, even with all our crowded craziness. David didn't have time to dwell on the loss of his sidekick, except to lament that Eddie wasn't available to help with the summer pole-barn project that loomed.

Meanwhile, Virginia announced that John McLennan had everything arranged for a wedding. The two had changed their minds a few times about when and where, but now their decision was final. They would be married on June 16, in Red Deer, Alberta, not far from Prairie—where Marilyn would graduate from high school just in time to be Maid of Honor.

Aunt Eleanor immediately wrote that the wedding could not happen without the Mother of the Bride present. And she tucked into the envelope $50.00, enough for Mother to ride the bus with her firstborn. Daddy didn't like the idea of Mother going without him, so he packed his grip and headed out the same day, saying, "I will meet up with you at the bus station in Spokane."

Daddy traveled his usual way, never holding up his thumb but believing God would tell someone to offer him a lift. He caught a ride to Tacoma and called on Art Berg. He was not surprised that Art just happened to be going to Spokane and would take him to the bus station. Meanwhile, Mother and Virginia rode a Greyhound to Seattle and spent the night at the elegant home of Laverne Nielsen. When the two arrived in Spokane, Daddy was waiting. Mother handed to him an envelope from Laverne who had said to her, "Arthur needs to travel on the bus with you to the wedding."

Daddy was not surprised by Laverne's donation, nor was he surprised that it was large enough to cover the cost of his ticket and pay for a pair of shoes to replace the ones with holes in the soles. He had believed God for both.

Not all aspects of the preparation were going as smoothly, however. Virginia was marrying John against his mother's wishes, and Mrs. McLennan wore a frosty face. Virginia found out why when she received a letter that had first gone to the Farmhouse before Elizabeth had forwarded it back to Virginia at Three Hills. The return address showed Mr. and Mrs. Arpad McLennan.

Dear Virginia,
John will not be put off from this plan to be married. I ask that you
call off the wedding. We always hoped for a daughter, but want
John to finish his schooling first and go to the mission field.
                    Sincerely in our Lord, Mrs. A McLennan[80]

Nothing was said about the letter, but later Virginia learned that her unhappy mother-in-law-to-be had once replaced her picture in John's wallet with a picture of a needy African.

When the day arrived, however, John's parents—wearing appropriate faces—sat on the front row. The Mother of the Bride, looking every bit the part with her handkerchief in hand, sat near Uncle Emil, Aunt Hazel, and Cousin Don. Marilyn wore an aqua green dress Mother had sewn, and a white hat and sandals that Gin had purchased for her. Ken Pendergast, the Best Man, was ready to walk Marilyn down the aisle on his arm, but Daddy told him not to. He quoted the verse—the same one he used when there was talk of dancing—"It is good for a man not to touch a woman."

Virginia, dressed in a navy blue suit, a lacy hat, and John's $12 corsage, walked down the aisle. Next to her, strutted Daddy, looking dapper in his only good suit and brand new shoes.

An hour later the wedding was over. In the handshakes and hugs that followed, Mother welcomed John into the family, "God bless you and give you and Virginia a good life together."

Cousin Don and his cohorts tied cans and streamers to the tailgate of the get-away car. Our first sister and her new husband rattled off to their honeymoon.

Daddy, Mother, and Marilyn left after the wedding and rode the bus the rest of the day and through the night, as far as Ellensburg, Washington. They stopped to visit Aunt Vera, Uncle Harold, and a couple of our cousins.[81] Mother was anxious to get home to Elizabeth and the youngsters, but agreed to take time for plane rides in the private plane that several of Uncle Harold's family knew how to fly. She said she could understand how much Marilyn wanted to get a plane ride for the first time.

Back at home, sixteen-year-old Elizabeth said she was the "Wreck of the Hesperus" looking after the household and six of her siblings, ages three to thirteen. Her biggest fear had been that one of us would get hurt, or there would be an emergency and she wouldn't know how to get help. That hadn't happened, but she still found herself frazzled and fidgety for the return of Mother.

Elizabeth didn't enjoy the pressure of being in charge, but word of her skills as a nanny had traveled. Mrs. Harper of the Harper Funeral Home in Port Angeles came to the house to ask if Elizabeth could live with them and watch their children. Elizabeth said, "That should be easy compared to this commotion of kids."

It must not have been easy. She only worked there a couple of weeks before she quit and came home to help her brothers and father with the pole barn, which was occupying them full-time. Elizabeth took her turn with the draw knife to pull bark off the poles and helped put together the frame. She gave a hand to shake splitting after Daddy and the boys had cut the lengths from cedar logs that had lain in the woods for decades. For the shake-splitting task, one of the crew held the wooden handle of a fro—a flat wide blade—while another banged it with a wooden mallet fashioned from a section of pole. When the shake began to crack apart, they slid the blade down the grain until the piece split off. The straightest pieces without knotholes were stacked for the roof, while the scrubbier shakes would go on the sides, and the scraps would be turned into kindling.

Penny and her brother Gary arrived while the roof on the barn was being finished. Penny was ready to play, so a bunch of us headed off to the creek. The muck from the spring flood was everywhere. Our clay sculptures kept falling apart, so we slid down the slippery bank into the creek. We caught trout and gathered craw daddies—that's what we called the smallest crayfish. Phillip built a fire and roasted the catch. Penny said, "No crawdads for me. They stink."

Thanks to Penny, I was able to defer also, without being called a "yellow-belly."

Penny and I sat on the Johnson's fence—a homestead-era type fence that was fashioned of hand-hewn rails, notched and stacked in a zigzag pattern that didn't require nails or spikes. We kept our eyes alert for the Johnson's pink-nosed bull that was especially mean, while I taught her about the rest of farm animals. I explained that we took our cows to visit the Nyholms' bull so they would have calves in the spring and told her about my sisters' experience in the Nyholms' pasture. "Bulls don't like people, especially girls," I said. "They just like cows, especially Daisy. Only we don't have her anymore."

We sat in the trees and I taught her about the woods and the wild animals. I explained that cougars sounded like babies crying. Later, we heard that yowling in the night and were too petrified to go to the toilet under the pitch dark trees. So I showed her how I'd made my own toilet place close to the corner of the Farmhouse where no one could see me. I started to tell her how one terrifying winter night I'd had to go Number Two so bad, I had messed my underpants. But I changed the subject so Penny wouldn't know what a coward I really was . . . at least about having to go to the toilet in the woods.

Once when we sat a long time in the corner where Grauel Road met the highway I told Penny about my other fear—that I was afraid of smashed-raspberry cars shaped like upside-down tubs. I even urged her to duck out of sight when one came around the corner. She wanted to know why, so I told her about diving in the ditch when David and I were carrying boards. I said, "But that's not the only fright I got. Sometime after that, maybe a year or two, the boys and I went to the end of the driveway. It was starting to get dark and we were close to the bus-waiting shed, when one of those cars turned into our road."

I stopped the story to pick a clover and began to suck on its spikes. She urged, "Go on. What happened?"

"Well, David said, 'Shh', so we stood still. Two men with guns got out of the car. One of my brothers—I don't know which one—said, 'Run.' So David picked up Merton and they all took off like maniacs leaving me way behind. I bawled to Mother that they ran away and I couldn't keep up. And David said the men were hunters and I was silly to cry."

As I talked about that phobia, I got an idea and said to Penny, "I'm tired of my chicken heart. I think if I watch a long time and count as many bloody-red cars as I can, I'll get done with that fear."

After that, with her by my side, we'd watch for cars and I didn't dive for cover. Though I admit, for the next few years—when I was by myself—I still felt the heat of fear rising inside.

We were headed back from practicing my bravery with cars when we saw a torch of fire shooting towards the sky. It looked close to the house—perhaps it was the house! Then we saw Phillip, Merton, and Gary come running toward us. "There's a fire by the toilet and we can't put it out!"

The fire was very close to the newly constructed toilet—our first one with a side for boys and a side for girls, and two holes in each compartment. Just a few feet away, a tall rotted cedar stump was ablaze, the fire shooting high in the air. All of us grabbed buckets, but we couldn't even get close enough to throw water at the inferno. Mother saw us and joined in. We dumped water onto the toilet, onto the woodshed, and around the edges of the stump to keep the flames from spreading. Then one of the neighbors who'd noticed the sparks and smoke came by to see if we'd lost our house, and he joined in the water brigade. Eventually, the blaze finished off most of the dry cedar, and died down enough that we could douse the coals. However, embers kept reigniting the needles under the trees and Mother said the toilet and wood shed were still in danger. If those ignited, the trees would go up in flames and the house would catch on fire. So the boys were not permitted to leave the scene, at least not until supper. At the table, Phillip told Mother—whether true or not, "It was Gary who lit the match when we were clearing brush."

Mother said he and Merton were equally to blame. She told Gary not to worry, that the fire was out and no damage was done. But Daddy informed the boys that they would have to sit by the toilet all night with containers of water to be sure no flames started up again.

The three-some set up camp and prepared for the long night. But, first, they commiserated on the loss of the stump. It had been the site of many adventures, the most recent being the experiment of eating raw eggs. Gary had been the instigator of that event, telling Phillip he'd heard that people sometimes ate raw eggs so they would grow bigger and stronger than everyone else. Gary had tucked a dare into his description—a dare which Phillip had no choice but to meet. So they had snuck into the hen house and taken two freshly laid eggs to the stump. Out of sight, they cracked open the eggs—each holding off as long as possible. They sucked out the yellow part first. It wasn't too bad, since it was like soft-boiled egg. But the white was revolting. Phillip swallowed and gagged, put his hand over his belly and swallowed again. He didn't dare look over at Gary for fear he'd never get the rest down, and what was down would come up. After both egg-eaters had finalized the bet, they ran for a water faucet to rinse the mouth and top off the slime in their stomachs. Phillip didn't actually say it to his two fire-guarding cohorts, but thought to himself, *Well, there's one good thing about the stump being gone, I won't have to try that experiment again.*

At midnight, Phillip was still musing on these things and trying to find a comfortable spot near the toilet, when Daddy came to tell the boys they could return to their beds.

The next day, Daddy reminded all of us fire was not something to play with. Mother changed the subject to remind all of us our little fire was nothing compared to the flames of warfare swelling in other continents. There was conflict escalating in Korea, and troops—including our uncles and cousins who were career pilots and commanders—were being sent. And Mother once again brought to our attention we should thank God the draft wouldn't call Daddy who was too old—more than 36—or the boys who were too young—less than 18½ years.

In spite of the uncertainty in the world and such unexpected events as stump fires, life on our land didn't let up. It was a full time job for everyone. The Johnson's seven-acre field—the one they'd *loaned* to us for the year because the flood had destroyed their fill—was ready to harvest. We could get to it by way of the Phillips Road with just a little repair to the split-cedar plank bridge that covered a smaller stream. Someone—maybe Harold Baar or Walter Johnson whose farms were on the west side—had cut the field for us, and then we did the rest.

Penny and I weren't much help, except to ride on top of the loads, clinging to a pitchfork during the bumpy ride along rutted roads back to the barn. We weren't allowed to pitch the hay into the barn since there were no walls yet. David said, "You'll waste too much if you throw it out the sides—and you'll just be in the way."

During the haying, the Bergs came from Tacoma and took Marilyn to be nanny to their three daughters and work in berry fields nearby. After the summer she would begin attending Nurses' School. We didn't see her again for months. It was as if she had gone back to Alberta, though she was just a few hours from home.

After the rest finished the haying, Daddy told us we couldn't play or even sleep in the barn until walls were built high enough. "Besides," he said, "the hay is not as good for the animals if you are in there too much."

Penny wanted to go in the hay when Daddy and the boys were in the woods and wouldn't see us. I told her we'd better not, but then we did it, anyway. We'd been in the barn for a half hour when my conscience got the best of me and she went to ask Daddy for special permission. Meantime, I crawled to the window and jumped out. "Yow," I yelled, and then wailed like a banshee until helpers came running from the house and the woods. I had sliced off the end of my second toe on the scythe, which was lying unsecured beneath the barn. Before long I was situated on the porch davenport with my bandaged foot elevated on the armrest. I kept on whining—I liked the sympathy I got—until Mother said, "You can be quiet now. It'll get better."

Penny sat on the couch with me. She said she had seen enough real blood that we didn't need to make any more pretend blood out of blackberry juice for our doctoring practice. Phillip went to the barn to retrieve the tip of my toe. He showed me the find and—reminiscent of what his sister Marilyn had once said to him—suggested, "If you like, we can roast it for dinner."

That reminded me how sad Marilyn would be that she had missed out on my medical emergency. Same as the time she had missed out when Elizabeth got a crochet hook stuck more than an inch into her leg, and *that* injury was really gross, even though it didn't bleed as much as my cut-off toe.

So through all of these events, and fears, and accidents, Penny was my second self. No one in the entire world knew as much about me as she did. I could hardly bear to tell her good-bye when she went back home and left me with *no one* to talk to.

Our lives, whether healthy or injured, or blessed by friends, were intertwined with the lives of all the creatures on our Old-MacDonald-had-a-Farm. Along with the fattening pigs, there were numerous chickens and their baby chicks, two ducks, two cows, a few rabbits, a calf, and way too many cats—probably double the number needed to control the mice. One cat in particular irritated Mother because it liked to eat baby chicks, and she gave David permission to use his .22 on it.

Until that challenge, David had only shot grouse and a few squirrels. He had hunted for the mountain beavers that gnawed on the fruit trees and left holes in the ground, but they never showed up when he had the gun in hand. Rising to the challenge, he watched for the cat and saw it run under the little barn. Lying down on his stomach, he peered between the foundation beams. Two yellow eyes shone back at him, and David fired. Out from the other side of the barn zipped the cat Mother had designated for destruction, while beneath the barn was crumpled the body of a cat all of us liked.

Another time, one of the cats got its tail caught in the gears under the washing machine on the porch. When we freed it, every speck of fur had been removed from the tail. The poor feline looked like a naked-tail rat for the rest of its life, which wasn't very long.

We loved our dogs too. Dogs were our companions and friends. We felt responsible to feed them, and they felt responsible to guard us. It was a dreadful day when Tiglathpileser took his guard duties beyond the acceptable limits. John's neighborhood friend liked to tease Tig with sticks or jump out to spook him. One morning, this boy crept around the corner and startled the sleeping dog. Tig jumped up, snarled, and grabbed his arm. David yelled and tried to pull him off. But, John, without a moment's thought, grabbed a baseball bat and whacked Tig on the back. Tig yelped and fled, as did the neighbor boy, clutching his bleeding arm.

Daddy was away, but the boys knew he would say we could not keep a dog that bit anyone. So they led Tig to Walter Johnson's place and asked him to shoot our pet. Phillip mourned a long time, "Tig was such a buddy. When John or I would call, he would run up side of the eight-foot stump and we would reach over to pull him up the rest of the way. He knew how to climb ladders too, and he never left our sides when we were working or playing. He was the best friend ever."

I agreed, but I couldn't even say so. My eyes were spilling over when I thought how I would never be able to hug Tig's neck and feel his wet tongue kissing my face; how I would never feel him sit on my muddy bare feet and warm them up.

After Daddy returned home, he went to see the neighbors whose boy had been bitten. They had taken the kid to the doctor and there were medical bills to be paid. We had no money to give, but Daddy said we had to make it right. So he took them our calf—the one that was to be our beef for the next year. To David it seemed wrong, not right. We had lost our dog because a boy teased him, and then we lost our calf to people who didn't need it and wouldn't care for it. No, it was definitely not right.

In the midst of our misery, we were cheered up twice. First we got a little dog named Kim. He would never make up for the loss of Tig, but his puppy dances helped us remember how to smile. Then Mother began to read a letter from Naoma. She'd not read more than a sentence when her hand went up. She looked toward the ceiling, and said to herself—as well as to any within hearing—"We are going to have a car!"

Naoma's letter explained that she had turned in her 1931 Chevrolet to the dealer as a down payment on a new car. On her way home—in an automobile that didn't need cranking to start and had a functional heater—a thought had banged her in the head. *Here I have a new car and Margaret doesn't have any at all.* So she'd returned to the dealer and bought her former Chevrolet back, and would Arthur please come and get it?

The big black touring car with the spare tire attached to the side arrived at our place. Naoma had filled it with a load of items she thought Margaret could use: Shoes, household goods and even a coat labeled for Mrs. Johnson who was stout like Naoma, not thin like Mother. Mother wrote a postcard to thank Naoma for "Chevvy," the name she gave her special gift.

> Dear Naoma,
> Chevvy made her first trip in for a jail service and several calls (to see people). It was wonderful! And I believe the story of Chevvy brought a blessing to several as we told it. Arthur and Dave have a heater installed now—one we had. Chevvy has a place of honor on the back porch until we can build a shelter. I have been looking over shoes that you sent and I can wear all but one pair. Where to put all my goods!! Thanks for everything– M. PS. Neighbor did appreciate the coat.[82]

So many changes for us came with a car to call our own! It had been six years since Daddy sold the Whippet for fifty dollars, and five years since we had discarded the car Mother said needed to be dumped at the junkyard. During our no-car years we had traveled only by bus, with friends, or in loaners. With Chevvy we could go places and do things without depending on others—and that's what we did. One of Chevvy's first safaris was to the beach to gather driftwood planks. The men needed the lumber to build the floor of the cow stanchions and the manure trough. The planks did not fit in Chevvy, so Daddy and David tied them onto the outside with ropes that we held tight through the windows. The barn floor of salt-water preserved planks was made to last, though there were complaints that the crooks, cracks and warps made mucking out the manure the worst barn job to be assigned.

There was another truly wonderful change Chevvy brought into our lives. Instead of having our own Sunday meeting, we began to attend Sunday school at the home of Virginia and Fred Pennoyer in Port Angeles. With a car of our own, we could all go at the same time—all nine of us stacked on top of each other or on the floor behind the second seat. It was an outing we younger ones anticipated all week long. There would be other families there, but most important to me were the girls my age, Lillian and Joann Pennoyer, and their baby brother Douglas. Going to church in some place other than our living room, was a new experience for me.

When we couldn't get there—either because Daddy was gone or because Chevvy was having a bad day—it was heart breaking. On one such occasion we got as far as the steep, switch-back hill on the east side of the single-lane Elwha Bridge when she quit. Daddy coasted her back by inches to park at a passing corner on the cliff side of the road. He kept cranking, hoping the car would start. Phillip and I looked over the side of the bank. It was straight down—almost as far as we could see—to the rocks and river below. By the time Daddy got the car started, Phillip's knees were shaking from fear of falling, and I was fretting that we would arrive too late. Which we did.

Chevvy would require frequent repairs, but she was a car, and she was ours.

Arthur Margaret and Chevvy 1950

CHAPTER EIGHTEEN
The Education
(Fall 1950)

After the arrival of Chevvy we were back in school. Phillip and I were both in third grade. Mrs. Tripp, our teacher in the first and second grades, had asked Mother in the spring if it was all right to skip me ahead, since I had already completed the books for both grades.

Phillip was used to me in the same room doing the same assignments, but with me jumping ahead to his grade, his deal was even worse than Marilyn's had been when Elizabeth skipped a grade. I would be in the same room every year, not just alternate years. But worse for Phillip—worse than having me in the same class—was having Mrs. Tripp again. Both of us had been looking forward to a new teacher, but that lady had switched classrooms too, and was now teaching third and fourth. We kidded that she liked us so much that she followed us. We said we didn't like her so much. I didn't like her because she wouldn't let me talk, and Phillip didn't like her because she wouldn't let him goof around.

As the year got underway Phillip became intrigued by her effort to teach us how to write in cursive. He was left handed so the writing lessons didn't do him any good at all, just gave him fodder for foolishness. Mrs. Tripp told us to watch how she moved her arms at the blackboard. She said, "It's important to make smooth, watery letters that flow into rippling words. You have to roooooll your arms like this."

As she *rolled* her ample arms, the flabby skin underneath flapped back and forth like the wings of a blue heron attempting to get airborne from our creek. When Mrs. Tripp's back was turned, Phillip copied her movement in the air. His arms had no extra skin, but the rest of the class snickered approval of his covert demonstration.

If Phillip was entertained by her, though, I was tormented. Mrs. Tripp asked questions, and I couldn't seem to help blurting out the answers. My mouth would open and words fly out—unbidden, unrehearsed, and unwelcomed. I wasn't used to raising my hand at home—not with so many voices going at once—but the teacher said I needed to at school. It wasn't too long before I knew Mrs. Tripp decided I would be her go-to object lesson for the rest of the class. The minute I spoke out of turn, she stomped back to my desk with a strip of adhesive tape—the kind used to wrap ankle injuries. Then, until recess that day, I had to sit in my desk with my mouth taped shut. Since the tape was stuck to my lips, I had to bite my tongue instead, or else risk multiplying my mortification by crying in front of two whole classes *and* my brother. It was a lesson I learned early that year, so I never got the adhesive treatment again.

On the other hand, my sister Elizabeth never got in trouble like the boys and me—not at home or at school. This year, Elizabeth was a senior in high school. She was such an angel that Daddy had trusted her to go to events the previous year even though she was only fifteen. So, when her friends, including Vern, a boy she liked, urged her to get permission to go with them to a Halloween party, she asked Daddy. She wasn't keen on the party, but didn't want to be somewhere else if Vern was there. She knew how that boy flirted with every other girl when she wasn't around. This time Daddy said no. "Halloween honors evil. It's not something to which we give tribute."

Afterwards, Elizabeth was relieved she had not gone. Policemen came to school. One by one, guys who had been at the party were called into the principal's office and questioned. The police didn't leave until they found out who had barricaded the highway during the night with a stack of railroad ties. Elizabeth forgot her jealousy about Vern, saying to herself, "I would have died of fright if they'd called me in."

It was the season to butcher our pigs. Daddy made his appearance after the shooting, in time to help dip the animals in the 55-gallon drum of steaming water—hot enough to loosen the hair, but not hot enough to cook the meat. Mother wasn't interested in the blood or the head parts, but she asked us to save the fat for her to render into lard. Mr. Johnson said we could cure ham and bacon in his smokehouse, as long as the boys would help to keep the fires smoldering.

Trips back and forth to their farm were common, so this was no hardship to any of us. However, on one tour of duty, a calamity confronted John. Mr. Johnson took him to see their new brood of puppies. John was hesitant, since their fierce, female guard dog was not tied up. All of us knew better than to go in the yard if *that* dog was loose. John was with Mr. Johnson, however, so he thought he would be safe. Moments later, the creature raced at high speed from across the field. She let out a ferocious growl and lit into the boy's leg. Mr. Johnson grabbed John's arms and swung him and the dog in a circle until the dog let go. The injured lad felt the pain of the deep wounds, but even more the embarrassment that in his fright he'd wet his pants.

John thought the Johnsons would have to kill their mean dog, like we'd had to do with Tig, but they didn't. John fumed, "Where is the eye for an eye, tooth for a tooth?"

What he meant was, "Where is a dog for a dog?"

Winter was beginning to blow in and much of the barn was still open to the weather. There was talk between the boys and Daddy about the need for more cedar logs for shakes, but we'd already used up the ones in our woods. There was our one cedar snag—the one in the "Y" of the creeks—that would have been an excellent source. However, we had no saw big enough to cut it down. Ours was only seven feet and we would have needed at least a twelve-foot old-timers type to work through the base of that snag. One day, we came home from school to see smoke rising from just a shell of the 50-foot-tall icon. "What happened?" David wanted to know.

When the story was told, we learned that Daddy had decided to burn out the rotted middle so it would be easier to saw and pull off the sides for shakes. Merton, at only five might have wanted to stop his father, but by then it was too late.

The fire started with a single match and roared into a sky-high torch. There was nothing Daddy or Merton or Mother could do but watch as the snag went up in flames, leaving only a remnant standing. The barn would have to wait for another year and another source for the rest of its walls.

The wood supply for the household that winter was also wanting, but it could not wait for another year. The job of cutting would fall to David. Marilyn wasn't around, Elizabeth wasn't as tough, and John was temperamental. David, as per usual, was thinking . . . and thinking . . . and thinking of ways to facilitate that chore. He had seen neighbors use a powered buzz saw to cut their firewood in a fraction of the time it took us. Their buzz saws zipped trees into blocks, while we labored for days and weeks with a hand-pulled crosscut saw. *Here we are*, he lamented to himself, *in the middle of the twentieth century, using the same technique as the earliest loggers and settlers that came to homestead seventy years ago.*

David was cogitating and ruminating on the value of a buzz saw when an idea emerged. He said to his dad, "We can make a saw out of the Packard."

The two-transmission Packard tractor had been dead of late, so Daddy let the boy continue. "Mr. Tieche would know what to do."

And Mr. Tieche did. In his machine shop he milled a set of flanges to mount on the end of the Packard transmission. Daddy and David attached a circular blade to the flanges. They set a carriage on rollers so one *man* could push the wood toward the blade. On the other side of the blade, his helper would reach over the side frame into the part where the cab had once been, to lift off the 16-inch block. The invention was as dangerous as a guillotine, with its wide-open and unguarded 30-inch spinning razor edge. Yet it was an ingenious set-up that sliced off a firewood length in seconds and left smooth, level cuts that were simpler to split. With the buzz saw, the boys finished the woodpile in record time, and even took a supply to the Tieches in gratitude for the machining that had made it possible.

What a shame Marilyn didn't come home during her Christmas break to see the buzz saw spinning through the wood. At almost nineteen, she was going through an impossible time, with her head in a quandary—a confused frame of mind where thoughts, plans, and hopes spun round and round like the blade on the buzz-saw: *What to be? What to do? Where to go?*

Marilyn was broke, she'd had trouble with her father, and she was facing the end of her dream to be a nurse. Everyone with whom she spoke offered a different opinion, and all the options became competing voices in her head. The director of the Seattle nursing school offered her a scholarship to continue, but that required a commitment to stay as an employee for four years afterwards. Marilyn said, "I can't make that promise. I am going to be a missionary."

Should she go with Aunt Ethel Berg—who wasn't really our aunt—to Indonesia? Should she drop out of school and get a job? Should she apply to the Bible Institute of Los Angeles (BIOLA)? Should she move back to the Farmhouse and wait for direction?

On March 23, 1951, Marilyn caught the Greyhound bus for home, and the very next morning she grabbed a pick from the tool shed and put her restless energy to good use excavating a stump. She laid a strip of linoleum—left behind by the Brucks—on the stove end of the kitchen floor. She helped us color Easter eggs, then hid them all around the yard for us to find. She went with Mother and Daddy to the jail and Rest Home to assist with the music. And she started on a diet of eggs and prunes. As per her usual approach—if a little is good, a lot is better—she ate far too many prunes.

BIOLA, like nursing school, was too expensive, so Marilyn decided to get a job. Daddy took her everywhere they could think of to apply for a medical position. On her birthday, she called eleven places to ask for employment. As a last resort, she took a job in Seattle as office secretary to Mr. Pike, a businessman. She knew she could be a successful secretary. She could handle customers in place of patients, a Dictaphone instead of a stethoscope, files instead of a chart, and a typewriter instead of bedpans. But she also knew it was the death of her dream to be a nurse. She moved into an apartment with her friends, Louise and Caroline.

To drown her sadness, Marilyn filled the summer with after-work and late-night activity. She attended two churches, sang in two choirs, led youth ministries, counseled at a Billy Graham Crusade, made party plans, went on picnics with boys she liked and boys she didn't. She answered late night phone calls from the boy she liked best. Caroline was fed up with Marilyn—all that social life when she herself had none. Caroline quit eating the food if my sister cooked it, and left the room when Marilyn came in. Then, one morning, as Marilyn went out the door, the roommate said, "You have to move out. You're not welcome here anymore."

Marilyn sent an urgent message home. Within a couple of days, Daddy and Mother moved her into the home of Mr. and Mrs. Kimble—people Daddy knew from his many travels, and Marilyn had only known from the stories he told. While Daddy helped unload his daughter's belongings he listened with an affirming nod to her many ministry activities. She knew better than to tell him about the boys. Mother just reminded her she really ought to get enough sleep to be able to stay awake on the job.

The basement room at the Kimbles was as warm and inviting as the friends' apartment had turned cold and dismissive. Whatever the Kimbles had, she was free to use. Why, Mr. Kimble once even let her drive his brand new car across the ferries—back when you had to stay on narrow planks from the terminal dock to the ferry deck.

At the same time, Marilyn was beginning to think about returning to Prairie to attend Bible School, and to stay with Virginia who'd said earlier that they had room for her. The nursing school plan had fizzled, the office job was going nowhere, and she needed to get training for missionary service. She'd not be able to run a medical center, but she still could look after orphans in a foreign land. She wrote to ask if Virginia and John just might be able to put her up.

Virginia responded immediately that, of course, John and she would welcome Marilyn. She went on to say, "We'll just be one happy family of four. I was waiting to tell you and Mother that I am going to have a baby close to the time Prairie classes begin in the fall. But now you know."[83]

Soon after that all of us knew we were going to get our first niece or nephew. It was exciting news—news that went right along with other exciting events at our home and school.

At Joyce, David graduated from eighth grade and Elizabeth from high school, both at the top of their classes. Elizabeth gave the valedictory address. She had practiced it for the cows, for the chickens, and for us until we could quote her phrases. At the ceremony, when her name was called, she stepped onto the podium and stood on her tiptoes to peer over the top of the lectern at the audience spread across the gymnasium.

How brave she was and how smart her speech sounded. She talked about how a liability is really an asset, and how we should be thankful for hard things like disabilities. She told the story of two soldiers with amputated arms—one who took his pension and sat on a couch, and the other who said he would not allow his injury to slow him down. She talked about Demosthenes who learned to speak over a mouth full of pebbles, and about John Bunyan who wrote *Pilgrim's Progress* when he was locked up in prison for his religious beliefs. She concluded that we should not be discouraged by the things that happen to us, but that we should let the spirit within us rise above the obstacles.

Immediately afterward, Elizabeth went to Seattle to stay with Marilyn at the Kimbles and to look for a job. It only took two days for her to forget her own speech and to become discouraged by the things that *didn't happen* to her. With no job offers, she returned home to clean cabins at Rosemary Inn on Lake Crescent.

Meanwhile, Mrs. Courtwright invited me to go to Black Lake Bible Camp with her, along with her grandkids, Penny and Gary. I was ecstatic—and frantic with fear that I'd disobey Mother or Daddy and be denied the trip.

Mrs. Courtwright was the nurse at the camp, located near Olympia, Washington, and we settled into a small cabin reserved for the four of us. She brought out a shiny chocolate cake with eight candles to celebrate my birthday and brightly colored skeins of thread to teach Penny and me to embroider. After I had eaten two big slices of cake, I came down with a sore throat and a headache. Mrs. Courtwright gave me a cough drop to suck on and then left to take her grandkids to the chapel. I had seen where she left the Ludens Menthol Cough Drops box, and I helped myself to several during the next hour. They were sweet like candy, which was a rarity in my life. However, the sweetness turned bitter when I burned with fever throughout the night—and burned with the knowledge that my fever was punishment for eating too much cake and sneaking cough drops.

The next morning, Mrs. Courtwright shipped me off to Tacoma with a staff person. Aunt Eleanor met me and took me to the doctor. The nurse, in her stiff white hat and starched dress, held my hand and led me into a narrow room. She lifted me onto the tall bed, stuck a thermometer in my mouth, and told me the doctor would be right in. A window with shades drawn almost to the bottom let a wave of sunlight wash the pale green walls. A big round light bulb seemed to move back and forth above me as I rotated my head.

When the doctor arrived, he took one look in my throat and said one word to the nurse: "Tonsillitis."

Nurse brought in a bottle of liquid sulfa and gave me a big spoonful of mustard-colored goo. I had never tasted anything so foul in my life. It was worse than turnips from Mrs. Johnson's garden, and even worse than the liver Mother sometimes made us eat because she said it was good for us. But I never whined when Grandma or Aunt Eleanor spooned the medicine for me during the next few days. For just the second time in my memory, I was an only child receiving undivided attention. The first time had been when I was about four and was helping Mother in the garden. She had tossed a can out of her way and it hit me in the forehead. That injury didn't hurt as much as the tonsillitis, but Mother had felt so badly that she hugged me on her lap for a very long time, and for once she didn't let Merton shove me off. I never thought much about getting—or not getting—the special attention, since I never really expected it at home. But when it came to that time with Mother and the time with Grandma, it brought a flood of warm feelings that started in my heart and reached down to my toes and up to my eyes.

While recuperating in Tacoma, I visited Naoma and her famous fluffy cat named Malty. I walked across the tall bridges on both sides of Grandma's hill, seeing the bay to the north and the mountains beyond. I sat in front of Grandma's flower garden so Aunt Eleanor could take my picture. Then Daddy came with Chevvy and took me to visit Mr. Skaugseth at the Ruston Smelter and to see Grandma and Grandpa Corey at their house. We stayed only a short while, and that was okay by me, because my nose hurt from Grandpa's cigar smoke and I couldn't think of anything to say to him.

The rest of the summer back at the Farmhouse, I mostly entertained myself. I'd only had one day at camp with Penny and she didn't come to play with me at home. My older sisters were working elsewhere, and the boys were toiling outside. I usually helped Mother with the little kids and did the dishes, but she liked to see me doing needlework and sewing on the treadle machine. I told her she could assign to me the chore of sewing, even though it was fun. Still I was surprised when she didn't call me to do dishes since I was embroidering pansies on tea towels. After that I sewed her an apron from a daisy-decorated flour sack because it was pretty and because she always wore an apron, and

I took two other matching flour sacks to sew myself a nightie, which turned out to be scratchier than I had expected. So it was that with Mother's blessing, the 1911 White Rotary Sewing Machine and I became inseparable as I gained skill as a seamstress of flour-sack clothing.

As much as I loved to sew, I could be pulled away from the sewing corner—especially when the boys called to go scrounging for bottles along the highway. In those days, most people kept their cars clean by tossing their trash in the ditch. All of the bottles, except whiskey and wine bottles, had value. Sometimes Phillip, Merton, and I hauled a fifty-pound gunnysack, just in case we found a stash, and sometimes we walked all the way to Bill Lennon's store and back, or even all the way to the Baars' store at Joyce. Once, Phillip and I found beer bottles with dregs in the bottom and no bugs, so we dared each other to take a drink. Neither of us wanted to, but a dare is a dare. We promised never to tell anyone that we had tasted alcohol in the ditch next to Highway 9A. And we promised we'd never dare each other to do that one again.

We usually turned in our collection at Salt Creek Store. Pop bottles netted two cents each, and beer bottles a penny. I bought black licorice sticks that cost a cent, and Phillip gnawed on a Big Hunk candy bar for which he paid a nickel. He selected a Big Hunk because it measured the largest and lasted the longest. Phillip's goal was to get enough coins to buy some real fishing hooks—you didn't lose so many fish on real hooks—and still have enough money for candy.

Once Phillip came upon a wino's hoard of empties squirreled away in the woods above the Johnsons. Since the store would not take wine bottles, he brought them home to Daddy, who had begun to brew root beer. At first our father didn't want to use the wine bottles—he anticipated they might offend one of the neighbors or cause someone to stumble. However, too many canning jars had exploded in Daddy's quest for the optimum-aged root beer, and Mother was at the point of shutting down his brewing for good. So Daddy overcame his concern-of-conscience and bought corks to fit the bottles. After that there were fewer geysers of fermented yeast, sugar, and extract of Hires Root Beer behind the stove or under the sink. And Daddy could share with us, and even with neighbors, a full stock of root beer from dark green or brown wine bottles.

Most days, though, Phillip and John preferred to focus on fishing instead of bottle collecting. About the time they had several real fishing hooks and were ready to head upstream, Mrs. Johnson came to tell us that she had seen a mother bear with two cubs in their yard and big tracks in the gully. She emphasized, "We have put bear traps in the ravine, so no one should go up our creek."

So the two boys took their fishing gear up Grauel Road beyond the Johnsons, and began fishing downstream until they came to the big logjam just inside Johnsons' fence. On the lower side of the logs they discovered a protected pond glimmering with large silver and pink rainbow trout. It wasn't long before the boys returned home via the road—not chancing an encounter with the Johnsons' guard dog or bear traps—laden with their record catch.

A week or so later, Mrs. Johnson came by to complain that someone had gone on their property and caught the trout she had been feeding since the previous summer. She reminded Mother, "I know I made it clear that the pool was off-limits."

Mother replied, "It couldn't have been my boys; they wouldn't fish where they have been told not to."

When Mother told the boys of the neighbor's visit, John said, "We did catch the fish by the logjam, but Mrs. Johnson never told us we couldn't fish there and she never told us about the pool. She just told us about the bears."

Mother's jaw dropped at the realization that Mrs. Johnson had not been fully honest with her. Perhaps that is why my mother never felt obligated to say anything about the incident to Mrs. Johnson or Daddy. Besides, by then the fish had provided more than one fine meal, and what was the point in bringing it up.

John may not have felt guilty about the fish, but he often felt guilty for other reasons. Once he sat on the bank, looking over the creek and feeling the strongest urge to do something he knew was wrong. At the same time, he knew his father would find out. And, even if Daddy didn't find out, God would see. John had heard his father quote the verse many times, "Be sure your sin will find you out." John's worst temptation—the one he never could manage—was his temper. Every day he was nagged by the plaque on the dining room wall that read, "Be quick to hear, slow to speak, and slow to wrath."

He knew the opposite was true of him, that his wrath was the quickest of all. He knew Mother worried and prayed about him. She'd say, "I wonder what will happen to you if you can't control yourself and get victory over your fits of rage."

Later that summer, John and Phillip went to Black Lake Bible Camp. John carried a load of guilt over his will to do wrong and his quick temper. When the speaker asked if anyone wanted to be sure he was a Christian, John was the first out of his seat, but it was Phillip who would carry the clearest memories of that camp. He was miserable and cried way too much, so one day the counselor offered to help. "It's okay, you can tell me," he promised.

Phillip blurted out, "Every night I wet my bed and I can't help it!"

That evening, when all the rest of the nine to eleven-year-old boys were gathered in the room, the counselor announced to everyone, "The reason Phillip cries is because he pees in his bed."

The boys burst out laughing, then proceeded to tease Phillip about it every time they saw him. He cried all the more. John tried to console his brother by saying it had happened to him at least twice, but that he had hidden the problem and not told anyone. Phillip wished he could have kept it a secret as well.

When camp was over, the boys were prepared to ride back with the man who'd brought them. The nurse found John and said, "Your dad called to say he will pick you and your brother up."

The boys waited and waited. All the other kids and most of the staff left. Phillip was in a state of anguish when Chevvy finally pulled up. Daddy said he had not called the nurse and didn't know where she had gotten that idea. But at least he didn't blame the boys. During the trip home, Phillip and John got to arguing about which of them was more important and had the best abilities. Their father interrupted, "Let another praise you and not your own lips."

So they switched to arguing about who was the worst. "I am worse," Phillip said, "because I don't do my school work and I tell Mother I am too sick to catch the bus."

"No, I am a lot worse," John argued, "because I lose my temper and throw things at people."

After a few minutes of their inventive self-deprecation, Daddy said, "Stop arguing. Don't you know that 'a fool's lips enter into contention, and his mouth calleth for strokes?'"

The boys were quiet the rest of the trip home. Phillip fell asleep in the back and John mulled in his mind if he would ever be able to do or say the right thing—if he would ever be able to act like a Christian.

On September 1, Mrs. Tieche came across the valley to tell Mother that she had received a phone call from John McLennan. She said, "You're a grandmother now. Virginia has had a baby girl."

Mother, thinking how sorry she was not to be at Virginia's side, asked, "Everything went okay?"

Mrs. Tieche nodded, "I'm sure of it. They named her Virginia Star, but will just call her Star."

What a pretty name for my first niece, I thought.

We were still getting used to the idea of our sister having a baby when it was time to head back to school. This year, Merton started first grade, while Phillip and I moved to the upper grade side of the third and fourth classroom. We hoped rowdies such as Billy Hart and Ronnie Krieg (or perhaps the two of us) had worn Mrs. Tripp out the previous year and she'd gone back to first grade where she'd get our little brother. Or, better yet, she'd moved to another school.

However, it was not to be so. Quite the opposite, in fact. She was sturdier, stronger, and stricter than ever. It was said about this teacher, "Some people are tough enough to hunt bear with a switch; Mrs. Tripp is tough enough to hunt bear *without* a switch."

Most of the time Phillip and I got along with each other in the classroom, but sometimes we squabbled. I threatened to tell on him for getting in trouble at school, and he told me to shut up. "Shut up" was not permitted at home, so I said I'd remember his bad language in case it came in handy.

He countered with, "I'll tell on *you* for saying 'darn.'"

"Go ahead," I taunted, "I'll just say that I was talking about darning my socks."

Mrs. Tripp made Phillip sit in the front and me in the back. When that failed to produce studious behavior from him and a quiet mouth from me, she drew a circle on both ends of the blackboard and told us to stand with our noses inside those rings. In third grade I'd nearly cried when punished. This year I danced around the blackboard ring and made noises at Phillip, until the teacher threatened to send me to the principal.

Phillip had his own issues with Mrs. Tripp. She followed the boys to the bathroom and stood just inside the door to keep track of their behavior. When he acted badly there or in the classroom, she picked up her paddle, took a hold of his ear, and hauled him to the cloakroom at the back. Everyone in the class was quiet, listening to hear if the spanking brought forth a cry, but instead Phillip yelped like a wounded animal, "Yip, yip, yike, yap, ow, ow, yip, yip!"

Sometimes the whole scene played to his advantage. When Phillip had behaved for a few days, Mrs. Tripp—perhaps thinking he was turning over a new leaf—let him take the blackboard erasers to the furnace room in the basement for cleaning. Mr. Reeder, the bus driver and janitor, supervised Phillip's use of the buffing machine that took off the chalk powder. Then he let Phillip follow him around the basement and talk. Phillip could think of lots of subjects, and Mr. Reeder never hurried him back to the classroom.

It was Mr. Reeder who, more than once, salvaged a batch of our school pictures from the pile to be burned and sent them home to Mother. The janitor must have known that she could not afford them, and that they would be a treasure. Mother set five of these pictures on the open two-by-four cross pieces and leaned them against the scraggly boards of the Farmhouse. I had my hair in pigtails and the boys showed fresh haircuts, the upside-down bowl type that Daddy did with the hand-powered clippers. But the pictures didn't have frames to keep them in place, and Mother didn't want to pound nails through the photos, so every gust of air that came near, knocked them to the floor. Mother boxed them up, saying. "Someday, when we have a house with finished walls, we will get frames for these."

I tried to imagine what our finished walls would be like. I knew they wouldn't have slivers, torn-off scraps of wallpaper, and nail holes all over the place like those of the Farmhouse. Maybe they would be painted wood like our neighbors' walls, or painted plaster like the walls of our friends in town. Whatever kind came to mind, I could see those pictures hanging in a row with my face next to the faces of my brothers.

Late that September, Daddy drove Elizabeth to Seattle Pacific College where she had been granted a scholarship. For the insecure, anxious teenager, the day turned into an ordeal that undid her, completely erasing all memory of the text of her valedictory speech about not giving up.

The registrar sorted through files and papers. Elizabeth watched as a frown creased the lady's forehead. "I can't find any record of a room for you," she said. "Your papers are here, but there's been a mistake. If you can wait awhile, we'll find you a place to live."

Elizabeth felt the flush of fear flood her face. She had known all along she was not ready for this kind of place—a place where there were so many kids she didn't know, and so many decisions she would have to make by herself. She couldn't—wouldn't—let Daddy leave her there all alone.

"No," Liz said. "I want to go home."

Daddy smiled at her and said, "We'll go see Marilyn."

They drove to the Kimbles, and Elizabeth told her sister what had happened. "I just don't know what I'll do now," she fretted.

Marilyn was quick to suggest an alternate plan—an idea that had been in and out of her mind while she brooded over Elizabeth having a boyfriend she didn't approve of. "You can go to Prairie with me. We'll be in the same classes, only you'll be smarter. We can share the bed at John and Gin's. They won't mind. I *know* they won't."

Elizabeth agreed. Staying with her sisters would be much safer than going off to college on her own. There was no time to write ahead, however, so they decided to make it a surprise to their older sister. They packed their belongings into Chevvy and Daddy drove north to Alberta. When they arrived at the house in Three Hills, Virginia opened the door—and opened her eyes even wider. She had been expecting one girl, not two. Elizabeth told them what happened at SPC, and John said, "It will work out. Come in!"

John and Gin lived in a dreary downstairs apartment below his parents. They slept in the living room with weeks-old Star, giving Marilyn and Elizabeth the bedroom. A honey bucket in the lower entryway served for bathroom needs, while the kitchen table and four chairs were used for dining, studying, and writing letters. The adults pooled their resources to pay for food and came to agreement on all purchases. Well, except one. Virginia said, "Liz, you just have to accept that I need to buy brown sugar for the rolls I make for my hubby. Brown sugar is a necessity, not a luxury."

And oh! Those cinnamon rolls! How Marilyn loved them. *So gooey, so buttery, so melt-in-your mouth delish.* One Saturday morning, Marilyn was savoring a roll, peeling off layer after layer, holding the center out in front, when John flipped out his hand, popped the piece from underneath, and catapulted it straight into his mouth. He said, "I thought it would look better on me than you. If you let me eat the sweets, maybe you wouldn't have to work so hard to take off the pounds, and we wouldn't have to listen to you beat the lard off your behind on the walls and the floor!"

That was the way it went. Teasing, teasing and arguing, arguing. Not a bit different than at home, except that Marilyn had met her match. Marilyn's egging on and John's unflinching disagreements may have helped him retain his sanity, but not that of his wife whose head ached from the shrill voices and the raucous laughter. However, when John wasn't being obstreperous, he taught Marilyn the trumpet and how to drive on icy roads, and gave Elizabeth lessons on the saxophone.

At home, it seemed strange that all three of our older sisters had moved so far away, yet there were still plenty of us. And there was still plenty of activity to occupy our hours: the farm work, the classes, and the homework, along with a new interest—basketball.

In December, basketball season began at Joyce, and David, now in ninth grade, was turning out for the team. Floyd Kautz, a bus driver who had graduated a few years earlier, came to scrimmage with the boys. One day in the locker room, David heard Floyd say, "I wonder if one of you guys might be interested in buying my Model A pickup."

David looked around at the other boys who acted like they hadn't heard or didn't care. He asked, "How much ya want for it?"

"Just ten bucks."

"Let me ask my dad. I'd really like it."

At home, David checked his savings pouch. He always stashed whatever cash came his way and didn't fritter it on licorice or Big Hunks. Mr. John Johnson, his most frequent employer, paid him a dollar an hour for helping him hay and for doing odd jobs. The odd job this year had been to climb on the roof and jiggle tire chains inside the chimney to knock down the soot.

David approached his father, eased out his breath, and measured his words. "Dad," he said. "Mr. Kautz has a Model A pickup for sale. He just leaves it at school twice a day while he drives the bus. He only wants ten bucks."

"What would you do with a pickup? You aren't even old enough to get a license. It's probably a piece of junk that would be more work than it's worth."

"It runs well and looks real good to me. Just think how much help it would be to haul wood and stuff around the place. I would learn more about mechanics to keep it running. I have enough to pay for it myself and buy the gas."

Daddy shrugged, then drove David to the Kautzes about five miles west. Floyd had the truck parked on a hill. He told David that coasting was the easiest way to start the engine, though there was also a weak battery starter and a crank that sometimes worked. So David was forewarned.

The Model A had no muffler, and the exhaust pipe ended beneath the floor boards, so the truck rendered a remarkable racket. For entertainment, David would take John with him to the top of Grauel Road and along the logging roads, where the roar would scare up the grouse that they planned to shoot. On the way down the hill, David would accelerate on the straight stretch by the Johnsons, lift his foot from the gas, and move the ignition lever to "retard." The engine back-fired with dynamite-force explosions and belched torches from the exhaust pipe. Mrs. Johnson told Mother it disturbed their cows and asked her to tell the boys to quit driving that way.

On one trip near the top of the mountain, the Model A stalled and refused all encouragement to start. David and John pushed and coasted to the bottom of Grauel Road and into our creek valley. The head gasket had blown. Mother remarked, "Could it be that Mrs. Johnson prayed your lesson would be learned?"

David fixed up the Model A and put it back to its rightful use—hauling wood. On one of the loads, a splatter of gas leaked onto the winter pond. The rainbow-colored streaks twisted across the surface like a whirling dervish.

Phillip watched; then lit a match. The flame chased and consumed the rainbow lights clear to the middle of the pond. He said to no one in particular, "I wonder if this is what the lake of fire in hell looks like."

By the time Christmas vacation rolled around, the Farmhouse was wall-to-wall sickbay. Four or five of us had broken out with chicken pox. We were feverish, wretched, and whiny.

"I need a drink. My mouth is dry."

"My back itches."

"My head aches."

"I'm burning up."

Mother said she couldn't keep climbing the stairs to answer the never-ending calls. So she set up an infirmary of mats, couches and cots in the living room and hung blankets over the windows to protect our eyes. She told us we wouldn't get a Christmas tree—there was no room for it—and, to add insult to illness, she said we were pesky, and she was exhausted. We would celebrate after everyone got better—if we would celebrate at all.

On Christmas Eve it began to snow. We pressed our faces under the coverings on the windows. How could it snow on Christmas Eve when we were all sick? It never snowed on Christmas Eve, and there we were, stuck inside! By the next morning there were several inches of fresh powder on the trees, tall mounds on the fence posts, and a glittering blanket on every green thing. Acting as if I were back to normal, I put my clothes on for the first time in days. "No, you can't go out in it," Mother said.

"Why's she such a poor sport?" I mumbled.

Mother leaned against the sink and wiped her forehead. She looked exhausted. "Arthur, it's time to call the girls at Prairie and give them the news."

I wondered why Daddy needed to make the trip to the phone, since my sisters already knew we were sick. Or why would he need to tell them about the snow? They had plenty of their own snow in Alberta.

Without a word, Daddy buttoned his overcoat, tugged on his galoshes, and picked up his hat. He didn't seem in a hurry as he pushed through the snow on the bridge and climbed the hill toward Tieches. He would borrow their phone, but it was not a "We wish you a Merry Christmas" call that he needed to make.

The phone rang at the elder McLennans where the household was eating roast duck and Star was taking a nap. John answered. Our father's message was simple. "Tell the girls that their mother is expecting a baby. She thinks it will be in April."

Marilyn was incredulous. *Mother is expecting another baby—and it will be younger than Gin's!* The livid nineteen-year-old vituperated under her breath, "How could he, how could he do that to her again? She's nearly fifty!"

Marilyn and Elizabeth conferred. Who would go home to help? Liz insisted she was the one. "You're going to the mission field and I don't have that call. I'll go ahead on my assignments and leave school early—in time to help Mother."

Two days later, on Daddy's birthday, he decided to check on his parents and Grandma Phenicie in Tacoma. It had snowed there too, and Mother thought they might need his assistance. She told him to take Phillip, the first pediatric patient to have improved from critical care to crabby convalescence. She said, "I can manage the rest with the crankiest one gone."

Phillip stuck close to Daddy while he repaired Grandma Corey's oven handle, then helped him shovel sawdust at Grandma Phenicie's. They visited Daddy's sister Aunt Esther as well. When they left for home, Daddy stopped at a dairy stand and bought Phillip an ice cream cone. As they savored the treat, Daddy said one of the ladies they'd helped told him to "buy something special." Phillip thought, *Daddy got that right. Nothing could be more special than an ice cream cone to eat all by yourself.*

Upon returning to the Farmhouse, Daddy took the boys with him across Grauel Road to check on the Tieches. Mr. Tieche had been sick for months and he was getting weaker. Daddy sat with him all afternoon as he had on other occasions, allowing Mrs. Tieche and Rose to get to town. The boys shoveled their road, refilled the firewood bin by the stove, and went home. Daddy asked Mr. Tieche if he was ready to die and followed up with, "It doesn't matter how bad you've been or what you've done. God loves you and sent Jesus to die for your sins."

The hard-headed neighbor listened, and then his eyes began to blink. Daddy prayed aloud, then leaned forward to be closer to the man's parched lips, to be able to hear Mr. Tieche's whispered words. When Daddy came home he told us, "I believe Mr. Tieche is ready to meet the Lord."

We didn't get much Christmas that year, but we believe God did. We believe he got our neighbor's heart. Two weeks later, Mr. Tieche passed away.

• • •

CHAPTER NINETEEN
The Baby
(1952)

Elizabeth came home with a notebook of school requirements, ready to help with the household. Mother was relieved to have her back in plenty of time, and was pleased with the gifts she brought from her daughters at Prairie—especially the winter pants Gin had sent.

One day, as Mother stirred soup on the stove and chatted with her friend, Virginia Pennoyer, Daddy walked through the kitchen, only to stop in his tracks and ask, "Margaret, what are you wearing?"

Daddy addressed Mother by her first name when he wanted her full attention. She turned to face him as he reminded her, "The Bible says, 'The woman shall not wear that which pertaineth to a man.'"

"Well, Arthur," Mother replied, using his first name to show that she meant business as well, "these are *maternity* pants that our Virginia sent home with Elizabeth. They are warm, and they are comfortable!"

Daddy glanced at the belly that filled the loose hanging smock. Then without another word, he turned and walked away. Our mother often wore pants after that and, as far as I know, he never again reminded her of the verse.

Virginia Pennoyer had come to Mother for counsel as she had many times before—as a teen who walked seven miles to Sunday meetings and helped out with the children; as a young woman dating Fred; and as a new wife when Daddy baptized her husband in our creek. On this visit, Virginia told Mother that Fred had asked her if she would be willing to leave everything and go to the Philippines.

Mother spoke to the young woman in front of her, "If God is calling Fred, and God has called you to be his wife, God will take care of you and your children."

So the Pennoyers joined New Tribes Mission and began preparations to go to the Philippines. They set aside a few belongings that they would ship overseas; then cleared out the rest. To our home came a couch, a chair, and an up-to-date Whirlpool refrigerator with an ice box on the inside and turquoise trim on the door. We would be able to make ice cubes and store ice cream—at least for an hour. But that was a big improvement over the last refrigerator, which wouldn't freeze anything . . . with the exception of lettuce. Daddy moved that one to the Separator Room and dedicated it primarily to the storage of cream for the Port Angeles Creamery. For Daddy it also had a secondary purpose. Behind the cream he stashed the jars of fermented fruit—ones not sealed property—that Mother would have thrown out. When she questioned how he could swallow the spoiled pears and fizzy juice, my father claimed that it was medicine prescribed by the Bible for his "stomach's sake and . . . oft infirmities."[84]

It was next to this refrigerator that Marian got the shock of her young life. She was standing in the doorway watching as Mother prepared cream for delivery to the creamery. Mother took a full gallon from the shelf of the fridge and turned to pour it into the galvanized can. At that instant, she banged the lip of the can with the jar, breaking off the bottom and sending the rich, thick cream cascading down her front and splattering all across the room. "Oh, darn!" She exclaimed.

Marian's eyes jolted wide at the shock of hearing her mother use the forbidden word. Mother looked equally shocked as she jerked her left arm across the mouth that had issued the expletive. Marian glanced around to see if anyone else had heard, and turned back toward Mother, whose face was flushed and whose right hand still held the upper part of the jar.

Mother faced the cream-covered floor, "It's gone—the whole gallon is gone. Such a waste. So clumsy of me!"

Marian understood the value of the cream and its role in helping to pay the bills, but hearing Mother say that word—well, that was just plain stupefying. Marian backed away, thinking to herself, *I'll keep Mother's secret forever, but I sure hope God doesn't hold that slip of the tongue against her.*

On February 18, a car full of people drove into our yard. As usual, we ran out to see who was visiting us. We were surprised to see Grandma and Grandpa Corey in the back seat, along with Aunt Vera. Uncle Harold and two of our cousins were in the front. We stood back, waiting for them to get out. Elizabeth went to the window, "Mother and Dad will be home soon. They took David and John to town. You can come in."

Nobody but Uncle Harold got out. He chatted with us for a few minutes, then climbed back in, started the ignition, and drove away.

This trip was the first time Grandma and Grandpa Corey had ever come to see us. Why did they leave without waiting for our parents to return? They didn't say, but I was dreadfully disappointed we didn't get to show them the house, the barn, the animals, and all of the gadgets in the Separator Room. We learned later it was Grandma's 82nd birthday and she had wanted to see her son Arthur and his family at the farmhouse in the country.[85] That led us to speculate that Grandpa had argued against the trip and had only given in to please her. Or perhaps he was shocked to see the place we lived in—a barn—and he didn't want to use the place where we went to the bathroom—an outhouse.

If we were sorry, Mother and Daddy were all the more disappointed. They returned an hour after the relatives left, having been gone just a short time to take the boys to get their school shoes repaired in town.

That day, John came home from the repairman without his shoes—they would take an extra day to be fixed. Since he had only one pair, the next morning he headed off to school barefoot. David couldn't believe that his kid brother would be seen barefoot in public, and warned him about the teasing that was sure to come. "If I were you," David suggested, "I'd just stay home."

John wasn't one to think twice about such things, however. And within a few days, his classmates had begun showing up at school without *their* shoes. It soon became a trend, forcing the principal to send out a memorandum declaring that all students going barefoot at school must bring a note from home.

Mother was counting days until time for the baby to be born. "Such a weight on my tired feet," she reminded Daddy as she asked him to pull out the wicker bassinet that had been used to store bedding since Marian was born.

Early on April 22, Daddy took Mother to the hospital in Port Angeles. She had a different doctor this time—not one who looked at her like, *Oh, it's you again Mrs. Corey.* That evening Daddy came home to tell us we had a little sister, Janice, to whom they had also given Mother's middle name, Lenore. Janice Lenore Corey. I thought it had a nice ring, rather like poetry.

Phillip told his teacher and friends at school. "I have a baby sister now. I'm so excited!"

Mrs. Tripp made a remark about too many kids already and Phillip didn't say any more. He couldn't understand why she couldn't just be happy with him.

Mother didn't plan to stay in the hospital as long this time. She was already recovering well, and was concerned for Elizabeth with such a tribe to look after and such a grind of work. She needn't have given it an ounce of consideration. I was almost nine and could cook up a batch of the best-ever cookies without any help. If Mother had been there, she would have told me to use chicken fat as part of the shortening and to add cinnamon and cloves to disguise the flavor of rendered poultry. The boys never found fault, but I said that even with spices, the taste of chicken fat reminded me of the barnyard at butchering time. When Mother was gone, however, I just used margarine—the white kind that came with a squishy yellow bubble to mix in—and *no* chicken fat to stretch it out.

I was smitten by Janice—by the baby whose hair matched mine and whose eyes were a much deeper blue. I told Mother, "I will look after Janice. You can take it easy and make Liz watch the rest of the kids."

I was holding the baby when Mrs. Tieche brought us a pot of soup. She also brought an outfit she had purchased for Janice and dresses she had sewn for Marian and me. Mrs. Tieche was not known for fine-touch tailoring. But she sewed clothes out of brightly-colored new fabric, rather than from missionary barrel outfits and flour sacks like we mostly did. After Mrs. Tieche went home, Mother let me help her redo the seams that puckered and fix the hems that didn't jive. I thought altering a new dress to fit was just as much fun as sewing from scratch, and Mother said it didn't cost anything and she was glad to let me take over that part.

Mrs. John Johnson also came by. Mother hadn't forgotten that neighbor's words of faith and wisdom spoken just weeks earlier as Mother faced the arrival of child Number Ten. As old Mrs. Johnson held Janice, Mother thanked her again for the comfort of her counsel. "You'll never know how God used you to bring peace to my spirit."

With Mother back at home, and me helping out, Elizabeth went to work at Lake Crescent Lodge. Janice outgrew the white bassinet, so we shuffled the beds upstairs. Mother moved Marian out of the crib and into a bunk bed of the dormitory. Daddy returned the crib once more to his and Mother's bedroom. I moved out of the second guest bed—in the curtained alcove under the eve of the charred trusses and shingles—into the first guest bed in the room Elizabeth had left. John moved out of a bunk into the second guest bed that I had left. Phillip moved up to a mattress in the attic that had been vacated by David, who moved to a cot in the tiny side room on the north wall of the second floor, next to his tinkering table.

The tinkering table was where he kept his collection of screws, wires, small motors, and parts of all sorts. He was trying to make Mother an electric mixer using a pair of beaters he had found, and to assemble a doorbell with a buzzer. David lacked parts for the mixer and batteries for the doorbell, so neither invention was ever put into action. Late into the night David messed with his contraptions or read issues of Popular Mechanics he'd received as a gift. He was analyzing welders and deciding on the best way to convince Daddy we should get one. Such thinking and tinkering and contemplating took lots of time. Mother would find David at his table when she got up to feed the baby and take other children to the chamber pot. "David, what are you doing? Turn off the light and get yourself to bed."

"Just a sec, Mom . . . "

For decades—ever since Marilyn was a toddler—Mother had awakened those with weak water control to go to the toilet during the night, in hopes of reducing the frequency of wet beds. She even tried other measures—permitting no drinks after supper, or serving a piece of bread sprinkled with salt. Nothing brought success. In fact, some mornings Phillip threw his sheets straight out the attic window and down to the laundry porch, hoping no one would know where they'd come from. He muttered, "I'll never be able to quit wetting the bed and I'll never be able to get married."

Once, when Marian wet her bed, she hid in a trunk by the closet even though she knew Mother wouldn't punish. She didn't want to see Mother shake her head and groan, "Not again, not wet again."

With a new baby to care for, Mother told Daddy it was hard for her to keep the boys on task, fix meals, do laundry, and get the rest she needed. "I'd appreciate having you around, at least during the summer months," she said, "and maybe you can do something about our drive."

Our driveway was always a mess—deep muck and puddles whenever it rained, and a series of dusty corduroy ridges the few weeks of the year it was dry. David showed Daddy clumps of crunchy clay mixed with rocks and shale down by the creek, past the steep hill, next to the Johnsons' fence. To haul the filler to the driveway, however, we would need a road.

For several weeks, we slammed picks into the bank, hacked at roots that stuck out, and shoveled dirt and rocks over the edge to build up the lower side. The road with a switchback curve grew until it opened a passage—not only to the gravel pit, but also to the bridge crossing the creek. David tested the road with the Model A, and when it held up, the boys began to shovel load after load of crumbly creek bank, first into the pickup and then back out of the pickup into the driveway.

David leaned on his pick and pondered aloud. "Hmm—if I turn this Model A into a dump truck, it'll be half the work."

Daddy said, "It can't be done."

But *can't-be-done* usually can. David made the dump feature by pivoting the bed near the middle of its length and placing a rod at the front to secure the bed so it wouldn't unload itself at the wrong time. "The secret," he said, "is to balance the load so we can lift the weight and let the dump bed do its job."

The task of driveway enhancement was similar to the task of supplying wood for winter before we had the buzz saw. The boys could never get enough rocky fill to build up a base that would last through more than one or two big rainstorms. But at least the new road and the redesigned Model A dump truck made it easier.

The Model A did nothing to help in the hayfield that had been taken over by thistles. Those grandiose purple topped stalks had become even more of a nuisance than the daisies. The neighbors told us these thistles were introduced along our highway when the military donkeys that traveled by in the 1940s were fed hay filled with thistle seed. Anyway, it didn't matter so much what kind they were or how they got there—they just had to be gotten out of there! Daddy sent the boys with the same shovels they'd used on the gravel, telling them to chop off the thistle below the ground. He said if they cut low enough, the root wouldn't send up shoots fast enough to ruin the hay for the cattle or go to seed before harvest. The shovels were faster at removing the stalks than hands had been at pulling daisies, but the task had to be repeated several times during the season, and again the following years.

This same summer Daddy began to talk in earnest about building a house. Mother was skeptical that there would ever be funds to construct, but agreed to walk the property in search of a site. It had been eight years since the two had first walked the land that had become ours, the land upon which Daddy had visualized a real house with bedrooms for everyone. Since that time, two more children had been added. Furthermore, the Farmhouse constructed as interim living quarters was more crowded than the Grange House had been. As they walked, Mother said, "I want to build for southern exposure so the sun will shine in our windows all year long."

There was one such location and Daddy laid out kindling sticks to mark Mother's selection. A few days later, the Public Utilities District (PUD) came through with a survey to establish the right of way for a new power line heading west. They hacked marks in trees and pounded stakes in the ground directly through the sun-swept site Mother had chosen. Daddy was away that day, but upon his return, he pursued the same path the power company had taken and yanked out all the stakes, one by one. He fumed, "What right did they have to trespass in this way?"

Mother didn't discuss his action, but God must have spoken. Daddy tried to replace the stakes, but he couldn't locate the spots where they'd been placed. He told Mother that what he had done was wrong—he had not taken his provocation to the Lord before acting on impulse. He decided to go see Mr. Miller at the PUD.

The results confirmed that Daddy was right to listen to God. Mr. Carl Miller was the General Manager of Clallam County PUD. He was also Aunt Edith Phenicie's brother. After speaking with Daddy, Mr. Miller had his crew return to our land and put survey markings on a different route. The power line would not impact the building site, but would actually widen the sun exposure for Mother, and open up her view of the Olympic Mountains.

With the survey complete, Daddy told the boys they could cut down the trees that were on the part of the right of way that traversed our property. He said the PUD crews would just shove the timber out of the way and leave a mess, but we could make good use of the wood. He added, "Some of it you can cut into four-foot lengths to sell in Port Angeles as pulpwood."

David and John took the crosscut saw to the trees on top of our hill not far from Phillips Road. As they dropped and limbed the timber, David took a hatchet and marked four-foot lengths to saw for pulp. They had already cut a few of the pieces when Vern, Elizabeth's boyfriend, came by. We'd seen Vern quite a few times when he'd come to visit Elizabeth after she returned from Prairie. Now that she was working at the resort on Lake Crescent, he usually brought her home for her day off. This time, he walked up the trail to see what the boys were up to. Vern said to the loggers, "That's a slow process. How about I bring a chainsaw next week and give you a hand?"

With that kind of incentive in mind, David and John worked as many hours as time would allow—toppling trees, laying them in rows and marking the lengths. Vern showed up as promised and began to saw the sections. "You know," he commented, "I don't think these are the length required by the pulp mill."

Sure enough, when he measured those that had already been cut, they were a hair under four feet. He said, "They're actually supposed to be a couple of inches *more* than four feet, not a half inch less."

David questioned, "Should I make new marks on the rest of the logs?"

"Nah," Vern said, "They'll probably not notice. But if they do, you can just act like you didn't know any better."

So Vern cut the whole slew of logs to less than four feet. David and John split them into acceptable thickness and hauled them in the Model A dump truck to the Farmhouse yard. When the piles were big enough, they called on Mr. Gerber, who lived near Bill Lennon's store, to bring his flatbed truck to make the delivery. They didn't warn him that the cuts were not up to standard and that the mill might deny his load, so David's mind paced in circles of uncertainty. *What if the mill workers make Mr. Gerber take the load back? What if Mr. Gerber comes to tell me off? What if all the work is wasted and there is no money?*

David watched for Mr. Gerber's return. What a relief when the truck returned empty and Mr. Gerber handed over the check. The mill had accepted the stack despite its length deficiency.

Because Daddy was around more, he gave additional attention to our spiritual well-being. He and Mother took John with them to hear an evangelist near Sequim Bay. John said the message helped him commit his life to serve the Lord wherever God would send him. John suspected his father made a commitment that day as well. One evening, after punishing John for misbehavior, Daddy said, "What you did was wrong and you needed to be punished. But I was angry and not in full control of my spirit. Will you forgive me?"

John was confused by the turn of Daddy's tone. He knew he deserved the spanking, and was accustomed to his father's angry words. Now the man he'd placed on a spiritual pedestal was admitting that he was wrong—that he had sinned. It had never once entered John's mind that it was sin for Daddy to be angry when he administered punishment. This revelation shredded John's heart, and he couldn't help but think about it all the time. *Daddy is a man of God and he sometimes sins by losing his temper like I do. Then he has to be humble and seek forgiveness. Maybe, just maybe, there is hope for me.*

One day John was talking to his best friend, Dan, about being ready to die, when Dan said to him, "I'm a better guy than you are. If you get to heaven, I will get there before you do."

John said to himself, "Dan is right—he *is* a better guy. He is always kind and never loses his temper. But he isn't right that being a better guy will get him to heaven."

John reasoned that a public commitment might help him with self-control, so he told Daddy he wanted to be baptized. In follow-up to John's request, Daddy took five of us to the beach—to the mouth of Salt Creek where the incoming tides of Crescent Beach flowed over the sand and silt to form an estuary of warmer water.

We lined up in age and took turns wading to where Daddy stood. First David, John, Phillip. When it was my turn, I told Daddy I believed in Jesus—that I had believed as long as I could remember. He held me by the shoulders and laid me back under the water. He didn't tell me to hold my nose, and I came up snorting water and coughing. I thought my spluttering and choking was quite irreverent.

After me, it was Merton's turn. He didn't tell Daddy whether he did or didn't believe; instead allowing John to be his advocate. "Sure," John offered, "Merton believes."

When Merton came out of the water, he felt nothing but guilt. At the same time, he was relieved that no one—not even Daddy—found him out. His lie was safe. He would make sure it stayed that way.

At the end of summer, Elizabeth's job at Lake Crescent ended and she started attending a business college in Everett, about three hours away. She had decided to become a bookkeeper.

Five of us were back at Joyce: David in tenth grade, John in seventh, Mert in second, and Phillip and I in fifth. This was the year I took a brand new pair of roller skates on the first day. I had saved birthday and Christmas money until it added up to $3.00, enough to pay for a pair of clip-on skates at the

Coast to Coast store in town. At home there was nowhere to ride except the cow-messed warped and ridged barn floor. But at school I could whip down the sidewalk as fast as the other kids, even those who had real shoe skates.

On the bus home from school one day, my classmate, Alva Sands, invited me to see the kittens in her barn. Mother gave permission and I talked Phillip into coming along with me—I still didn't like going on the highway by myself where I might encounter a smashed-raspberry-red car (my exercises with Penny just hadn't provided a cure). I told Phillip if I wore my skates, he could run and we'd get there in no time. The Sands' kitties were the fluffiest, cutest babies I had ever seen, coated with a colorful variety of stripes, splotches, and speckles. I asked Alva if I could take one home, saying, "I don't think Mother would mind."

Mother did mind, and she made me take the kitten back. But not before I had passed it around to Merton and Marian. After three days, I had sores like a necklace of fiery coins plastered to my neck—all the places the kitten had snuggled. The sores itched and burned and grew and spread. Even though it was a hot September, I wore a collared shirt buttoned up to hide them so I could go to school.

At home, no one paid much attention to my skin problem because Marilyn was coming from Three Hills with our sister Virginia, her husband John, and year-old Star. We hadn't seen the McLennans in almost a year and a half and never had met our first niece. Mother said we had to get the house ready, and I said, "It won't be good enough for Marilyn, she'll just do it all over."

Every day I jumped off the bus and ran as fast as I could up the path, hoping to see a nice car in the yard. Finally, there it was and I hollered back to the rest. "They came, they're here!"

Star had deep dimples, curly honey-colored hair and skinny legs like a colt. Marilyn seemed strong and soft when she hugged us, but Virginia was as scrawny as the refugees we had seen in the missionary magazines. We learned how difficult that year had been; how her baby was often sick; and how the baby's crying tried John's patience until he said he had no idea this was what having babies was like or he would have opted out. Gin could find nowhere to hide while John and Marilyn engaged in non-stop debate and teasing. Later Gin's little family moved away from Marilyn into a house infested with bedbugs, about which the owner scoffed, "Bedbugs are normal." It's no wonder Gin was so puny and worn out.

Of course, we couldn't imagine that John's teasing wore anyone out—at least not yet. We laughed at his joke about the first time he visited—the joke he told every time he came. "I'd never seen so many kids in one family," he said. "You just kept coming and coming and coming. At first, I thought you were going around the house and coming out the door again. It took me a week to learn all your names."

We were still laughing at him when Marian shouted, "Train, I hear the train!"

Phillip, Merton, and I took off for the knoll overlooking the creek. Marian followed but was left far behind. "Wait for me, wait for . . . " she wailed.

But we couldn't wait. The train hardly passed by anymore and none of us wanted to miss it. John McLennan saw that we ignored Marian. He caught her up, tucked her onto his shoulders, and raced the rest of us to the look-out spot. Marian's trip to watch the train from the neck of the tallest man in our household was imprinted in the recesses of her brain. And lucky for her, because that was one of the last times we waved at the train, saw its cloud of smoke, and heard it rumble over the trestle.[86]

We were barely back from the train when Marilyn caught a glimpse of the sores on my neck. Mother told her, "We think it's ringworm."

"We'll try tincture of iodine," Marilyn said. "Iodine cures everything."

Oh, that burned. Worse than the stove, worse than the iron, worse than a blistered sunburn, worse than kerosene on the itch. I ran down the hill and into the creek, clothes and all, to cool it off. Merton and Marian had ringworm too, but I shrieked so fiercely Marilyn didn't use the treatment on them. I had not seen my sister for ages, and I wasn't sure I liked her to come home with her ideas of medicine. While I was getting over it, Marilyn set the house in order from top to bottom, even though I had already cleaned. I didn't say to Mother, "I told you so." Instead I went to bake cookies for the picnic we had planned. No way could I be upset for long. *We were going on a big family picnic.*

David had returned from a high school trip and Elizabeth arrived from Everett with her boyfriend Vern. The morning of the picnic, the whole entire family gathered for breakfast. Mother served Danish pastries—treats from the sack of bakery throw-aways we called Pig Bread. We'd been getting Pig Bread for a couple of years from a bakery in Port Angeles—pulled-from-the-shelves bread designated for farm animals. We weren't exactly animals, but we did live on a farm, and we did eat what wasn't smashed, smelly or moldy. After Mother had heated them in the oven, nobody would have guessed where they came from, and nobody needed to tell—not that knowing the source bothered a single one of us Coreys. The week of the picnic, Daddy had brought home a bonanza. There were enough salvageable pastries for all of us to get a taste of butter horns, donuts, or maple bars.

At noon, we drove in a caravan to Crescent Beach. Daddy let Marilyn drive Chevvy which was stuffed with the most wound-up of us kids. Vern carted Elizabeth and a few more, while John and Virginia filled their borrowed car with Daddy, Mother and the babies. I couldn't get from the car to the beach fast enough. Phillip, Merton, and I chased each other out into the breakers. We jumped waves and fell flat in the frigid ocean until our skin was red from the cold. We raced back to the Salt Creek slough and belly-flopped into the warmth. John was trying to roll a log from the bank into the slough. He called to David for help and the three of us younger ones went running to get in on the last push over the edge. We jumped on the log and it sank, so we had to take turns. The tide was coming in, so any who stayed on the log got a ride upstream. That is, until the log rolled over and the riders fell in.

Meanwhile Mother laid out a blanket in the shade of the wind-gnarled trees, and propped five-month-old Janice on her tummy so she could watch the activity. Virginia sat Star in the sand nearby and handed Marian a few digging utensils. "Here, you can help Star make a sand castle."

Daddy and John McLennan stood near the car and talked scriptures, until John said, "Wait a minute." He opened the trunk and brought out two badminton rackets and a couple of birdies. He handed one to his father-in-law and they walked to a flat sandy stretch. Daddy soon learned that he was no match for the pro and handed off the racket to Marilyn. Marilyn was no match, either, and fell down as often as she hit the birdie. Then Marilyn said, "Enough of this," and threw the racket at John.

"Hey Liz," she called to her sister who was walking with Vern toward the rocks of Tongue Point. "Give me a hand with the food."

The two smoothed a red and white checkered tablecloth on top of a board held up by a stump, and laid out the food—sandwiches, Kool-Aid, and cookies. Before they could even call, we pushed the log to the side of the slough and ran to get our share. Daddy called on his son-in-law to pray and we were patient while John gave his spiritual oration, naming every single one of us, and blessing Mother and Dad Corey who had welcomed him into the family like one of their own. I wasn't averse to his praying, except I wished he could pray in a voice we and God could hear, but not the people playing in the sand half way down the beach. Marilyn divvied up the lunch. Satisfied for the moment, we started toward the water when John McLennan called us back. "Wait! Let's get a picture of everyone together."

Elizabeth held the dog and looked toward Marian, who hid her face, while Phillip clowned and Merton frowned. I hoped there was still a smear of zinc oxide disguising my ring worm, and was relieved to see that the sores were not bright red. When John had everyone in the screen of his camera, he handed it off to Vern and ran around the back to stand next to Virginia and Star. Thus, there was recorded in black and white, a photo of the big picnic when we were all in the same place at the same time—all ten brothers and sisters from Virginia down to baby Janice, along with our parents and the two newest members, John McLennan and little Star.

The following morning we sang our hymns, one after another, holding onto the completeness of the family for as long as possible. In the yard, John McLennan took one more photo and we finished our get-together weekend with the tearful farewell song: "God be with you . . . "

As Mother looked around at her children—a few preparing for missions, others for careers, and the rest growing up so fast—she wondered aloud. "When *ever* will we all be together like this again?"[87]

She mulled these thoughts as life moved on, bringing with it a series of reasons to rejoice. She rejoiced with the sale of another round of pulpwood—up to standard length—that allowed for a new typewriter for writing letters to her three daughters, her mother, her sister, her cousin, her in-laws, and the multitude of others she cared about. She rejoiced in the outcome of the elections in which General Dwight D. Eisenhower was voted in as president.

Eisenhower—besides being Mother's distant relative[88]—was highly respected by Daddy as a man of faith and conscience.

Greater joy came that same month when word came that Elizabeth had ended her relationship with Vern. During the previous summer, Daddy had preached to Vern about his need to accept the Lord and, since then, Mother had prayed that her third daughter would realize that the non-believing—and rather shiftless—guy was not right for her. Marilyn had been praying too, since Liz had opted to stay in Washington and was still seeing Vern, instead of returning to Prairie for school. After the break-up, Elizabeth had written to her sister:

> Vern showed up unannounced one evening, but I said I would not go out with him that night. He argued, so I told him I just could not break my commitment to sing in the revival choir. So he stomped out the door and roared off in a huff. I really don't expect to see him again and it's hard for me right now. But it's better this way.[89]

It *was* hard for Elizabeth. But she began to turn her depression into determination, and by Christmas had put together a plan—a very big plan. She told Mother, "I am going to help you get a new house. When I finish school, I'll be able to work full-time. I want to set some aside every month towards the building fund."

The family picnic 1952

CHAPTER TWENTY
The Building Fund
(1953)

What a wild-wacky Christmas promise. We would have a *real* house—one with an indoor toilet, doors on the bedrooms, and insulated walls. There would be cooking, eating, and living space big enough for family and guests. Elizabeth would make it happen. She would get us out of the shoddy shack of a farmhouse that should have been turned into a barn for the cows long ago.

In January 1953, Elizabeth completed her schooling and landed a permanent bookkeeping job in Everett at a concrete and construction company. She moved from the boarding house to Lloyd and Grace Troupe's home in Snohomish. She put her income in the bank, setting aside a percentage for what had been named "The Building Fund."

Mother pondered the news that her daughter, at eighteen years, had made such a decision. Her daughter was the age to be thinking of marriage and having her own home, and her salary was only a mite above the minimum wage of 75¢ an hour. Daddy didn't question, however. Instead, he just waited for affirmation from the Lord—what he called "The Witness of the Spirit."

We grew up knowing that God spoke to our father, if not audibly then at least clearly enough that he needed no further instruction. It was the same principle when we asked Daddy for permission. Before responding, he would listen for that witness. Perhaps that is the reason I sometimes chose to do what I wanted *without* asking, despite the likely consequences. Who could argue with the *Witness of the Spirit* or the *Mind of the Lord* any more than with the father who heard such messages?

Within days, Daddy assured Mother that he'd received the *witness* that God was the author of Elizabeth's commitment.

About the same time, the agency assigned to clear the right of way for the power line established a contract with Daddy. The agreement said the company would pay us $700 to fell and remove the trees. It didn't matter to them what we did with the wood. Daddy cashed the payment and bought a blue Titan 40 chainsaw. What an impressive invention that was. It whipped through trees like they were matchsticks.

But the Titan 40 was also cumbersome and complicated. The boys had to rotate the blade in the right direction for cutting, and clamp the rotator tight, or else gas would flood the engine and run out on the ground. The saw was so difficult to start that once it was running, it was best to just keep cutting until the gas was gone or the daylight disappeared. However, once Daddy and the boys learned the Titan's ins-and-outs, it paid great dividends. The new saw made redundant both of our other saws—the arm-wrestled cross-cut saw and the treacherous cut-off saw linked to the Packard's two-transmission tractor engine.

Purchase of gas for the chain saw and payments to Mr. Gerber—the neighbor who delivered the pulpwood to the mill—took a chunk out of the profits, but there was enough left for Daddy to buy himself a pair of heavy duty caulk boots—often called cork books—and fill the 300-gallon farm gas tank at eighteen cents a gallon. He ordered a living room wood heater that Uncle Al, Aunt Hilda, Cousin Kurt, and Grandma Corey delivered to our door.[90] This time Grandpa wasn't along, so Grandma was permitted to get out of the car and stay long enough to see the animals and the construction site, and to join us in the Farmhouse for lunch. She didn't explain why she'd been denied the opportunity on the previous trips—just said to Mother, "You really have fixed this up for your family. I am proud of what you've done."

This heater was topped with a brown porcelain grate you could sit on while the fire heated up. The quickest kid down the stairs in the morning got first dibs on it for devotion—ideal for me since I jumped out of bed the minute I heard Mother open the firebox door, crinkle the paper, and put in the kindling. The other benefit to me was the placement of the treadle sewing machine right next to the heater. When I sewed, I hardly ever needed to wear a sweater.

During that season, David could give extra hours to woodcutting with the Titan 40 because he had dropped out of basketball. That had not been his plan. He had wanted to play and was turning out for practices, until the afternoon Daddy stopped him at the door. "I have an issue with the basketball schedule and want to make something clear before you start the season. You have to get home earlier from the games. No coming in at eleven or midnight."

David was in a dilemma. The team played against some schools more than an hour away, and players wanted to stay for activities or dances after the games. David didn't know how to negotiate with his father, and didn't know what to say to Coach Jorgensen and the team. So he simply quit and never told anyone why.

On March 24, David turned sixteen. He'd been counting down the months and days until he could get his license. Daddy took him to Port Angeles for the exam, and a confident—even cocky—teenager took the wheel of Chevvy with the testing official seated next to him. David drove for the test just like he did at home, with his elbow out the open window. He didn't fully stop at the stop sign, and cut the corner when turning left. He turned the wheels the wrong way when parking and didn't use the correct turn signal with his arm. It was the quickest flunk the instructor had ever given.

Several weeks later, a chastened David, with all arrogance erased from his attitude, took the exam again and managed to pass.

Chevvy had done her part to help David get his license, but in recent weeks she had been developing her own old-lady maladies. Her parts could not keep up with the demands placed on them. Her crank didn't function half the time, so she required several humans pushing her backside to get her started. Her crankcase bearings knocked, her burned valves leaked, and her piston rings made the engine drink oil by the quart. Her steering mechanisms were so loose she could scarcely keep her wheels in her own lane on the road, especially when the driver forced her brakes—mechanical brakes that were connected to each wheel with worn down rods, pivots and levers.

Mother was frank with the Lord, "We need a new car. A station wagon would hold the whole family—if that's thy will."

God answered her prayer for a car, but not the part about a station wagon. Instead, Daddy came home from the John Johnsons with a '41 Plymouth Coupe. David remembered having seen in Johnsons' shed this dark brown shiny car—the manicured Plymouth that for years had been driven once or twice a week to town or to Joyce Store. Mrs. Johnson had told David once how this car had seemed like a miracle after their years of using a horse-drawn carriage on the all-day journey to take their produce to the market.

It felt like a miracle to us too. The Coupe had a bench seat for two and a half adults, some lap room for cramming in extras, and space behind for a couple of tots to stand. It boasted an oversize trunk—a trunk big enough with its lid open to carry four or five of us on trips up the mountain or to the beach. No, the Coupe was not a station wagon—maybe next time—but it had wheels with good tires, a heater that warmed up, and an ignition that started with a button on the floor. It had brakes with hydraulic fluid and steering that took the car in the direction chosen by the driver, rather than the ruts on the road. And it had a cigarette lighter with which Marian created a frightening display of smoke when she dropped in a penny and tried to hide it under the coiled heating mechanism.

With payment from the mill for pulpwood, Daddy paid Mr. Johnson most of the $300 for the '41 Plymouth Coupe. He pushed the 1931 Chevrolet—Mother's Chevvy—under the lean-to roof of the barn. "Its highway days are done," he pronounced.

David saw the forsaken vehicle sitting idle when he went to milk, when he hauled wood, and when he came from school. Possibilities began to spin and spin in his mind. "Dad," he said, "Would it be alright for me to fix up the Chev so I can have a car to drive around?"

With permission granted, David bought $50 worth of parts.

His first priority was to get the engine repaired and running, so he replaced the connecting rod bearings and crankshaft main bearings. He fixed or replaced engine valves and installed new piston rings. He ran out of savings, so the steering and brakes would have to wait. He figured he could drive with adequate space for the Chev to wander and plenty of distance for it to stop.

Dave—we usually called him Dave now that he had his license—tried not to act superior when he drove the showpiece to school, though it was impossible to entirely keep the spring out of his step and a grin off his lips. Dave could see that his dad was proud too, so he used the moment to broach a subject he had studied at his tinkering table for more than a year. He opened the scrappy pages of the Popular Mechanics. "I was wondering about getting our own welder. It sure would be a help to fix our machines when they break down."

Before his father could dampen his determination, he explained. "See this 28-volt surplus aircraft generator with the adapter kit? If we bought it, we could take the cut off saw out of the Packard and use the tractor to power the generator for a welder."

Apparently it made sense to Daddy and he wrote a check to place with Dave's order for the kit. Within days of the packet's arrival, Dave and Daddy had removed the cut off saw from the base of the two-Packard tractor and had installed the mechanisms for a welder. Dave reviewed the manuals and—wasting no time—donned the welder's helmet and tried out the new device to weld together two pieces of scrap iron.

The welder was sitting proud when, on Memorial Weekend, a gang of guests arrived from Snohomish. Elizabeth came, along with Lloyd and Grace Troupe and their five: Alan, the age of Phillip; Kay, my age; Dale, Merton's age; and Ann and Joy, whose years sandwiched Marian's. Bob and Ruth Richardson brought their three boys too.

On Sunday morning, the Farmhouse was bursting full for church. Daddy preached one of his longest sermons. Mouths moved and heads bobbled in agreement—these guests were staid and steady Baptists who didn't say "Amen" out loud. They had been sheep of our father's itineration for many years and didn't seem to care about the length of the sermon.

We wiggle worms on the stairs cared about the length, though. We wanted to eat the food these people had brought. Our stomachs growled; we shifted, twisted, and squirmed. Hours later, it seemed, church was over and we could dig into a feast of more food than we had ever seen in one place: Turkey, ham, fruit salad, store-bought rolls, and potato chips. We roasted hot dogs and marshmallows, pigged out on watermelon, and spit seeds at each other. We finished off with ice cream from the salt-and-ice-packed machine. There were so many people that meals were served by installments with dishwashing in between. Lucky for me, one of the ladies put her hands in the sink and shooed me out the door to play with the other children.

Food wasn't all the Snohomish people brought. A carton of toilet paper was divided and stashed in the outhouse—actually more rolls went to the girl's side for obvious reasons. Mother warned us not to use too much, and Daddy followed up by declaring that two small sections ought to suffice. Some disagreed with his premise, but chose not to continue the discussion.

A couple of the city slickers who came had no experience with farm life. One boy followed Phillip and John to the milking stanchions and Phillip told him, "I need you to pump the cow's tail so she will let down the milk."

After the kid had pulled up and down for a few minutes, Phillip said, "You can slow down for awhile so I can rest my hands."

George and Jim Richardson, rural ruffians like us, roared at the gag they'd pulled.

Several photos recorded the Memorial Weekend gathering. In the back row, Bill Richardson stood the tallest. At 20, he was a sophomore at Seattle Pacific College on scholarship for basketball and baseball. Bill was known for his ability to throw a left-handed curve ball, and had even been offered a major league contract straight out of high school. But most incredible in our eyes was his interest in Elizabeth.

Bill had first met my sister in January when she showed up at First Baptist in Snohomish with Grace Troupe. He asked her to go riding with him, and she liked seeing the countryside and the foothills of the Cascades. However, she didn't like the way he talked. "I'm through with women. They are just a nuisance and more bother than they are worth."

For all his grumbling about females, he nevertheless asked Elizabeth on a date to the Seattle Pacific Spring Festival. It was an event to remember, not because she said yes, but because he ended up having more than one girl lined up for the same date.

Bill borrowed his Granddad's 1940 Ford and picked up Elizabeth. They walked into the auditorium at school and had barely found their seats when Gus, one of the Bill's friends, tapped him on the shoulder. He whispered, "Jen is waiting for you at the dorm lounge."

"*What?*"

"We set you up with a date with Jen. You better not disappoint her."

Bill's mind raced. He did like Jen, and didn't want to make her mad, but he liked Elizabeth even more. Perhaps he could avoid hurting *anyone's* feelings. So he told Elizabeth that there was an emergency and he would be back right away. He then found Jen and ushered her to the auditorium, onto the balcony where the two girls would not see each other. Throughout the concert, he made up reasons to hustle back and forth between the main floor and the balcony. By the end of the evening, he was soaked with sweat from his shirt to his socks, but neither girl had been the wiser.

A few weeks after Bill got over the nerve-racking date, the opposites-attract principle convinced him that Elizabeth was a made-in-heaven match. He was talkative, she was shy. He was big, she was little. He sang bass, she sang soprano. And she was the answer to a request he had made to God.

That answer had come when Bill was in the hospital after major reconstructive surgery for basketball injuries to his ankle. Elizabeth had said she would go to the hospital if she could get off. Another girl had told him the same thing. Bill puzzled whether or not one of these was the lady God had in mind for him, so he prayed, "Will you bring the right girl?" He came out from under anesthesia, and there was Elizabeth, holding his hand. Bill said nothing of his request to God, but called on her at the Troupes, sat with her at church after they performed in the choir, and took her on dates.

A few weeks later, he asked her to marry him. She was dazed at the speed of his decision. "I don't know . . . it's too soon," she replied.

He persevered until she explained one reason for her uncertainty. "I've promised to put aside money from my salary until my parents have built a decent home. I can't break that promise, and I can't marry you unless you agree to be part of that commitment."

Bill could not have known the ramifications of that pre-nuptial contract. He was a student about to lose his sports scholarship; he was recovering from surgery and unable to get a decent job; and he was broke. But he promised, "Yes, I will."

All summer long, Bill and Elizabeth traveled back and forth from Snohomish to the Farmhouse, often with a full car of us going east, or Troupe girls and Richardson boys coming west. Bill was like one of the family—just a big tease. Sometimes too big, sometimes too much tease. One day he pestered Marian until she took off after him. As she chased him through the back door it slammed shut on her face. Her front tooth connected with the door knob and broke. She howled with the pain. Mother comforted her and exhorted Bill to watch out for the little ones. "You need to remember your size and strength when you go chasing."

For a long time, Marian held her hand over her mouth when she laughed. But she loved to laugh, and eventually had to give up the effort to hide her broken tooth.

Mother's suggestion that Bill slow down a bit with the teasing did not transfer to his dealings with the boys, as they would discover for themselves. Not long after Marian's accident, Phillip and John led George and Jim on an exploration of the abandoned Smith place. That was where we kids went, at the right time most summers, to eat Gravenstein apples from the left-behind orchard. Daddy had said we couldn't bring the apples home, but he didn't tell us we couldn't eat them. So we ate as many as we could and stashed the extras along the trail, using our one brilliantly-decked vine maple tree as a marker.

However, the adventure with the Richardson brothers this trip had nothing to do with apples. Instead, the boys were rummaging around in the weathered barn when George got the idea they should take home the pioneer wagon with its wooden-spoke wheels. Phillip agreed there would be numerous uses around our place for such a well-built tall-wheeled machine. John and Phillip knew better than to take it home without permission, but with the other boys taking the lead, what else could they do? They took hold of the two front poles of the tongue that would have connected the wagon to a horse and pulled it out of the barn and through the weeds. The Dempsey Road was downhill all the way and too steep for an easy trip. So they sliced off alder saplings with pocket knives and fashioned brakes to keep the wheels from rolling out of their control. All four were laughing their heads off when they pulled the wagon into the driveway. Daddy met then. "Where did you get this?"

Phillip explained about the Smith's property where no one lived, and started on the part about "it would be very useful . . . "

His father said, "It doesn't belong to you and you will take it back the way you brought it."

There was no argument. They turned back, pushed and pulled the wagon out the driveway and up the gentle slopes of the highway. The Dempsey Road was another story. Once a logging road into the foothills of the Olympics, it was a series of nearly vertical inclines topped with unstable gravel and pock-marked with potholes.

Four of them could not make the wheels go forward. So they placed the alder poles in the spokes and stood on them, using body weight to force the wheels. They put rocks in back of the wheels so they could rest before continuing to inch up the mountain. They had been sweating at this exercise for hours it seemed when David and Bill came up the road in a car. Those two guys, especially Great Big Bill, howled and hooted as if they had never seen anything so humorous. "Come on, you clodhoppers, where's your muscle?"

"What a nursery of crybabies you are!"

The taunting went on way too long. George said, "Let the wagon go; that'll wipe the stupid smirks off their faces and shut their fat mouths."

John shook his head. "No! We'd just be in worse trouble if we wrecked the car and still had to push this monster back up again."

After Bill and David had enjoyed their own hilarity long enough, they used the car to pull the wagon to its final resting place at the old Smith barn—which is what Daddy had sent them to do. Phillip was miffed for months, *What a waste of a perfectly good wagon. What a waste—the whole day shot! And Bill should learn to talk nicer.*

Bill and Elizabeth left, but Jim and George were still at our place when tragedy struck. Betsy didn't come when the boys called at milking time. Phillip and George found her lying between two spruce trees on the hill above the barn. She tried to get up but couldn't seem to get her feet under her. The boys went to find Daddy who came to her side. He prayed, one hand raised and the other on Betsy's head. "You can raise her up, Lord. You know the family needs her milk, and you have promised to hear when we ask."

The boys watched until it got dark. Betsy lay on the ground, her sides heaving. The next morning when the boys checked, Betsy was dead. John hurried back with the news. The first words out of his father's mouth were, "Praise the Lord."

John was puzzled, and shook his head in disbelief. He had heard his dad's prayers of faith that the cow would live. *How could Dad, or anyone, be thankful in such a disaster? We need the milk, and we can't replace her. How could Dad quote 'The Lord giveth and the Lord taketh away; Blessed be the name of the Lord' at such a time?*

It was another of those lessons John thought about a lot. *If Dad prayed in faith and God didn't answer, what did it mean? Was Dad's faith too small or did God have another reason to deny what had been asked.* John could only conclude—*God's ways are sometimes hard to understand.*

Daddy gave John and Phillip the responsibility of burial, and they shared shovels with Jim and George. The ground was parched and rock solid under those trees, and the cow was bloated to twice her size. They dug for hours until they thought—well, hoped—the hole was deep enough. It took all four of them to roll her in, but she still stuck up over the top. There was no way to dig deeper, so they poked holes in her gut to let the gasses out. They finished the burial with a mound over the top that they knew would sink down as she decayed underneath. Phillip commented, "I hope I am not around if she explodes under there and blows off the cover."

I mourned the loss of Betsy. She'd entered my world in 1946 and was part of my earliest memories. Mother whispered, "Maybe a vet could have saved Betsy."

After Betsy was laid to rest, we got a new calf. Such a beauty she was—a Jersey with round soulful eyes and curly eyelashes. We named her Delilah. We would indulge her with the same affection we had given her predecessor, at least until time to teach her the art of sharing her milk. But that would be awhile.

Each day, Phillip and George would finish their assigned tasks and go off to play, with Merton tagging along. They climbed cedars and slid down the outside branches as if they were carnival rides. They made bows from cedar poles and arrows from narrow strips pulled off the Johnsons' hand-hewn homestead fences. Phillip had one real arrow tip, possibly an Indian artifact found after the flood, or perhaps from the cache left behind when Fred Pennoyer went to the Philippines. Otherwise the boys tipped their arrows with nails or spent bullet casings, then attached chicken feathers on the back ends. Phillip bragged about hitting a rabbit with an arrow, but George countered, "Sure Phil! It was totally by accident."

They formed fishing poles from iron bush and strong twisted string that came on packages. Fishing was what they loved best. They fished nearly two miles up the creek and three miles down the other side. They fished at The Falls and they fished in the Salt Creek slough, where once they caught so many fish on the incoming tide that they couldn't carry them all home.

Then it was time to ask Mother if they could camp overnight. They reminded her that Bill had once taken them camping on the island at Tongue Point—off Crescent Beach—and they assured her they were ready to go on their own. When she agreed, they carried their poles, tackle, and overnight gear down Camp Hayden Road, past the army base now overgrown with salmonberry, and out onto the island at low tide. They scraped mussels from shells for bait, fished for kelp cod, and watched the tide come in until they were surrounded on all sides and the waves lapped at their feet. They crawled up the slippery bank and built a fire in the same pit Bill had used on their first trip. They fried fish and wolfed down piping-hot blackberry-bread-sugar pie, then climbed into their bags.

So far, so good—but after that, the night ran like a spooky story. The sky turned pitch black, and noises multiplied in the darkness. The two boys needed Bill. He wasn't afraid of anything and told stories all night long to keep the fear at bay. But Bill wasn't about to show up, and the boys had to listen all alone to the waves crashing higher and higher on the rock walls encircling them, terror mushrooming in their minds of what would happen if there was an extra-high tide or if—*God have mercy*—the high water included a tidal wave that washed the whole island out to sea! Hour after hour they listened to the crashing cymbals, pounding drums, and wailing woodwinds of the night. Hour after hour they looked through the bending, creaking trees towards the sky, searching for the first sign of morning.

When the sun crept up the horizon, they ridiculed their jellyfish hearts, caught more rock cod, and headed for home—but they didn't camp there again for several years. Nonetheless, Phil's fishing adventures with George netted him a new nickname, "Fish." The moniker spread as Fish returned to school in the fall, and schoolmates and teachers caught the whiff of leftover bait and gear in his pockets.

Mid July, Marilyn headed home from Montana, where she'd gone from Prairie to teach rural Vacation Bible School. With her was her boyfriend, Allen Thompson, who had been working as a hired farmhand a few miles from where she had boarded. Along the bus route back to the Farmhouse, Allen, a lifelong lowlander who was born in Cuba, gawked at the tall firs and the rugged mountains. Meanwhile, Marilyn nagged him to pay attention to her instructions on how to act. "Make a good impression, especially with my dad. And don't overdo your infatuation with me in front of my brothers and sisters."

When the bus dropped them off at our driveway, she took off running, only to lose her footing on the log bridge and fall flat. She jumped to her feet, crimsoned-faced, as an entire family of welcomers poured out of the house.

The *trueloves* tried to scurry off by themselves. Marilyn said she wanted to show Allen the entire farm. Penny Courtwright, who'd arrived the week before, and I snuck up on them at the creek, hoping to see them kiss. I kept pestering Allen to tell me if he already snuck a smooch when I wasn't looking, but he just teased—he loved to tease—and kept me wondering. When Marilyn wasn't going for walks with Allen, she was showing him all the girly stuff like crocheted doilies and embroidered dresser scarves in what she called "Our Hope Chest"—even though Mother said she wasn't really engaged. I didn't think Allen cared much about that stuff, but he acted like he did to please my sister. I thought he would have had more fun hanging out with all of us than looking at linens.

When we could pry Marilyn's attention away from her boyfriend, she told us about the Vacation Bible Schools in Montana where she and her friend Barb had taught. She said it was kind of like our VBS at the creek, except that every week they went to a new place—a different one-room schoolhouse. Each day they told Bible stories, led songs, and played games. They met the families and had programs at the end of the week. Parents took an offering and donated the sum total of thirteen dollars to the young teachers.

I was most impressed, however, with her adventures. She said, "You should have seen the rattlesnakes. They were everywhere—on the roads and under the porches. You know that people die from rattlesnake bites. Sometimes I dreamed they were chasing me. But the mosquitoes were even worse. They came in swirling clouds and swarmed up from the grass. They left honking big welts wherever they bit. I scratched until blood came, and then the welts were even bigger."

She stopped to catch her breath and make certain we were impressed, before continuing, "At one place, I tried to play the piano, only to hear a thud with each key I pressed. We took the front off the piano and there was a nest full of baby mice. The whole time it was so hot you could hardly breathe. Then a storm would come up, knock out the power, and turn everything into mud!"

Marilyn had hardly unpacked and ironed everything—including her underwear—when she began to repack, telling us she would be spending the remainder of the summer in Montana, managing the house at the Miller Ranch during harvest. She and Allen left the Farmhouse five days after they came, not even staying long enough to see Elizabeth or meet her Bill. "What's wrong with her head," I muttered to myself. "Why would she go back to Montana with its rattlesnakes, mosquitoes, and sweaty heat waves?"

Five days had been plenty of time for me to take a shine to Allen, however. His main virtue was that he never told me to shut up when I talked too much. The day after they left, I wrote him a post card. "Ha ha ha. I know you are going to marry Marilyn. So there. Ha ha. Love, Eleanor Joy"[91]

A few weeks later, we received some packages. Allen had collected retired power tools from the Jackson farm where he worked. They were implements that ran off a direct current battery system, charged by windmills—the kind of system farmers used before the Electrification Act. There was a bench grinder, a heavy-duty drill, and a welder. The welder would improve the functioning of the Popular Mechanics aircraft adapter model, so Daddy and David augmented the first model with the donated DC welder. To that same generator system they could have connected the grinder, but David said it wouldn't be convenient. Instead, he stripped the internal parts out of the grinder, installed a pulley, and powered it with an external 110V AC motor. With all the new, *old* stuff, our lean-to began to resemble Mr. Tieche's machine shop. David and Daddy may have known what everything was, but to the rest of us, it looked like a mulligan stew of whatsits, doohickeys, and this-and-that's, some hooked up and some not.

On July 27, we heard on the radio that the Korean War was over. Mother dabbed her eyes with her apron and said to no one in particular, "Thank the Lord the troops can come home."

I didn't think so much about the war on the other side of the world, because my battles were with my sister Marian. Mother told Penny and me to play with Marian, but instead we climbed a stump that was too high for her and whispered so she couldn't hear. When she sniveled, I called her a crybaby and she cried harder. So I chanted my version of a ditty I had heard at school, "Sticks and stones may break your bones, but names will never hurt you."

The tears of the little girl and the meanness of my teasing gave me guilt beyond belief—not that day, but the day I feared my six-year-old sister was gone forever.

It happened part way up Grauel Road in July when Mother and a few of us had gone wild mountain blackberry picking. The best berry patches were on the inclines where the loggers had left a crisscross maze of fallen trees that they couldn't sell. Briars, nettles and wild vines grew over the logs and covered the deep holes beneath. The boys headed off to the ridge, balancing along the big logs and scuttling up the steep parts as they carried their lard or coffee cans suspended under bent clothes-hanger handles.

Penny, Marian, and I stayed close to Mother, picking a patch that was just out of sight from the road. Marian had been right there with us all along—until she wasn't.

We began to call and to search up and down the road. We checked a gutted, rusty, Dodge truck that sat in the overgrown path. The sun was high in the sky, and the heat of the day could be seen in waves down the mountainside. Drying grass and wildflowers produced the dead-sweet smell of summer. "Marian! Yoo-hoo! Marian!"

Silence, except for the droning of a thousand insects, met our ears.

"Mother," I asked, "Could a bear 'uv got her?" Penny and I knew there were bears around; we had seen the smashed berries and the purple droppings.

"No, she's here somewhere, close by. We'll find her."

"B-but, we've looked everywhere and . . . "

"That's enough. God knows where she is, and He will show us."

I knew my mother believed that, but she was rubbing her hands the way she did the time John and Phillip did not come home from fishing before dark.

I wanted to ask Mother if she had heard a truck come up the road earlier. I knew if a bear hadn't gotten Marian, then the big man in his noisy truck had grabbed her with his hand over her mouth and taken her away. We would never see her again and I wouldn't be able to say sorry for climbing on the stump with Penny and taunting my little sister who was too small to climb up. I really wanted to tell my mother what I was feeling, but her eyes told me I was not to say anything more.

"Oh, Jesus," she breathed. I hugged my chest, shivering even in the heat.

We yelled louder, "Yoo-hoo, Marian, yoo-hoo!" the sound of our voices reminding me of the howl of coyotes and the call of crows.

The boys scrambled from behind the ridge, over and under logs, holding their waving buckets high in the air to keep them from spilling. "Marian is lost," Mother told them. "We've not seen her for at least an hour."

Our brothers scoured the area, tromping on the road, calling, and listening. Mother told John to run home and tell Daddy to call the sheriff. We knew it would take a long time, as he would have to call from the Tieches' and wait for the sheriff to drive out from town. "But run as fast as you can!" Mother urged.

The sun moved behind the trees. Our stomachs were empty from hunger and sick from anxiety. We heard the Coupe before we could see it. Following behind Daddy drove the sheriff in his patrol car. The men got out, concern etched on their faces. In response to the sheriff's question, Mother turned and pointed toward the knoll where we had been when Marian was last seen. At that same moment, as we looked where Mother was pointing, we all watched a small girl crawl up out of the ditch and onto the road—not even a child's stone-throw from where we stood. Marian had been sleeping for nearly four hours, oblivious to our frantic calling, and hidden from sight by the weeds in the ditch.

We all began to blabber at once. Marian rubbed her eyes. When the hullabaloo settled down, she said, "I was scared to death when I couldn't find anyone. I didn't know where to go and no one answered when I called. I heard a truck on the road so I climbed into the ditch and lay completely still so no one would see me. I guess I fell asleep."

I wanted to hug her, but we Coreys didn't hug each other except when someone was going far away. Instead I told myself, "For the rest of my life, I will always be nice to my sister."

While Penny and Gary were still at our place, Virginia, John, and Star came home to the farm. They had finished a tour across Canada providing music for the preacher, Oswald J. Smith, and they were beginning to raise support to travel as missionaries to St. Vincent.

Mother told them to leave Star to play with Janice while they called on people in our area, and she assigned Penny and me to watch the toddlers. We took the girls outside to play in the woodpiles, but we were distracted. Two-year-old Star and 17-month-old Janice disappeared from under our noses. We thought they were hiding, so we checked all the trees nearby, using a teasing voice to get them to reveal their whereabouts. No answer. So Penny and I searched the barn and ran along the creek, calling and calling. My heart hammering with anxiety, I hurried into the house, "Mother! Come! Help! Star and Janice are missing. We've looked everywhere. We don't . . . "

Mother came running—just as two men rounded the driveway carrying Star and Janice. The children squirmed free and ran to Mother who wrapped them in her arms. The tallest man explained, "We came around the corner in the logging truck and saw these two children sitting in the middle of the highway. They were eating blackberries out of their cans, oblivious to any danger. There was barely time enough for us to stop." He ran a hand through his ragged hair and tugged one of the sleeves of his dirty jacket.

"Thank you, thank you! God bless you!" Mother exclaimed.

She handed the little girls off to us; then reached into her apron pocket for a nose rag—that's what we called the torn pieces of fabric we used to blow our sniffles. I needed a nose rag too, but didn't have one so I used my sleeve instead. The men walked back toward the highway. Mother stood still for a moment; then turned to us. "Those men smelled like alcohol."

Penny and I were silent with guilt and shame. I could hardly stand to think what might have happened if the men had not been able to stop soon enough or if they had been really bad men. I expected to be punished, but it never happened. Penny and I promised each other we would never, *ever*, be so careless again.

Back at the Farmhouse, we cleaned the dirt and berry stains off Star and Janice in the new bathtub. Yes, the new bathtub! A few days earlier, about the time Penny came, Daddy brought home a porcelain claw-foot tub. He put the tub under the stairs at the side of the kitchen, on top of the strip of linoleum we'd laid the year before. He made a sidewall using one of the Sears cupboards, then installed pipes along the other wall from the water tank behind the stove. He anchored a rod on which Mother hung a heavy canvas curtain with just a few small holes. Penny and I fretted about what the boys might be able to see through the holes, so we fixed folds in the fabric or sewed on patches to ensure our privacy.

Besides improving the bath arrangement for all of us, the tub also supplied another spigot for washing hands when everyone came in from outside at the same time. The luxury would have been overwhelming if the tub had been smaller or the hot water heater large enough to give more than an inch or two of lukewarm water. Nonetheless, there were few complaints.

With the school year approaching, Penny and Gary went home. Marian headed off to first grade and Merton got Mrs. Tripp for third grade. Phillip and I warned our younger brother that if Mrs. Tripp had thought the two of us were bothersome, she would really have her hands full with him. Within the first few weeks, Mrs. Tripp had pinched his ear several times and led him off to the cloakroom for an encounter with her paddle.

That was the year I decided, for the first time, to get off the bus with a new friend and walk from her house to mine. I said to Phillip, "Tell Mother I'll be home in half 'n hour."

My friend Betty lived in the Doll House, the bungalow that bachelor John Udd had built during homestead years, the same house in which the John Johnsons lived while they built their home up Grauel Road. I thought it was the cutest place—I could see it from the highway, and wondered what it might look like on the inside. As Betty and I climbed down the steps of the bus, John and Phil said in unison, "You better not."

I knew what they meant. At our house, you asked permission first—but I didn't like that rule. Later that afternoon, Daddy was waiting for me at the Farmhouse door. I don't remember what he said, but I do remember the trip to the woodshed. *But so what!* I thought. *Seeing the inside of the white dollhouse was worth it*. In front of Daddy, I acted remorseful for my willful act—not because I was repentant, however, but because I was afraid he would say I couldn't go to Mrs. Myers' for Pioneer Girls and play games, make crafts, and eat sweets with my friends. Sometimes you just had to put up with the punishment if you wanted to have any fun.

With the ninth child in school, Mother was left with only Janice at home. Her relative quiet lasted for only a few days, and then she was given three more charges all at once: Timmy, Brent, and Laney Miner,[92] ages nine down to four. Their mother had died and Mr. Miner said to our parents. "I can't care for these children and go to work. If you'll look after them, I will help pay for their food and expenses."

For the next several months—months that began to seem like years—we all moved over and made room for the Miners. In total, we were nine kids under the age of thirteen, of which two were babies. Laney wasn't *technically* a baby, but the stringy-haired four-year-old sure acted like one. Brent, with wavy hair and freckles, was quiet and withdrawn, while Timmy, the curly-haired blond, was an artistic dreamer who could draw cartoons. Neither boy could do his school assignments. Mother said they were just slow and I said they needed to be in special schools.

I also thought the boys were cruel to our pets and needed to be punished. One day, Timmy and Brent picked up our baby ducks and threw them over the fence onto the Johnsons' side. The fall broke at least one leg on every duckling, and we had to kill them all. "Why do we have to keep these kids?" I stewed to Mother.

She didn't answer me, but she stewed to Marilyn in a letter. "This morning Brent just missed the bus. He was as slow as usual . . . but Dad had a rule that anyone missing the bus would stay home and work. Well—it's more work for me to have to keep him busy. Worst of all, his father is coming out today to help Dad. Sometimes he is as slow as his kids."[93]

Mr. Miner never brought any money. However, he did pay to have his old car repainted. He showed it off, pride oozing from his voice. Then he brought Mother the *gift* of a coffee pot that he didn't need and Mother didn't want—she already had one. Anyway, she preferred instant Nescafe, which was cheaper per cup than ground Folgers. We were stuck with the Miner kids, though, no matter what. Mother had given her word that the children could stay, and Daddy was not one to insist on payments of debts when he was the holder of the note. "'Do good and lend,'" he quoted, "'expecting nothing in return.'"

Across the Puget Sound, Bill Richardson was recovering from surgery and sealing his relationship with Elizabeth. She began wearing an engagement ring—a ring he bought with money borrowed from his granddad.

Mother wasn't pleased that Elizabeth was engaged so soon after her big break-up with Vern. She commiserated in letters back and forth to Grandma and Aunt Eleanor that these youngsters needed more time. Shouldn't Bill have a paying job to help cover the expenses of a new household? But what could Mother do or say? She could only remind herself as often as necessary, "I *will* trust the Lord for all my children, and will *not* be afraid."

In September, Bill and Elizabeth arrived for a visit with news that signaled the next phrase of their pre-nuptial agreement. Bill said, "When we drove past a place east of McDonald Creek, I saw an old sawmill for sale. It looked like it might be a good one."

Daddy nodded and agreed to check it out. Bill and my father had already looked at two others, but the price had been too high. By this time, it was a foregone conclusion that the next step towards building a house was getting a saw mill to cut our own lumber. It was just a matter of finding the right one.

Marian Janice and walkway to outhouse

CHAPTER TWENTY-ONE
The Sawmill
(Fall 1953)

"Seven hundred dollars," the owner of the rusty sawmill told Daddy and David. "But," he added, "For two hundred more you can have all of the accessories."

He pointed out the extras—a gas-powered yard donkey, along with pulleys, conveyor belts, cables, a cut off saw, and much more. David took stock of it all. He was in his element, and Daddy knew it. David nodded his head in a way that told his father that the hodgepodge of equipment would be worth far more than $200. Still, nine hundred dollars was an inordinate amount of money, regardless of what hoard of tools it might purchase. Daddy told the man he'd pray about it.

After he prayed, Daddy said he knew that God would supply enough for this mill and the accessories. Elizabeth agreed. And on her next trip to the bank, she withdrew $900 from the funds she had been depositing each payday for nearly a year.

Daddy delivered the full payment to the owner, only to be met with an additional condition for the sale. "You must get this moved off my land and up and running on yours by December 3rd."

The mill had stood idle for years. Its parts were rusty and stiff. The boys were in school. Daddy would have to do most of the tear down and transport, and the deadline was only a few weeks out. So every day, except Sunday, he made the fifty mile round-trip from the Farmhouse to the site of the sawmill. Behind the Coupe, he pulled a trailer he'd cobbled together with parts from the Packard tractor. Back home, in the evenings, he helped the boys excavate a road to the mill assembly site. They'd chosen a flat area on top of the ridge to the southwest of the barn, overlooking the Johnson's gully. Crowbars, picks, hoes, and shovels—this road demanded more muscle power than had the road to the gravel pit by the creek. Mother lamented the time these projects took. "I wonder if we've bit off more than we can chew," she said on several occasions.

Just when it seemed impossible, God built the road. Well, not God alone. He sent his workers, only they didn't know they'd been sent—unless my father told them later, which it stands to reason he did.

It happened that the men, who had earlier cleared the right of way for the power line, came to pick up their bulldozer. They couldn't get it started. In their attempts, they flooded the engine and ran out of gas. Daddy said, "I have enough gas in my farm tank. Shall I bring a can?"

A gallon or two was all they needed. Daddy chatted with the men as they prepared to leave, and assured them, "No, you don't owe me anything." However, the second time they offered to pay him, he ventured, "Well, do you suppose you could drop your blade and push some dirt along this road as you head out?"

Mother watched from the back porch as the driver traversed the hill for the next 45 minutes, cutting into the wall with the massive blade, lifting stones and pushing the dirt and cedar roots over the edge of the slope. When the man chugged back to the highway, the new roadbed to the sawmill site was wide, smooth, and level.

All that was needed after that operation was gravel—and tons of it. The boys took the Model A dump truck across the highway to the railroad grade and picked up load after load of real stone pebbles, not the clay mixture from the creek. The new road to the mill and the driveway to the house sucked up gravel like quicksand, such that the boys lost count of the number of trips in the Model A.

When there was a day free from school, one of us would accompany Daddy on his trips to the mill site. I wasn't much help, but I could talk to him along the drive so he wouldn't be bored. Talking was what I did best. "Dad," I whispered. "Dad, Dad." I was practicing a new grown up name for him. Heart fluttering, I repeated loud enough for him to hear, "Dad?"

"What?"

"Dad, how soon do you think you will be done moving all this stuff, Dad?"

He answered me, but I wasn't listening. What mattered was: I had graduated to calling him "Dad," the same name my older brothers and sisters used.

I didn't travel much with Dad. I'm sure he preferred the boys who could wield a wrench. Or Mother, for another reason. One morning, Dad said to Mother, "I need you to go with me today—now—please!"

Mother didn't have a trip to the sawmill site on her agenda for the day, but Dad insisted. He demurred at telling her the full reason, simply saying, "Your presence is a blessing, and it will help to keep the distractions at bay."

Before long, Mother discovered the source of the distractions was Mrs. What's-Her-Name, wife of the mill man. The woman would watch for Dad's arrival, and when he drove in the yard she would pull on her coat to accompany him. She would sidle up close to talk, and Dad would speak to her of the Lord. She was happy about that. In fact, she was happy to talk about anything. Eventually, my father came to realize that it wasn't his Bible message the missus was after. Daddy told Mother that none of the rest of us was as good as she was in "keeping the distractions at bay." So she would pick up her coat and galoshes and follow Dad to the Plymouth Coupe, teasing as they went, "You're still the handsome man I married. I'm not surprised she took a liking to you!"

So while there were distractions at the mill-disassembly site and a mess of pieces dumped on our hill, there were also never-ending interruptions. "For the life of me," Mother wrote to Marilyn, "I can't see how they can get all those parts together again to form a mill. Besides, interruptions eat up more time than the mill-moving operation. So naturally it's taking longer than anyone figured."[94]

The biggest interruption this fall was hunting. David was determined to bring home wild meat—one of his first seasons to hunt for big game. He went out day after day, first with his .22 rifle, then with a borrowed shot gun. No big game accompanied him back home. Mother told him it was not a hunting season for him to write his sisters about, but she could—and she did: "David was out hunting yesterday, using Don Nordstrom's gun . . . he saw a bear enjoying himself eating berries. The bear was still – didn't hear David. So David fired— and missed. Buck fever they call it. He said he just got excited and didn't aim good. And it would have been such an easy shot. Was he ever disgusted![95]

Another day, Phil went hunting with David out west, near the Gossett home, and he was also able to testify to the bad aim. "David's eyes are blind. He can't see a thing out there in the woods. Let me tell you. We'd just gone around behind the Gossett's house and I could see as plain as day a four-point buck. I tried to get David's attention without spooking the deer, but the guy never saw that animal and never got one bang out of the shotgun."

Phil paused for effect. "Yup, David's eyes are bad—he must need glasses."

Donny Nordstrom, Glenn Duncan, and most of the other school-age hunters filled their deer tags, but not Dave.[96] He only got ducks and rabbits that he pumped so full of buckshot they had more lead in them than meat. Mother told him, "Don't bring them home. There's nothing left to cook."

She said the grouse—*dickey bird*, David called it—was not too bad. "But you need to shoot at least three at a time for everyone to get a taste."

David was discouraged with hunting, so he took the boys and me clam digging. We carried the Coleman lantern and didn't get home until past midnight, owing to the tides. Dad told him not to stay out so late, but that owed—not so much to our sleep habits or safety—as to Dad's frequent comment about clams, "as far as I am concerned, one clam is one too many for my liking." I agreed with him on the taste score, but the midnight dig on the rocky beach was just fine by me.

And then there was a butchering interruption. Not at our place, but at Mrs. Tieche's. "Do you think you could butcher our goats?" She asked David.

David had never butchered goats before, and neither had Bill who'd come to help with mill transport, but they said they would. They headed across the road and David handed Bill the .22 rifle. Remembering his hunting failures, he said, "I don't want to shoot them, the target is too small."

Bill took care of that part. Then the two realized they had not set up any place to hang and skin the carcasses, so had to drape them on the fencepost. They took the butcher knife in hand and hacked the quarters apart until the hunks were small enough for Mrs. Tieche to package. The boys joked afterwards that they had never let on to Mrs. Tieche that they were clueless. And Mrs. Tieche never let on that she was well aware of that fact.

Yes, the interruptions were many. They continued beyond hunting and butchering; beyond a death and a wedding; and even beyond the mill man's deadline.

On November 13, Mr. John Johnson died. He had been sick for a long time, and his daughter Margaret and her husband Orben Ellis had taken over management of the farm. We hardly saw Mrs. Johnson anymore, but when

Mother heard the news, she said she needed to pay the widow a visit. She wanted to tell Mrs. Johnson how much she and her husband meant to us, and how grateful we were for their generosity, and for all they'd taught us while we stumbled along as novice farmers.

Mother returned home down Grauel road, past the Tieche's and past the hayfield. She turned west on the highway, still musing about the life that we'd led because the Johnsons had been such magnanimous neighbors. As she looked ahead toward the mailbox, she picked up her step almost to a run. Sitting there were several large boxes. Her thoughts immediately switched gears. These were the packages she'd been waiting for—packages sent by Allen Thompson. They were bulky and heavy—almost more than she could carry. When she arrived at the door, she was met by Marian, who'd stayed home from school with a cold. When the six-year-old saw the mysterious packages, she spoke right up, "I feel better already!"

Mother, Marian and the little kid, Laney Miner, opened the boxes to discover a set of sixteen plates, saucers, cups, and bowls in the most modern of materials: Melmac plastic, guaranteed to last a lifetime. The silky, chip-free, stain-free service came in three soft colors: A pale, pinky peach, a spruce-tree green, and a lemon-drop yellow. Melmac wouldn't crash to pieces like Mother's Admiral Bavarian wedding dishes, most of which had already been destroyed. Melmac wasn't elegant like the gold-rimmed blue with floral garlands of Grandma Phenicie's Oxford design by Noritake. But they would serve sixteen at a time and survive even the three-times-a-day heavy-duty usage of all us kids.

Mother pushed to the back of the shelves her chipped porcelain plates and bent tin. She joked to Marian, "We will have to tear down these cupboards and build bigger."

"Can I wash all the new dishes? Please? Please? Laney can dry."

At dinner, even the boys wanted to set the table and choose a favorite color. Janice pointed to her choice and baby-babbled, so Marian said to her, "Say 'pink,' Sweet Pea, say 'pink.'" The toddler puffed her lips and popped a *puh* sound. We laughed and she giggled. Janice—or Sweet Pea, as Marian called her—was at the age where she tried to repeat everything we prompted her to say. And we prompted a lot.

Mother wrote to Allen and sent a carbon copy to Marilyn and Virginia, whom she knew had helped to inspire the purchase. "I was wondering if using such dishes would help this family to improve table manners. You know, Allen, Dad mentioned something about a "dowry for our girl!" You could have had <u>her</u> without a dowry. But a question, do the Cuban boys pay the girl's dad for the girl?"[97]

The dishes had arrived at the perfect time—just in time for the biggest event our Farmhouse had ever hosted. Elizabeth was getting married, and had selected Thanksgiving week for her wedding. It was a hurry-up decision—you know the kind that says two people can live cheaper than one. It was much quicker than Mother had hoped, but she said we would be ready. So with the new dishes in place and the cupboards tidy, she welcomed those who came the day ahead to help.

On Wednesday, November 25, we arrived from school to see the Farmhouse all gussied up. Liz and Bill had hauled in armloads of cedar boughs they draped over the two-by-fours and rough boards still splotched with left-over patches of Grange House wallpaper. It smelled of Christmas.

All of the Richardsons and Pastor Sanford from Snohomish arrived that afternoon, as did Elizabeth's friends from Joyce High School, Beverly Hanson and Doris Thors. This was the first wedding I'd been to, so I dressed in my finest outfit which included a gift from Aunt Eleanor—a new pink Orlon sweater with pearls and rhinestones. I sat in the front row of chairs facing the backdrop of cedars, where the pastor and Bill waited. I'd never seen Bill dressed up before. Oh my, did he ever look handsome in the swanky suit he'd bought with all his money (which is why he'd borrowed from his Granddad for the engagement ring.) Elizabeth eased down the steep stairs in her fancy white wedding gown, taking care that the layers and layers of netting didn't snag on the rough walls. Dad met her at the bottom of the stairway and ushered her the distance of three steps toward Bill. I looked back and forth at the two, taking it all in and trying to decide which of the boys from school or Snohomish I would one day marry. After the pastor finished with the readings from his black book, Dad finalized the ceremony with a benediction. There was a big announcement about Mr. and Mrs. William Richardson, followed by a long kiss—which, in turn, was followed by Phillip's voice calling from the stairs, "Ha ha ha! I wore my PJs under these scratchy pants!"

Thus, the solemn ceremony ended with rounds of laughter, after which the quote about the PJs was immortalized through many repetitions as we finished off the snacks served on the new dishes. Bill and Elizabeth left in their car—the 1940 Ford that had been Granddad Richardson's—for a two-day honeymoon. They would spend Thanksgiving with Grandma Phenicie, and from there settle into a stamp-size apartment they had rented in Snohomish. Elizabeth would be back at her office job, while Bill would return to his classes at Everett Junior College where he had transferred after his injury cost him the sports scholarship at Seattle Pacific.

The following weekend, Mother and Dad were invited to a reception in Snohomish for the newlyweds. Before leaving, Mother sent Timmy, Brent, and Laney Miner home to their dad, and put me in charge of the kitchen. The first night, I made a canner-size pot of soup from jars of beef broth along with carrots and potatoes from the root cellar. It was simmering along nicely until the lid fell off the curry powder while I was shaking it over the pot. I dug out as much of the gold-colored spice as I could; then stirred in the rest. I pulled biscuits from the oven and went off to read a book. David came in, checked the pot, and remarked, "This soup *might* cook a little quicker if you put wood in the stove and keep the fire burning."

Letting the fire go out was nothing compared to hearing the boys snipe about the flavor of the fiery soup that I served for dinner that night. I had added milk and a can of peas, but the broth still burned all the way down our throats and left a strange taste in our mouths. We weren't used to curried East

Indian cuisine—and this was *curried*. When Mother came home, she poured the leftover soup into the dog dish, where he took one sniff and trotted off. My brothers offered helpful comments like, "It was great soup . . . if curry is your favorite flavor," and, "maybe you should stick to making biscuits."

I expected that the Miner kids would come back once the folks were home, but they never did. I didn't say it out loud, but I figured they all ended up in a special sort of school they all needed.

All December, I practiced for the school Christmas program in which I had a singing part. Then the day came. I told Marian not to rehearse with me because I couldn't hear my pitches very well, and I didn't read a book to Janice when she brought it to me. I jabbered at Mother, until she—having reached the point of exasperation—told me to get kindling for the wood box. It did seem like a good idea to work off a bit of my hyperactivity, so I went out to the woodshed and took the hatchet to a cedar stick. A couple of chops later, the blade glanced off the side of the wood and connected with the inside of my knee. I could see the bone before the blood found its pathway. Then what a mess it made. Mother pulled the gash shut and covered it up with the usual piece of bed sheet held with adhesive tape. Lying on the couch, I bit my nails and fussed that everyone would see the patch. Mother dismissed my sniveling with the brush of her hand and told me I'd be fine.

Well, I wasn't fine. Six hours later, up on the stage at Joyce School and smack in the middle of my song, blood began to ooze out from below the bandage. I could feel it dripping down my leg, past the hem of my almost new red and white dress with the circle skirt. I twisted my leg inward, hoping no one would notice. I finished the song with blood drizzling into my shoe. The teacher made me sit at the back of the stage for the rest of the program, my leg elevated on a chair. I didn't even get to stand up at the end and take a bow for the audience.

At home I also missed some of the festivities. Mother wouldn't let me go with the boys to get a tree because my knee would bleed, and she let Marian climb the highchair and put the star on the top. But she did let me organize the Christmas cards—of which we received many. I loved the peaceful portraits of Jesus in the manger, the fresh scenes of snow highlighted with a red cardinal bird—a kind I'd never seen in real life. I didn't care so much about seeing the photos of relatives I didn't know. First, Mother opened the envelopes and checked for donations. If there was money it meant she could go Christmas shopping. The more cards we received, the better our Christmas. As soon as my knee got a good scab, I hung the Christmas cards all around the nook in the living room and on strings across the windows. After Christmas we wrote thank you notes and Mother let me keep the best cards. I was especially pleased when people wrote their letters on separate paper and left the colorful pictures undamaged by handwriting. The clean ones I could make into ornaments or cut and glue onto construction paper to design our own cards—the ones we could send the following year to people important enough to warrant the three-cent stamps: i.e., those friends and relatives who were inclined to provide us with something tangible for our celebration. I was still sorting the

Christmas cards into piles of cards-for-crafts and cards-for-ornaments when David rushed through the door. "It looks like Tieches' house is on fire!"

We ran out and stood on the top of the hill overlooking the creek. On the other side of the valley flared an inferno of red, orange, and yellow flames—iridescent against the silhouettes of the trees, and sending trails of sparks sailing into the clouds. Within minutes, the brightest torches had died down. Gone was the home of Rose and Mrs. Tieche. Gone—the workshop where Mr. Tieche machined parts for our welder. Gone—the former dwelling of Seth Davis, his goats, bees, and tubs of honey. Gone—the Ramapo School built in 1915 for the children of the first settlers.

What a relief to hear that Rose and her mother had not been home when the house burned, and to learn that someone had heard their barking dog and freed him from his pen. The Tieches lost everything, but not their lives or their pet.

Friends from the community and Joyce Bible Church[98], where Rose and her mother attended, began to build a new house. The Himples, the Wetheralds, the Myers, the Halls, and others pitched in, and within a few weeks the shell was up. Energetic Mrs. Tieche worked alongside, and when the others left, she finished the project.

Dad checked in on them and reported to Mother that he wasn't needed. He was way behind on the mill transport and edgy from dealing with the mill owner and What's-Her-Name. Then it snowed half a foot and he couldn't travel at all. School was closed too, so everyone else was on edge. That meant David was at home, however, and he suggested that we put together the yard donkey, since the parts were under the roof of the lean-to. The yard donkey would be needed in the logging operations to haul trees after they were downed and to pile stumps for burning.

To reassemble the donkey, the boys found skid poles on which to attach the machine so it could be pulled wherever needed. They rigged up the four-cylinder Buda truck engine that had been part of the original mill accessories and soon the donkey was ready for action.

The snow melted, and Dad returned to his fifty-mile round trip with pieces of sawmill. On one of his final trips, he lugged back the John Deere stationary engine that filled every corner of the rickety little trailer and likely weighed a ton or more. Merton watched Dad drive past and thought, *How in tarnation did they ever load that engine—and how did the Coupe survive the weight it had to pull?* Well, the Coupe made it, but that was the end of the trailer.

Once unloaded, the engine joined the jumble of sawmill pieces—pieces that included the gears, pulleys, rollers, beams, carriage, track, drive mechanisms, and who knew what else. Dad looked at David, shook his head as Mother had, and said, "I can't imagine how we will put this back together."

David agreed it was a conglomeration, but he had seen it all intact. He shrugged in his nonchalant style. "We can sort out the parts and start over."

The task of reassembly would be David's job—but not yet. He was a starter on the basketball team, practicing every day after school and playing one or two games every weekend. The previous year, David had quit because he didn't have the courage to mitigate the differences between the coach's time schedule and Dad's curfew. Now he was a year older, a year bolder, and a year more experienced in negotiations.

The mill assembly was on pause, the house construction was delayed, and Mother's hopes were on hold. Perhaps it was the break in activity that prompted Mother to begin her new project, or perhaps she was thinking that at the age of nearly fifty, she was having a hard time keeping track of everything she needed to write to her daughters. Or perhaps she had a vision that one day, someone, somewhere would want to know about us. Whatever the reason, on May 28, 1954, Mother began to keep a diary.

'41 Plymouth Coupe and pulpwood by the cord

Dressed for Church
Star Eleanor Janice Arthur Marian

CHAPTER TWENTY-TWO
The Diary
(Spring 1954)

Mother recorded her first entry.

> Eliz. and Bill from Snohomish about 8:30 with Troupe and
> Richardson children. Got them settled with boys in the barn.
> Sunday was Baccalaureate. John finishing 8th grade. Folks got
> Dad and me to go . . . and what a surprise awaited us when we
> got home. A real celebration for the 25th anniversary. Gave us a
> beautiful wool blanket.[99]

It was a party worth writing about, the likes of which we'd never given our parents. There was a flower-decked, three-tier cake that they fed each other like newlyweds, a corsage for Mother's silky dress, and a wisecrack by Bill's dad, Bob Richardson, about not getting too cozy under the new blanket. I had never heard anyone make such remarks to Dad, and I didn't know whether to be shocked or to laugh with the guests. Dad's grin reached his ears and— double shock—he grabbed Mother for a passionate kiss. After which came shock number three: He followed Bob to the kitchen, donned Mother's apron, and the two men did the dishes, all the while chuckling about the Bible verse with the words, "as a man wipeth a dish . . . turning it upside down."

Bob was good for our father. We watched him make light of Dad's no-nonsense nature and saw our father turn jovial, almost carefree, as the two men labored, talked, and communed together.

The following Saturday the school held its annual end-of-year picnic at Crescent and Agate Beach. Before the day was over, word spread that the young Dimmel boy, a child with mental disabilities, was missing. The searchers scoured the area until the tide was in and it became too dark to see. On Sunday, Dad, David, and John went back and joined the search parties. A shock reverberated through the community when it was discovered that the youngster had fallen to his death on the rocks below the cliffs to the west of Agate Beach.

Mother was still reeling from the news about the young Dimmel child when Merton, age eight, came in from outside, crying and covered with blood. Earlier, Dad had sent Phillip and Merton to dispense with two-hundred thistles from the hay field before they could go fishing. The youngster managed to snuffle through his tears that they had filled a Spam can with worms and that near the knoll by the water line he had caught his foot on the end of a log and gone flying.

What a mess the sharp-edged can made of him! Blood was spurting from his head and hand. Mother sat him on the kitchen table and patched him up. The sight of the splattered blood everywhere made my head woozy, so I sat down too. No way was I going to make a fool of myself like Virginia did when John cut his hand. Mother, well aware that a ripped bed sheet and tape weren't going to be sufficient in this case, was in a hurry to get Merton to the doctor for stitches. Dad went out for the Coupe and remembered David had taken the car to his friend's. Mother said, "We'll have to take the Chev. We can't wait."

On the highway, Dad wrestled the floppy steering wheel with white knuckles, and rammed the brakes again and again. His lips were thin as a thread. Mother prayed for the car and Dad's patience as much as for her injured child. Merton white-knuckled his injured hand the same way Dad held the steering wheel. They made it to the clinic without incident, and Merton didn't fuss when the doctor put eight stitches in his thumb and three in his head, or when he got a tetanus shot.

What a shame, in a way, that the medical emergency happened without Marilyn at home to administer the first aid. But she was on her way back home from Homer City, Pennsylvania, and we were full of anticipation. For the previous six weeks, she had been doing laundry and cooking for dozens of guests. She had been scrubbing floors and toilets in a hands-on boot camp at West Indies Mission headquarters. Under the watchful eye of her future in-laws, she had been proving herself to be a worthy missionary appointee and an acceptable candidate to marry their son, Allen Thompson.

She burst through the door two days later and we blabbered at her about Merton's accident and the excitement she had missed. "That's alright," she said. "I'm not in nursing anymore, anyway, but I about burst a blood vessel wanting to nurse little Star back to health when I got Virginia's letter that the child was so desperately sick with dysentery—and so far away! I begged them to send her on a plane from St. Vincent to Florida where I could meet her."

Mother said, "Well, I am thankful to the Lord that all of them are coming home. It's just been one thing after another down there in the tropics, and that makes me think it's not the right place for them."

All of my oldest sister's family was coming home, and soon. In fact, Marilyn hadn't even gotten our place in order when Dad and Mother took off for the Vancouver airport to meet Virginia and her two babies. Her husband John would follow later.

Marilyn was in charge, of course. Before going to town with David in the Chev—The Beast, Dave called it—to pick up groceries, she commissioned a cleaning detail of us girls, including Kay Troupe who'd come to play with me. Marilyn said, "Virginia is bringing her babies and we have to get the house ready. You know Star has been so sick she almost died, and Virginia needs to get some rest."

The dishes, the floors, the windows, the stove, the tables, the chairs, the porch, and the toilet. We said she expected of us what Mr. Thompson had required of her at the mission home. We protested that we had no need to prove anything to anyone, but that didn't stop her from bossing. "Philtoose, you grind the wheat for bread. Mertie, you stay inside and keep that cut covered. It'll get infected and never heal."

When Marilyn got back from town, she fussed at Merton for loosening the bandage and making his hand bleed, complimented us on the cleaning we had done, and then went about to finish our job, since it was "still lacking in some small corners," she said. Then she set me to fixing beans.

"I'll sure be glad when Mother gets home," I lamented.

Marian agreed, "Mother isn't so picky."

The fact is: We could have readied the house at a slower pace because Dad and Mother were delayed. They got home the next day with reports of red tape at the border because Gin's youngest, little David John, had been born in St. Vincent.

We weren't to have much family time, even with the arrival of Virginia and her babies. That same day, after Mother had just situated the little family, Dad said he wanted his wife to go with him to Seattle. "We need to hear Allen's father preach and it's a chance for us to get acquainted with him."

Mother didn't argue, but moaned in her diary, "Arthur not content to settle down it seems, so he and I left at 5:00."

Two days later they returned to hear Marilyn announce that she would be off as well, for years and years. She told us all, with Virginia nodding, that she would be going to Pennsylvania to get married and then she would go overseas. Mother said, "I don't see any way your father and I can go so far. Can't you stay home for the summer and have your wedding with all of us around?"

Dad added, "Your Grandpa and Grandma Corey need fulltime care now. I'm sure there would be some money in their account to pay for your assistance until the wedding."

But Marilyn's mind was settled. Allen had wired her enough money for a ticket, and she couldn't wait to get back to his arms. She was in such a hurry we didn't even sing, "God be with you 'til we meet again," before she scrunched into the Coupe next to Mother and Dad, and they drove off to take her to the bus station. It was all too strange. She used to be sad about leaving, but not anymore. *What's wrong with her*, I wondered. *Why doesn't she listen to Mother and stay here for the wedding so we can celebrate like we did with Elizabeth and Bill?*

We had just said goodbye to Marilyn when word came from Snohomish that Bill had been listed as "physically unfit" for military service. The medical officer had checked Bill's reconstructed ankle and declared him 4-F. The five-hour operation had left Bill with pain and a limp, which meant he would never be called up.

We kids might have gone to visit Bill or our other Snohomish people, except that Mother declared most of us kids "medically unfit" to leave the Farmhouse. We had the "itch"—a recurrence for the umpteenth time. It had been only five years since we first got what we called "The Seven-year Itch," that we later learned was really scabies, and scabies didn't necessarily follow a seven-year schedule. We were subjected again to the kerosene treatment. Kerosene burned, but nothing like the tincture of iodine on ringworm. Kerosene stung just enough to feel like it was doing its job as a cure. Our eyes watered with the sizzling pain at first, but the relief from itching that followed was worth it.

So Bill was unfit, we were unfit, and then David announced that the '31 Chev was also unfit. It was a hazard to him and to anyone sharing the highway—not to mention the danger to those of us who tried to hang on to the fenders while it bumped around the yard. He rolled it into the lean-to and fixed the brakes, but the steering repair was far more difficult. He described the process to me in detail—all about kingpins and bushings—I acted like I understood. He groused about not having something called a reamer tool to shape the bushings, and having to force in the kingpins with large clamps. In the end, the Chev's steering troubles were reversed—David had to wrestle the steering wheel to make even the smallest turn, and wrestle it back to go straight ahead.

He'd about finished the car repairs when Mother declared that our dog, Flopper, was "behaviorally unfit." Flopper had come to us in dire straits. We could relate—dire straits was where we lived. Dad had seen the dog's pathetic face and floppy ears more than once while driving along the highway near the Place Road. One day he had brought the hound home in the trunk of the Plymouth. We gave the critter scraps of bread, soup bones, and whatever we could scrounge, but Flopper never seemed to fill up. Once he devoured an entire chicken that had been near death, after which the poor dog lay comatose for an entire day. When he wasn't eating, Flopper chased rabbits. He whooshed forwards and sideways, nearly tripping over his own feet, and barking his guttural *Huuu Huuu Huuu.* He'd rest a few minutes and then head out again, sniffing for a new trail.

After Flopper suffered an accident on the highway, he could only use three legs in the chase. That put him at an even greater disadvantage with the rabbits. If he had been able to supplement his diet with wild meat, perhaps he would not have committed an unpardonable deed, which he did while we were unloading groceries from the back of the car. In a flash, Flopper grabbed a package of wieners, and wolfed it down whole.

"This is the end of one of us," Mother declared. "Either Flopper has to go, or I do."

She gave her reasoning, "It's bad enough that we owe money at the Co-op and can't pay our bills, let alone having a dog eat us out of house and home."

We were sorry for Flopper, but we understood why Mother could not with clear conscience support a dog who would steal what she had rationed for us. Mother no doubt felt unfit too, as she reminded us about our debt to the Co-op for the purchase of fuel for car and farm, grain for our bread, feed for the cattle, and scratch for the chickens.

Day after day, week after week, the negative numbers of the Co-op bill—posted on a two-foot wide blackboard by the kitchen stove—nagged at her; as did the verse Dad had written below them, "But seek first the Kingdom of God and His righteousness, and <u>ALL</u> these things will be added unto you. Matthew 6:31"

Mother, though not doubting the truth of God's word, commented to Dad, "The time seems unnecessarily long for some things to be added unto."

She sighed, but nevertheless thanked the Lord, when *added unto* meant Elizabeth telling Dad to take $103 from the Building Fund to pay the Co-op bill.

Then again, *added unto* meant something entirely different when Mother received a letter from her sister. "Could you put up a house for Mother (Phenicie) on the farm? I am planning to get married."[100]

Our Aunt Eleanor—our adored, glamorous, dental assistant Aunt Eleanor—was finally planning a wedding at the age of forty-two. She had been courted numerous times by excellent candidates, but this one was the real deal. Mother and Dad left for Tacoma the next day to get the scoop. They learned our aunt would be marrying Dr. Howard Koon, a dentist whose children were grown and whose wife had divorced him.

Our parents were not convinced about the wisdom of the choice, but Mother said that her sister had cared for their mother twenty-five years, and now it was our turn. We would build a bungalow to specs acceptable to soon-to-be Uncle Howard. He would pay for a place designed for our grandma—our tiny grandma who was bow-legged with arthritis, who couldn't climb steps, and who would have to depend on a cane to get from her chair to the kitchen and back.

John McLennan arrived to join Virginia and the two children who'd settled in at our place after their return from the mission field. Within a short time, John was accepted as Pastor of a church in Irondale, near Port Townsend. This meant their family would be located only a ninety-minute drive, rather than off somewhere between one Canadian coast to the other, or in St. Vincent of the Caribbean. John and Virginia found a Pontiac to purchase and secured a loan of $300 from Elizabeth, the banker, who said they could pay it back over the next ten months without interest.

John's arrival was good news for Grandma's house. John Mac—so as not to confuse him with our brother—seemed to know more about architecture and construction than all the rest of us put together. He brought an artistic touch to the Coreys' typical hand-to-hammer approach to building. By the end of August, the structural design had been approved; the site cleared of stumps; the foundation poured; and a truckload of lumber delivered. Merton walked around the pile, breathing in the fresh wood fragrance and rubbing his hands along the smooth, nearly knot-free, planks. He said he'd never seen so many boards except when Dad drove him past the lumberyard.

The boys measured the lumber to length. It was a slow go, cutting those boards with the carpenter hand saw. The cut off saw had been removed from the Packard for the welder adaptation and the chainsaw would have mutilated the lumber, so Dad took part of the money earmarked for materials and bought a Skilsaw. It was revolutionary. The boys could rip a straight cut through a board in seconds. The house, built with new lumber, new nails, new windows, new sinks, and a new toilet, was coming together in record time. We were so busy that we hardly noticed when September 7 came and went—Marilyn's and Allen's wedding day in Pennsylvania. We were reminded a few weeks later when the pictures arrived. The bride beamed, even in black and white photos, and I was sorry we hadn't been there to hoot and holler when Allen kissed her.

On September 19, Aunt Eleanor and Uncle Howard were married in Tacoma, doubling the pressure to get Grandma Phenicie moved. Within a month, the new well was dug and hooked up, the septic installed, and the house sealed against the rain and wind. Dad and Mother tripped back and forth to Tacoma, helping Grandma pack her belongings and choose what to bring to her new home. After each stressful trip, Dad and Mother returned to a never-ending list of things to do at the Farmhouse.

In spite of the overload, my parents were never too occupied to drop their workman tools or kitchen tasks when people called on them for help. One such set of needy people, Martin and Gladys Mansfield, arrived the same day my exhausted parents returned from yet another trip to Tacoma. We'd known the Mansfields for a long time. Dad often stopped at their place near Port Townsend to give counsel and pray. In gratitude, Mr. Mansfield would share his catch of seafood or invite my brothers to go fishing, crabbing, or boating from their waterfront place. Mr. Mansfield helped Daddy repair and maintain the car, and was an all-around generous man. His wife was something else entirely. She started her raspy ritual of harping the minute she walked through our door. She censured the church hypocrites that grated on her nerves, then switched to whining about her knees and back, even as she eased her bulk into a chair and served herself to a third helping of bread and jam. I marveled how Mother and Dad could be so long-suffering. I thought, *Why don't they just say they have stuff to do, or take the Mansfields outdoors to help with the jobs? That would send them home in a hurry!*

The Mansfields sometimes brought one or two of their three sons. But they came alone on this visit, for reasons easily understood. Mrs. Mansfield said to our parents, "We can't control Delfred anymore. The neighbors have said they don't want to see him in the neighborhood and that they don't trust him around their families. Would you be willing to let him live here with you?"

As if we needed that kind around our family. Oh brother!

Yet, less than a month later, Delfred—Del for short—moved in. Mother put a second mat on the floor of the attic so he could share the space with Phillip. He would attend the same classes in school as John. The Mansfields wrote a check for Mother to get Del school clothes and glasses and promised a monthly payment of $40.00. They gave her five honking geese—and I mean honking as in truck-horn-loud honking. Those geese took ownership of the pond and came after us if we got too close, once grabbing the backside of Phillip's pants and a beak-full of the skin underneath.

After the Mansfields left off the honkers, Mother's tone was sad, "Gifts can never make up for how I feel about Mrs. Mansfield's rejection of Delfred."

We thought the Mansfields hadn't done much better with their other two boys. We felt sorry for Alvey, who was hospitalized with a medical condition, and we were awed to learn that Davey was locked up in a lunatic asylum. Some said he was insane, but Mother told us not to use that word.

Grandma's house was ready by Thanksgiving. Dad, with a couple of helpers, drove a truck loaded with her things, and went back a day later to bring Grandma. It took them longer than Mother expected, but she was glad to hear they had delayed the trip to give time for Grandma Corey to see them off.

Meanwhile, Mother and I spent part of the day getting Grandma's new house ready. We washed the dust off the counters and wiped out the cupboards. We hung curtains that I'd hemmed, and I tried out the toilet a few times to make sure it worked. I talked about how excited I was that Grandma would live in this house, so close to us. Mother told me, "It's a good thing that we have the house ready for her so she can get settled. Your grandma has lived for so long in one big place this small space will take some adjusting to."

Then, there they were, the men helping Grandma out of the car and up the single step to the door. I was in a dither, but held it in because Mother reminded me that Grandma would be tired after such a long trip. Once I'd said hello, Mother sent me across the yard and up the driveway to help Elizabeth fix dinner.

Then Christmas came in a hurry. For a gift, John and Virginia gave us an electric clothes dryer which we didn't use much because electricity was expensive, and it cost nothing to hang everything outside, on the porch, and behind the stoves. Mother cooked the bonus turkey that came with the dryer—a turkey we figured was a gift from God to replace ours that had fallen dead in the night. When it was ready, along with the trimmings, John Mac and Dad took the car over to Grandma's, helped her get in, and brought her across the yard to eat Christmas dinner with us for the very first time.

I suppose there were other gifts that year, along with the turkey and the dryer, but none compared with the gift of having Grandma sit at our table and then go home to her house next door where she was so close we could see her every day.

And we did see Grandma every day as she sat at her table with the yellow and green butter-cup stencil, looking out the picture window, and waving her hand when we waved to her. Or we would see her with her coffee cup in hand, talking with Mother and asking about us. After all these years, Grandma could ask questions and get immediate answers—no more letter writing to her daughter, Margaret, and waiting two weeks for a reply.

Twenty-fifth Wedding Anniversary

Grandma Phenicie's New Home

CHAPTER TWENTY-THREE
The Resident
(1955)

Mother sat at Grandma's fold-down table—with a cloth over the butter-cup stencil so it wouldn't fade in the sun—and said, "David took Phillip, Eleanor and me to the basketball games last night at Joyce. It's the first time I've seen Dave and John play. What a surprise when Arthur said he would stay home and watch the youngsters so I could go."

"How did the boys do?" asked Grandma, "Were they pretty good?"

"Well, of course, *I* thought so. John is still getting a handle on the game but David is pretty fast on his feet. It was quite entertaining to watch him hassle the boy he was supposed to guard, knocking away the ball or causing the player to travel."

For the rest of the season, if the game was at home, Mother gave the report according to what she saw—how well the boys did, what team won, and the scores if deemed worthy of remembrance. When the boys didn't do well, Mother gave reasons: i.e., the refs were at fault, or the team was short of players who had taken sick or fouled out. She gave second-hand reports about games that she couldn't attend because they were at other schools. And Grandma never seemed to tire of learning about the athletic prowess of her grandsons.

News about the girls was equally important. Mother reminded Grandma that the first family birthday of the year would be Elizabeth's. She'd be turning twenty-one on March 3. "She hopes to be up a few days after and we can celebrate it then. I hope you'll feel like joining us."

"Oh, I'm sure I will," Grandma said. "But, in the meantime, I have something to give you."

Grandma stood and shuffled with her cane toward the table behind the brown recliner that had once been Grandpa Phenicie's. She pulled out two one-dollar bills. "Will this be enough for you to call Elizabeth for her birthday?"

Mother looked up, surprise in her eyes, "Oh, you don't need to do that. We'll see her in a few days."

Mother could see Grandma meant business, so adjusted her response, "But, yes, that will be enough. I'll go to Mrs. Tieche's first thing in the morning and place the call."

Because the rest of us were in school, three-year-old Janice got to spend extra time with Grandma. She'd go across the yard with Mother every day and sit on the floor, building towers with blocks that Grandma pulled from the black hutch by the door. Then came the day that Janice got to stay all morning with Grandma while Mother and Dad went to town. Grandma half filled two dainty teacups with hot water from her kettle on the back of the wood burning heater and filled them with milk. "Come here, Janice," she said. "We'll have a tea party."

Janice left the block pile and climbed up on the chair, where Mother usually sat, and Grandma gave her a spoon to stir in the sugar. Together, Grandma and her youngest granddaughter sipped milk tea, nibbled on lady finger cookies, and talked about the pond, the frogs, and the spring flowers that were in bloom already.

When I went to see Grandma, I talked about important matters, like how Ellen had surprised us with her second calf and Delilah with her first, and that we didn't know if the in-heat cows had been bred in their scheduled visits to the neighbors, or when they had broken through the fences. I knew Grandma wasn't used to talking about those farming kinds of things, but she didn't seem to mind hearing what I knew. We commiserated about David having to break in Delilah as a first-time milking cow, how Delilah kicked whatever her hoof could reach—usually the pail or Dave's arm—how she swatted her tail in his face; how she was so jumpy Dave had to milk with one hand, hold a pan with the other, and dodge the flailing foot; and how even the cats missed out because he couldn't aim straight at their mouths. I said, "David has to milk Delilah because John would get too mad and pound on her, Phillip would give up, and Merton would blow his stack and spill all the milk."

Grandma laughed, "Well, it's a sure thing I wouldn't know what to do with a cow like that."

"Me neither," I agreed.

Grandma didn't make it over for Elizabeth's birthday celebration. That morning a snow storm hit and Grandma told Mother she felt too unsteady on the slippery ground, even to get in and out of the car with help. Mother didn't push since there were so many people there to party—twenty to be exact—and it would be mayhem. "But," she said. "I'll send Elizabeth over to visit and bring you a slice of her birthday cake. She has an announcement to make and wants to tell you personally."

"I think I can guess what *that* is," Grandma answered.

This spring the McLennans came from Irondale to spend every other Monday at the Farmhouse. John Mac was working on a design for our New House and talked at great length with Mother to be sure he was incorporating her desires. When he wasn't sketching plans, however, he was forming a musical band of four of us: John, Phil, Mert, and me. Elizabeth loaned me her saxophone. John Mac loaned a baritone horn to John and an E Flat alto horn to Merton. He gave a guitar to Phil, who switched to a smaller baritone horn in short order. "Because," Phillip said, "John expects me to learn to read all the notes and play melodies on the guitar, but I just want to strum chords."

John Mac gave us individual lessons and showed us how to tongue, read notes, and hear pitches. He arranged hymns and taught us how to blend with each other—sort of. He called us "The Corny Corey Corchestra."

The sound of our practicing made for bedlam in the Farmhouse. But Mother encouraged us by humming along whenever she managed to recognize the melody amidst our squeaks and squawks. If we were doing music, she said our chores could wait.

Until John Mac's horn lessons, most of the music in our house had come from our voices and the piano. Mother had given each of us piano lessons, at least until she gave up the battle of wills. The battle was won by the boys within a few months—even though Phillip promised her he would keep on as long as he didn't have to play with two hands at the same time. The older girls had been given a good start with Mother, and Virginia went on to become a virtuoso while taking lessons with the professionals at Prairie. We younger girls never did quite catch up with our eldest sister, although Elizabeth, after a time, became a proficient piano teacher to dozens of local kids.

David, as with many things in life, took his own path when it came to music. He didn't want to play a horn and didn't want to take lessons like the rest of us, so he picked up Mother's accordion and took it to the barn. He began to teach himself, the same way he'd learned the piano—by experimenting with the sound, not bothering with too many written notes. David practiced all the songs on the accordion he could play by memory in the key of C. He only needed a few chords, so he just kept doing the same things over and over.

That's because he could not concentrate on anything else. Just a few weeks earlier David had learned that his grades were the highest in the class and he would be Valedictorian. And being Valedictorian meant giving a speech. So while he played songs in the Key of C, his mind kept regurgitating. *I can't give a speech, I can't write a speech. I don't want to be Valedictorian. I can't give a speech. I can't write a speech . . .*

He knew Mother would ask him, as she had already, "Have you thought of a topic?"

And he would have to say, "No."

And she would make some suggestions. And he would shrug his shoulders and think, *How brainless of me to get the best grades—making a speech is no honor, it's a penalty!*

We all knew that he had to give a speech. We talked about it in the kitchen and reminded him how smart Elizabeth had sounded. Mother talked to Grandma and wrote to her daughters and Aunt Eleanor. It had been broadcast across the continent and even beyond. David couldn't rid himself of the talk, except in the barn, and then the voices nagged from within. *Everyone knows I have to make a speech. I wonder if I can get sick enough to skip out.*

Oh, he'd started a few times with a pencil and paper, but gave up after only a few words, wadding the paper into a ball and tossing it in the stove. His dilemma was solved when, for his birthday, his sister Elizabeth sent him the best gift the smartest kid in school could have received—her graduation speech. It is possible that Liz or Dave edited a few words, but it is on record that both used the same examples of individuals who had succeeded in spite of adversity. It had been four years since her graduation, so who would remember? David practiced the speech—instead of the accordion—in the barn. He wouldn't have to invent an illness.

Phillip knew how to invent illness. He didn't have to give speeches, but how he hated school. He would make himself vomit, or he would breathe pepper, sneeze, and put on a cough. It meant he could stay home, even though he got well right after the bus had gone by. He was most happy to miss the day of the vaccinations that the nurse gave at school, even though Mother would make him get the shots later. None of us wanted shots, but she would say, "I don't want any of my children getting diphtheria that nearly killed me when I was your age, or whooping cough that almost took John from us. And you know what polio does to people."[101]

This spring Mother didn't even talk about Phillip faking his illness. He was needed at home. Dad was traveling and McLennans had left Star and David John with us while they went to a conference. Little David was at the stage of into-everything and better-watch-me-every-second. Star, three and a half, and Janice, barely three, sweet-talked to each other one minute and picked at each other the next. Mother said, "Phillip, it's time to teach those two how to pull together."

She set the toddlers facing each other and holding hands. Back and forth she and Phillip had them pull, had them clap, and had them raise their hands—all the while singing,

> If we all will pull together, together, together;
> If we all will pull together, how happy we'll be.
> For your work is my work, and our work is God's work.
> If we all will pull together, how happy we'll be.[102]

Just when it was time for the urchins to go home, Virginia got sick and they stayed longer. Phillip hung onto his ailments as long as Mother needed him to run patrol on three little ones. He extended his sick leave beyond that to clean up the chicken house for 100 new baby chicks. Then Mother made him go back to school. The longer he stayed home, she said, the harder it would be for him to get caught up with his assignments. Not that he cared about that. Moreover, he knew that Dad was getting ready to start with the most exciting project we'd ever do—dynamite the stumps. Phillip told Mother, "I'll go to school, but please don't let Dad blow up the stumps when I am gone. Please! Please?"

Phillip needn't have worried. All of us got in on the blasting brigade, at least as observers. The first stump—a three-foot fir—was the practice run. Dad dug between the roots and opened up a narrow tunnel. He waved us off while he tucked in a few sticks and packed dirt over the hole. He checked to see that none of us was in the line of fire and then lit the fuse with a match. He hurried behind a tree. Poof! Out puffed a bit of smoke followed by a spray of dirt, and the stump toppled over. No big deal.

The eight-foot tall, six-foot wide charred fir was another story. Its roots, the size of trees, were anchored in at least six feet of hardpan. Dad assigned the boys to dig the hole between the roots and under the trunk with a pick, a crowbar, and shovels. They dug for hours. This time Dad sent us all far away. Phillip, Merton and I ran toward the Farmhouse to tell Mother, Marian and

Janice to watch. We hid behind the trees, while John and David headed toward the barn. Dad stuffed in a large wad attached to a three-foot fuse. By the time he had the dynamite hidden in the recesses of the hole, only a few inches of the fuse were visible. He lit the fuse and ran to get out of the way. We watched, and we waited. "I don't think it's going to work," Phillip complained. "Taking too long!"

Still, from our cover 700 feet across the yard, we dared not blink, just in case. We were rewarded. Smoke and dirt exploded from all sides, and the earth shuddered. Then K-Boom!

Pieces of wood flew in every direction. Our eyes followed the propulsion of a hunk that landed on the barn roof, 500 feet from the explosion. The vibration broke a window in the Farmhouse and Marian dove behind Mother. "Woo-hoo," Phillip yelled, and Merton and I echoed, as we three ran back toward the scene.

After the smoke cleared, we could see that the stump had split in several sections. The largest piece had rotated, using its root as an axis, to station itself in the middle of the construction site. We could still smell the blasting powder. It was a fragrance we came to love, for it symbolized the heart-pounding thrill of blasting stumps to bits.

Once the stumps were loosened, the yard donkey was put to work. Our forerunners in the logging industry had used live donkeys to pull on the cables to winch out the roots. Our yard donkey—the one the boys had assembled at the lean-to—was powered by a gas engine. Using the wire rope cable of the donkey, Dad and the boys winched the machine on its sled logs across the yard to the clean-up site. The back end they anchored to a solid stump. They set up a pulley high on a spar tree and strung it with the cable from the donkey. On the opposite end of the wire they attached a choker to a hunk of stump. They powered up the engine that turned the drums that began to wind up the cable. We watched amazed as the rope tugged loose the chunk of stump and dragged it to the site of the burn pile, all in one simple motion. What a change from all the inefficient human labor of former days.

By the time we finished clearing stumps from the building site and the nearby field, we had several barn-size burn piles we turned into splendid pyres that flared and smoldered for days.

The next job was to excavate for the New House foundation. As usual—through trial and error—Dad and Dave invented a dirt-moving tool—a slip. It was quite a marvel on which one of the boys would ride for weight while Dad pulled it with the donkey. After the slip hit rocks or roots a few times, catapulting the boys through the air, they learned to jump off and get out of the way. With the slip, Dad and his crew dug and transferred yards and yards of dirt, clay, and rocks until they hit hardpan.

Then David went off to put the final touches on the Sawmill—which by now had earned a capital letter for its name. He and Dad poured in the fuel and turned the starter wheel. It took some fine-tuning, but before the day was over, the John Deere two-cylinder engine spoke up: Kapoot-kapoot-kapoot, and the 35-foot belt that would run the log-moving pulleys flap-flapped around and around. Anyone within hearing distance of the kapoot ran up the hill to see the machine in action. Like a convocation of eagles we gathered near the engine, not daring to get within flapping distance of the belt.

"It's working!" I shouted back to Marian still coming up the hill, with Janice's hand in hers.

Mother clasped her hands together. "Praise the Lord!" She said.

David grinned, just slightly, so as not to show unnecessary pride. Yet he—and all of the rest of us—realized that the boy had done it once again: Tinkered until his machinery came to life.

"Can we cut a board?" John asked. He had been dragging logs to the site for weeks in anticipation of this very day.

So Dad and his two oldest boys, with a little help from the two youngest boys, pushed a log onto the rollers. We all watched, breath abated, as the log was guided towards and through the spinning blade. John dropped the slab. Merton and Phillip pulled it out of the way before Dad and David pushed the log through to peel off the opposite slab. Then, they did it! They sliced the first piece of lumber.

On Saturday May 21, 1955, Mother recorded: "We cut the first piece of lumber—but mill needs much adjustment and work on it yet."

"The Sawmill needs work;" or, "they spent the day working on the Sawmill so cut no lumber;" or, "they couldn't get the Sawmill started," would be the story she would note over and over again. But for now the *kapoot-kapoot-kapoot* and the single board held the hope of lumber for the New House.

A week later, David celebrated his engineering success by giving his—well, Elizabeth's—graduation speech without even a stutter or a stumble. Mother told Grandma about it and added, "David's talk was the best given—much better than the main address of the evening. Of course, I don't suppose I'm partial."

She paused. "Nobody even knew that it was his sister's."

Grandma said, "The brains are all in the family, you know."

Grandma said that most of the time when Mother talked about her offspring. And Mother would counter with a grin, that it was from her husband's side of the family, not hers. And Grandma would say that she knew her grandkids didn't get their smarts from her, "But, Margaret," she would add, "You're no dumb-bell yourself."

So David graduated with honors and went off to work for the summer with Bill Richardson on the other side of Puget Sound, while Merton, Marian, and I went off to Vacation Bible School at Joyce Bible Church. We had not participated in a community VBS since the time eight years earlier when the bus didn't run, I sang a solo, and Phillip kissed a girl. That had been about the same time that people had left our home services after the altercation and had started the new church at Joyce. [103]

During the years in between, we passed Joyce Bible Church every day as we rode the bus to and from school. We had friends who attended and talked about the good messages and the outside ministries, including youth going away for Christian education, and missionaries leaving to serve overseas. During those years, we had attended Sunday school at the Pennoyers in Port Angeles, or met in our own home. So it was a new day when Dad told us we could go to VBS at Joyce. Dad said he respected the new pastor, Don Hindman, who had been an acquaintance of Virginia's from Simpson, and had once come by with his wife Dolores to visit Gin and meet us.

Each day, Mrs. Myers or one of the Wetheralds picked us up for VBS. I reveled in the excitement of hanging out with an accumulation of kids in the rustic lodge-style sanctuary or in the upper side room. Mother and Janice came to hear our program at the end when we sang our songs, recited our memory verses, and raced through the pages of the Bible to locate the references of the Bible Drill. During this summer of 1955, a renewal of relationship with those who'd left our place had begun in earnest.

Also during this summer on the home front, there were milestones and there was routine. Mother celebrated her 50th birthday, but since I was in Snohomish picking berries, Phillip baked a cake and John followed up with a blackberry pie. There was a kerfuffle going on between them as to which baked dessert would be the celebration treat with candles. So Mother told the boys she wanted to eat their gifts that day, not wait for her birthday. She said, "I'll make another cake on Sunday." And so, with the Wisdom of Solomon, she ended the feud.

The next week, Phillip, without the Wisdom of Solomon, played with an abandoned firecracker at Crescent Beach. It exploded in his hand, and he had to get a tetanus shot, Mother saying, "I lost a relative to tetanus after he was injured by fireworks.[104]

On July 13, Elizabeth gave birth to Michelanne. Dad took Mother and the white bassinet of our babyhood to Snohomish. He left me in charge of the household and John in charge of the boys outside. While Mother and Dad were gone, Aunt Hilda and Aunt Vera brought Grandpa and Grandma Corey to visit. For the second time they didn't come into the house and, for the second time, we were bewildered that after such a long trip they would ignore six Corey kids from John down to Janice, all waiting to show them around. We learned later that Aunt Vera had wanted to stop by on her way to Alaska where her husband, our Uncle Harold, was installing a radar station in the Yukon and had invited our grandparents to ride along.[105]

On Labor Day weekend, David came home from his summer job in the forest service. He was heading to South Carolina, where he would attend Columbia Bible College and live with Marilyn and Allen. Dave had been planning to take the bus across country but was able to purchase a plane ticket because his boss had given him a bonus. Dad took David to check out the Model A dump truck. "I can hardly get it started, but once I do it just cuts out and stalls."

David put his hand on the hood and said, "I could probably fix it if I had more time. How about I remodel the Chev to replace the Model A as the utility vehicle?"

So David cut off the cab of the Chev and turned the back seat into a truck bed. The 1931 Chevrolet, once Naoma's touring car, Mother's Chevvy, and David's run-about, became the farm workhorse.

Two days later, Dad and Mother took David to catch the flight. They made a couple of stops, dragging out the inevitable as long as possible. They bought a suitcase at Sears—since the airline required it—for David's one extra pair of shoes, two pair of pants and three shirts. They had supper at Grandpa Coreys and headed to the Seattle-Tacoma Airport, arriving just as people were checking in for the flight. There was no time for farewells, just a blessing and prayer for safety. Then he was gone. He would land to change planes or wait for refueling three times, taking all night and all the next day. Mother and Dad watched from the window as the four-engine prop plane taxied and headed into the sky, where it caught the final rays of the setting sun. Mother looked at Dad. "I'm feeling the butterflies in my stomach with him flying so far. It never gets any easier for me to send off our children."

She paused, "I can't imagine how you will manage all the work on the farm with Dave gone."

Dad nodded—his eyes still on the sky. And then they turned to go. Mother wrote the next day in her journal, summing up her feelings in the words: "I will go wash Grandma's windows as I am feeling quite alone."

There would remain a David-shaped gap at our table that only he could fill, but John had already begun to fill the outdoor leadership shoes. It hadn't been easy to come out of the shadows while David was still there, especially since Dad listened to him most. But John had learned well. During the summer while Dave was at the forestry job, John had become chief in the hayfield with assistants Phil, Mert, and Delfred. He drove the Coupe with the hay trailer behind, even though he was still too young for a driver's license. He, Phillip, and Dad put the finishing touches on a sawdust disposal system that automatically shuffled the mess away from the Sawmill and out to a pile.

After David left for South Carolina, John fashioned a roof to keep the rain out of the converted '31 Chev and helped Dad weld on another set of wheels to increase traction. He rigged up the donkey so he could tow the Chev to get it started and take Mrs. Tieche and Mother to pick apples at the Johnsons. John and Dad took the back end off the defunct Model A dump truck to build a trailer—one to replace the Packard-axle trailer that had been ruined in the delivery of the Sawmill engine.

It became readily apparent that John did not lack inventive mechanical know-how, and Mother said on more than one occasion, "That boy has really stepped up to the plate!"

Mother also noted that John's skill at hunting was equal that of David's, both of which might have competed for the lowest shooting average in the neighborhood. She wrote in her diary: "At least he got one rabbit with a rock after he missed it with the bullet."

News was arriving from many parts of the country. David had been given 4-D draft status as a ministerial student, even though he had no intention of being a preacher. John McLennan had been called as an associate pastor to Rockford, Illinois, and he, Virginia and the children would be leaving Irondale. Bill was returning to Seattle Pacific College to get a degree in Education since he'd come to realize that forestry would demand too much of his injured and reconstructed ankle.

Bill and Elizabeth came with little Michaelanne—whom we called Micki—for Christmas vacation, arriving in time to help us trim the tree. Liz reminded Marian and me there was only one right way to decorate with tinsel made of aluminum foil. "You have to hang each icicle by itself without it touching another branch or another tinsel strand." She told us to be careful not to break the foil or the pieces would be too short and there wouldn't be enough to cover the tree equally on all sides. Marian and I chose to let her finish by herself.

Delfred, who was still living with us, was in trouble at school and at home, and Mother was ready to send him back to his parents. But she got word that his brother Alvey had passed away from complications of diabetes, and she decided to hold off a little longer. She told Dad, "Just take him home for the week of Christmas vacation. We'll have the Richardsons and McLennans, and I need to catch my breath."

Dad and Bill left with Delfred shortly after Christmas breakfast. The drive was less than 90 minutes each way, and Mother expected them back to eat turkey dinner. The McLennans arrived, but not Bill and Dad. "I wonder what could have delayed those men," Mother worried.

We waited for an hour or so. Then sat down at the table. Mother didn't eat. She said her stomach hurt and she went out to the toilet several times. All of us were on pins and needles. It was Christmas Day. We just knew Dad and Bill would have come home for dinner—unless something awful had happened.

Hours later there was still no car in the driveway. Mother told Virginia and Elizabeth, "If I knew who or where to call, I'd go to the Tieches. But who would I call?"

It had been dark for five hours when the men finally arrived. Dad was driving the Coupe, and Bill followed in the 1940 Ford that had once been Granddad Richardson's. They told Mother they had dropped Del at his parents, only to realize that they were almost halfway to Snohomish where the thing was parked. Dad said, "It just made sense to get it so we could redo the welder during vacation."

Mother understood the need for the Ford. Still, she faced him. "I was sick, wondering what happened to keep you when so many of the family were here for dinner, including John and Virginia for the last time in who knows how long."

She added, "We have to get a telephone. We can't wait until the New House is built. Even if it means borrowing from The Building Fund, I must have a phone so when you get a notion to go off like this, you can call."

Furthermore, she thought to herself, *I'd be able to call my children who keep moving so far from home.*

Corny Corey Corchestra

'31 Chevvy turned farm truck broken down
Bill John Arthur Marian Janice Margaret

CHAPTER TWENTY-FOUR
The Telephone
(1956)

We had stored the decorations and taken down the Christmas cards when a late one arrived from Mother's cousin Charles Phenicie. In the envelope was a check that Mother said was her answer about the phone. She put in the order on January 4—which was also the day we got a new dog we named JaFo for having come on that day. Within a few weeks, the telephone was installed. What a change that invention brought to the Farmhouse. We received a call from our brother-in-law, John McLennan, when Virginia delivered her baby, Marilyn Dawn, in Illinois. Then, on our sisters' or David's birthdays, we could call them and talk for up to three minutes—at the lowest rate. Sometimes we kids listened to party-line talking while we waited for the speakers to get off the line, but usually we hung up and tried again and again, hoping the talkers would hang up when they heard the clicking. No, the party line did not at all match the reputations that party lines sometimes got. On the other hand, there was no gossiping from our phone, except when Mother let me call my best friend from school on her birthday and talk for five minutes—since it was a local call—even though I had seen her that day at school.

But there were calls of much greater impact. We learned that Grandpa Corey had suffered a stroke and was having difficulty speaking. So Dad left to check up on his father. He returned home a few days later and told Mother that Grandpa didn't have much time left. "But I spoke with him about his relationship with the Lord and I know he is ready to go."

Mother replied, "I've felt that his heart has grown more open to talk of spiritual matters. He seems to have reconciled with the call on your life to minister."

Two weeks later, a telegram told us that Grandpa Corey had died on March 27. Dad and Mother left a few days later to participate in a memorial held by the family. Mother noted in her diary that the service was especially blessed, and that Mother Corey seemed held up by the everlasting arms.

We'd never known our Grandpa Corey well—he'd seemed aloof, and hadn't talked much to us kids. But we'd known that he and Anna Phoebe Wheelock[106] were the parents of eight children. We'd also known that he had been harsh with his offspring, and had been angry when Dad chose a life of sacrifice and ministry. However, after the funeral, we learned more about him than we'd ever heard before. We learned how his father—our Great-grandfather Henry I. Corey—had been a civil war veteran of several battles, and had built a respected banking business in New York State. How the son, our Grandpa Merton Henry, had moved from New York in 1869, ignoring his father's expectations for him to continue in the family business, and we learned of his successful career in the insurance industry as well as the roles he'd played while serving two terms in the state legislature soon after Washington became a state.[107]

Mother was back at home, and Dad still tending to family matters, when he called from Tacoma to our phone. Dad said he was bringing his mother and sister Hazel to spend a couple of days. Mother replied it was nice to have the forewarning so she could fix up the nook of the living room and hang a curtain. Her decision to have a phone installed had paid off in multiple ways within just a few weeks.

I was thrilled to have Grandma Corey come. I could only remember one time when I had visited her house and Grandpa's cigar smoke had given me fits of coughing. Then two times they had come to our place and not even gotten out of the car. I was sure, on those trips, Grandma had wanted to stay awhile, but Grandpa had not been in favor. So when Grandma came once with Uncle Albert, and this time after our grandpa had died, she seemed free to do whatever she wanted—and she wanted to be with us. Grandma Corey fit right in, and we were having such a grand time, Mother reminded us more often than usual to "keep the noise down."

To which Grandma responded, "Have you forgotten that I raised eight children, one of whom is your offspring's tempestuous father?"

We had quite an old folks' party when Dad brought Grandma Phenicie across the yard to eat lunch. Our two grandmas talked about how long it had been since they sat together at a table, but neither could remember just when that had been. Grandma Phenicie sympathized about Grandpa Corey's passing and reached out to touch Grandma Corey who thanked her for the kind thoughts, saying, "I, well, all of his family, miss him a great deal. But during these last months he was so miserable. Now I know he is in a better place."

Grandma Phenicie nodded, and the other grandma changed the subject. "How has it been for you to live close to Art's and Margaret's family?"

"At first it was hard for me to leave Tacoma and the other relatives . . . you remember, you were there to see me off . . . but the welcome here has more than made up for that loss."

To which Grandma Corey replied that she was glad to be here to get acquainted better with Art's children and, "Aren't they just so smart?"

Once Grandma Corey went home we were back to the normal projects and repairs. We hauled logs, repaired the donkey, sawed lumber, fixed the mill, and dynamited stumps. In fact, we blew up so many stumps, Marian and Janice hardly came out from hiding under the bed. Dad replaced the green power insulators that the blasts or the flying pieces broke, and Mother told him to cover the broken windows with boards until he was done with dynamite. The boards over two gaps in the Farmhouse wall remained in place forevermore after that.

Setting off dynamite was far more fun than any other land-clearing job. Phillip decided to take care of a stump not far from the chicken coop. He and Delfred lit the fuse and watched it sizzle along between the roots, waiting for the stump to be blown to *kingdom come*. Just then a hen flew to the top of the stump and landed. *Tuh-whoomp*—up in the air sailed pieces of stump. *Plucka-plucka-plucka*—the chicken flipped up with the stump, flapped its wings, and flopped to the ground, leaving behind a folly of feathers fluttering through the smoke of the explosion. *Plucka-plucka-plucka*—it cackled back to the chicken house. It survived the ordeal with just a plucked-bare wing and a naked tail to remind us of its blast into space.

That was the last blasting for several months, until Dad discovered a pile of leftover dynamite, crumbling in an open package in the barn. David who'd returned from South Carolina said, "I'm not sure it's safe to use that."

Dad said, "The best idea is to blow out the stump in the way of Mother's new garden."

The stump was a grand and elegant fir—eight feet tall and eight feet wide. Why, if it had been a cedar, it would have been ample enough in the olden days to have been hollowed out for a house or a post office.[108] The boys spent umpteen hours digging under the roots as far as they could; then Dad stuffed in the entire damp, broken-apart box of dynamite, after which he added the normal charge of new dynamite sticks and packed the hole. He sent us all out of the way. Way out of the way.

What a blast! It was like nothing we had ever seen before, and we had seen some doozies. Roots exploded through the air in all directions. Chunks hit the new construction; a slab landed as far away as the highway; and a piece shot straight up, shorting out the PUD power lines that curved across our property. We watched in awe as green fire arced and rolled on the high-powered wires. When the show was over, we surveyed the crater—fifteen-feet wide and eight feet deep—which would serve to remind us of Dad's epic dynamite demolition. Years later, we learned that there had been an unidentified power surge in the area that summer, causing damage to homes and televisions. And, by then, not one of the Coreys felt it necessary to 'fess up.

At the Corey property, explosions weren't limited to the outdoors. Two days after Dad's big event, I came into the kitchen to show Mother the dress I was wearing for an end-of-year program at school. It was a flowery black dress with a white bolero that Aunt Eleanor had brought when she came to visit Grandma earlier that week. Mother was near the stove where she had a ham boiling in the pressure cooker and turned to look. "That fits you good. Are you sure you don't want to save it for the grad—"

Just then a blast louder than dynamite rocked the room. The ham bone hit the ceiling, scraps of meat burst forth and stuck to the wall, and broth showered the floor and doused the front of my dress. The explosion was so powerful that it punched a hole in the cast iron stovetop, and flames flared through the gap. Mother whirled toward the stove and back toward me, alarm in her voice. "Were you hit? Are you burned?"

I held out the front of my skirt. "No, just a mess down here. What about you?" I asked. When I saw that she too was okay, I exclaimed, "Now *that* was some display of firepower!"

I helped her pick up the meat and place it in another pot. When she started the floor cleaning, I rinsed the front of my skirt while still wearing it and said, "It's a dark enough color. No one will notice it's wet." I shrugged, "Be dry by the time I get to school."

Dad took the stovetop to Wils Myers' welding shop in Port Angeles. Afterwards the iron griddle top sported a rough ridge that got in the way of cooking. Mother groaned, "We'll have to get a new stove I suppose, but they are so expensive."

Dad checked the prices of stoves and when he couldn't figure how to buy one—even on installments—he came home with a new hand cultivator from the Co-op. Mother frowned a little, but didn't question the decision—at least not in anyone's hearing. Then after she saw how the cultivator tore up the sod for potatoes and cleared the way for the rest of the vegetables, she said, "Does that machine ever make short work of gardening! I'll just get used to cooking around the crooked part of the stove."

On June 5, 1956, Phillip and I graduated from eighth grade. Phillip had a fine hand-me-down suit and I wore a bright blue dress I had made from store-bought fabric. Dad gave the invocation and benediction at the ceremony. He made certain that those in attendance heard God's name used in a respectful way. I was relieved afterwards that his prayers were short and to the point without a sermon attached.

About the same time, Phillip was concerned for his relationship with God. He'd battled doubts since he was baptized, which he knew he'd done to please Dad, not because he knew he was ready. Over the years, he'd not questioned Dad's messages. He'd agreed with the preaching of the pastor at Joyce Bible Church where John, Phil, and I went for the evening service. Phillip still wrestled with thoughts that a step was missing: *Maybe God doesn't hear my prayers, maybe I've faked my faith all along.* So one Sunday evening when the Joyce preacher asked if anyone wanted to be sure of salvation, Phillip jumped to his feet in a flash. Wils Myers walked over and stood alongside until the pastor dismissed the service. Then the two sat on the pew. Wils questioned if Phil had asked the Lord to forgive his sins and if he wanted to live for God. With assurance that boy meant business, the two prayed together. Then Mr. Myers said, "When you leave here tonight, you should tell someone of your decision."

Phil ran through the door of the Farmhouse and bubbled over to Mother, how he had prayed with Mr. Myers and knew he was saved. She looked surprised. "But you were baptized. I thought this was taken care of a long time ago." Phil was disappointed his mother didn't seem as energized as he felt. It reminded him of the teacher at school who dumped a bucket of ice water on his enthusiasm after the birth of his littlest sister. But at least *he* knew his commitment was for real.

Phil affirmed his pledge of faith as he, John, and I attended the Joyce Bible Young People's outings. For the rest of our high school years we belonged to that Friday night group. We became leaders—inviting our school friends, and planning progressive dinners, hikes, lake trips and full-clothed swim dares in the frigid water at Crescent Beach. After the fun, the youth would circle a campfire and sing choruses like "Kumbaya" and "Peace in the Valley" with the three of us taking the vocal lead, after which someone would give a message. My eyes were no doubt more on the boys who came for the fun, than on the Lord, yet this was a season of my life when I realized I wanted to do whatever God asked of me—even though I just knew before I could serve God I would have to confess to stealing ice-cream dimes from the Girl's Club till at school.[109]

This summer Dad made a deal with Mr. Sands, another of our neighbors. Mr. Sands plowed our field, gave us hay for the cattle, and a calf to replace one that had died. Dad's part of the agreement was to saw into boards the large timbers Mr. Sands had salvaged from the trestle that had crossed the Salt Creek chasm until the trains quit running.

Not a profitable exchange. Those trestle under-girders were hard like petrified wood and laced with hidden metal. Dad and Phil had only cut one or two lengths when Screech! Crunch! Crash! They jumped back as teeth from the saw flew like bullets through the tin roof. No one was hurt, but a half-inch square spike in the wood had been cut clean through and the saw was busted. Repairing the Sawmill consumed more hours during that operation than actually slicing the superstructure of the trestle.

Mr. Sands took his son Murray and our brother John to a one-day logging job near Joyce. The teens worked so hard they were hired on for several weeks. To honor his 16th birthday, John took the day off to get his driver's license and got it on the first try. Mother told him it was a present, even though he paid for the license. She said, "Now that you are working in the woods with Murray you are richer than we are."

Money was in short supply—as per normal—even though we'd started marketing a few dozen eggs each week and continued our sale of cream. And though the exchange of jobs, like that with the Sands, brought certain benefits, few paybacks helped to balance the budget. After Dad and Mother figured out what supplies would have to be bought for the construction of our house, she wrote in her diary: "It's enough to give one heart failure. Would that folks would pay us some of what they owe. That would be a blessing."

It is hard to imagine that others were in debt to us. Yet Mother cared for kids whose parents didn't help with the bills, and Dad did jobs without receiving promised payment. When Mother asked about these debts, Dad reminded her again of the scripture: "Do good and lend, hoping for nothing again; and your reward shall be great."

In July, Lillian Pennoyer, the daughter of Fred and Virginia, came to stay with us. She had returned from the Philippines where her parents were missionaries. Lillian and I were once again childhood chums, as if she'd never left. She entertained me with stories of the tropics, and I sewed clothes for her to wear to her new high school.

Lillian got in on lots of family fun and folly—like when Phillip and I conducted a medical experiment: how to dispense with the warts on our hands. Dad had not given us the same diagnosis of cause (attitude) and cure (change attitude) he had given to David, so Phil and I were left to our own devices. We used the following protocol:

- Stand by the stove in the kitchen with a box of matches—the kind with three-inch sticks.
- Light a match and hold it close to the wart until tears run.
- Pass the match to the other person to use on his wart so you don't waste the fire.
- Dump the spent match in the stove before it burns your other fingers.
- When the pain subsides, strike another match and go back to the same wart.
- Compete with each other to see how long you can burn yourself. Eventually, after four or five matches, you will see a blister form under the wart and in a few weeks you can pull it off.

However, there was a contraindication: The treatment did not get rid of plantar warts. Fact is—it made them spread and hurt worse.

Phil liked to show off to get my friend's attention, all the while thinking to himself, *I wonder if some day I will marry Lillian Pennoyer.* So with that in mind, he amused himself by teasing. But sometimes his jesting backfired. Late one evening, we girls had finished washing the dishes and had flopped on the bench of the trestle table just as Phillip came rushing in from outside. He blabbered in the high pitch of a girl, even though his voice was changing, "You should have seen the eyes of a creature I just saw in the woods. I'm sure there is a bear or a bobcat out there—out behind the toilet. Those eyes watched every move I made!"

"You're kidding."

"No, it's for real. I had to keep my eyes fixed on it and creep backwards all the way to the house."

He spun the story until our faces froze with fright, and he had worked himself up into a state of trepidation. Lillian and I didn't say as much to each other, but I knew that neither of us would dare go as far as the outhouse before bedtime.

Mother had been listening to the conversation, however. She turned to face him. "Phillip Raymond Corey, you will now walk with the girls to the toilet. And you will wait outside until they are ready to come in."

Mother usually had wise words for her children, but she didn't feel so wise in another matter—a matter that had become a churning concern for several months. Delfred Mansfield had become a burden to her. She did not trust him—not around the house, and certainly not around her daughters. Yet when she had spoken to his parents and with the authorities at school, there seemed to be no other solution than to keep him longer. Instead of sending him off, she had agreed to keep him indefinitely within the legal foster care system.[110] She knew she would have to trust the Lord, both for him and for the safety of her family.

After the school year ended, however, and Delfred was home all day every day, Mother realized her capitulation to pressure had been a mistake. It was impossible for her to keep an eye on him every minute. She called the judge assigned to Delfred's case and told him Del could no longer live under her roof. The judge promised he would see to the matter, but he never followed through. Since Dad was on a trip, Mother called the Mansfields, who came that day. Mr. Mansfield, though a stepfather to Delfred, would have taken him home with permission from the judge, but Mrs. Mansfield did not agree, saying "We can't control him and the neighbors have said they will call the police if he is seen on our street again."

So Mother sent a Special Delivery letter to Bill's and Elizabeth's address, hoping to catch up with Dad. She wrote of her escalating unease with Delfred and the lack of response from the judge, asking if Dad could please find out if there is a place at King's Garden where Delfred can live?

Mother was still waiting to hear back from Dad when Delfred acted out in a way that could no longer be hidden from any of us. One hot afternoon, Lillian and I had gone into the bedroom to change into shorts when we discovered grains of sawdust on the covers. I stepped onto the bed and rubbed my hand over the ceiling. "Look at this," I said. "Holes have been drilled right through the boards. Peep holes!"

Lillian asked, "Well, who could have done that?"

"Delfred," I said. Even as I looked up at those fresh, rough holes, I flashed back to a recent experience. I had entered the kitchen to pick up a stack of laundry, and the instant I turned to leave the room, Del had walked out from behind the bathtub curtain, stark naked. I had wanted to tell Mother about that incident, but hadn't known what to say or how to say it. Now I had moral support, however, so Lillian and I went to find Mother. I blurted, "There is sawdust in our bed. We can see that holes had been drilled in the ceiling. It looks like they are right under the blankets where Delfred sleeps."

Mother followed us to the bedroom. She rubbed her hands together as she did when she had to make a hard decision and was uncertain of the outcome. Her mind made up, she went downstairs, looked for Phillip, and told him what had happened. "I need you to find some boards and nail them over the holes." Then she turned to Delfred who'd heard most of the conversation. "Mr. Corey will deal with you when he gets home."

Del opened his mouth as if to say something, but then he turned and went out the back door. No one followed. Dinner time came, and Delfred did not return. Mother sent the boys to look for him. It got dark, and still Delfred was nowhere to be found.

Mother became alarmed and called the sheriff to report that the boy was missing. She called again on Friday night, and again on Saturday morning and Saturday afternoon, but there was still no sign. The sheriff told her they would be sending out search parties. We couldn't imagine where he had gone—his mother didn't want him, and he had no home but ours. Dad returned in the wee hours of Monday morning with news that there was no place for Delfred at King's Garden. The school was full, and there were no resources to manage or meet the needs of a troubled teen.

On Tuesday afternoon, the phone rang. Mother picked it up after the first ring. I could hear the anxious tone in her voice, "Hello?" She listened for a few moments, and then her free hand lifted to her cheek. "Ohhh—oh no!"

She hung up and turned to us. "The sheriff says they found Delfred hanging from a tree along Salt Creek, some distance below the culverts. He's been dead for several days." She paused. "May God have mercy on him."

After the news came, the boys took their nervous thoughts to the barn to see if he had taken one of our ropes. He had. I had nervous thoughts too—thoughts of relief that he would no longer be sneaking around and setting my nerves on edge. I supposed I should have been sorry, but somehow I couldn't get past the freedom I felt.

The funeral was held in Delfred's hometown, and my parents attended. Only a few others were present, and no mention was made of the suicide. However, before Mother and Dad returned home, Mrs. Mansfield said, "We don't hold you responsible for Delfred's death. We just ask that you not tell his other relatives what happened."

When Mother reported to us Mrs. Mansfield's words, John said, "That's not right. His family didn't want him, but we gave him a home. I did my best to help him in school, and even stood up for him against those who were mean. How can she even imagine that it is somehow our fault?"

Phillip added, "I don't know what we could have done different. We treated him like a brother. I took him fishing, and helped him with his part of the chores. I don't know why he would do bad things when we were all trying to help him."

Phil didn't reveal his additional thoughts. *I don't know if I'll ever be able to go fishing by myself in that part of the creek, where I would have to look at the big maple trees, and imagine him struggling to breathe and then hanging for days.*

Mother packed up the boy's things and sold the four remaining geese—we had eaten one—that had come as part of the Delfred foster care package.

Then, to transform the muddled maze in our minds, Dad and Mother took us to the beach late at night to see sparks in the water, a rare phenomenon Mother called "phosphorus."[111] We kids took off our shoes and walked into the Salt Creek estuary which was lukewarm on the incoming tide. With every step we could see the sparklers spin away from our legs. I made small circles, then wide ones, first with one leg and then the other. In the clear water, the sparks were one bright color, while in the murky water their colors changed.

The water chilled, and we sat on a log to dry our feet. We turned our eyes to the stars in the sky, Lillian and my brothers pointing out the North Star and other constellations they knew. In the water and up above we could see the lights God had placed to remind us that he loved us, and that he loved Delfred too—no matter what he had done. Delfred had lived with us for nearly two years, but he was gone and there was nothing more we could do for him.

A few days later, more signs from the skies appeared. Thunder rumbled and lightening hit so close it caused a red glow at the mill and turned on the lights. Mother noticed that even Dad was startled by the display. It appeared to be a sign for us to get on with it. There were logs to haul, boards to plane, machines to fix, and laundry to do. We needed to get back to work.

Summer ended. Bill, Elizabeth, and Micki came home from Seattle Pacific. Even though Bill had not graduated, he would be teaching school at Joyce on an emergency certificate. The Korean War had caused a shortage of male teachers, so permits were being issued to education majors who would commit to summer classes until they graduated. It would take Bill several summers.

Bill and Liz went back and forth, filling their brand new, shiny black '56 Ford pickup with their belongings, and, on the final trip, bringing their two-ton piano. They stashed everything on our back porch and in the corners in the living room. They slept in my room—the first guest room—as did all other guests of importance. Early each morning Bill and Liz left Micki for me to babysit, and went the four miles each way to paint the Hall's house where they would live for the year.

After they were settled, I continued babysitting at their place. I don't think they ever paid for that service and I don't think I ever thought they should. It was such fun to take care of my sweet niece in a warm house, far from the commotion and confusion. I dressed her in my ruffled crinoline slip and took her picture on my little camera. I combed, curled, or braided her long brown hair. I baked treats and gave her nibbles. I sang all the nursery rhymes I could think of and made up my own. Then I listened on the Hi-Fi player to my new favorite records—Rhapsody in Blue, The Grand Canyon Suite, and Beethoven's Fifth Symphony. As the orchestra music swelled, I picked up Micki to waltz all around the room. I was babysitting my niece, experiencing classical music for the first time, and swirling without inhibition. I was in heaven.

David, after returning from South Carolina, had worked all summer with Bill in Seattle. Then in the fall, Dave sent his application to Seattle Pacific College, hoping to continue his studies closer to home. He would be around to help on the farm and fix machines until classes started. After that, he could come home on free weekends—if he had money for the bus fare, or if he could hitch a ride and had enough to pay for the two ferry rides[112] each way.

David immediately put together a cut off saw for the mill from the original accessories and new parts he purchased. The cut off, attached to the mill mechanisms, would be used to shorten timber, trim the rough ends, or cut the exact lengths of boards. Most of Dave's inventions worked the first time. This one was different. He and Dad fired up the motor and had just started testing the speeds of the saw when a pulley broke. Pieces of cast iron shot out in all directions. David woke up on the ground with blood covering his face, a gash in his kneecap, and a loose tooth in his mouth. So Dad took his son to town for repairs—X-rays and stitches.

David hobbled around college for months on his lame leg. And his discolored tooth would remind him for years to come, that God had protected him from a much worse outcome of that accident.

Not long after the injury, Dave, Bill and Dad were working on additional mill repairs and it wasn't going well. Dad picked up a hammer to pound a part into place and brought the tool down full-force onto his thumb. He sucked in his breath with the pain and laid down the hammer. The two younger men watched as Dad walked away from the mill, holding his bloody thumb. Bill shook his head in amazement, thinking, *If that had happened to me, I would have thrown that hammer clear across the gully.*

Dad had not gone far when he turned back to the mill. He said, "I didn't pray before we tackled this problem."

Then he looked toward heaven, "Now, Lord, you know the beginning from the end, and you know what is wrong here. We ask you to reveal the solution. Amen."

Immediately, he showed the two bystanders what needed to be done, and they did it. After that, Dad went to the house for repairs to his thumb. Bill took Dad's lesson to heart, thinking how he lacked that kind of faith—a faith where he sought God for answers—preferably before God had to speak in a loud voice.

Dad didn't get back to work on the Sawmill or the cut off saw for several weeks. The needs of the extended family on the far side of Puget Sound called to him. Grandma Corey had moved into an apartment and asked Dad and Mother to help clean out her house and get her things ready for movers. It took them several days during which they also visited others who needed encouragement. As emissaries of Grandma Phenicie, they went to see as many of her relatives as possible. They checked up on her sister Lottie, who had been placed in a rest home. They visited Aunt Mabel Kent Phenicie and her sister Elsie, and went to the hospital to encourage and pray for Cousin George Phenicie who was a paraplegic and had been suffering debilitating pain. They sat with Aunt Edna and Uncle Elmer, both of whom were also failing in health. Mother found it disheartening to see so many of her mother's generation coming to the close of their lives. And she didn't like to be away from home so long, but she said to Dad, "I am encouraged, though, that most of them seem to have found God's comfort in our prayers."

The folks returned home and found Grandma Phenicie in pain. She had injured her knee and could not get out of her chair. I felt badly because I had checked on her just the day before and she had seemed fine. Mother stayed with her, helping her get to the bathroom when needed, and fixing her meals.

Meanwhile, Dad worked on a buzzer system that he'd bought through Uncle Albert's store. Once he had it hooked up, and Grandma was able to hobble around on her own again, Mother returned home to stay. Even so, she was on alert through the nights, listening for the buzzer to go off, and feeling uncertain whether or not it would function should Grandma push the button.

They were still futzing with the buzzer system, when we heard that Marilyn and Allen were on their way home. Thinking it was about time, I talked Marian and Janice into waiting with me at the corner above the culverts. But the couple didn't come that day, or the next. About the third anxious day, we heard the welcoming *yap yap yap* barking of JaFo and ran out to meet them. As soon as Marilyn stepped out of the car, even before the greetings, we could see she was hiding her *condition* under a maternity smock. Her first full sentence to Mother was, "Virginia gave me the top when we visited there and I made her promise not to give out the secret."

Allen and Marilyn moved into my bedroom and I moved out. I couldn't believe how long it took her to get everything put in exactly the right place. So fastidious, so punctilious, so . . . well . . . nitpicky. First she hung every shirt and dress in its proper order. "I'll get everything organized and then take them down stairs to iron," she told me.

She folded her underwear in an emptied drawer of Aunt Eleanor's vanity, the one that had come to my room when Grandma Phenicie's house was sold. She found places for socks, and set each of their shoes in the closet—*just so*. She left the room and came back with two small dresser scarves to smooth carefully on the dresser to hold her face creams, her hair brushes, and even her make-up—it was a subdued color that she hoped Dad would not notice, she admitted. Then, after everything was in its place, she straightened out the bed I'd *already* made up for her, and headed downstairs.

Marilyn spent hours ironing—first all of hers and Allen's clothes, then she sprinkled water on the things in Mother's ironing basket, so she could do those later. When she washed the living room curtains, I warned her, "You can't iron those . . . they're made of plastic." And she rolled her eyes.

She cooked dinner alongside Mother and cleaned the floors and windows, all the while talking and talking. During those hours, Mother felt a growing irritation with the West Indies Mission. How could those people send her daughter to Cuba when there was no place for her to live and the baby was due in January? Mother couldn't help but remember the anxiety she felt when Virginia was in Trinidad with a baby so sick she almost died. Besides, Marilyn's doctor had advised against travel at this late date in the pregnancy, and the family wouldn't be able to come home for at least four years.

Mother acted on her feelings. And a few days later, a telegram came from Mr. Thompson, the mission director.

TO: J ALLEN THOMPSON
FROM: ELMER V THOMPSON
IF UNWILLING TO GO NOW, RESIGN[113]

Allen was mystified. He looked at Marilyn. "What does this mean?"

Marilyn looked equally confused. "I have no idea."

Allen handed the telegram to Dad, who read it aloud. Mother was quiet for a moment; then confessed. "I wrote to Allen's dad, and asked them to reconsider."

After an ear-splitting silence, Dad spoke, "What you did was wrong. You should not have taken the liberty to write without checking with me."

He drew in his breath. "Have you forgotten that Marilyn is under the authority of her husband, and that Allen has chosen to follow the direction of the mission?"

Mother's eyes were lowered when she spoke, "I'm sorry I stepped in. I . . ."

She stopped, realizing that any further argument would only bring more words of correction. Allen spoke up. "Thanks, Mom, for thinking of us. It'll be all right. I'll call my dad to let him know there was a mistake. We are still planning to travel as scheduled."

And so the matter was laid to rest and nothing more was said—at least not in Dad's hearing.

All too soon, Allen and our sister were packed up to leave. There were tears and the singing of "God be with you 'til we meet again." We would not likely meet again until our sister's baby would be nearly old enough to go to school. Allen and Marilyn drove out, leaving behind a subdued and saddened farewell committee. But I'd learned to handle stress by keeping busy, so I changed my sheets and did the laundry. Mother, too, went right to work. She took a roast from the fridge and stopped short. "Oh, I forgot to tell you," she said to Dad. "Bill and the boys are planning to butcher all of the animals this weekend."

With four animals—two pigs and two beef—the task took all weekend. But Bill was there to take the lead, much to Dad's enormous relief. Afterwards, there was so much meat we had to rent an extra locker in town. And there was so much hide off the largest beef, Dad got the idea we should turn it into leather. Phillip agreed, "I can think of a lot of uses for leather."

Dad told Phillip and Merton to get the hide ready—to scrape off all the gristly, slimy tissue and fat. It took days. He picked up tanning chemicals for $12.50 and put the pelt to soak. For a week or more the boys rotated the bulky skin and added more lime solution to loosen the hair. We—even Mother, Marian and I—took blunt knives to scrape and stretch and pound. Phillip said he had no idea it would be so much work, or he wouldn't have been so agreeable.

The year wrapped up with a larger-than-usual Christmas program at Joyce School. It was quite a production, with Merton as narrator, John singing a duet with Judi Anderson during a pantomime, Bonnie Carter singing a duet with me, Elizabeth leading from the piano, and all of us playing our instruments with the band. At Joyce School events, Coreys tended to be everywhere.

For Christmas, we received a new kitchen stove from Elizabeth to replace the one that had been damaged by the pressure cooker. I was tickled by it. A person could cook with wood on one side and cook above electric elements on the other side. I suggested that Mother could use the wood part and I could use the electric—and together we could serve the main course of the progressive dinner for the Joyce Bible Church Young People, and Mother agreed.

The year closed with a Watch Night Service at Joyce Bible Church, and we entered into the New Year of 1957—the year in which I made the only childhood resolution I can still remember. It was a wager with Phillip, recorded in black ink inside the front jacket of a lock-and-key five-year diary I had received for Christmas.

From the woods to the saw mill

CHAPTER TWENTY-FIVE
The Wager
(1957)

The diary was covered with red leather and was held together with a matching strap and golden lock. I just knew I would use it every day. I wrote in the jacket:

"Phillip thinks I won't keep it up for five years. Signed, Eleanor Jan 13, 1957. P.S. Just you wait and see Mr. Corey."[114]

Thus, at the age of thirteen, halfway through ninth grade, I began a ritual of penciling three lines across the top of each fifteen-line page—the same page that could be used on the same date until the year 1961.

Mother kept her diary at the typewriter in the corner of the kitchen where I had learned to sew; mine was beside my bed. Mother and I mostly wrote about the same events, but she detailed the construction, the machine breakages, Dad's trips, the people he saw, and the meetings in the Rest Home and jail. I described the myriad of outfits I designed for my younger sisters, their dolls, and myself; bow ties and shirts I sewed for my brothers; clothes I made for friends who brought me the material; and the quilts I pieced from the remnants of all of the above. I wrote about the boys in school and about problems with the teachers. I wrote how hard it was to keep on a diet; how hard to stay out of the raisins, and how impossible to stop globbing cake batter into my mouth when I baked.

Mother and I both wrote about having to complete book reports for English. I wrote about my reports, while she wrote about doing the drudgery on Phillip's so that he didn't flunk English. He told her, "I just don't get it. How can you read a boring book and figure out what the author is trying to say? It's a stupid assignment."

She stopped pinching the pimples on his back long enough to make a point, "Well, Phillip Raymond, either you do what they assign and get passing grades, or you don't play basketball."

Mother made cookies to bribe him, and—long into the night—she sat prodding, cajoling, and urging. I didn't like writing book reports either, but grades were grades and my gut told me to get A's. So I did the required reading and reporting—plus an extra book, just in case my score needed a boost. And I told my diary all about it.

I wrote about the kids in my classes in school. They were the same ones that I'd been in class with all through grade school, mostly obnoxious boys. The worst was Ronnie Krieg. One day in science class he called me a bad name. Mr. G chortled at the jab and said, "Go ahead, Eleanor, slap his face."

So I did, with enough force to pay back multiple infractions that had stockpiled since first grade. My fingerprints signaled we were even. "Ha," I wrote in my diary, "that ought to show him."

That year, Elizabeth, Bill, Dad, and Mother went to lots of PTA meetings. They encouraged the school board to voice dissent against the military using a location nearby as an ammunition dump which to the community's relief never happened. They also pointed out violations of safety on the buses and questionable behavior by a couple of teachers.

I, too, was peeved about school leadership. I gave Mr. Krattli, the Superintendent, my opinion that teachers were not prepared for the classes. He nodded but made no comment. Then I gave suggestions to Mr. G on ways to improve the direction of the high school. Mr. G looked at me, the youngest in the freshman class, and said, "Eleanor Corey, I believe we can run this school without you."

I was shocked to silence. My eyes filled but I held them wide open so they wouldn't spill as I walked down the hallway. I quizzed myself later as to which was the most depressing: Being told I wasn't needed, or realizing that my logical analysis was going to be ignored. The next day I told Mr. G that I was sorry for giving my counsel on administrative matters. I felt better after confessing, but it didn't change my opinion of him and what I perceived was his lack of dedication to the quality of my education. I dictated to my diary that I would not be attending Joyce High School after this year. How could I learn what I needed to learn if lesson plans weren't ready, tests were useless, and boys disrupted the classes? I just knew that on all these accounts—plus more I expect—my academic success was at terrible risk.

In the meantime, I would make use of what respect still remained with my classmates. They voted me to be Head Engineer of a new oil refining business. My job was made-to-order—I was in charge, and no one could tell me I wasn't! Sylvia Durrwachter was voted to be my assistant. She and her twin sister, Dianne, lived two miles or so from us so John took me to design plans and strategy with Sylvia while he hung out with her brother Dale. Sylvia and I worked on our project for months, and I was too busy to be bothered by *that* teacher, Mr. G.

Marian, in fourth grade, was making a terrible fuss about an assignment to write a poem. "Nonsense," I said, "It's easy."

I opened the dresser drawer and pulled out my hand-written treasury of stories, poems, and illustrations. Some copied, a few created, most convoluted. But all in the style of the ten-year-old who had compiled it a few years earlier. "Here's one you can use," I offered, handing her the wrinkled paper.

Marian copied and turned it in to her teacher. It went something like this:

> Dora pour a cup a tea
> Eva give it back ta me
> Amanda hand a plate to Flo
> Nicka pick a rose to go

All was well until Mrs. Krattli asked Marian, "What does this mean, 'Amanda hand a plate to flo'?"

Marian blushed tomato red. "I-I-I don't know."

"Well, it doesn't make sense. What is 'flo'?"

Unable to answer her teacher about her *own* poem, Marian demanded an answer of me after she got home.

"Sure it makes sense." I tossed my ponytail. "Flo is a girl's name. You forgot to use a capital letter, silly!"

Marian walked away, mumbling. "Next time I will just do my own work, even if I don't know how."

Bill, too, was having issues in the classroom. As big as he was, and an athlete of repute, he could not figure out how to make certain boys behave. He'd learned positive reinforcement psychology in his education courses and he tried to use the method. "But," he said, "These knuckle-heads don't understand sweet talk."

Bill went to see the miniature Miss Larson, Professor of Practice Teaching, at Seattle Pacific, and told her about his struggles with discipline. The tiniest hint of a smile accompanied her confident answer.

"You can do it, young man. Let them know the rules. Then, at the first infraction walk slowly to the front of the room. Take off your jacket, hang it on a chair; take off your tie and your dress shirt, and hang them too. Walk back to the errant kid, lift him off of the floor by the back of his shirt, and remove him from the room. Make a production of the discipline, but never, ever lose your temper."

Bill returned to class determined to use Miss Larson's lesson. It paid off. Even Merton agreed the procedure worked, but he protested that *Mr. Richardson*—who was really just Bill—liked to use the three-foot board with the holes on his relative more than on any other boy. Buzz Thompson disagreed with Merton, saying he'd experienced equal or worse discipline. However, the two cohorts agreed that Mr. Richardson did not always carry out his punishments quietly without losing his temper, and they learned to muffle their errant behavior at the early signs of fire in their teacher's eyes.

But for all of us, the school afforded benefits beyond discipline and education. One such benefit this year was an eye screening. Three of us needed glasses, but I got the first pair since my eyes were the worst. The optometrist charged $32.50 for the test and glasses, but he said we could make time payments without interest.

I saw a brand new world—a kaleidoscope of shapes and particles. I saw individual needles on the firs, not just the color green; the Small Dipper, the North Star and trillions of lights in the Milky Way, not just a handful of stars. I was amazed at snow appearing as flakes, not fog, and birds nesting, not just flying. There were trees on our mountains, and the moon had a *man* in it. I couldn't stop looking to see what I could see. I said to Mother, "I can tell that Dad and John are working with the mill, Phil and Mert are by the pond, and Grandma is sitting at her table."

The trips to the eye doctor were fine, but not so the trips to the dentist. Dr. Marquardt gave Dad and Mother a good deal—he would charge nothing for our check-ups and little, if any, for fillings. We figured he filled teeth on the cheap because he didn't use Novocain, or anything else, to kill the pain.

I got my first filling in the spring of 1957. I thought my brains would rattle out of my head with the screeching and grinding of the drill. I wanted to yell, but my mouth was sealed wide open. My siblings also had never-to-be-forgotten visits to the dentist. Marian didn't think she would survive the pain of her first filling, but she looked at Mother and could see that she was suffering too. Mother told how she once had all of her teeth pulled so that they could be replaced by false teeth. "But," she said, "They put me to sleep for that, so the pain didn't come until afterwards."

When my first tooth was filled I got black and white saddle shoes—the kind the stylish kids wore and that you polished every day, carefully keeping the black off the white and the white off the black. Mother paid half of the $6.50. I paid the other half and used the rest of my $9.00 savings on shoe polish and yards of bright red crinoline. I cut the netting in strips, gathered and sewed it in tiers to fluff out my circular skirt with its green stripes and red roses. June Liljedahl had the nicest crinolines, at least four or five, to wear at the same time. I wanted my red one to stick out as far as hers, so I treated it with a pasty mix of cornstarch or a sticky syrup of sugar water every weekend. Monday mornings it was full and stiff and scratchy, but by Wednesday it was flat.

Saddle shoes and crinolines were not enough, however. I told Dad I needed to get high heels. I needed them to sing with Judi Anderson and Elizabeth at the church banquet. Dad said no to the heels. He also told Mother she couldn't accompany the trio, even after she had practiced with us.

Then he changed his mind. Perhaps in these cases, Dad's first response had not been his final answer. Or perhaps he wanted to make amends for speaking harshly. In any case, before the week was up I got two pairs of high heels—a black pair from the store and a white pair from the missionary barrel. Furthermore, Dad took Mother to play at the banquet and asked her afterwards, "Wouldn't you like to stay for the movie too?"

Since Dad seemed to have loosened his restrictions, my next move was to smuggle to school a lipstick sample that Aunt Eleanor had left at our place. I rationalized that lipstick would make my lips look fuller, my nose look smaller, my freckles less conspicuous, and my mousy hair less mousy. Red lips would also accent my eyes, which I had just come to realize were not blue like I always thought, but had turned green when I wasn't looking. And maybe—just maybe—no one would notice that I was gaining too much weight.

My rationale didn't convince anyone. John, with Phillip's nod of approval, told Dad and Mother I was painting my lips at school. Dad gave me a lecture for wanting to look worldly, and Mother agreed with him. So I just filled in my eyebrows with a lead pencil and curled my lashes with a paring knife. My brothers never figured that out.

Other—far more significant—news happened this spring: Debi Sue was born in Cuba to Marilyn and Allen. Micki, at 19 months, fell off a stool and broke her collarbone. I learned to drive the converted '31 Chev truck, even rolling it down a hill and popping the clutch to get it started. David and Elizabeth bought a 1940's Farmall Cub tractor to help in the farm work. Mr. Myers welded our yard donkey so we could pull felled trees out of the woods to saw for lumber or to sell as pulpwood—the latter being necessary to pay for cement and nails, since everyone insisted that we should buy new nails and not use rusted hammered-straight ones like those that held the Farmhouse walls together.

In cutting down trees, the boys dropped so many that Mother, to her dismay, could see the toilet from the kitchen. She said she wished they would have left at least a couple of trees for privacy, especially since we were expecting multitudes of guests this spring. "Oh, well," she rationalized, "If it means there are boards for a house with an inside facility, so be it."

"But," she said to Dad, "It would be helpful to sprinkle lime out there. Maybe a new hole won't have to be dug this year."

We agreed with her, since lime cut down on the fumes and aided in the breakdown of pit's contents. The New House was coming, slowly but surely. Well, slowly at least. So for the time being, we'd use the same toilet pit, and hold our breath as long as we could.

Bob Richardson came during Easter vacation with carloads of construction workers and their families from Snohomish—most of them from the Baptist Church—with plans to donate a week to the foundation and framing. There were so many people, we put up a camp-meeting tent donated by Naoma, and filled it with squeaky wire beds for all the boys. One of the boys was my heartthrob from as many years as I had known him—Alan Troupe. He had tan skin, dark eyes, and the broad smile of his mother Grace. And he ignored me completely. He never knew how much time he spent in my dreams, never knew how many times he was talked about in my diary, and never knew that I wanted to ask if he liked my hair in a ponytail.

Mr. Richardson allowed for no slacking on his construction team. When one of the guys pontificated one too many times, Bob snuck up from behind and nailed the sole of blabbermouth's shoe to the floor. The fellow jerked around to see what had happened and fell over. Everyone cracked up—until they realized the character had broken his ankle. Sympathy oozed from those who went to his aid, but others went back to their posts, continuing to grin about the punishment rendered for foolhardiness.

Outside of that distraction, Bob and his volunteers finished the floor joists, sub-flooring, studs of two walls and several window frames. We could see from as far away as the Farmhouse that the New House was taking shape.

At school, May was filled with band concerts led by Mr. Longfellow. The band went to Clallam Bay, Neah Bay, and Dry Creek, and those schools sent their bands to play for us at Joyce. Elizabeth directed our high school girls' chorus and we sang popular songs of the 1920s.

To raise funds for our trips, the PTA put on three plays and the band played between performances. Mr. Longfellow needed to change costumes for his part in the productions, so he asked me to conduct the band for three songs. Being in charge of all those horn blowers and drum pounders was my ideal role. I told Mr. Longfellow, "I think I will be a music director when I grow up."

Mr. Longfellow didn't answer, but I liked the way he moved the music stand—as if he was in full agreement that my plan had validity.

When school was out, we Corey kids went straight to work. Merton at twelve years and Marian, on the day of her tenth birthday, went to pick strawberries for a week in Snohomish. I started working in the Anderson strawberry patch, close to where the Myers lived. I was there every day, picking as hard and fast as I could, and earning up to four bucks on a good day. By my 14th birthday on June 18, I had earned enough to pay for repairs to a ring Aunt Eleanor sent to me. After the jeweler handed it to me, I held the ring in the sun and watched the colored lights reflect from the stone onto the ceiling. It was real grown-up jewelry, not the fifty-cent kind in the Five-and-Dime Store. At home, I put it in my velvet jewelry box next to Aunt Eleanor's gold childhood locket with the engraved E she had given me when I was ten. I couldn't wait for Sunday so I could wear both of them to the evening service, though I was terribly disappointed when I got dressed for church that the glittery ring looked completely wrong on my hands, all stained and scratched from strawberry picking.

John and Phil were working on New House construction when Bill Richardson's dad, Bob, came with a truck full of windows that he had gotten on a good deal. He returned a second time, pulling a boat and bringing us a calf. The calf was a Holstein, born to the prize-winning cow in the best dairy farm in Snohomish County, maybe even in the state. We talked about what to name her. We'd named Betsy for Elizabeth, Ellen for Eleanor, so we named her Marianne for Marian. Janice said, "That's not fair. I want to name the calf."

Marian said, "You're only five. You'll get your turn next."

Bob Richardson launched the 14-foot wooden boat with the boys at Crescent Beach and Bill mentored them in the art of rowing with oars and managing the fishing lines in the choppy water. If four were rowing hard and steady, two could fish or fix their tackle.

The boys were short on fishing gear to snare the ocean-size fish, however. So when they weren't working on the New House, they contrived to set up a makeshift factory in the lean-to of the barn—a factory to make their own fishing tackle. They carved a variety of holes in blocks of wood to serve as molds for different sizes of weights, and they salvaged lead from dead car batteries. Then they fired up the blowtorch, melted the lead in a ladle, and spilled it into the molds. After the weights hardened, they dropped them from the molds and cooled off everything with water.

One Saturday, David, who was home for the weekend, raced in from the barn. "Lead blew up in John's eyes!"

We found John on his knees in the barn, holding his hands over his face and moaning in agony. The molten lead had exploded when it hit the cold water. Mother raised her apron to her cheeks. "Jesus," she breathed.

Dad pulled John into his arms and said, "Lord Jesus, save this boy's eyes. For your glory, amen."

Then he looked up at Mother, nary a doubt in his voice. "God has heard."

Next came the orders. "Margaret, call Dr. Moore. David, bring the car. We're taking John to get his eyes washed out."

Dad and Mother arrived at the clinic, leading John who held a moist cloth over his eyes. Dr. Moore helped him onto the examination table and directed him to lie down. The physician peered in one eye and then in the other. He looked up at Dad and shook his head. "I'll do the best I can, but am unable to tell you what might be the long term effects of this injury."

He put drops in one eye, propped open the lid and picked out nearly a dozen scraps of lead, then repeated the process with the other. When he finished, he wrote prescriptions for ointment and pain medications. But John slept well the first night and never needed any pain pills. By the second day, he could see from both eyes. The doctor said, "This recovery of sight and health to these eyes is beyond any expectation I could have had."

He turned to John and said, "I want you to wear dark glasses for a while, and rest your eyes every day. They have experienced a severe trauma."

Dad had not doubted that this would be the outcome, but his faith had been affirmed to others—including us. God had done a miracle.

Next time John went fishing he caught a 22-pound halibut as the others rowed. However, when he hoisted the fish into the boat, it thrashed against Bill's tackle box and sent the contents flying. Most of Bill's best tackle and our hand-formed sinkers sank to the floor of the ocean.

Soon after, Bob Richardson brought us a 5-HP Johnson outboard motor, and the battle of the oars ended. With the updated, powered wooden boat, Bill ran a regular chartering service for the family. We had to take turns, but no one got skunked. Even Mother, Liz, and I pulled in cod or salmon. That season there was so much fish, the boys made a smoke house, padding the walls with batting, and drilling holes in the roof. They made trays from chicken wire and situated the wooden structure next to the outhouse. The smoke house provided a screen—a smoke screen. It buffered Mother's panoramic view of the toilet, and masked the rank odor that even lime could not allay during the summer rush of visitors.

The first guests to arrive were John McLennan, Virginia, their three kiddies from Illinois, along with John's parents from Canada. John had resigned his position in Rockford, and they would be moving in two weeks to pastor a church in Cresskill, New Jersey.

John Mac took up his ribbing routine the minute he walked through the door. He teased Mother on her 52nd birthday. "My, but you look young. Could there be a more wonderful, marvelous, lovelier mother-in-law anywhere on earth, than the one I got when I married your most beautiful daughter?"

Mother said, "Pshaw," and tucked her more-salt-than-pepper hair into place.

Our brother-in-law always talked that way to Mother, but he wasn't always so kind to the rest of us. His quick wit could bite and I could just about imagine what Virginia had faced when her husband bickered day after day and evening after evening with Marilyn in the little Prairie apartment.

On this day, John's chuckle with Mother choked when word came from outside that Star and Janice had damaged the welder—that they had poured water into the gas tank of the 1940 Ford car engine that ran it. "But," Janice whimpered, "We were just playing house and getting the car ready to go to town."

Janice was only five. It was a car; it had a place to put in fuel, and water was pretend fuel. Both girls got spankings, but the hardest fell on six-year-old Star whose father told her, "You are the older one and should have known better."

Marian felt so sorry for the girls she spent the rest of the day giving piggy-back rides up and down the hills, across the creek, and through the woods.

The water killed the welder. Dave's aircraft generator-with-adapter welder, that had been switched out to DC welder from Allen, was dead-as-a-fencepost dead. The boys would drain the water, flush out the system and get it working again. But it hadn't been doing its job all that well before the mistreatment—and even less afterwards—so Dad stopped by Wils Myers' welding shop and explained what had happened.

Wils said, "I have something that might work for you."

He gave us a discarded heavy duty generator welder of his. We added one of the old car engines to turn the generator, and mounted the adapted apparatus onto a trailer that we'd built from the axle and wheels of the retired Model A Ford Pickup-turned-dump truck. We hooked up the Farmall tractor to pull the trailer with its mounted machinery to weld equipment anywhere it broke down. Once the welder was functioning, it was time to upgrade the Sawmill. The carriage had tended to stall under the weight of the logs because of worn out buffers. Dad and David cut a pile of five-inch circles from the home-cured leather and stacked them like spools, then laid them on their sides in place of the buffers. The friction of the new leather pieces kept the carriage moving forward no matter how heavy the logs. Dad bought a planer to smooth the boards and shave them to the right dimensions. Efficiency reigned at last.

The pile of lumber grew, as did the stack of slab pushed aside to be cut for firewood. Phillip had an idea. "Dad," he asked, "Can I have some of the slab to make a cabin?"

Over the next few weeks, Phil—with a little help from Merton and me—constructed his own shack next to the gully of the small stream. He cut strips of homemade leather for hinges, put in a chimney, and built a cement-and-rock stove. He stood back, looking at his masterpiece, proud as any 15-year-old house builder and masonry expert could be. The following day, he gathered a few of us around to watch him crumple the paper and build a teepee of kindling inside the new stove. When Phillip lit the match, I was thinking how fun it would be to cook trout in his little cabin above the creek. The paper flared right up and by the time the kindling caught, smoke was spilling out the sides. "It'll be fine after I get the wood going," Phil said. But it wasn't. Smoke never lifted out the chimney. It just filled the cabin and spewed out the doorway and through the cracks.

Marian loved to hang out in the house that Phillip built—without the fire of course—so he told her it could be her playhouse. Phil was kind to her when others weren't. He warned when there were bats in the attic, so she wouldn't be frightened, and answered her questions about the birds and the beavers without making fun of her. On the other hand, Merton teased her and roughhoused until she cried. Janice would say to him, "I am going to tell on you, Merton." And then she would print on the blackboard next to the Co-op bill, "TELL ON MERTON. BAD BOY."

Marian didn't want to get her brother in trouble, so she would snuffle her nose and say. "No. Don't tell. I'm okay. I'll give you a piece of candy if you erase the board."

So, Mert would get off easy, and Marian would go visit Grandma for a cookie, or hide in Phillip's house, not only from Merton, but also from the jobs to be done, or just because other things weren't going well. That's what happened when she announced to Mother, "I am running away from home."

Marian pulled our largest leather suitcase from under the winter coats on the second floor. Mother asked, "What do you think you will need to take? Shall I help you pack?"

Mother watched the ten-year-old drag the suitcase down the path toward the highway and veer right to Phil's cabin. Mother would have known that fear of the road and the truck drivers would have kept the child from going more than a short distance from the safety of the house. She watched for the child's return—it only took about half an hour—and met her daughter at the door. "I'm glad you came home. I missed you."

Mother carried the suitcase up the stairs. "Let's unpack your bag and pack a smaller one so you can go visit your cousin Kathleen."

The next day, Mother and Dad took Marian along on a trip to Tacoma and left her to play with Kathleen Corey, the daughter of Uncle Albert and Aunt Hilda. Kathy was Marian's age—one of the few cousins not older by a decade or two or three. Aunt Hilda took the two girls to a shopping center. Marian had never been any place so exciting, nor had she ever ridden on an escalator. While Aunt Hilda shopped, Marian and Kathy rode up and down, up and down, and then they searched out more moving stairs.

Aunt Hilda caught up with them. "I have been looking everywhere for you two!" she panted. "You should have stayed where I left you and not wandered off."

Catching her breath, she went on, "You know, Marian, I *had* planned to buy you something special to take home. But now I won't. Maybe that will be your lesson."

All of the fun of the day drained from the child's heart. She wanted to run away again. Instead she had to wait for Mother and Daddy to pick her up, and to wonder for the rest of her life, what nifty necklace or new toy Aunt Hilda might have given her, if she just hadn't been caught up in the exuberance of riding escalators.

Meanwhile, back at the Farmhouse, Lillian Pennoyer, who'd come from Seattle, was helping me run the kitchen. We fired up the stove, and made goulash. I told Lillian to choose the spices, since I didn't want to risk a curry powder accident. When that was ready, we pushed it to the side of the stove and added more wood to the fire to make it hot enough to can fruit and bake pies. It was hot enough for certain. I stepped out the back door to cool off and saw flames creeping along the roof. "Fire! Fire!" I screamed at the boys. "The house is burning. Hurry! Get the hoses from the garden. Hurry!"

Phillip and John hauled the hoses onto the porch roof and to the upper level. They doused the shingles until the pump ran dry. Mert checked the attic, while Lillian and I sat on the roof until no more sparks flew out the chimney. What relief that the house had not burned—yet it felt like triple trouble when we returned to the kitchen and realized we'd left the pies in the oven until they burned. When we tested the goulash that had simmered all day, it was stuck on the bottom and tasted of burned meat and spices that Lillian realized was paprika. She had dumped in a heaping tablespoon of that spice instead of the teaspoon the recipe called for.

The next day we didn't want to fire up the stove and chance any other disasters, so Lillian and I packed ourselves a lunch of sandwiches filled with lettuce and Kraft Miracle Whip. Lillian had never tasted lettuce and mayo sandwiches before and thought they were quite yummy. I said, "Add peanut butter and you won't believe how good they are."

And Phil added, "I'll pick dandelion leaves and you can put those in your sandwich—it's as good as lettuce."

Upon Mother's return, she wrote as if to reassure herself: "Found *all well here* but (they) had had a fire in the roof on Tuesday. Well was pumped dry and Phil and John are digging that."

"All well here." When Mother returned from travels, *all well here* was the most repeated phrase in her diary. She knew God had called her to support her husband, and knew by the end of a trip—even if she hadn't wanted to go—that God had used her to bless others. She also knew God would care for the children in her absence. Yet, she seemed happiest of all to return home and find *all well here.* So that August 2, 1957, *all well here* meant the house had not burned, no children had been injured, the well would recover, and she was just plain glad to be home.

She was also glad to be home to show Elizabeth and Bill where to stash their stuff upon their return from summer school in Seattle, and to remind Lillian and me to move out of my bedroom so the Richardsons, including their newborn son, Dennis John, would have a place to sleep.

There was one benefit of Liz and Bill taking over my bedroom. I got to go stay with Lillian at her family's cabin on the beach. We cooked what we wanted to eat—except the chicken that Lillian had left on the counter to thaw until it rotted. We had the whole seashore and ocean to ourselves. No bosses, no brothers, no babies. We could listen to the Lyre River, the surf, the sea gulls, and each other's stories. We talked nonsense and told dumb jokes until Lillian said, "I remember your Dad quoting a verse about bad men who creep into houses and lead captive silly women."

That ended the feather-brained talk by me. No way was I going to jeopardize my safety at the beach house. So we read Grace Livingston Hill books that we'd brought from the Book Mobile and talked about marrying rich men so we could live in beautiful mansions and have servants. And if it really went well, we could live next door to each other and drink tea and eat shortbread made with fresh butter.

Lillian went back to her boarding school in Seattle, and I went home to teach Vacation Bible School at Joyce Church. Alice Myers helped me. She was older and more spiritual than I, but not as talkative and bossy. There were nearly twenty wriggly five and six-year-olds that *needed* bossy, and they wore us out. Even so, after the Friday session, I went on a hike at Mt. Angeles with Phillip, Merton, the Myers girls, and a few other young people.

We got a late start from Hurricane Ridge with plans to hike nearly fifteen miles to Lake Dawn along the ridge below Mt. Angeles. There were two trails. We girls took the bypass trail at a lower elevation, while the boys went closer to the top that jutted up to 6,500 feet. We were still far from our destination when it got dark. No flashlights, no moon, and no stars to light the way. Our steps got shorter and shorter, as we crept along trying to keep our bearing on the narrow path shaved into the steep wall. My knees knocked and I quit talking—the others had quit even sooner—even though I liked the sound of my voice more than the sound of the pebbles sliding from the path off the cliff and into the blackness below. My heart pounding, I began to pray under my breath that I would not accompany the shale into the chasm. Hours later, the trail flattened out and I could see the waiting cars with their lights turned our direction. My knees half-buckled all the way to the car and shook during the drive home. There was a ton of chattering, but not from me. I was done in.

Mother met us at the door of the Farmhouse. She said she had wanted to call someone, but didn't know whom. On top of that, she would have had to go to the Tieches, since she'd had our phone disconnected a few weeks earlier when the monthly fee went up.

That night in my nightmares—it seemed like all night—my legs wobbled and jiggled until I pitched off the precipice into the pit that had no bottom.

John hadn't gone on the hike with us. He had begun to build a stone chimney in the center of the New House, and it was his total commitment. He didn't even stop to help us rake, shock and bring in the hay. Often by himself for hours on end, John piled rocks in formation and mortared them with a mix of sand from Crescent Beach, and cement and lime from the store. The chimney was more than four feet in all directions when Mr. Samuelson came by. The gentleman, with his salesman smile, said to John and Dad, "I will bring a friend, an expert on laying rocks, to give you some hints."

The tradesman got down beside John and began to fit rocks in a pattern that squared the corners and made the walls both strong and straight. He said, "It is best to practice just where you will place the rocks, then lay them aside, cementing one at a time according to the plan. And you should use washed sand for your mortar."

He looked John in the eyes, exuding warmth and confidence from his own. "You will have a chimney that will be sealed, strong, and safe, even if it grows to thirty feet."

So, while John sculpted the chimney, we hauled load after load of stone from a rock cliff off Camp Hayden Road near the entrance to the Kreamans' driveway. We used picks and crowbars on outcroppings of a wall where it was too steep to stand. At the bottom we sorted what remained after each avalanche and hoisted them—some of them too heavy for one person to lift—into the back of Bill's pickup.

When the loads weighed too much and the pickup scraped bottom on our driveway, Bill spluttered about the ruination of his brand new truck. Then he shrugged his shoulders and went back for more.

So John just kept laying rocks, as if fitting the pieces of a puzzle, until the chimney reached the framework of the main floor.

Mr. Samuelson came again, taking time to affirm John's artwork, before handing Dad a check for $385 he said was for roofing. Dad went right to town to purchase rolls and rolls of tar-infused paper roofing. All of us who could wield a hammer made short work of that nearly 2,500 square foot surface. We had just finished when Mother walked over from the Farmhouse to check our progress. "Come up and look," Phillip said.

So Mother joined us in the review of the roof. She looked out over the fields and down through the chimney hole. Satisfied with all that she saw, she said, "Well, now, let's go have lunch and celebrate."

Later that day, Mother recorded in capital letters. "AUG 23. ROOF FINISHED AT 1:30 TODAY"

We were back to school a week later. John was a senior, Phil and I were sophomores, and Mert was in seventh. After we got home in the afternoons John occupied his time with the chimney, while Phil, Mert, and I began to pick fir cones to sell. The cones with the highest number of seeds in them were in the upper branches. Like monkeys in the jungle, we swung back and forth fifty feet up in the tops of the evergreens. We took deep breaths of the fragrant Christmas-infused air, and paid no attention as the pitch gunked up our hands, globbed in our hair, and glued us to our clothes.

We filled a dozen burlap gunnysacks and waited for the inspector to test our stash. He sliced through a few samplings from each sack. We held our breath hoping not to hear him say, "Not ripe. Too early in the season," or, "Not enough viable seeds." Either comment would have ended our cone collecting for the year. But this time his report was good, and we headed back out to the woods.

We knew a tree was perfect when we heard cones swishing through the branches and plopping in a heap. The squirrels were pelting the best cones to the ground. We tip-toed in to gather their hoard, hoping they wouldn't scare off and quit helping us. When hunting season started, we stopped picking cones. There were as many hunters in the woods as squirrels and we knew to keep out of their way—especially after we heard that a young boy, whose family we knew, had been killed in a hunting accident. But, we were farm kids finding our way in the business world, and seeking to earn a few dollars in whatever manner came available.

The three of us high schoolers took time from everything to go with our high school classes to the Puyallup Fair—a Washington State festival that had been entertaining guests every year since 1900, except for two years during the war when the military turned the grounds into an internment camp for Japanese-Americans.

For us country bumpkins, the Puyallup Fair was a place of fascination: A place to watch acrobats and animal acts, and to scream during the thrilling rides; a place to wonder at the nerve of the man shot from the cannon; and a place to spend our berry-picking and cone-collecting quarters. It was a place to hang out with our classmates, and also a place for some of them, like Phil and his girlfriend Alice Myers, to sneak off with each other. A freshman named JP thought he would try that with me—or at least try to earn a seat next to me on the bus. JP reminded me of a beaver—he had that sort of face—and he would sneak up behind me to get close. He said, "I will win you a teddy bear."

"Don't bother, because I won't sit with you no matter what," I told him.

But he went off with that goal in mind. I figured I was safe since JP was a worse shot at the ring toss than he was with a basketball back at school. But after he'd tossed most of his pocket quarters, he bought a black and turquoise panda, and insisted I take it. "Sorry," I said, "Just quit asking me."

But I liked the bear and decided to keep it—without obligation, of course. There was no way I would be that close to JP in a dark bus. Just thinking about him gave me the creeps—like the creepy-crawlies of fright I had felt a few days earlier, when he and another hoodlum had chased me to the end of the vacant school hall, where I managed to escape into Bill's classroom. I didn't know what they had in mind, but I was pretty sure I didn't want to risk finding out.

Anyway, at home in the sanctuary of my room, I secretly named the fuzzy animal "Sammy," after a boy I did like.

Influenza hit Joyce School right after the Puyallup trip. The teachers were dropping out one after another and, in some classes, more than half the students stayed home. Every Corey except Marian was sick with a variety of temperatures and complications. John's turned into pneumonia and the doctor prescribed medicine that cost $13.95. Janice got an earache and Phillip got nosebleeds and an ear infection. Mother ran a merry-go-round of juice and water, fever thermometers, wash pans, and hot water bottles up and down the stairs. She said if she had known it would go on so long, she would have moved everyone to the living room, like she did when we had the chicken pox.

School was closed until November 7 to stop the spread. We learned that Virginia and her little ones were sick on the east coast, and Marilyn was sick in Cuba. We were improving and Mother said to Dad, "I'm concerned about David. If I pack up a box of food, could you take it to him? It's been weeks since we have heard from that son of ours."

Dad drove to Seattle and found David at the rooming house where he boarded. Dad gave him a report on Marilyn and Allen and the rest of us. When he asked how Dave was getting on, his son told him he'd been sick too, and had to stay in the Seattle Pacific infirmary. "I felt so bad they even gave me an aspirin."

Dad ignored the part about the aspirin, but asked. "By the way, how much does it cost to rent this room?"

"Just fifteen a month. Seems reasonable to me."

Dad pulled out a five-dollar bill. "Here is something to help with your expenses."

David objected. "Dad, I've been able to make it alright. I work at odd jobs and get a little here and there. You have lots of mouths to feed at home and bills to pay."

"I know, but you are supposed to have this," Dad responded, pressing it into David's hand and waiting for him to take it.

David puzzled how to refuse such a gift and realized he couldn't. He took the money, and the conversation turned to other things. But later, after Dad had left, David thought, *That sacrifice speaks of a father's love he doesn't say with words; it speaks of his desire to do much more if he could.*

Dad reported back to Mother that David seemed well settled in with some friends in a boarding house and that he'd been too sick to write.

We learned later that the Asian flu and its complications killed nearly 70,000 people in the United States, and up to two million worldwide. When we were back on our feet, we received word that someone we knew and loved—our former superintendent Mr. Krattli—had passed away. We weren't told if his death was due to the same virus, but we grieved for him as we talked about the impact this man had had in our lives.

We high school kids remembered our final visit with Mr. Krattli, just weeks before his death, when he had climbed the ladder to check on our progress with the new roof. David remembered him as the counselor that had said, "Young man, you have the ability to do anything you set your mind to. You could become an engineer. You know, they make as much as $10,000 a year."

When David had applied for Bible College, he sensed Mr. Krattli's disappointment. However, David was glad that this year he'd been able to tell Mr. Krattli of his plans to study math and science at Seattle Pacific. The young man wished he'd also had courage enough to say more, wished he had said to that mentor, "You are the one who instilled in me the confidence to aim for a good education."

Others remembered Mr. Krattli for his flexibility. Bill told the story of how Glenn Duncan would come to school after hunting through the woods, usually late for the first class. He would sit on the steps, take off his caulk boots, and put on his slippers. Behind the door of Mr. Krattli's office he would stash his 30/30 rifle and Heavy Red Filson Mackinaw jacket. Promptly at 2:00 in the afternoon, Glenn would say, "Mr. Krattli? Got to get goin' home before too long or I'll never make it 'fore dark."

Mr. Krattli would get the gun, boots, and jacket and give them to the boy. And Glenn would head towards the woods behind the school. Rumor was that Glenn kept people in venison—people except for Mr. Corey who would not accept it if it didn't come with a legal hunting tag.

In the months to come, the students and community raised funds for a memorial to Mr. Krattli. By the end of the school year, a new time clock and dedication plaque were installed in the Joyce School gymnasium.[115]

Thanksgiving ushered in the basketball season. The coach had quit after a bout with pneumonia, and Bill had been approved by the school board to take over. Bill made me the official score keeper—a position that gave me a pass to all home games and to most away games. John's friend Dale Durrwachter kept the time clock, and I sat next to him with the scorebook. I marked a slash for each shot attempted and crossed the slash if it was made. I marked the fouls and the free throws. At the end of the game, I tallied and posted the percentages, making me popular—or not so popular—with the players.

Equally important at the games was my role as rooter. While keeping stats, I never allowed the paperwork to interfere with my shouting. "Go for it, Phil!" "Good shot, Gary!" "Whoo-hoo. Yay guys. Great steal, Sam!"

Sometimes I yelled at the refs, too, about their stupid calls, only I covered my mouth for fear that I might lose my job as scorekeeper. At the end of the game, the numbers would be posted, but my voice was gone. Aurea Schmitt, who taught me singing lessons said, "You would be wise to stay calm at the games and save your voice for singing at the Christmas program."

I agreed with her, but it would have taken Mrs. Tripp's adhesive tape to shut me up when the boys were playing. And, in any event, my hoarse voice did not hinder my performance with the Corey band that we now called "Corey Inc." We put on a Christmas concert for Grandma Phenicie. She was a captive audience, yes, but also appreciative—so beaming proud of the grandchildren and their talent!

The Pennoyers were there for the concert as well. They had returned on furlough after four years in the Philippines, and Fred and Virginia stayed with us most of December. Mrs. Pennoyer held us spellbound with her stories of life in the villages—stories of children whose lives were changed, and stories of families who were reunited after the parents heard the gospel. Mr. Pennoyer also talked of their ministry with a confidence and brilliance we had never heard in his voice before they went overseas. While they talked, a seed of commitment to missions began to sprout in my spirit.

As interested as we were in hearing the tales of foreign lands, Mrs. Pennoyer was equally interested in knowing how the construction of our New House was coming along. Mother and Dad were delighted to give the tour.

"Oh my, oh my," Mrs. Pennoyer said as the four walked into the new kitchen.

She grasped Mother's arm. "It is beautiful. So many big windows to let the light in."

They walked around the chimney, into the living room. "And, oh, what lovely rockery."

Mother smiled, "John has taken this chimney and fireplace on as his project, and has been working at it for months."

They walked through the hall where the bedrooms would be and Mother pointed out the area that would become a bathroom. They laughed together as Mother commented. "Can you guess how many years I've waited for an indoor toilet?"

As they walked out the front entrance, Virginia said, "I am so happy for you. I can't wait to sit at your table in this place."

"Yes, it is wonderful," Mother said, as she faced her cherished friend, "to know that we are coming into the homestretch."

New House back dropped by Farmhouse and barn

CHAPTER TWENTY-SIX
The Homestretch
(1958)

To all appearances, the construction was on track for rapid completion. But delays were standard, and Mother noted more than once in her diary: It's always something . . .

Some implement to fix—the cultivator, the tractor, the car, the welder, the donkey, the mill.

Some lack of funds—the Co-op bill, the cement, the nails, the toilet, the bathtub, the lights.

Some need for help—the plumbing, the wiring, the septic, the cupboards, the cabinets, the doors.

And always something else to be doing—who could engage full-time on a construction project with so many other things afoot? There was Phillip trying—and failing—to get his driver's license, and there I was, resolving to be nicer to my brother in his time of need. There was Merton's 13th birthday, celebrated with a cake and much razzing, rather like a Roast of Celebrities, only we were less kind. We called him Mergatroid, Myrtle the Turtle, and Knothead. And there was Janice's 6th birthday a few weeks later when we called her Sweet Pea or Pumpkin, Elizabeth gave her a child-size bike, Mother gave her a bottle of bubbles, and I made her a brand new dress. Such inequity.

At school there was basketball, the school band, and traveling concerts. And there were classes. Biology had become my favorite subject. For a term project, I went to the hospital to get my blood typed and watch the donors give blood. I presented the report and finished with the statement, "I plan to be a doctor someday."

Of course, I also wanted to be a singer. That year, for the first time, I sang at a wedding and, for the first time, I sang at a funeral—the latter turning out to be far more memorable.

Dad took me to the funeral home early. After practicing with the organist, I asked, "Where's the bathroom?"

"Down the hall to the end, go right."

Somehow—I'm not sure how—I opened a door just *before* the end of the hall. The room was cool, almost like a refrigerator, and heavy with darkness. I thought, *If I leave the door open a little I can find the light switch. Yes, I can see a string.* I moved toward the string and started to reach for it. At the same moment, I lowered my hand to the counter beneath.

I gasped. Resting on the counter was the shape of a mummy in a shroud. Unable to even breathe, I backed up and eased out the door, closing it with the stealth of a ghost. The bathroom was where it was supposed to be—at the end of the hall. I locked the room and sat on the tile floor, wondering whether my heart would slow down enough for me to sing. Somehow, when it was time, I managed to get the notes and words out, though my thoughts were elsewhere.

> One sweetly solemn thought comes to me o'er and o'er *(could've fainted in there and frozen to death)*
> I am nearer home today than e'er I've been before *(like that stiff body? No thank you very much!)*
> Nearer my Father's house, where many mansions be *(didn't see mansions. Please Lord, I can wait)*
> Nearer today, the great white throne *(nope, it was a white sheet)*
> Nearer the crystal sea. *(with a sign, no swimming allowed. Who'd swim in heaven anyway?)*[116]

On and on, I kept singing the hymn and re-seeing what I'd seen, re-touching what I'd touched, but managing to make it through my appointed verses.

The solos I sang that year and the next earned me a name in the community, such that when Pete Seeger visited Port Angeles for a concert, I was invited up to the stage to sing with him. Forever after, "Go Tell it on the Mountain" would bring back memories of that one-night honor.

At Joyce School others were also getting noticed for their achievement. Murray Sands, Steven Anderson, and Roland Pfaff in eleventh grade had won the first rounds of inter-school debates. We sent them off to compete in Spokane at the all-state jamboree. They didn't win, but we treated them like heroes. When Joyce high school students—of which there were fewer than forty in all four grades—made an academic or athletic mark outside our community, we all stood tall.

This year I had problems with Mr. W, the superintendent. And I wasn't the only one with an attitude. Teachers seemed to skip school as often as the kids. Jim Hill, my classmate, dropped out completely. A couple of students started attending classes in Port Angeles. Others went to the school board meeting to protest the way Mr. W treated them. My biggest gripe was that he gave me a B in geometry. Even after I had earned all A's on my papers and tests in the class I most hated, he still gave me a B. When I asked why, he told me, "I don't give A's to high school students. They don't know enough yet."

During class, and even in my diary, I drew cartoons of his square face with glasses hanging low on his nose and a curl that bounced in the middle of his forehead. Laugh at him I could, but it still took me a long time to forgive him for the undeserved B.

I took a remission from the aggravation at Mr. W by creating a new design for the Mother's Day Tea Style Show. The latest fashion to come out of Paris was a straight shifty shape called the *Sack Dress*. So I made dresses from gunnysacks, paper sacks, and flour sacks for my friends and me to model.

Dave came home from college from time to time. One weekend he arrived with four of his college friends on three noisy motor bikes, one of which was

David's new 1947 Indian motorcycle. So many college boys! I gave them names: Frank the goony, Jack the handsome, Louie the quiet, and Paul the tall. When the guys roared out at 4:00 AM the next day for the rest of their trip around the Olympic Peninsula, I was disappointed. None of them had said he would write to me.

Since the college boys didn't ask to hear from me, I wrote the next big news in my diary: "Dad drove home a Station Wagon. It's a '51 Chevrolet Station Wagon with wood trim on the sides."

We had seen Dad leave to take the Coupe to the mechanic. After he arrived in the wagon, Mother questioned, "Is this loaned to us while the Coupe is fixed?"

"No," he exclaimed, "It is ours!"

After that announcement, we hurried out with Mother to see. She opened the doors to look inside; then turned back toward Dad. "I don't understand. What about the Coupe?"

Dad explained that the estimate on the repairs was way beyond what he could pay. After negotiating, he'd agreed to buy the vehicle when Mr. Priebe offered an extra discount of $100, and Mr. Samuelson put money on it. "We will owe a total of $215 to be paid as we are able."

Mother's assessment in her diary that day was simple: "A Station Wagon at last!"

Mother had asked God for a station wagon since the grown-ups were babies. The Station Wagon. She spelled it with capitals same as she had her Chevvy and the Coupe, as if these cars were her people. We never saw the Coupe again, never re-mastered her into another machine, and never had a memorial for her. But we would never forget her five years of faithfulness— five years of Dad's trips in ministry; five years of trips to haul machines, hay, and supplies; and five years of carting us in her open trunk up the mountain to pick berries, or to the beach for a swim.

For the first road trip in the Station Wagon, Dad and Mother went to Tacoma to settle Grandma Corey into a nursing home, and to bring to us the extras from her house. In the midst of the move, Grandma asked Dad to read a portion of scripture for her. He held the Bible as far from his eyes as possible, but still could not make out the small print. She laughed, "You need long arms like your brother Lester."

Then she turned serious, "Arthur Wheelock, you are to get your eyes checked and send the bill to me. Do you understand?"

Dad gave no argument, and within days had followed his mother's orders. With his new glasses, Dad's arms were once again long enough to hold the Bible for reading. He wouldn't have to buy a big print version just yet.

One of the extras Grandma sent home was her television. When our parents were away, every kid who was at home watched hour after hour of shows on the one or two channels that came through. One Saturday afternoon, I watched my first TV movie—a movie about aliens putting people into pods where they turned into strange creatures that looked like themselves, except for the black almond-shaped gaps where their eyes had once been. After that I didn't sleep well for several nights. I closed my eyes and could still see those black holes in the place of eyes. Then I would be sucked into those holes and over the Mount Angeles cliff, like falling shale. I decided such movies were not a good idea—at least not movies like *The Invasion of the Body Snatchers.*

However, I did like *Leave it to Beaver* because something funny usually happened, and Mother liked *Gunsmoke* because it reminded her of John Wayne movies. Dad didn't much approve of TV, but he, too, could get caught up in programs. Then came the day he preached a sermon at Joyce Bible Church on how you could waste your brain in a fantasy world; how you could dissipate your energy for doing good; how you could whittle away at the time available to help others; and how that box could become an idol in place of God. A few days later, at the dinner table, Mert and Phil took Dad to task, "But we have a television, don't we? And you watch it, don't you?"

The discussion ended with the boys offering to help Dad carry the *thing* out to the hillside. Janice was not pleased with the thought of losing the TV, so they told her she could be the one to do the target practicing. Together, the members of the family headed out, so Janice could take her first shot with a gun. And her second shot, along with many, many shots until one actually connected with the larger-than-life bullseye. The television was no more.

Yes, it is true that Dad preached the sermon at Joyce Bible Church. By this year, our involvement at that worship center was all-inclusive. We helped host a farewell for Pastor Hindman and his family, and welcomed George and Elsie Woods. Elizabeth became the pianist, freeing up Mrs. Myers, who said she had only done it because there was no one else. Mother taught the toddlers' Sunday school class and Dad sometimes attended the evening service with us—even preaching when asked. It had been more than ten years since the church had formed at Joyce and Dad had returned full-time to his itinerate ministry. Dad's new commitment to serve at Joyce Bible—without authority—was best for him. He was available to help those who needed him, but he was not in charge of those who didn't. During those ten years, Dad had rebuilt relationships with old timers, and had become a spiritual mentor to new neighbors. He had continued to serve God's sheep in other places but, by this time, his local ministry had blossomed once again.

The stretching out of the homestretch persisted past all of these activities. However, one project that was finished in the spring was the chimney. John, with occasional help from others, had worked on it day after day until it passed through the main floor; until it formed a fireplace and its mantels were layered with flat sandstone from the hills in the Twin area; until it passed through the roof and received the finishing touches. The 30-foot masterpiece of art in polished shades of sienna, bronze, clay, and coal, could have stood proud in a first-class resort, and it had strength enough to withstand an earthquake. This chimney had taken nine months to complete.

John was proud of his accomplishment and we were proud of him. What a trophy to honor his graduation from high school just weeks later. At the program, John gave a moving salutatory speech—a speech on being committed to finishing what one starts. Although he didn't use his own example of the chimney, we knew that wherever John went, he would accomplish what he set out to do.

Mother post-scripted her remarks about John's graduation in her diary: "Hardly seems possible one more is out of high school and no doubt will be away from home."

And he was. John got a job in Kirkland as a carpenter's assistant to one of Uncle Howard's and Aunt Eleanor's neighbors. He planned to go to Prairie Bible School in the fall, where years earlier his sisters had attended. He was going to be a missionary.

As summer warmed, Phil and I were once again employed. Phil got a better job than berry picking or cone harvesting. He went with Bill to Joyce School where they cleaned out the water line, scrubbed the holding tanks, and closed up the mountain beaver runs. I went to pick strawberries at the Andersons with my best friend, Judy Price, earning as much as $5.00 a day if I didn't stop for lunch. On my fifteenth birthday, in the middle of strawberry season, I received several lengths of fabric for my birthday. I think if I compared my outfits at that time, I might have found as many made from new cloth as from pre-worn clothes. My younger sisters didn't fare quite as well, since I reconfigured my outgrown ones into their sizes. But my best gift of all was Grandma Corey's radio that Mother had held as a special present just for me. What a prize! That source of music became my space of bliss as I tuned in to hear the songs of the day and the symphonies of long ago.

Progress on the house forged ahead as friends brought a huge beveled mirror they hung under the skylight, and linoleum which they installed in the utility room. Phil, Mert, and I carried blankets to the building and slept on the floor, along with Dad or a few of our guests. Mother cooked huge meals and I helped when home from the berry patch. Mert took most of the responsibility for the cows and the woodpile, and went with Phil to work in the hayfield several evenings. Marian and Janice washed the dishes, fed the chickens, and gathered eggs. We all said goodbye to the Pennoyers who were headed back to the Philippines, and then took turns salmon fishing out in the boat. We picked the raspberries and weeded the garden. All of us were doing our part. But Dad still had his list of to-do's:

- Take trips to see Grandma Corey who is off-and-on sick and make calls on people along the way. Check.
- Bring truckloads of donations from Howard and Aunt Eleanor who are moving to Arizona. Check.
- Make cabinets with Mr. Aldrich and paint them. Check.
- Install toilet, bathtub, lights. Check.

- Test plumbing. No check. The pipe joints drip, the basement faucet cracks and the floor floods.
- Fix pipes. Check.
- Pick up Mrs. Courtwright at the bus. Check.

As if on cue, Mrs. Courtwright brought us a Kenmore Electric Portable Sewing Machine. She had promised months earlier to give us one and had in mind to deliver it before the Big Move. When Mrs. Courtwright left, Mother said to me, "The electric machine will be yours. You are a much better seamstress than I am now, and the treadle suits me just fine."

"I will make you the first dress on it." I told her. "And then I will make curtains for all the bedrooms in the New House."

On July 16, Dennis's first birthday, I woke with the sun to pack my clothes and get started on the curtains. Bud Duncan showed up to finish the wiring and turn on the power, while the boys deepened the drainage ditch for the gray water from the kitchen and utility. They unhooked the combination stove, lugged it across the yard, and attached it to the stone chimney. Trip after trip, load after load, we emptied the old space to fill the new, until finally—as Mother recorded in her diary: "We moved into the NEW HOUSE."

It was true. At last we were *in* the New House, the one for which we had yearned, prayed, and worked for more than twenty years. The New House was far from finished, but was it ever full of promise. After a week or two, we would complete the septic installation, put toilet paper in our bathroom, and declare that the outhouse and its catalogs were redundant. After an arctic winter or two, we would have shingles on the roof, insulation in the walls, tile on the floors, carpets in the bedrooms, and a telephone. We would have doors on the bedrooms, cement covering the dirt in the basement, and ducts to deliver furnace-heated air to the rooms. We would have varnished cedar walls, made from our own lumber, where Mother could hang our pictures that had been saved from the school furnace—pictures framed just as I had once imagined.

Before the New House, we had lived through two decades during which we could have been miserable. There had been a time when we'd eaten beets for three days in a row, or oatmeal, because there was nothing else, not even flour to make bread. We'd had no running water, no electric lights, and no indoor plumbing. Wind had blown rain or snow through the cracks in our makeshift homes, and the bedrooms had been as cold as the outside toilet.

We had lived through two decades during which we could have been mortified. Our clothes were made from throwaways and our shoes worn down or outgrown. For many years we had no car and had to beg rides on the country highway. Our father had been exacting with us and irascible with others.

Misery and mortification. Oh, we'd been tempted to feel sorry for ourselves, but we'd never had the time to dwell in sadness. We'd had work to do, games to invent, songs to sing. Our father had required of himself what he'd expected of us. Our mother had been patient with him—with us most of the time—and she'd prayed. She'd borne his children, one after another, until we were ten brothers and sisters in the same quest—the twenty-year quest, not only for a better life and a bona fide house, but for a haven to fill with song and—in time—our own families.

One might think a life of leisure lay ahead for the Coreys. Not so. There would be the blackboard above the stove to remind everyone that the Co-op bill needed funds and the taxes were due; there would be difficult foster children who brought with them the scars of abuse and neglect; and there would be anxious prayer for family members who chose to follow detours instead of the straight-and-narrow.

But for now, on July 16, 1958, we could rejoice that God had provided for all of us what he promised to Dad on the Wilcox chicken farm in 1937. And we could celebrate with song, our voices joined from high to low, youthful to grown-up:

> Oh Lord my God when I in awesome wonder
> Consider all the worlds thy hands have made.
> I see the stars, I hear the rolling thunder;
> Thy power throughout the universe displayed.
> Then sings my soul, my Savior God to Thee,
> How great thou art, How great thou art.[117]

• • •

CHRONICLE THREE
July 1979

CHAPTER TWENTY-SEVEN
The Reunion
(July 1979)

It was the year of my parents' fiftieth wedding anniversary, and the question traveled to the far reaches of the earth. *Could we—all of us siblings, spouses, and successors—pull off a family reunion?*

The response, representing sixty people scattered across six countries, was unequivocal. And so the gears were set in motion. We would come together in July on Whidbey Island, Washington. There was a retired World War II army camp there, now run as a retreat center by Seattle Pacific University. Camp Casey would have everything needed to host such an energetic clan.

Marilyn and Allen, who served as directors of West Indies Mission in Miami, Florida, were the first to arrive. David, who was a civilian health physicist at the Bremerton Naval Base, met them at SeaTac airport and drove them to his place in Port Orchard. Dave's wife, Violet (Traina)[118], worked with Marilyn to stockpile two vehicles with food—gallons of homemade spaghetti sauce; boxes full of jars with canned beans, applesauce or plums; and sufficient mix for thousands of pancakes. Next to the food they crammed in seven kids: The Thompson two, Debi and Shari, and Dave's and Vi's five: Marilyn Ruth, Carolyn, Jacki, Steven, and Ty.

They'd just gotten underway when David's jeep broke down. Marilyn jumped out of the passenger seat to help. Standing beside her brother and staring at the engine, she bit her lip and fretted under her breath, "I *so* wanted to be there early to have the place organized."

She needn't have doubted. David had been fixing worn-out vehicles since the Model A in 1951, and they were soon underway. Marilyn smoothed the hair in her carefully-coiffed bun and changed the subject. "I like the modern look of your sideburns—how they curve around to form a line with your mustache."

Dave smirked. "These days it seems there's more hair to trim on my face than on my head."

Once at the camp, Marilyn scrambled to systematize the larder before Elizabeth and Bill Richardson arrived to unload their contributions of meat, fish, canned goods, straight-from-the-cow milk, and fresh-from-the-garden produce. Bill's and Elizabeth's children came too: Four by birth, Micki, Dennis, David, and Karen; two Korean adoptees, Kim and Daniel; and three black siblings in process of being adopted, Melissa, Linda, and Phillip.[119]

All afternoon the relatives arrived, including my husband, Ron[120], our three children, and me, who'd come from Ecuador, South America. I surveyed the scenery. It had not changed much since Ron and I came here for Seattle Pacific orientation as college students many years earlier. The center displayed before us more than three hundred acres of groomed lawns, army-toned soldier barracks, white-washed officers' quarters, stands of trees, remnants of gun installations, and oceans of water, all back-dropped by snow-tipped mountains. Above us, clouds changed formation against the background of blue, and bald eagles soared on the wind. In front, people of all ages were pouring out of cars, and two of our children, Jeff, eleven, and Joy, eight, ran off to greet their cousins. I saw my sister Marilyn scurry towards us, drying her hands on a towel, and I knew we were in good hands. She pulled the accommodation list out from under her arm and directed each arriving group to its pre-assigned place, allowing, of course, sections of one barrack for the gaggle of teenage girls and another for the bevy of youthful boys.

Aunt Eleanor, along with Dad and Mom—that's what we called her now—stood at the doorway of the barrack to which they were assigned, their faces lit with pleasure. Aunt Eleanor's hair was nearly white, and her beautiful face was the essence of elegance and grace. Mom's white hair, no longer tucked in the perennial donut-shaped roll, was short. She wore a pink and blue flowered top over polyester pants, with no apron on the outside. Dad's tanned face, beneath his fedora, showed permanent smile wrinkles. I stopped on the stairs in front of them, seven-month-old Janell in my arms. "Isn't this something? Who'd have thought they could get every one of us Corey kids together at the same time!"

Mom nodded, reached out to take Janell, and kissed her on the forehead. She looked toward Dad, "Our youngest grandchild. How precious she is."

How precious to my heart was the profile of Mom's lips touching my infant daughter's face. I put my arms around them both as Ron shook hands with Dad and reached around his shoulder to pat him on the back.

We gathered at 6:00 for dinner in the mess hall. The bell sounded, and everyone pushed in from all sides. We—the middle generation—had always been loud, but with the addition of our children it was bedlam. When the room was filled, David called on John McLennan to bless the food. John raised his hand and blessed—not only the food—but all who had gathered, thanking the Lord for those who had brought the event into being. He blessed Dad and Mother Corey, reminding us—and God—that they were the source of this most amazing of all families, of which he was proud to be a part.

That night we ate vats of spaghetti, bushels of salad, and trays of garlic bread. Kids were beginning to wander out the doors when they were called back to sing "Happy Birthday" as a decorated cake was placed in front of Mom to honor her seventy-fourth birthday. She blew out the forest-fire of candles, after which there were compliments and teasing that made her blush; there were cards with humor, and cards that brought tears.

We cleaned up and settled into our selected bunk beds. It was late in the night by the time all the giggles and the chatter petered out. In the silence of the wee hours, there was a crash and yelp. A flashlight revealed that Karen Richardson had fallen off the top bunk and landed on Jacki, who had been asleep on the floor, having already fallen out of the lower level. The family reunion was getting literal.

The next morning, the kitchen rattled to the beat of an African dance. John, who'd come from Ethiopia with his wife Jeanette (Hawkinson)[121] and their five daughters, Melodie, Reenie, Shari, Debbie, and Joycie, hummed and hammered away at the steaks, while Marilyn—feeling the rhythm—slapped pancakes on the industrial iron-topped stove. The rhythm John and Marilyn made together in the kitchen had been a very long time coming. John stopped the pounding. "Last time I saw you, Marilyn, was when you were headed to Cuba."

Marilyn turned with her spatula high in the air. "That was 1956. You were just a school kid with a crop of curly hair, John. Now you've got a forehead almost as tall and bare as Dad's!"

John ribbed back by suggesting that perhaps his sister used artificial means to ensure that the genetics of gray hair did not show on her head. Marilyn flipped the pancakes, turned back to make eye contact with John, and changed the subject. "Seriously, John, I'm so glad to finally meet Jeanette and your girls. How I grieved for all of you when your little Nathan died. It must be hard to think that you won't be going back to the land where he is buried."

It had been nearly eleven years since Nathan, a toddler at the time, had choked on a peanut in Burji, an isolated village of Ethiopia, where John, Jeanette, and their first three children were living. Nathan had struggled to breathe throughout the night. By the next morning, when a bush plane could transport him to a hospital, pneumonia had done irreversible damage to his lungs.[122] John spoke briefly about the loss, and the fact that Ethiopia had recently come under communist rule and was closed to foreign missions.

Then he changed the subject, "It's interesting that I became the missionary to Africa, just like Mom's vision, even though you used to tell her you would go there to run an orphanage or a clinic for lepers."

Marilyn chuckled. "Well, my heart was in the right place. But, just so you have it straight, I would have gone to take care of lepers in China, *or* I would have opened an orphanage in Africa. Back then, I didn't know I would be called to marry Allen and we would go to Cuba." She paused. "We loved Cuba. What a sad day for us when Castro took over with his revolution and we had to leave. Even though Allen had been born in Cuba, our very presence as Americans made it dangerous for the national pastors with whom we worked."

Marilyn brushed a stray hair from her eyes, and returned to an earlier theme. "I'm just glad you never wavered when God took you to Africa, instead of me."

My hungry baby called me from eavesdropping in the kitchen, where John and Marilyn recalled how their trips back to the farm had never coincided, even though each of them had connected from time to time with all of the other family members. Later, I returned to the mess hall to help with the dishes. It turned out the dish pit was covered, but I stopped to enjoy the bantering in Spanish between my brothers, Phillip and Merton. Nearly half of us at the reunion interchanged the Spanish and English languages as if they were hats. Phil had a hold of the sprayer hose in the camp-size sink and was whipping through the dirty dishes like a pro. Mert pinched the corner of his Fu Manchu moustache and shouted over the noise, "Ay, Felipe, cuidado del agua. Por favor, lavar los platos, no la cara mía!" *Hey Phil, careful with that water. Wash the dishes, would you, instead of my face!*

Phillip was quick with a reply. "Caramba, pensaba que habías olvidado de bañarte esta mañana." *Shoot, I thought you forgot to get a shower this morning.*

Phil and his wife Darlene[123] managed a camp and conference center in the Dominican Republic. They'd flown out of Santa Domingo with their four: Two birth children, Mark and Melanie, and two adopted Dominican toddlers, Tim and Jenny. Merton, with his wife Debra,[124] had come to the reunion from Colombia, where he was a pilot and mechanic with Mission Aviation Fellowship and Debbie worked in the base office. After high school, Mert had taken a tour of army duty in Viet Nam, repairing helicopters. When his military service ended, he returned to Joyce and married the hometown girl who'd waited quite a few years for him to make up his mind.

That morning of the reunion, after the breakfast dishes were done and the cooking laid out for the next meal, we had a meeting in the chapel. I was reminded of the home services when I was a child, except now I was of the older generation and sang with a grown-up vibrato, bobbed my head, and sometimes said "Amen" out loud. Virginia played the piano and her husband John McLennan blew on his baritone, just like former times. The McLennans had brought Dina, their youngest, and Dan with his wife Barb. Star brought her two little ones—Mom's and Dad's first great grandchildren—but not her husband Tim, the only family member to miss the reunion. David John, who added his guitar or keyboard playing to the music, had come with his wife Becky. And Dawn, who was six months pregnant and proud of her growing baby bump, was there with her husband Doug.

Mom and Dad sat near the front of the room. It was a new era for them. Their children were leaders and the two of them were privileged participants. We sang hymn after hymn, Mother mopping her eyes and Dad glowing with what seemed to me to be the full joy of the Lord. Next to Dad, Marian sat with her arm draped around his shoulder, her face showing an uncertainty—almost a distraction. At Mom's side, Janice, who had come to the reunion with her son Tony, wiped the corners of her eyes with the knuckles of her fingers. In the years after our move to the New House, my two youngest sisters had both experienced some hard knocks in their short lives, and both had been through miserable marriages and devastating divorces. There at the family session of the reunion, they were owning the love of our parents, and my eyes filled with empathy.

On the floor, a clutch of young cousins sat reasonably still for the first hour of singing, then fidgeted through an uncle's lengthy message. At last, *por fin, gracias a Diós*, the speaking was over, the last song sung, and the doors opened for play.

Such play! The huge field, designed for military drills, was soon filled with our riotous relays. Kids from age four to age fifty-two leaped and chased and rooted and howled. We teamed up to pass cherries held between the upper lip and nose or apples pinched beneath the chin. There were piggyback races, volleyball, soccer, and even a basketball game in the swimming pool. Bright plastic Frisbees sailed across the field like flying saucers, and soap bubbles swirled in the breeze until they popped.

After dinner that evening, I left our two oldest playing with cousins and walked with Ron, who carried our baby, to the knoll overlooking the waterways to the west. We could see the ferry from Port Townsend cutting a trail through the dark waters of the Straits of Juan de Fuca. Behind the ferry, Victorian structures graced the cliffs of Port Townsend and created a shadow over the port below. The late sun played hide-and-seek with the clouds, reflecting its brilliance on the mirror of water below and its changing colors on the slopes of the Olympic Mountains. My thoughts returned to childhood, and I could see again those peaks from our Farmhouse and the New House; I could once more climb Grauel Road into the foothills to pick wild blackberries; and I could trek the trails of Hurricane Ridge, and camp by Blackwood Lake. Ron, too, had hiked under those peaks, sometimes with me while we were newlyweds, and sometimes to higher elevations with my brothers. I drew him into my remembrances, saying, "I never quite saw the rugged grandeur of the Olympics that were our backyard until I returned home from my first year at Prairie. Funny how much of the beauty of this place was taken for granted until I had lived elsewhere. Why, even the peaks of the Andes in Ecuador are no match."

The bell rang, calling us back to the reunion. I tucked the blanket around Janell, who'd fallen asleep on Ron's chest and we hurried toward the center. That evening was dedicated to jokes and skits. Virginia's son Dan, a church youth director, took charge. He volunteered several contestants, including my brother, John. Blindfolded, each player competed to eat the most bananas. Urged on by raucous cheering and clapping from the audience, John shoveled in banana after banana until the bell rang. He whipped his blindfold off, only to discover that everyone else had been in on the skit—John had eaten nine bananas, while the others hadn't eaten any! With a shout, he took off after Dan, though his legs were no match for those of his young nephew.

I'd wondered how this brother, the one who'd battled an explosive temper for the first half of his life, and who'd seemed to take his calling to missions with the most serious dedication, would respond to being made a fool. I needn't have given it second thought. John had let his hair down—what hair he had left—and he, along with the entire crowd, sported faces flushed with laughter. Throughout the jokes, skits, and funny tales, Dad cracked up like the rest of us, while Mother and Aunt Eleanor slapped their knees and wiped their eyes. Rounds of entertainment rattled the walls long into the night.

The next day, with the younger children supervised by older cousins, we siblings—with our spouses sitting beside us—met in the chapel. There we began to dig deep, not into the soft, shell-speckled sand near the ferry dock, but into the vaults of our memory. There were all kinds of memories: Of eating green beans when there was nothing else, compared to later memories of using steak knives on t-bones from our beef; of haying with a scythe and hand rake, followed by memories of tractors and a hayfork lift; and of the frigid outhouse, before the heated bathroom. Other memories had remained unchanged through the decades: Games invented for play; prayers of faith that brought healing; and singing of hymns that filled our hearts.

The sharing turned from nostalgia to poignancy. We ten had grown up in more than one generation, the oldest gone before the youngest were born. Never before had all of us, in one place, addressed our propensity for teasing, pestering, and brow-beating. Now was the time. Phillip pinched the edge of his bushy moustache and brushed his hand past his chin-length sideburn. He fidgeted, acting as if he had something to say. Everyone turned in his direction as he spoke up, "I felt like I was growing up with six or seven mothers—all telling me what to do and when to do it—and a sister who tattled."

He was speaking straight to my soul, for I was the sister who threatened to tell—even if I didn't. "I'm sorry Phil, for being such a brat. Will you forgive me?"

My brother grinned and nodded toward me. But I had a bone to pick with him as well. "All these years, even though I tried not to hold a grudge, I carried sadness in my heart that you had butchered my pet hen, Peep. There had been plenty of other chickens. Peep was just an easy catch—plopped down to be picked up and cuddled. She didn't know to run away."

I paused as the impact of that remembrance hit me; then I added. "Remember how I couldn't eat poultry for the rest of my childhood? That's why." Phil said he was sorry, and as I looked at him, I knew he meant it.

Once the ice was broken, I listened as others worked through their confessions and forgiveness. John and Dave talked about the difficulties of growing up—John explaining how he couldn't measure up and David telling how hard it was for the two to get along when John's temper would explode. We girls talked about the unkind words, the name-calling, and the hurtful teasing of our brothers and brothers-in-law. I could tell that they, too, were touched by the honesty of our feelings.

Then Janice brushed back the chestnut wavy hair from her attractive young face. She sucked in her breath and started telling how our parents had driven to Montana to rescue her and her three-year-old son Tony after they had been deserted by her husband. She looked towards Dad, whose hands clasped his Bible, and whose face brimmed with affection. Then she turned toward Mother, who'd pulled off strips of toilet paper to wipe her raw-from-blowing nose, and said, "When we got home from Montana, I told Mom, 'I don't know how we'll survive. I wonder if my life will ever amount to anything. You probably should have quit with nine.'"

Janice sniffled, but kept going, "Mom looked me straight in the eye and said, 'Janice, your life is a gift from God. When I realized I was expecting you, I told Mrs. John Johnson how hard it was for me to go through this pregnancy, how hard to face the talk again.'"

Janice stopped to catch her breath. She looked down, as if embarrassed that she, who rarely spoke up in public, was giving an entire speech. She continued. "Mrs. Johnson told Mom, 'God has given you this child. This baby will grow up to be a blessing to you in old age.'"[125]

We were silent—hearing for the first time Mother's story of the neighbor's prophetic blessing in 1952. But our sister was not done yet. "That conversation with Mom helped heal my heart."

Janice turned toward Bill Richardson. "Then one difficulty piled onto another, until I was back in the dumps. It was then that Bill told me the trials weren't my fault, that God was just testing me. So today I want to thank Bill publicly for helping me accept who I am."

John was out of his chair in a flash. He hugged Janice tight for most of a minute; then held her at arm's length and caught her eyes straight on. "You *are* special! You have a sweet spirit of love that reaches out to everyone. Jeanette and I so appreciate the warm letters you write to us."

Others joined John in a chorus of kind words to Janice and then to each other. For some of us, hugging felt peculiar. In fact, as the hugging went on around me that day in the chapel, I remembered the first time as a grown-up I'd hugged Dad. He was leaving me at Prairie when I was eighteen, and as he told me goodbye, I walked straight to him and held out my arms. He lifted his arms and returned the hug, and I felt a barrier lift. After that, it became easier for me to initiate hugs with my parents and siblings.

There at the reunion in 1979, hugging and speaking kindly to each other was a new phenomenon. Phil shook his head and whispered in my hearing, "I never realized before that we could be affirming. We're so used to one-upmanship that it's hard to know what to say."

Our family had a history of treading in new territory, but now the many beautiful things we were discovering were not in the landscape, but in each other. We were saying things we'd never thought expedient before. Of course, there had been no doubt of our love, and there had been times we'd apologized for hurting another, but this was very different. We were openly sharing our affection for each other in front of every member of our immediate family, including Mom and Dad.

Rolls of toilet paper were passed around the room. I could see chapped noses, bloodshot eyes, and roughed-up lips to match mine and those of my mother and aunt. There was a hush, punctuated only by the sound of sniffing and blowing; then Dad's warm tenor voice started the song:

> Amazing Grace, how sweet the sound
> That saved a wretch like me!
> I once was lost, but now am found,
> Was blind, but now I see.[126]

This same day, a semi-circle of small fry gathered in front of their Grampa Corey—my father—in preparation for a service of their own: A baptism. Grampa had already spoken with each one individually to ascertain that the child had accepted the Lord as Savior. "Do you understand that baptism means you are showing others that you love the Lord and want to obey what he says in the Bible?"

Heads nodded and hands lifted in affirmation. After Grampa followed up with a few more questions, he said, "Well then, let's go."

He led the way across the cracked, uneven cement walkway toward the swimming pool, while two assistants, David McLennan and Dennis Richardson, came next. Eleven Corey progeny filed behind, hugging beach towels or worse-for-wear Casey Camp rags around their swimsuits to protect against the chilly, northerly wind on that overcast day. These children, no longer the same rambunctious cousins that had hollered themselves hoarse on the playground, moved in a serious, steady, follow-the-leader line. Joycie, one of the youngest, started to falter and looked back to her parents, John and Jeanette. Her mother caught the message and went to take the child's hand. The rest of the children seemed to appreciate the adult in their midst, and moved in rhythm to sit down cross-legged at the end of the pool. Older cousins and parents bunched along the sideline, readying cameras so as not to miss a moment.

Meanwhile, Grampa kept right on walking, down the steps into the pool. Once in the water, he discovered he was still wearing his single pair of good shoes, an oversight which made him chuckle and Mother shake her head.

Since the water was as cold as the wind, and Grampa knew the youngsters would soon be shivering, he motioned for an assistant to bring the first candidate to meet him in the shallow end. Off to the side of the pool, we couldn't hear Grampa's voice, but we could see his lips move and his eyes connect with each child as he spoke a sentence or two. Then he, with the aid of a helper, dipped the youngster back into the water in the same manner I remembered from the Salt Creek slough when he had baptized me.

The cousins baptized that day were Debbie, Shari, Joycie, Mark, Melanie, David, Kim, Karen, Jeff, Joy, and lastly, Tony, the eight-year-old who—with water dripping from his chin—looked up with a broad grin and spoke for the rest, "Thank you, Grampa."

The children pulled their towels close as Grampa turned to face the audience. "These youngsters have chosen to follow the Lord in baptism. They must be taught in the way of the Lord, so that when they are old, they will not depart from it. May God help each of us to be an example and a teacher. Amen!"

That afternoon there was music and more music—at least for those who were inclined to read the shaped notes and syncopated rhythms of the Arkansas book. *Those so inclined* were primarily of my own generation. Those of a younger generation still in the room soon lost interest in this impossible-to-read music, instead running outside to play games and explore.

After dinner, we sang around a campfire. Virginia pulled out a song—the one memorized by my three older sisters so they could accompany Dad to the Tacoma rescue mission in 1937. Around the campfire, however, it belonged to all six of us sisters—and to David who accompanied us on the accordion. "How about the key of C?" he suggested, since he still had those chords down pat from the hours he had practiced in the barn instead of writing his valedictory speech. With some negotiation and a little practice, he agreed to the key of G.

And so we sisters sang—our hearts in tune and our voices loud enough to be heard by the passengers on the Port Townsend ferry.

> There's not a friend like the lowly Jesus,
> No, not one! No, not one!
> None else could heal all our soul's diseases,
> No, not one! No, not one!
> Jesus knows all about our struggles . . . [127]

At the end of the song, David handed off the accordion to Virginia who wasn't as limited with the keys, and the singing carried on with everyone joining in "Great is Thy Faithfulness" and the Gaither favorites, "He Touched Me," and "The Family of God." Fidgety boys and their dads poked at the fire and added sticks. The wind picked up, blowing the smoke and sparks into our faces, but still we sang—until babies needed to sleep and children complained of the cold.

After tucking my youngest into bed, I returned to the chapel, where others were continuing the songfest. I had just found my place when Vi came through the door and tapped Marian on the shoulder. Marian turned her head, and Vi handed her an empty candy wrapper, saying, "A young man outside gave this to me. He said *you* would know who sent it."

Marian jumped up, threw a sweater around her tall, narrow shoulders, shook loose her short curly hair, and went out. When she returned after fifteen minutes, she didn't tell whom she had met and we didn't ask—though we all wanted to. I wondered if the faraway look in her eyes and the quietness of her presence that I'd observed had something to do with that clandestine encounter.

The singing didn't end that night, didn't end with our Sunday service, or when we left Camp Casey. It simply took a breather until two days later when we gathered at a church near Seattle with other relatives and friends to celebrate Mom's and Dad's anniversary. We performed the songs we'd practiced at the camp, including the six-sister rendition of "No, Not One." We told our parents, in front of a larger audience, what they meant to us, and how their commitment to God had been our example.

We'd not always followed that example. Some had made poor choices, had become involved with wrong people, or just simply ignored God's voice.[128] But Mom and Dad had been on their knees; they'd recounted God's promises; and they'd known—in God's time—that all of us would choose His way. As we celebrated their fiftieth anniversary, the radiance on their faces showed that they knew God's promises had been fulfilled—that all ten of their children were walking in faith.

We left the church, but the party wasn't over. A day or two later, most of us converged on the New House, by this time known to one and all as "Gramma 'n' Grampa's." It was to be base camp for a pack of Corey trekkers, excited to head out for Blackwood Lake in the Olympics. It was time to test the mountain mettle of the next generation. And test it they did—but that adventurous story is for them to tell.

Meanwhile, back at Gramma 'n' Grampa's some of us were getting to know the man with the candy wrapper who had called Marian away from the reunion. We learned that Dennis Alwine had been standing outside the gate at Camp Casey, listening to the music, watching the light surround our family, and feeling himself to be in outer darkness. By that time, Marian had known Dennis for at least a year. They had dated and he had become a believer, but then he got sucked into a relationship that led him away from trusting God, and from listening to Marian's counsel. Realizing his mistake, and desperate for reconciliation with God, he had looked for her that night of singing. Within the next few days, Dennis had broken off the damaging liaison and was back in God's—and Marian's—good favor.

So Dennis was on hand, along with my sister, to welcome home the campers, rain-soaked, and mud-splattered after a night of pouring rain in the mountains. His eyes sparkled with amusement as he watched Marian's nieces and nephews, including Elizabeth's multiethnic tribe, as they slithered out of the cars. He chuckled, "It looks more like the United Nations than a family."[129]

He was right. We were representatives of many nations—not so much for the color of skin, but rather for our international ministries. After all the campers returned, those of us who had been missionaries to other lands provided two full evenings of slides. Our stories were sequels to spell-binding tales told by missionaries such as the Pennoyers, whose lives of commitment had been an example to us when we were first learning to be obedient to God. These were stories we brought back because others, including Mother and Dad, had prayed and sacrificed so we could go.

As we shared together, we could see the wall-size world map, complete with stickpins Dad had placed where each of his missionary children was living. We watched as Merton flicked through slide after slide: He and Debbie smiling in front of a Cessna 180 that he'd repaired on the base of Mission Aviation Fellowship in Colombia; a lush, green tropical forest, striped with ribbons of rivers, photographed from the cockpit; and a jungle-ringed, dirt-covered airstrip where a cow stood, and grinning children surrounded the aircraft wings.

Phillip took over with slides of the West Indies camp center in La Vega, Dominican Republic, where brown children flew through the air into the swimming pool; where a marketplace overflowed with tropical fruits and vegetables; and where raggedy children played in the dirt.

John clicked on shots of women with enormous baskets balanced on their heads, next to children whose swollen bellies spoke of poverty; a meeting place filled with children of all sizes, white-shirted men, and brightly-wrapped women; the boarding school in Ivory Coast where his four younger daughters would soon be living. John finished with a slide of ELWA radio station in Liberia near where he and Jeanette would be serving.

The sound of clicking continued as Ron showed our efforts with a radio station—HCJB—in Ecuador, where I was involved as a musician. He clicked on a series of medical shots—shots of people with lumps on their backs, elephantiasis of the limbs, and smoky-white spots over eyes turned blind. Ron told of discovering in the western jungles the disease of River Blindness that brought on these life-threatening problems—the disease that he felt God leading him to research towards a treatment.[130]

As those of us who served as missionaries told our stories, there was one thing we all understood as a certainty: Growing up a Corey had prepared us to care for people who knew nothing other than grinding impoverishment—people who didn't even have catalogs in their outhouses, if indeed they had outhouses at all, and people for whom a treadle sewing machine offered a way to earn enough for their soup.

The reunion was coming to a close. Mother and Dad sat in the dining room, at the wedding table with the ends still pulled out for the large group that had come home to reunite. They looked out over the land—our Promised Land. It was the farm where we had milked cows, raised animals, and planted gardens. It was the homeplace where we had fixed machines, welcomed friends, and served neighbors. It was the treasure island of memories: Making new clothes out of old, making ends meet in the kitchen, and making music every day.

At the table, my parents held documents in front of them. Mother shook her head, "I can't understand how they did it—how they figured a way to set up a trust that would guarantee this house and land would provide for us and still benefit our children and the generations to come."

Dad was thoughtful. "God knew to bring Dennis Alwine, with his experience in real estate, to us at just the right time." His eyes twinkled as he had a second thought, "I should have said, God brought Dennis to Himself, and we received some benefits!"

Mother grinned, "Back in the forties when we had nothing but a raft of kids, and God gave you the promise of this land, I wondered how he could possibly supply $1000. Just look at all he's provided!" She paused, twisted the pen in her hand, and spoke again. "How much more significant than the provision of this place, is what has gone out from this place.

Dad agreed. "To God be the glory, great things he has done!"

And then it was over—the reunion that brought all ten siblings together with Mother and Dad; the anniversary celebration that honored our parents for their faithfulness to God and their example of sacrifice; and the camping safari of cousins, aunts, and uncles. The singing, the sharing, and the remembering all drew to a close. Only God knew when, if ever, we would be together again. So, as we said our goodbyes, we set in motion the plan to reunite in ten years, "if the Lord tarries."[131]

Mom and Dad stood on the porch, watching the last of their children and grandchildren drive around the bend and disappear behind the trees. They stood there for long minutes, their arms interlocked, listening to the silence, and thinking of the miracles that had transpired since God called them into fulltime ministry: The lives changed in the neighborhood and around the world; the children God had entrusted to them; the grandchildren so full of energy and possibility; and the children of those grandchildren yet to come.

Then Dad walked down the steps, picked up a cedar stick that had been dropped from a child's hand, and moved toward the wood box. Mother turned, entered through the French doors into the kitchen, and walked to the corner desk where her typewriter awaited:

> July 27, 1979. Altogether it's hard to describe what has come about on this 50th anniversary. May God bless and keep each one.

Celebrating family

All Twelve 1979
Back left: John Back right: Phillip
Middle: Janice Merton Marilyn Elizabeth Marian
Front: David Virginia Margaret Arthur Eleanor

The Baptism

THE EPILOGUE
2014

I am brought back to the present and to my grandchildren, whose interest in the icons of the past inspired the telling of this story. In the family room, the White Treadle Sewing Machine still sits without a belt; in the bathroom, the model outhouse collects dust; and in the hallway between those rooms stands the piano on which my mother took her lessons. And I am brought back to thoughts of my precious parents, about whose passing I write these final pages.

Margaret Phenicie Corey was the center and the heart for all of us. When we were away she wrote us letters and filled her diary with snippets that she'd heard from us. When she knew we were on our way home, she called everyone within a hundred miles to help her welcome us back. If we were late, she waited up—waited to hug us and tell our children how tall they had become. She fixed us dinner and talked with us until the wee hours. When we left again, she wiped her eyes and wrote in her diary: "How long will it be 'til I see them again."

Our mother was a pillar of strength to our dad, from the days when he was stern with her and strict with us, until the Spirit of God and experience of life had softened him. Through all of their years together, Dad's affection for Mother was palpable. I could see it in his eyes when he looked at her, and hear it in his voice when he talked about her. And I can still read it in his words, written on the occasion of her eightieth birthday and their fifty-sixth anniversary:

> It's not been smooth for you to do;
> Five decades and a year or two
> To raise ten siblings; that's not few,
> With all the hardships that you knew.
>
> Fourscore years have come and gone
> Regret them? No, they've not seemed long;
> To see the way that God has led
> Much light upon my way, He's shed.
>
> I know the best is yet to be.
> Comes yet, "The perfect day," I'll see
> The heritage God's given me
> Is mine for all eternity.[132]

Mother's final two years were marked by illness and suffering. Yet, her humor burst through even when pain deepened the creases in her forehead. With a smirk on her face and a croak in her voice—and to let us know she wasn't worried about the future—she would sing:

Oh, they cut down the ol' pine tree,
And they hauled it away to the mill
To make a coffin of pine for that old gal of mine,
Oh, they cut down the ol' pine tree.[133]

Mother didn't linger in the humor of the lyrics. Instead, as thoughts of heaven took over, she transitioned to a favorite hymn:

When all my labors and trials are o'er,
And I am safe on that beautiful shore,
Just to be near the dear Lord I adore,
Will through the ages be glory for me
Oh that will be Glory for me . . . [134]

I was alone with Mother on a Sunday afternoon. Sun poured through the window and lit the living room where she lay. I straightened a fresh pink blanket over feet that faced inward, pigeon-toed as they had always been. I fluffed her pillow, wiped her face, and swabbed water onto her tongue. Her eyes thanked me as I sat down at her side. Mother's grip was weak. Her skin was no longer calloused from planting peas and scrubbing floors and canning beans. It was soft, and the fingers wrapping mine felt like those of a sleeping newborn.

The ambiance of the room was changing. I sensed it in the breathing in and out of my mother, and in the way the warmth seemed to swell. Her fingers loosened on mine, and I could see that she had moved into a deep sleep. I walked to the open window and took in the scenery that had been part of my first memories—the Olympic Mountains peeking through the evergreens on the hill, and the grassy plot overlooking the stream as it flowed into a smooth-as-glass pond. I listened to the birds in the trees and a cowbell in the distance.

I moved back towards Mother and began to sing into the silence. We knew the words by heart, my mother and I, and so I sang them without conscious thought, blending with what seemed to be the presence of angels descending around us. While Mother listened, her eyes shut and her mouth at rest, I sang to her the story of a shepherd and his chosen sheep. I sang of pastures green, of still waters, and of paths on which she had walked with purpose and peace. And I sang to her of the valley through which she was moving—a valley for which she had no fear, a valley through which the rod and staff of her shepherd would bring comfort until she emerged on the other side, where a feast of celebration awaited her arrival.

Mother slowly raised her hand—the one I'd held—toward the ceiling, her pale fingers opening even as a lily opens to the sunshine. I sang the song again, and began to pray inside, "Please Father, bring Dad home in time."

He did. Minutes later, Dad came through the kitchen door, chattering to Mother about the flowers he had brought home from the church potluck. "Dad, come!" I called, raising my voice beyond what felt right in the sanctity of the moment. "Come now! Mother is going."

He dropped the flowers on the table and hurried into the room. I heard alarm in his voice. "What do you mean?"

I looked toward him and motioned for him to sit on the opposite side of the bed. I spoke without wavering. "Mother is dying."

He took her left hand, looked at her, looked at me. I nodded, and he leaned in. "I'm here, Margaret," he whispered.

Her breath was coming slowly. We watched, Daddy and I, as the blanket across Mother's chest lifted and fell. Lifted and fell. And then was still.

"Is she gone?" Daddy asked.

He reached forward and took her hand in his. Inside his fingers, hers looked as if they were once again the fingers of a young Margaret being courted by an adoring Arthur. There was a moment that stretched back to their beginnings.

Then Daddy lifted his wife's hand up to his face, her fingers to his lips. And it was in that pose—touching, together, partners as they'd been—that we watched the light drain from Mother's cheeks and the furrows fade from her forehead.

But the light never left the room. That light covered Daddy and me as I put my arms around him and we wept silent tears together. Our cherished one had gone to that beautiful shore, to be near the dear Lord she adored.[135]

We would all miss her terribly. The hole she left could never be filled by another.

A few years later, Dad came to the close of his life. Weakness and complications of a stroke confined him at home. Since he could no longer leave, people came to visit him. People for whom he had prayed came to pray for him; came to sing, to study the Bible, and to sit in his presence. We, his offspring, also came. We took turns with night-duty, and slept in a bedroom down the hall—all the while tuned in for a call from his room; all the while ready to provide the strength he needed to get from the bed to a walker and down the hall to the bathroom. We bathed his deteriorating body; we fixed his breakfast, and fed him when he could not feed himself. Dad expected that God would heal and restore him, believed that God would take him home with his eyes undimmed and his body in full health. And yet when God allowed him to remain weak in his limbs and vulnerable to infection, he did not dispute God's sovereignty. Instead, a brand new revelation swept over him, and he worried to Bill Richardson one night, "Is God going to let me into heaven?"

Bill was shocked to the core at that question, but his father-in-law went on, "I have been teaching something wrong all my life!"

The younger man shot up a silent prayer to heaven, "What do I say to Dad?" Almost immediately, the answer flowed from Bill's lips. "Did you ever willfully sin against God? Did you ever willfully go against scripture? But, even if you did, God will forgive . . . "

Dad interrupted, "Oh no! I believed it all along—I believed it completely. I believed that if you had faith enough, God would heal you. Now I know that is not true. Now I see that God sometimes has plans for us that need to be worked out in our weakness, in our infirmity."

After that, even though Dad—and all of us—could remember how God had often chosen to fully heal those for whom he prayed, my father no longer expected that God would restore to physical health his aging, decrepit body. Dad simply sang of the realization that "through it all, he'd come to trust in Jesus and come to depend upon His word."[136]

It was that Word—the Word he'd hidden by poring through his dog-eared, marked-up Bible day after day for more than seventy years—that sustained him when he could no longer read it for himself.

It was that Word he used to encourage others to keep the message going out—that the work begun in his life would continue even beyond his death. It was that Word he used to commission his children and his grandchildren to keep the fire burning.[137]

Dad had other revelations come while he was confined to the recliner. He began to make amends with anyone he knew he had offended. This included one of his first employers, some seventy-five years earlier, whose vending machine he had rigged so he could use it without spending any of his own money. "Vi," he asked. "Would you find the family of this man and try to make restitution for me? I calculate I owe him more than $100."

Vi did the footwork and spoke with a relative, but Dad never asked again. He had unburdened his heart, and the remembrance of guilt was gone.

Dad apologized to Virginia for not believing that her eyes were bad enough to warrant the cost of glasses. When he asked me, I told him he didn't owe me any apology, though I reminded him that the spanking I got for climbing on the chicken coop roof—after he told me not to—hurt quite a lot. Since he'd asked about these things, I went on. "Dad, do you recall how you wouldn't let me wear make-up in high school? Well, I remember the first time you asked me to put some color on Mother's pale cheeks."

He answered. "I wanted my daughters to be taught of the Lord, not to be influenced by the world."

He paused and his eyes twinkled, "But I suppose there is some truth in the saying, 'If the barn needs painting.'"

His youngest didn't talk about rigid rules, but brought to his attention what she'd wanted to hear from his lips. Each time Janice stayed with him, she would say, "Dad, I love you." He would smile, but say nothing. Then came the day that Dad, a huge grin covering his face, exclaimed for the first time, "Janice, I love *you!*"

Dad went on to bless all of his children with those three simple words. But to Marilyn, the daughter whose gusto for life he'd not understood, the daughter he'd punished with unreasonable severity, he spoke more than three words from his recliner. He pulled down her head, looked deep into her eyes, and said, "You are a good girl, Marilyn, a *good* girl, and I love you."

On January 25, 1998, David and Vi were preparing to leave after a turn at caring for Dad. But first, as was customary, they spent half an hour close to the recliner. They sang with Dad, one song leading into another. The room began to flood with the presence of God, and Vi felt compelled to raise her face and her hands in worship. Nearby, in her chair, Aunt Vera[138] sang, too, perhaps not fully aware of the significance of the words of the song they were singing, but fully aware that she was worshipping God. David also sensed that something was different—that the singing was not only their voices.

> My sin, oh the bliss of this glorious thought,
> My sin not in part, but the whole,
> Is nailed to the cross and I bear it no more.
> Praise the Lord, Praise the Lord . . . [139]

"Yes!" Dad interrupted, even before the chorus began. "Yes! *All* of my sins are forgiven. They are *all* forgiven—even the sins of my youth!"

His voice, strong and powerful and confident, led into the chorus,

> It is well with my soul,
> It is well, it is well, with my soul!

And then there was silence—silence, but for the murmurings of praise, of joy, of peace, and of rejoicing. A few minutes later, the frail body of the man in the recliner could no longer hold him back, and God ushered home his faithful shepherd and our beloved father, Arthur Wheelock Corey.[140]

THE APPENDIX

Before these chronicles come to an end I wish to bid farewell to some of the key players and express my gratitude for their contribution to our memories.

Grandma Anna Wheelock Corey passed away on November 19, 1958, just a few months after we moved into the New House. From Grandma's desk came notes with details of my father not recorded elsewhere. Perhaps it was this grandmother from whom I received the gene of leadership—considered bossiness by some—that gave me the fortitude I needed for this task.

Naoma Spottswood, Mother's closest cousin and our beloved benefactor, died on January 27, 1967, at the age of seventy-two. Besides a treasure chest of love, Naoma left behind her hoard of Mother's letters that brought coherence to Chronicle One.

Grandma Edith Chappell Phenicie lived next door to us until she could no longer care for herself. She died in the Port Angeles Convalescent Center on August 25, 1969, at the age of ninety-three. Grandma Phenicie saved a few of Mother's early letters to her, but later became an inside part of our story as, from her little house above the pond, she watched us toil on the farm.

Aunt Eleanor Phenicie Koon, Mother's sister, departed on September 27, 1993. Our dearest aunt brought us joy and humor and laughter like none other. Her record of our early years in priceless photos will remain an inheritance, not only for this book, but also for future generations.

John McLennan, Virginia's husband of 60 years, passed away on October 29, 2010. John Mac left his creative touch on so many elements of our history. He taught us music, designed Grandma's little house and our New House. For sixteen years, prior to John's death, he and Virginia lived in a home they established next door to that Farmhouse which still stands—barely. Across the yard, in similar ramshackle condition, is the pole-and-shingle barn.

On September 19, 2012, my brother John Wayne Corey died at home in Portland, Oregon. During wakeful nights of his treatment for multiple myeloma, John emailed his memories to me, many of which are included in the story. John also left a legacy of training national pastors—The Romans Project—that has multiplied since his death.[141]

There is also a legacy, not of the human sort, that speaks to the ever-present wisdom of Corey inventiveness and frugality. Besides the Farmhouse and the pole-and-shingle barn there are also pieces of equipment, vehicles, implements, gadgets, and renovations from the 30s, 40s, and 50s that still remain in our possession today.

Naoma's 1931 Chev that became Mother's Chevvy, then became a pickup, then became the framework of a welder, and finally became a trailer. Its axle and wheels are featured in a sculpture of scraps next to a blackened stump.

The Double-Packard Tractor, which supplied the power for the buzz-saw, became the first home of the welder made from an aircraft generator and adapter. Its axle became a trailer to transport the Sawmill. The shaft, bearings, and couplings of the aircraft generator and adapter went to Ethiopia with my brother John, who attached them to a hand-crank grinder to crush grain for bread, and peanuts for peanut butter.

Floyd Kautz's Model A that David used as his personal mechanical school became a dump truck; then became the mount of a welder from Wils Myers, which now rests on Merton's farm.

The 1940 Ford, that Bill Richardson drove to court Elizabeth, was donated to run the DC welder, after which it became the second home to the aircraft generator-plus-adapter welder. The Ford hung out for a while in the bottom of the small creek canyon near the cedar grove, "keeping the banks from eroding," as Dad said. Merton pulled it out and stashed it among the cedars and firs on a parcel held by my brother, Phillip.

Nearby, the slab house of Phillip is scattered round-about his still-intact cement stove that made *heap big smoke, but no fire.*

The transmission and electric motor of the four-plunger washing machine was adapted to power the hand wheat grinder, which was subsequently used for years by the Richardsons, and continues to this day at the David Corey residence.

The Cream Separator has been duly separated. The bowl sits on top of David's wheat grinder, while Bill Richardson is the holder of the crank and Elizabeth is the guardian of the discs and spouts.

The DC-powered tools Allen sent from Montana have an incomplete history. The half-inch drill and the welder went to Ethiopia with John, who powered them by a windmill until the country closed its doors to missions; while the bench grinder remains in the basement of the New House, now belonging to David.

The blackboard that posted the numbers owed to the Co-op is held by Phillip, who also keeps tabs on the blackboard's original felt eraser and the pocket size notebook in which Dad recorded every gallon of gas he used on the farm.

The Sawmill that started, or not, with elbow grease and a prayer accomplished many things: Cutting the lumber for the New House, for the Joyce Bible Church addition, for Bill's and Elizabeth's home as well as for Dave's and Vi's home, and for countless neighbors and friends. Most of the mill has now found a resting place at the Richardsons.

Mother's diamond that was priced at the pawns, offered to Naoma, and loaned to Virginia to protect her from unwanted advances, found its long-term home on Darlene's finger when Phillip offered it to her as an engagement ring.

The Yard Donkey has more than one final home. The drums decorate the holdings of David, who has been gathering and gathering and gathering for his posterity, while the donkey's original engine motor has gone to roost at the Richardsons—or better stated—has become the roost for their chickens.

Last, but not least, the bassinet of our babyhood remains in semi-active duty. After serving most of us Coreys as babies, from the 1930s to the 1950s, we passed it around for sleeping at least twenty babies of two subsequent generations. Recently, I lowered the woven wicker bed from our attic, patched it up with duct tape, gave it a paint job, and fixed a new mattress so my youngest grandson, Niko Ibsen, could try it out.

END NOTES

1 At the time of writing, the family members include Jeff and Crystal Guderian; Joy and Aleph Fackenthall, Zaid, Zia, Zac, Zella; Janell and Luke Ibsen, Neveah, Nolan, Niko.

2 Anna Wheelock Corey notes.

3 Arthur Corey recordings, undated.

4 Audrey Bolling, who married George Thompson, was the mother of the only Joyce resident to become a member of our family. Their daughter Debra Jean is Merton's wife.

5 Gladys Bolling Maybee. Interview, 2012.

6 Bev and Joan McNally's grandfather, Manuel Wasankari, and other relatives filed claim in 1884, and by 1891 had gained title to their homesteads. Information provided to author by Beverly McNally Porter Simmons through interview and handwritten notes. In 1889, during the proving up years, Washington was granted statehood.

7 Photo of Ramapo Grange provided by Joyce Museum. Public Domain.

8 Highway 9A was later renamed Highway 112.

9 Described in Margaret's letter to Naoma, 1938.

10 In about 1905, the year of Margaret's birth, Edith Chapple Phenicie had gone to Paradise Valley on Mt. Rainer as was customary for many of her clan. On this particular trip, Edith did not feel up to hiking and stayed in camp. During the afternoon she strolled down a path and discovered a little waterfall. On the hikers' return, she took them to see it. No one could identify the falls, so her brother-in-law Joe found a board on which he printed, EDITH FALLS, and nailed it to a tree. The name remains Edith Falls officially to this day. From family history of Sarah Isabelle (Ford) Kent; Benjamin Franklin Kent and Julia Ann (Hoke) Phenicie; and Charles Augustus Phenicie. Compiled by Charles Kent Phenicie, 1995.

11 Charlie Smith, whose Finnish name is not recorded, and his wife Lizzie who was from the Wasankari clan, had lived there. Handwritten notes by Beverly McNally Porter Simmons. Used with permission.

12 Margaret to her mother, 1938.

13 Margaret to Naoma, 1938.

14 The Doxology by Thomas Ken and Louis Bourgeois. Public Domain.

15 Source unknown.

16 Onward Christian Soldiers, Sabine Baring-Gould, Arthur S. Sullivan, late 1800s.

17 Samuel Herbert (Bert) Phenicie, b. 1/9/1869, d. 2/25/ 1938.

18 Margaret to Naoma, 1938.

19 The first page of a letter was missing from this letter Mother saved out of Naoma's papers. It appeared to have included the explanation of what she had suffered in early summer 1938, but did not wish for anyone to uncover. Was it a miscarriage?

20 Three homes built in 1903 by Grandpa Bert Phenicie and his brothers, Charlie and Joe, were razed for the construction of Stanley and Seafort's Restaurant which stands today with its bright red neon sign above the Tacoma Harbor.

21 Margaret to Naoma, 1938.

22 Ibid.

23 Margaret to Edith Phenicie, 1938.

24 Margaret to Naoma, December 1940.

25 Ibid.

26 Ibid.

27 The detailed record and sales slip of her shopping was discovered in Naoma's papers.

[28] In the 1700s, explorers gave names to the waterways and mountains. In the 1850s and 60s, fur trappers came. In the 1880s Crescent Bay became Port Crescent with a logging industry in full operation. Many of our early neighbors laid claim after hiking inland from Port Crescent and often worked in the logging business while they settled their own properties. The town of Port Crescent had a short life, less than twenty years, as described in *Jimmy Come Lately, History of Clallam County,* Jervis Russell, Editor. Clallam County Historical Society, 1971. A symbol of former boom town is the Port Crescent Pioneer Memorial Cemetery where, next to the earliest of pioneers, are the tombstones of Arthur and Margaret Corey, her beloved sister, Eleanor, and other family members.

[29] Most of the installation at Camp Hayden was built underground or camouflaged in the woods. Barracks housed up to 150 soldiers. Forty-five foot guns, built on revolving turntables, stuck out over the straits. These guns could shoot a one-ton slug nearly 28 miles in any direction. (*www.clallam.net/CountyParks*).

[30] Don Bruck's Memoir: *A trip with Grandpa Bruck in Memory's Spaceship.* Not copyrighted or dated. Used with permission.

[31] From the matching description, it is perceived to be the one that they used in their move west some years earlier. A copy of the Wetherald memoir is located in the Joyce Museum Annex.

[32] Don Bruck's Memoir: *A trip with Grandpa Bruck in Memory's Spaceship.* Not copyrighted or dated. Used with permission.

[33] Margaret to Naoma, January 1942.

[34] Margaret to Naoma, 1942.

[35] The Grauel Road was later named Graul-Ramapo Road.

[36] Joan McNally Quigley.

[37] Beverly McNally Porter Simmons.

[38] Margaret to Naoma, April 1942.

[39] Ibid.

[40] Arthur Corey recording, undated.

[41] A century earlier the word 'sad' meant 'heavy" – from which the name was derived.

[42] Recreated by author and Virginia.

[43] Joan McNally Quigley.

[44] Lyrics to *Amazing Grace*, John Newton. Late 1770s. Public Domain.

[45] From the hymn, *O That Will Be Glory*, by Charles H. Gabriel, 1900. Public Domain.

[46] *No Not One*, by Johnson Oatman, Jr. and George C. Hugg. 1895. Public Domain.

[47] Ferry service from Port Angeles to Victoria took nearly two hours. Canadian Pacific Railway managed a ferry service from downtown Victoria to Vancouver until the 1960s. That leg took five hours. *www.BCferries.com/about/history.*

[48] Interview with Hannah Singhose, 2011.

[49] Margaret to Naoma, December 1944.

[50] Ibid. This is the last letter Mother saved from Naoma's hoard with the exception of a postcard years later.

[51] *Tea for Two* is from the 1925 musical *No, No, Nanette* with music by Vincent Youmans and lyrics by Irving Caesar. Public Domain.

[52] FDR visited Port Angeles September 30, 1937. Controversies accompanied his visit. He had established the Olympic National Park and loggers were angry at the loss of jobs.

[53] These six were the only recorded deaths on the mainland United States directly due to the war.

[54] Name of character in comic strip, *Gasoline Alley.*

[55] From a folk song attributed to William Swords, 1790.

[56] It became one of the most treasured family photos ever.

[57] Arthur Corey recording, undated.

[58] Message recreated.

59   Port Angeles Evening News Obituary on August 22, 1945, states that Elsie Grauel died after a three-month illness.

60   Arthur Corey legal documents.

61   Elsie was married to John Felix Grauel—originally from Germany—who became a Clallam County citizen in 1913. They lived up the mountain beyond the Johnsons and beyond the end of the road that bore the Grauel family name. Felix filed his will in 1926 but died in Germany in 1929. Census information and Port Angeles Evening News, Elsie Grauel Obituary, August 22, 1945.

62   August Peterson's 160-acre piece included the two parcels that the Coreys purchased from Elsie Grauel's family. August built his cabin on a portion on the opposite side of the highway as seen in the 1907 hand drawn map available at the Joyce Depot Museum annex. After Mr. Peterson sold the homestead, it changed hands back and forth between Jim Gallagher and his son Charles. Clallam County Courthouse records.

63   All through the property were railway spurs or skid roads that had been cleared or flattened. Early logging operations used wood-burning or gas-run donkey engines to winch the logs on skid roads from the woods to the railway spurs. Steam locomotives would then to deliver them to the port from where they went by boom to mills.

64   Marilyn's diary and Port Angeles Evening News, Article on Mike Laszlo's death, January 4, 1945.

65   Seth Davis was born in 1861 in Missouri. Seth traveled west in the 1880s to join an uncle already living at Port Crescent. Seth was a powerful lumberjack who tackled the toughest logging jobs. As a mule skinner, he drove the first teams of mules in the logging fields. As a choker setter, he fastened thick cables on immense logs to be dragged over skids into place for retrieval. Seth delivered supplies and mail for miles by foot to fellow dwellers in the Twin and Gettysburg settlements, where he also purchased property. In 1890 Seth served as a guide for railway engineers prospecting a route along the west coast of the Olympic Peninsula. From Seth Davis tapes recorded by John and Myrtle Gossett and Ed Lippert May 12, 1957, six months before Seth died. Also from MEN, MULES, AND MOUNTAINS Lieutenant O'Neil's Olympic expeditions, by Robert L. Wood, 1976.

66   John and Lena Johnson moved to the area not long after the Peter Johnsons, but they were not related.

67   In 1912, the owners gave Will and Margaret Willis permission to build a post office and a general store. Margaret Willis was the great aunt of Bev and Joan McNally. Apparently Margaret served as postmistress, although her husband had the legal position of Postmaster. One of the Possingers served a couple of years later as postmistress. In 1915 the Willises also built the two-room school house that served the local children until 1922 when Crescent Consolidated Schools opened. Beverly McNally Porter Simmons.

68   In 1970s to the 1990s, Arthur Corey was the pastor of local churches, first in Sequim and later in Swansonville and Port Ludlow, WA.

69   We also knew Rose's older sister Evelyn who lived in Port Angeles.

70   Clare H. Woolston, 1856-1927. Tune by George F. Root, 1820-1895. Public Domain.

71   Don Bruck's Memoir: *A trip with Grandpa Bruck in Memory's Spaceship.* Not copyrighted or dated. Used with permission.

72   Margaret to Marilyn, 1948.

73   Ibid.

74   Recreated.

75   Later became RR 1, Box 306. It eventually was given a 5-digit number.

76   From reminiscing with Penny Courtwright Tolson, 2012.

[77] Herbert and Edith Phenicie served as missionaries in Cuba until the take-over by Castro in 1960. Their sons returned the United States at different times for schooling.

[78] Arthur Corey recording, undated.

[79] Slim's story and the starting of the Rest Home ministry detailed in Arthur Corey recording, undated.

[80] Letter recreated.

[81] Cousins Dick, Phyllis, Stuart, and Roger are the children of Harold and Vera Corey.

[82] Margaret to Naoma, 1950.

[83] Letter recreated.

[84] Arthur experienced indigestion, often after returning from times of ministry. In later years, when there was no fermented fruit available, he kept wine in a paper bag labeled, "For Medicinal Purposes Only."

[85] Anna Wheelock Corey's notes.

[86] The railway, used first for passengers and cargo, secondly for spruce intended for airplanes in World War I, and thirdly for logs to the Port Angeles mills, was completely abandoned in 1953.

[87] This 1952 weekend is the only time all 10 siblings were together until 27 years later at the family reunion in 1979.

[88] According to Mother's comments.

[89] Letter recreated from diary.

[90] Anna Wheelock Corey's notes.

[91] Allen recently gave back the card written by Eleanor Corey sixty years earlier.

[92] Not their real names.

[93] Margaret to Marilyn, Fall 1953.

[94] Ibid.

[95] Ibid.

[96] After a few slim years, David became an excellent hunter and guide in the woods.

[97] Margaret to Allen, November 1953.

[98] Joyce Bible Church had been established soon after the people left our Farmhouse meetings in 1947.

[99] Margaret's diary.

[100] Aunt Eleanor Phenicie to Margaret, July 21, 1954.

[101] In Port Angeles, the family frequently visited a victim of polio who was kept alive in an iron lung.

[102] Source unknown.

[103] Rose Tieche, History of Joyce Bible Church, copy located at the Joyce Museum.

[104] C L Phenicie, 1864-1888. Dubuque Iowa newspaper clipping. Exact date of death not visible.

[105] Anna Wheelock Corey's notes.

[106] In 1889, Merton Henry married Miss Anna P. Wheelock, who had traveled from the same Chautauqua County to visit an aunt in Tacoma. Anna Phoebe had, from the age of 12 when her mother died, helped to raise her younger siblings. Anna Wheelock Corey was one of the founders of the Washington State PTA and its first secretary. She was active in social circles, politics and church. Information on Anna gleaned from a privately printed book compiled by Ellen F. Vose in 1932. The excerpt also details the descendants of Robert Vose, who was born about 1599 in England and immigrated to the United States near the mid-1600s.

[107] Information on Honorable Merton Henry Corey is summarized from a free online book, donated by The New York Public Library: History of Puget Sound Country. No Copyright.

108 Pictures of early post offices set in stumps can be viewed on the internet. Bev and Joan McNally's ancestors lived in a hollowed stump their first winter of proving up. Beverly McNally Porter Simmons.

109 While in college, the author returned to Joyce High School and confessed to the principal that she owed at least a dollar to the Girls' Club. He said to give it to the church.

110 Delfred had been assigned to the legal foster care system sometime during his years with us. In later years, Dad would often speak of the many (up to fifty) who stayed for periods of time. Some of them may have come from difficult homes, but most were our friends or children of our friends. In the 1960s several legal foster children lived in our home.

111 Phosphorescent sparklers are actually live bioluminescent organisms.

112 Prior to construction of the Hood Canal Bridge a ferry crossed the canal between Lofall and South Point. At that time the cost per walk-on passenger was well under a dollar. After the storm of 1979 sank the bridge, a ferry ran another three years across the canal.

113 Telegram recreated.

114 The diary ended four months before the five years was up. The author lost the wager.

115 Crescent Consolidated School Student Newsletter, 1958.

116 Phoebe Cary, 1852. Public Domain.

117 *How Great Thou Art*, based on a Swedish poem written in late 1800s, was made popular in the United States in late 1950s by Billy Graham Crusades.

118 David met Violet Traina while he was at Seattle Pacific College. She lived next door to Dave's landlady. They were married on September 23, 1960.

119 The Richardsons would, in time, adopt one more Korean child, Scott; two more black children, Sandy and Jerry; and an infant from India, Raman.

120 The author met Ron Guderian at Prairie Bible Institute. Both attended Seattle Pacific College and were married on 12/27/1966.

121 John and Jeanette (Hawkinson), graduates of Prairie Bible Institute were married on August 25, 1962.

122 Nathan John Corey, b. 5/5/1967, d. 12/3/1968.

123 Phillip married Darlene Howell on May 21, 1966, one year after their graduation from Prairie Bible Institute.

124 Merton and Debbie (Thompson) were married on April 7, 1972. Later they became the parents of two daughters, Alana Joy and Lydia Grace.

125 During bouts of nausea that accompanied Mother's final illness, Janice was holding a basin when Dad said, "This *is* the fulfillment of the prophecy by Mrs. Johnson that this baby will be a blessing to us in our old age."

126 Lyrics to *Amazing Grace*, John Newton. Public Domain.

127 From the song, *No Not One*, by Johnson Oatman, Jr. and George C. Hugg. 1895. Public Domain.

128 David had taken years to get his heart fully right with God. Merton was also slow to find faith. He lived his lie all through childhood and teenage years. He knew that Mother wondered if he would ever get control of his temper and set some goals for his life. God spoke to him in two near-death experiences, one out on the Straits of Juan de Fuca and the other when trapped in the creek under the tractor. After the second experience he heard God say, "This is your last chance." And Merton chose to commit his life.

129 Dennis and Marian were married eight months after the 1979 reunion on April 5, 1972. They are the parents of Megan, Joshua, Sara, Matthew, and Jonathan.

130 In 2014, The World Health Organization declared that River Blindness has been eradicated from Ecuador and Colombia as a direct result of the work of Ron Guderian that began in 1976.

131 The next reunion occurred in 1989, after which there were three more in the subsequent 16 years, and plans are in the works for another reunion in 2015. At the time of writing,

there are more than 250 family members that would count Arthur and Margaret Corey as their patriarchs.

[132] Arthur Corey, 1988.

[133] *They Cut Down the Old Pine Tree*. George Brown, William Raskin. New York: Vincent Youman, Inc., 1929.

[134] *When All my Labors and Trials are O'er*, Words and music by Charles H. Gabriel. 1900.

[135] Margaret Lenore Phenicie, b. 7/2/1905; married Arthur Wheelock Corey 5/25/1929; d. 6/25/1990.

[136] Adapted from the song, *Through it All* by Andrae Crouch, 1971 Manna Music Inc.

[137] Arthur's recliner commissioning of his granddaughter Jacki and her husband Pete Hise preceded the launching of Quest Community Church in Lexington, KY, that that has seen tens of thousands come to the Lord. It is also important to note that throughout decades of service prior to his illness, Arthur commissioned many other relatives and friends whose ministries have also touched multitudes. Perhaps their stories will one day be told.

[138] In 1991, Arthur married Aunt Vera, the widow of his brother, Harold.

[139] *It is Well with my Soul*, Horatio G. Spafford and Philip P. Bliss. Late 1800s. Public Domain.

[140] Arthur Wheelock Corey, b. 12/27/1904; d. 1/25/1998.

[141] In 2005, John began taking CDs of messages to Liberia, to donate as teaching tools to the national pastors. A few years later he began filling MP3 players with hundreds of hours of teaching, and by 2010 the ministry was named "The Romans Project." Strong leadership has taken up the challenge where John left off. More information available on the website: romansproject.com.

Photo by Ronald Guderian

ABOUT THE AUTHOR

Eleanor Corey (Guderian) holds a BA of Music Education from Seattle Pacific University, an MA from Azusa Pacific University, and a PhD in Management from Walden University. She has published professional articles, workshops, and newsletters.

After full careers in music, management, and consulting, that spanned twenty-four years in Ecuador and fifteen years in the United States, she and her husband Ron Guderian reside in Stanwood, Washington. They are the parents of three and the grandparents of seven.

Sticks, Stones & Songs is the author's story of surviving—even thriving—within a spunky, authentic, imperfect family of twelve in mid-century rural America.

Request for information on the ministries of Arthur and Margaret Corey

The author is compiling vignettes of the ministries of her parents for another book. If you or anyone you know was impacted in some way by the lives, teaching, or prayers of Arthur and Margaret Corey, please write your experiences, or contact the author for an interview.

Eleanor also welcomes humorous or poignant tales from the early years of her siblings and herself.

Eleanor Corey Guderian
PO Box 571
Stanwood WA 98292
www.eleanorcorey.com